Jet Combat in the Nuclear Age
Jet Fighter Campaigns—1980s to the Present Day

Martin W. Bowman

Skyhorse Publishing

Contents

Acknowledgements

I am indebted to David 'Mog' Morgan for kind permission to quote from his book *Hostile Skies: My Falklands Air War* and for all his help with proofing and photos. David Morgan became the most successful pilot of the Falklands war with four enemy aircraft destroyed and he was awarded the Distinguished Service Cross by the Royal Navy - he is one of only a handful of RAF officers to receive it and he accepted it with great pride and honour. He later became a commercial airline pilot. My thanks also go to Claudio Meunier for kindly providing Argentinian images and text and to Steve Rissi for kindly providing photos and information on his late father. .

Thanks also go to my fellow author, friend and colleague, Graham Simons, for getting the book to press ready standard and for his detailed work on the photographs; to Pen & Sword and in particular Laura Hirst; and Jon Wilkinson, for his unique jacket design once

Dedication

I heard the last B-52 stationed at Carswell AFB before I saw it. The eight turbojet engines have a distinctive sound at low altitudes and this one sounded much lower than I was used to hearing over that part of Fort Worth. Me and a few others working at Fort Worth Bolt & Tool Co. went outside and watched as the huge bomber trailing black engine exhaust, flew towards the Fort Worth skyline. As the pilot was over the centre of down town Fort Worth he gently rolled the B-52 back and forth rocking the wings to say goodbye to Fort Worth, which had been home to the 7th Bomb Wing and its B-52 crews and support personnel since 1958. Many people parked next to the runway to watch B-52s come in for a landing and see the big bomber deploy a drag chute from the rear of the aircraft. It was as sight to awe anyone, but the noise must have made living next to the base unfortunate for those needing some sleep or just some peace and quiet. The Dallas Fort Worth metroplex was not as the defense secretary of the time stated, a good place for nuclear bombers.

As I watched that last B-52 disappear to the east of down town Fort Worth I had a feeling of nostalgia, for the B-52 had been a huge part of my life though I never flew in one. My father had spent 22 years in the Air Force, as an engine mechanic on C-47s and then as a tail gunner on the B-52. My childhood revolved around the B-52 and its missions during the Cold War and Vietnam era. My dad was first stationed at Altus AFB in south west Oklahoma. Back then the B-52s were silver on top and white on the bottom to help reflect the nuclear flash away from the bomber if it ever had to perform its primary mission. The shield of the Strategic Air Command was on all the B-52s and SAC had the motto of 'Peace is Our Profession'. After eight years at Altus AFB dad was stationed at Columbus AFB in Mississippi. The B-52s there took on a new menacing look. The tops were camouflaged and the bottoms black to absorb searchlights when over targets at night. They were being prepared for war in SE Asia. The huge all black vertical tail fin always reminded me of giant sharks. My dad flew airborne alert two or three times a week. Every other week he would have to live at the alert pad near the end of the runway where three B-52s were fuelled up, loaded with nuclear warheads, ready to take off if the alert sounded. These every other week assignments, 24 hours a day for seven days straight, was hard on the families of the bomber crews. Picnic tables were set up outside the security fence of the alert pad and families could picnic with the crew members or just spend some time together. If the alert sounded the crew member had just a short sprint to the bombers that were ready for nuclear war with the Soviet Union. Once the alert would sound while we were there and off my dad ran. We watched as the B-52s started up and taxied to the runway. The crews, or families for that matter, never knew if it was real or just a drill to test the crews' readiness. Sometimes they did not know until they were in the air that it was just a drill. Life was nerve-wracking enough for the crew members and their families knowing that they were on the front lines of the Cold War. To make matters worse the war in Vietnam was added to the mix.

The first of two times the Bomb Wing deployed to SE Asia my dad came home from the base with a .38 calibre gun and holster. He was leaving for war that very day and the weapon which he brought home made it all the more real. We rode with him to a large hangar at the base and there all the bomber crews and their families were together as the crew members and support groups made the necessary preparations for departure. Then came the last hugs and kisses and off the fathers and husbands of the wing went on the B-52s and KC-135 refuelling aircraft to Vietnam. At first tours in SE Asia for B-52 crews were six months in duration. My dad's last tour was just four months. He flew over 200 combat missions during his three tours. He received a 'double bonus certificate' twice, when one of the B-52s in the formation had errors with its bombing computer and dad used the radar on his gun scope to line up the B-52 precisely behind his bomber. When his B-52 dropped its bombs, the B-52 he was guiding followed and this allowed more bombs on target than would have been possible without his assistance. He never had an opportunity to fire on enemy aircraft; very few tail gunners did until the end of the war when B-52s were striking major targets in North Vietnam. My dad has often said this was the best job he ever had. He used to tell me about the so called 'cat walk' that he would have to crawl from one end of the bomber to the other on and that it went along the length of the fuselage. As a drill in case of depressurization the tail gunners were timed on how fast they could crawl from the rear of the bomber to the front. He said some gunners cheated by running across the closed bomb bay doors but he was always afraid the bombardier would cycle the doors if he tried that and he might get some unplanned practice parachuting!

The B-52 determined how much time we had with my father and influenced where we had lived and what we experienced in the 1960s and 1970s. The nation has received its investment in the B-52 programme many times over. Part of the doctrine of M.A.D. (mutually assured destruction) during the Cold War, it let the Soviet Union know that we could and would hurt them at least as bad as they would hurt us in a nuclear exchange. It served in our wars with Iraq and Afghanistan too. The B-52 will be here long after my father is gone and most likely long after I'm gone.

Prelude

…'With the proper application of air and naval power', the Viêtnam War could have been won 'in any ten day period you wanted to but they never would bomb the target list we had'. If you look at the tonnage of bombs that we dropped in the Viêtnamese affair and compare it with what we dropped on Japan and that we dropped on Germany, you will find that we dropped more on Viêtnam than we did on Germany and Japan combined. Look what happened to Germany and above all, look what happened to Japan. There was no invasion necessary there. The only conclusion you can draw is that we were bombing the wrong things in Viêtnam.

General Curtis E. LeMay the Air Force Chief of Staff, who at the outset of the Korean War in 1950 had urged the Pentagon to 'turn SAC loose with incendiaries on some North Korean towns,' advocated an all-out strategic bombing offensive against selected targets in North Viêtnam too. In South Viêtnam on 20 December 1960 the National Front for the Liberation of South Viêtnam (NFLSV) (more familiarly known as the Viêt Công (VC) had formed in Tây Ninh Province after the Communists decided that a new revolutionary strategy was needed to overthrow the US-backed Sàigòn regime. Initially SAC argued that dropping conventional bombs in Viêtnam was not their 'business'. But, using large numbers of tactical fighter-bombers in-theatre failed to destroy the guerilla strongholds in the jungles of South Viêtnam. What was needed was a 'big stick' and only a force of B-52s carrying large conventional bomb loads could provide it.

On 1 November 1964 the Joint Chiefs of Staff (JCS) verbally recommended to Secretary of Defense Robert S. McNamara that the air force commence within 60 to 72 hours the systematic bombing of 94 'vital centres' in North Viêtnam. McNamara and Secretary of State Dean Rusk, fearful that widening the conflict would bring Communist China into the war as in Korea, rejected the scenario and advised a policy of restraint. During 1968-1972 there was no bombing of North Viêtnam above the 19th parallel. When bombings were resumed in 1972 during the first 25 days of October, 31,600 tons of bombs were dropped on North Viêtnam, the most intense period of daily bombing of the north thus far in the war.

All the B-52s in the Far East came under the control of the Eighth Air Force headquarters at Andersen Air Force Base on Guam, the largest of the Marianas Islands in the West Pacific which had been retaken from the Japanese in July 1944. Everyone on the island in the summer of 1972 was told that the Viêtnam War was almost over. Probably they would not fly the required twenty missions to qualify for an Air Medal. Then, each month, regular as clockwork, there was the '15th of the month rumour' that the G models were going home. Every month that is, until December. With each delay, frustrated crewmen started daubing epithets like 'Guam Sucks' on the inside of their B-52s and others, flying from Guam and U-Tapao reportedly destroyed their own officers' clubs and refused to participate in further missions. Then, there was an aircraft commander's meeting. For over a day, all bombing missions in Viêtnam were cancelled. The rumours really started flying: 'War with China', 'War with Russia' - 'G models going home'; 'Everyone's going home'.

Chapter One

The Eleven Day War

'This is your chance to use military power effectively to win this war and if you don't I'll consider you personally responsible...I don't want any more of this crap about the fact that [the air force] couldn't hit this target or that one.'
President Richard Milhouse Nixon in a message to Admiral Thomas H. Moorer, Chairman of the Joint Chiefs of Staff to begin a 'Linebacker II' bombing campaign against Hànôi on Sunday 17 December 1972.

Forty-one year old Lieutenant Colonel Donald Louis Rissi, a B-52G pilot and aircraft commander in the 97th Bomb Wing at Andersen Air Force Base on Guam, could be forgiven if he felt frustrated. He and his TDY (temporary duty) crew had been scheduled to rotate back to Blytheville AFB, Arkansas for their one-month break, first on 4 December and then again on the 12th. Rissi was a former B-58 Hustler pilot and F-4 Phantom jet jockey who on 3 June 1955 had graduated from the Naval Academy with a commission as a second lieutenant in the US Air Force. He had then completed Undergraduate Pilot Training and in August 1956 was awarded his pilot wings at Reese AFB, Texas. He deployed to Southeast Asia in February 1971 and served with the 389th Tactical Fighter Squadron at Phù Cát until September that year when he became a Mission Launch Control Officer with 7th Air Force at Tân Sơn Nhứt. After completing B-52 Combat Crew Training in March 1972 his assignment to the 340th Bomb Squadron took place in June that year and deployment to Andersen AFB followed in October. Two months on the

B-52Ds at Andersen AFBG on Guam. In December 1972 over 150 B-52s were positioned on the available ramp space on the five mile flight line.

8

'Rock' as the old volcanic mountaintop, 30 miles long and four to twelve miles wide was known, was more than enough for most men. December is the start of the dry season and this remote outpost 2,600 miles from Sàigòn is in Typhoon Alley. From early 1972 Andersen was the site of one of the most massive buildups of air power in history. The influx of bombers, crews and support personnel pushed Andersen's military population past 15,000. Over 150 B-52s were positioned on the available ramp space on the five mile flight line. Combined with other SAC bombers stationed at U-Tapao Field, Thailand, about 50 percent of SAC's total bomber force and 75 percent of all combat ready crews - equivalent to at least thirteen stateside bomber wings - were at the two bases. Billeting at Andersen was saturated and terms like 'Tin City' (un-air-conditioned) and 'Tent City' (of which there were three at Andersen with twelve men living in each tent amid dust, noise and tropical rains), became commonplace with improvised quarters set up in the open fields across from the flight line.

On Friday, 15th December Rissi was notified that their replacement crew had become snowed in at Loring AFB, Maine and when they did arrive, they were minus two primary crewmembers and would need 'over-the-shoulder' training before they could transition to a combat-ready status. It meant that Rissi, a devoted husband, who loved to fish and enjoy the outdoors around Collinsville, Illinois, would not be Stateside for Christmas 1972 with wife Joan and their five children. It was especially maddening for he was in line to become the new squadron commander on his return home. A quick tour of the flight line on Saturday morning revealed all the B-52s were being refuelled and loaded with bombs. Bomb loaders had to put in exhausting twelve-hour shifts in the hot tropic sun struggling to get the B-52s fully bombed up. All Rissi and the other aircraft commanders could tell their crews was that they should order two lunches and to get lots of sleep.

An aura of invincibility had seemed to pervade B-52 operations although some questions had been raised in April 1972 during the so-called 'special missions' over the North. Then, on 22 November 1972 the first B-52 combat loss in Việtnam occurred. Just after dropping its bombs

B-52Ds taxi out at Andersen AFB for another bombing mission.

Personnel at a North Vietnamese SAM missile battery. North Viêtnam began receiving Soviet SA-2 Dvina (SA-2F Guideline) missiles shortly after the start of Operation 'Rolling Thunder' in the spring of 1965. With Soviet help, the NVA built several well-camouflaged sites and also ringed them with anti-aircraft artillery (AAA), making them even more dangerous to attack. The SA-2 had a solid fuel booster rocket that launched and accelerated it and then dropped off after about six seconds. While in boost stage, the missile did not guide. During the second stage, the SA-2's liquid-fuel rocket propelled it to the target.

on enemy troops at Vinh, roughly 150 miles above the DMZ, two SAMs exploded beneath B-52D 55-0110, Call Sign 'Olive 02' commanded by 30-year old Captain Norbert J. 'Oz' Ostrozny of Lackawana, New York. 55-0110 was one of eighteen B-52s of the 307th Strategic Wing, whose crew were from the 96th Bomb Wing at Dyess AFB, Texas on rotation at U-Tapao. 'Olive 02' suffered numerous malfunctions of their ECM gear that prevented the EWO (electronic-warfare officer), Major Larry T. Stephens, 35, of Abilene, from ascertaining the exact position of the jamming transmitters. Secondly, high winds in the target area had blown the chaff corridor out of position and the entire cell was highlighted against the chaff. Just after bomb release at 35,000 feet Captain Philip A. 'Tony' Foley the 26-year old co-pilot, of Fair Haven, Vermont watched a SAM approach from 1 o'clock and disappear under the aircraft. Larry Stephens attempted to jam the Uplink/Downlink signals[1] to the missile in the blind but it detonated under the belly. Enemy radar had provided accurate guidance despite electronic jamming by the victim, the other two B-52s in the cell and three EB-66s orbiting some distance away. Throughout the approach, when the countermeasures were most effective and Ostrozny received additional protection from a chaff corridor created by two 'Iron Hand' F-105Gs and four F-4s,[*] the 'Fan Song' radar operator contented himself with passively tracking the jamming signal across his scope to determine azimuth (bearing) and elevation, using the normal operating altitude to establish the range and then verified the range by transmitting for a couple of seconds as he allowed 'Olive 02' to soar unchallenged to the release point. Then, as the B-52 turned sharply away after dropping its bombs, the wings formed an angle of roughly 45 degrees with the horizon and the strongest part of the jamming cone passed ineffectually beyond the SAM (Surface-to-Air Missile) site. At this instant, the 'Fan Song' transmitted just long enough to pinpoint its target before the missile battery launched the two SAMs that exploded beneath the B-52.

'Olive 02' caught fire in the wings and rear fuselage; all aircraft power was lost and Ostrozny and 'Tony' Foley had to read their instruments with a flashlight. They nursed the damaged bomber for 100 miles with one of the two F-105G 'Iron Hand' defence suppression escort but about five miles from the Thai border the last of the engines wound down at 10,000 feet but Ostrozny judged that he had enough altitude to glide the rest of the way despite a fiercely burning aircraft with no electrical power or flight instruments. In the gun turret Staff Sergeant Ronald W. Sellers 28, of Waco, Texas could hear but could not transmit on his radio. His compartment began to get hot as the fire in the fuselage took hold and he could see the fire in the right outboard engine pod and wing becoming brighter and the wings were gradually being burned away. Then these and other engines started flaming out due to fuel starvation from the wing fires. Sellers noted that the wing fires had turned a bright blue and had burned away part of the top of one wing. Soon he could see and count the internal ribs of the wing over the number eight engine pod. Then the last engine quit. Oztrozny asked his navigator, Captain Robert L. Estes, 32, of Abilene, Texas who was wounded by fragments of the SAM in his leg, how many more miles it was to the Thai border. The answer: five miles. The crew was alerted for an imminent bale out. Now for all practical purposes, they were a gliding torch, trying to trade

B-52D 55-0110 'Olive 02' was one of eighteen B-52s of the 307th Strategic Wing, whose crew were from the 96th Bomb Wing at Dyess AFB, Texas on rotation at U-Tapao. Insert: Captain Norbert J. 'Oz' Ostrozny commanding B-52 55-0110 Call Sign 'Olive 02' on 22 November 1972.

precious altitude for those last long miles to safety. The aircraft could explode at any minute. Since the engines had quit, all electrical power was lost except battery power to the bail-out lights and interphone. Oztrozny lost his flight instruments.

Sellers observed the tip tank area starting to bend and fold up over the outboard engine pod. As the navigator announced that they had crossed the Mekong River into Thailand the starboard wing tip broke away and the aircraft started an uncontrolled turn. Reacting immediately to the pilot's bail out signal, all the crew successfully abandoned their aircraft. Fortunately, an HH-53 'Jolly Green' from Nakhon Phanom was airborne and it managed to locate all six crew. 'Olive 02' crashed into jungle near Pla Pak/Mueang district border, fifteen miles south west of Nakhon Phanom. 'Tony' Foley suffered a fracture of his right ankle when he landed in the dark. Major Larry Stephens; Major Adam 'Bud' Rech, 35, also of Abilene, the radar navigator and Sellers were uninjured. The crew gave personal accounts of their experiences to meetings and fellow crewmembers. One of these was taped, permitting their story to be related to the entire bomber force. Ostrozny was awarded the Silver Star. Up until this time ten B-52s had been lost as result of combat operations in South East Asia but this was the first B-52 to be destroyed by hostile fire in more than seven years of war.

Richard M. Nixon, who on 7 November had won a massive presidential re-election victory, was determined to end the long drawn out war in Việtnam, even if it meant using them to bomb Hànôi, to destruction. As early as 1968 during a visit to Air Defence HQ, Hồ Chi Minh had predicted that the B-52s would come to Hànôi one day but Air Force plans to bomb Hànôi had always been pushed aside. On 30 November Nixon signalled his intentions to bomb Hànôi with B-52s, dismissing fears of losses. On 3 December the mayor of Hànôi began to evacuate civilians from the city. On 12 December the Paris peace talks reached an impasse. The North indicated that they might not even reach agreement on the release of American PoWs and on 13 December they walked out of the peace talks. President Nixon issued an ultimatum to Hànôi to return to the conference table within seventy-two hours 'or else' but Hànôi rejected his ultimatum. Nixon however, could turn to massive air power if he needed to. On Guam there were 150 B-52D and B-52G crews of the 72nd Strategic Wing (P) and another sixty B-52D crews at U-Tapao in Thailand. On 6 December Nixon had ordered the Joint Chiefs of Staff to begin planning for B-52 strikes against Hànôi 'as close as can reasonably risked' that would 'create the most massive shock effect in a psychological context.'

On the afternoon of 14 December Nixon turned to massive air power to begin the 'Linebacker II' bombing campaign against Hànôi. Admiral Thomas Moorer designated responsibility for 'Linebacker II' operations to General John C. Meyer (usually called 'J.C'), the chief of Strategic Air Command (SAC) at his Headquarters at Offutt AFB, Omaha, Nebraska. After approval by the JCS the plans were sent to Lieutenant General Gerald W. Johnson commanding Eighth Air Force at Andersen AFB and General John W. Vogt commanding 7th Air Force in Sàigòn. Meyer and Johnson had been among the highest scoring fighter pilots in England during WW2. B-52D/G attacks on Hànôi were to begin at about 1900 hours Hànôi time on 17 December but Nixon moved 'Linebacker II' back twenty-four hours to the night of 18/19 December because of fears of offending the Chinese who hosted a political visit by North Việtnam on the 17th. In any event not enough KC-135A tankers were in position to refuel the planned sorties by B-52s from Guam. It is 2,650 statute miles to Hànôi from Andersen AFB but combat routing lengthened the one-way distance to 3,000 miles; a 16-hour round trip, across South Việtnam, up through Laos and then a dogleg right on a northwest-to-southeast heading into Hànôi. Because of cockpit seat positioning limitations the B-52D had poorer refuelling visibility compared to the B-52G or H and it was underpowered. Added to this was an increase in drag created by 24 external bombs which the D model carried on the underwing stub pylons. Therefore a B-52D pilot who was able to get his full offload of fuel despite the loss of an outboard engine and an outboard spoiler group was considered a 'real pro'. [2]

The morning of the 16th there was a meeting at 8th Air Force headquarters, involving the

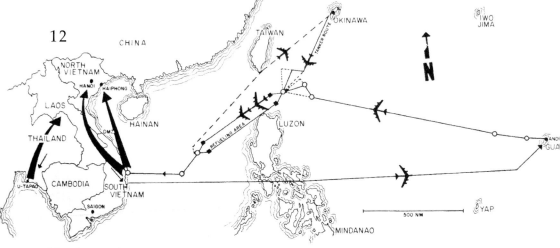

Map showing the routes taken from U-Tapao in Thailand and Andersen Air Force Base on Guam, 2,600 miles from Sàigòn by the B-52s and the re-fuelling area used by KC-135s from Kadena AFB on Okinawa. This meant that the 14-hour mission became an 18-hour one for some of the B-52 crews who had to fly close to Kadena.

division commander, wing commanders and the 8th Air Force staff. During the meeting, details were provided of the targets, routes to be flown inbound and outbound and an in-depth description of radar aiming points for bomb release. There was considerable discussion on enemy defences, supporting forces and target area attacks. Originally, the attendees were told to prepare for a three-day maximum effort. All personnel rotations to the States were to be halted and all available le aircraft were to be put in commission for the upcoming raids. A full colonel would be designated as the Airborne Commander (ABC) for each day's strikes. He would be held responsible for the successful completion of the mission. Colonel Thomas F. Rew, commander of the 72nd Strategic Wing was selected to lead the first wave on the first day. Forty-two year old Colonel James R. McCarthy, born in Memphis, Tennessee was selected to brief all three waves on the first day, plus the first wave on the second day. Each colonel on the operations staff and wing commanders were to take turns as ABC.

The most immediate task was to brief the wing staffs and the flight crews on how the missions were to be conducted. The wing staffs were briefed on the afternoon of the 16th and the flight crews were given a more limited briefing the next day. Lieutenant Colonel Hendsley R. Conner, commander of the 486th Bombardment Squadron, recalled the situation surrounding the briefings:

'Everyone was still hopeful that a truce would be reached in time for us to 'get home in time for Christmas'. All but a few bombing missions had been cancelled for 17 December. A meeting for all commanders was scheduled for 1400 on the 16th in the 8th Air Force Commander's conference room. What was in the air? Were they getting the airplanes ready for us to fly home? As I left the squadron on my way to the meeting, I saw several crewmembers talking together. One of them said, 'Colonel, are we going home? Let's hope you have good news for us when you come back.'

'As we gathered for the meeting, speculation was running about fifty-fifty that we would be going home. Others of us had a premonition and were saying nothing. The General came in and the meeting got under way. The briefing officer opened the curtain over the briefing board and there it was - we were not going home; not yet anyway. We were going North. Our targets were to be Hànôi and Hàiphòng, North Viêtnam. At last the B-52 bomber force would be used in the role it had been designed for. The goal of this new operation was to attempt to destroy the war-making capability of the enemy.

'The method of attack we were to use would be night, high altitude, radar bombing of all military targets in the area of the two major cities in North Viêtnam. We would launch a raid each night beginning on the 18th and continue with a raid each night. Each raid would consist of three waves of varying strength, each hitting their targets at four- to five-hour intervals. It would not be easy. We knew we would suffer losses. The Hànôi / Hảiphòng target complex was among the most heavily defended areas in the world. The combined number of SAMs, fighter aircraft and anti-aircraft guns that surrounded the target area exceeded anything ever experienced.

'As soon as the meeting was over I went back to the squadron area to begin preparations for the missions. As I approached the area, the crewmember who had wished for good news when I left was still there. He said, 'We're not going home are we?' We're going North instead. I can tell from the look on your face.'

It was the same scenario played out in *Twelve o'Clock High* when Gregory Peck tells his B-17 bomber crews that they weren't going home; 'they were going to die; in fact they should consider themselves already dead'.

On 17 December the 7th and 8th Air Force Commanders received the following message from the JCS: 'You are directed to commence at approximately 1200Z, 18 December a three day maximum effort, repeat maximum effort, of B-52/Tacair strikes in the Hànôi-Hảiphòng areas against the targets contained in the authorised target list. Object is maximum destruction of selected military targets in the vicinity of Hànôi/Hảiphòng. Be prepared to extend operations past three days if directed.' Plans called for the B-52s to attack at night, from 30-35,000 feet, with Air Force F-111A and USN A-6A aircraft following up by day. All available B-52s would strike against 34 previously restricted targets, against rail yards, power plants, communications facilities, air defence radars, the Hảiphòng docks, oil storage complexes and ammunition supply areas - over 60 per cent of them within a 25-mile radius of Hànôi, which were to be bombed in any weather using radar rather than visual aiming. SAC retained control over the choice of targets and also drew up the plans for the direction of attack and the bomb loads to be carried.

Plans for 'Linebacker II' B-52 strikes drew upon the experience gained during the spring of 1972. The enemy antiaircraft guns had proved so deadly against 'Rolling Thunder' fighter-bombers so the B-52s would fly beyond reach of even the 85mm weapon. At these altitudes,

B-52 crew briefing at Andersen AFB on Day One of the Christmas bombings on 18 December 1972.

B-52 crews look tense and focused as the details of the raid on Hànôi are read out.

SAMs were their most dangerous, but the bombers would maintain the three-plane cells which thus far had provided adequate countermeasures protection. To avoid mid-air collision, the cells kept two minutes apart. At the beginning of 'Linebacker II' only a limited amount of Chaff screening was available. This and other factors limited the approach and exit routes available to the Stratofortresses. Plans called for the B-52s from Andersen to fly over the Pacific and into South Viêtnam then fly through Laos where they joined Thailand based B-52s and the procession would then proceed north towards the Chinese border before turning east into North Viêtnam. Then they would head southeast down the Tam Đào mountain range known to US pilots as 'Thud Ridge' to Hànôi. The southeast target approach was to take advantage of the 100-knot jet stream tailwind blowing from the northwest. After bomb release the B-52s were to swing in wide turns which, it was hoped, would take them out of SAM range as soon as possible. The stream of three-aircraft cells was compressed to enhance ECM protection and keep the B-52s within the Chaff screens. The crews, who were unfamiliar with flying in large formations at night, were under orders to manoeuvre as little as possible to avoid collisions.

The bombing campaign would begin during some of the worst weather of the year, the middle of the north-east monsoon. Low cloud covered the Hànôi region for most of the day. The general staff briefing noted an ominous stand-down in B-52 activities in the south and the report radioed by an American weather reconnaissance aircraft flying above the city was intercepted. Hànôi's air defences went on the alert. The region was the responsibility of the 361st Air Defence Division. It had numerous radars and anti-aircraft guns, but its heart was three SA-2 'Guideline' SAM regiments: The 261st Regiment was responsible for the area north and east of the city, while the 257th and the 274th Regiments covered the south and west. Each regiment had a number of early warning radars and was assigned three SA-2 missile battalions, each one equipped with its own early warning 'Fan Song' missile guidance radar and six SA-2 missile launchers.[3]

John Petelin, a B-52D pilot flying from Guam, said that 'It's real easy to describe the SA-2 as a telephone pole with a fifteen foot stream of flame behind it... You don't actually see the missile until it's very, very, very, close and then you can see the outline, if there's any moon at all. And the biggest thing you see is the tail of the thing. And, of course, the next biggest thing you see is when it detonates... a nice big elliptical ring of fire that's shooting steel ball bearings out at you... Actually, it's real pretty if it doesn't kill you.'[4]

At U-Tapao at 11 o'clock in the morning on Monday, 18 December crews crammed briefing rooms to hear Colonel Donald M. Davis tell them what their target was. At Andersen the 'D' Complex ('Arc Light') briefing room was packed with over a hundred crew members. All came to attention when Colonel James McCarthy entered. 'As the crews filed into the briefing room there was the usual milling around and small talk between crewmembers, made the more so by the large numbers of people. Since I was selected to give all three briefings on the first day, I tried to come up with some words or phrases that would convey the message of the importance of the targets to our national goals; yet I wanted to keep it simple and uncluttered. After a few minutes' debate with myself, I chose the simplest of opening statements. As the route was shown on the briefing screen I said, 'Gentlemen, your target for tonight is Hànôi.' It must have been effective because for the rest of the briefing you could have heard a pin drop. Having sat through 1,200 pre-departure combat briefings myself, I can truthfully say that the group of combat crews was the most attentive I have ever seen.'

The briefing for Wave II was conducted in the midst of the flurry of excitement surrounding the Wave I launches, but it went smoother than the first briefing; the weather, intelligence and target briefers having 'polished their presentations.'.

Aircrew morale prior to 'Linebacker II' was quite low. Boredom and lack of motivation were common, especially among the crews that had been on several other SE Asia TDYs in recent months. When 'Linebacker II' began, morale improved immediately. The initial aircrew response

Pre-loaded M117 bombs waiting to be attached to the underwing pylons of a B-52D on Guam.

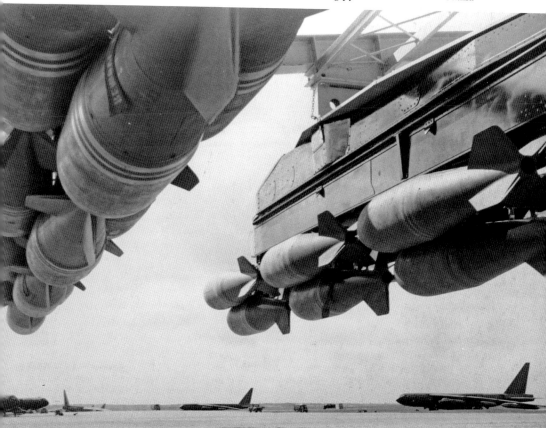

Loading wing mounted bombs on a B-52D at U-Tapao. B-52Ds could carry 42 750lb M117 bombs internally and 24 500lb Mk.82 bombs on the underwing pylons.

to the information received that B-52s were finally going to hit targets in Hànôi and Hái phòng was a mixture of apprehension and approval. Captain Gerald T. Horuchi summed up their overwhelming sentiment in this statement: [The attacks] 'were long overdue and something that needed to be done. Go in, kick ass and get it over with. The guys were anxious, nervous, even scared but morale I think was generally high.'[5]

'Reminiscent of *Twelve O'Clock High* episodes' recalled Captain Robert P. Jacober Jr., an experienced B-52 pilot who logged 64 combat sorties flying the Buff.[popular acronym of the B-52 meaning Big Ugly Fat Fucker]. 'The briefing officer stepped to the centre of the stage and said, 'Gentlemen, your mission for today is ...' A pause. Then the viewgraph machine projected an image of a small portion of a map on the screen. The map scale was such that 'HA' was on one side of a city and 'NOI' was on the other. The mind did not fuse the words until the briefing officer said ' Hànôi'. Dead silence was followed by everyone talking at once. Dramatic and impressive, yes. Scared, yes. Eager, yes. As a combat wing, this was the highest I had ever seen morale. We were about to really contribute to the war.'

Major Arthur Craig Mizner, from Texas, the B-52 pilot of crew Carswell E-57 in the 659th Bomb Squadron during 'Linebacker II', recalled: 'They told us...'We're going downtown; we're going to take the Buffs down with us...'Because the Buffs were relatively vulnerable in that they had to keep on for the bomb run, they had to be on a relatively straight line as they would come into the target and drop the bombs for that finite period of time...It also made it really easy for a MiG to come up and tap them because they could see the contrails and they would just follow the contrail and at the end of the contrail, there's a big airplane... I went back and gathered my crew together and I told them to be prepared to go downtown and start making your final arrangements to do that. And I think we all called our wives that night. Of course, we couldn't tell them that we were going into Hànôi, but I think we all just called and said how things are going and how's the children and kind of small talk to make it possibly a last contact with them.'[6]

Nick Hinch, a B-52G radar navigator on Guam who holds the distinction of being qualified and flying in every position on a B-52 crew with the exception of gunner, was philosophical about the raids. 'I basically... made my own peace and said, you know, I've had a great life. It's been good, yeah. I've got a wife... I'd just been married in May of '72, so here we're into six months. But you know, I said, those poor devils have been up in Hànôi getting the crap beat out of them for six or seven years. I mean, if it's going to take me to let them have the rest of their life, that's the way it goes, you know?'

The first raid would be with 129 B-52s in three waves with four-to-five hour intervals

A B-52G getting airborne at Andersen AFB.

between each wave. The long time lapses between waves was designed to keep Hànôi's population awake throughout the night but it would also enable SA-2 crews a chance to engage the first attack and then re-arm their missile launchers to meet the next two raids. The Guam based B-52D/G units were to attack 48 targets including the extensive Kinh Nỗ storage area north of Hànôi which contained four key targets and the rail yards at Yên Viên, all in the Hànôi area. Because of their shorter endurance the 'Wild Weasels' and other support aircraft could stay in the target area for only about an hour so the support packages had to be split into three groups rather than operating as one large force. The first wave of 48 B-52D/Gs would arrive just after dark, the second wave of thirty aircraft striking at midnight and 51 aircraft of the third wave attacking Hànôi at 0400 hours on the morning of the 19th. Seven cells made up of 21 aircraft from U-Tapao were detailed to bomb MiG-21 'Fishbed' bases at Hòa Lac, Kép and Phú Yên.

The bombers would fly almost identical routes, in single file, to Hànôi. Captain Jim 'Bones' Schneiderman, a B-52 co-pilot who attended the first briefing, was not impressed. 'It was clear before we even took off on the first mission that the tactics were really dumb, everybody coming in from the same direction, same altitude, same exit routes,' he says. 'It was so much like the image of the British in the Revolutionary War - all lined up, marching in straight rows making easy targets - that it was bizarre.'

While the weather on the ground was cold and rainy, above the solid cloud deck it was a beautiful night, with clear skies and a full moon that reflected on the clouds. As they were bussed to their waiting bombers Wave II, which would begin taking off at 1900 hours received their briefing. Lieutenant Colonel Hendsley Conner and his staff had worked almost around the clock getting the schedule prepared, notifying the crews, ordering meals and the transportation and preparing flying equipment, so that thirty crews and aircraft plus spares were assigned to Wave II. Conner, who had flown over 200 missions in Martin B-57 Canberras and who now commanded one of the provisional squadrons on Guam was Deputy Airborne Commander (ABC) to the second wave. He would occupy the fold-down jump seat behind Major Clifford B. Ashley and his co-pilot, Captain Gary L. Vickers on the flight deck of B-52G 58-0246, Call Sign 'Peach 02' whose crew were from the 2nd Bomb Wing at Barksdale AFB, Louisiana. The rest of the crew were 1st Lieutenant Forrest E. Stegelin, navigator and Major Archie C. Myers, radar navigator, Captain Jim T. Tramel the EWO. Master Sergeant Ken E. Connor was the gunner. By not having any crew duties, Conner could concentrate on how the mission was progressing and be aware of any problems the wave might encounter. Sitting on a jump seat for eleven hours trussed up like a turkey with a 40lb PCU-10P parachute pack is highly uncomfortable. Colonel Conner would have to wear his parachute at all times because the jump seat was not fitted with an ejection device. In emergency he would have to disconnect oxygen and interphone, un-hitch from his seat, go below and wait to bail out through a hole in the floor of the compartment after the navigators had ejected!

Shortly before departure each crew was given three large black briefcases full of information such as Mission 'frag' folders radar offset aim-points and imagery of target areas divided into 'low threat' and 'high threat' areas depending on the numbers of SA-2s and the risk from MiGs. In order to maintain the sortie rate crews of six ground-spare B-52s pre-flighted up to the 'engine start' point for 'abort' standby had to be prepared to fill in for any of three other cells. Each therefore received nine 'frag' briefcases.

Lieutenant Colonel Don Rissi and 24-year old 1st Lieutenant Robert J. 'Bobby' Thomas, his substitute co-pilot from Miami, Florida climbed up the ladder rungs of the enormous B-52G 58-0201 codenamed 'Charcoal 03', grasped the 'fire pole' and scrambled through the floor hatch opening into the narrow corridor to the subterranean flight-deck. Physically, the B-52 was cold after several hours of high altitude flying. The seat cushion did not cushion after several hours and the cockpit was cramped and uncomfortable. Underneath the flight deck the two navigators - both from Maryland - Major Richard Edgar 'Dick' Johnson from Oceanside and 25-year old Captain Robert G. Certain the radar navigator, from Silver Spring, took their seats in the windowless bombardier-navigator team compartment, where, illuminated only by their instruments, they were always very busy during the whole flight. Bob Certain was also the bombardier who armed the missiles. Senior Master Sergeant Walter Lee Ferguson the 43-year old gunner who was from Detroit took his seat in the forward cabin next to the EWO where a TV camera assisted him in sighting and he operated the tail gun position remotely. (On the B-52D the tail turret gunner was particularly effective in being able to monitor SA-2 SAM missile launches and approaching MiGs from the rear). Because Ferguson and Captain Richard Thomas Simpson the the 21-year old electronic warfare officer or 'E-Dub' (the interphone call sign for EWO) faced backward, their ejection seats were equipped with a 'hatch lifter', which converted the hatch above them into an air brake and held it out of the way as they ejected upward or climbed out. In an emergency the pilots would eject upward, the navigator and radar navigator ejecting downward. If the pilots' seats failed they had to unhitch and shin down the 'fire pole' to the bombardier-navigator team compartment and bail out. Having flown tactical aircraft on four previous tours in Việtnam, Simpson, who was from Anderson, South Carolina was not happy about being in a Buff. 'They were too slow; too vulnerable. This was not just another mission - we were going to the heart of the threat.' He wondered aloud, 'Are we really doing this right, going straight and level across the target at 35,000 feet?'

'Charcoal 03' was in the fourteenth cell of three aircraft in the first wave but when 'Charcoal 02' was taken out of line because of an equipment malfunction, Rissi's aircraft became 'Charcoal 02' and one of the ground-spare B-52s filled in. During engine start Rissi bluntly observed that if all of the B-52s were to line up and advance their power at the same time, they 'could break this end of the island off.' Shortly thereafter, while taxiing, an urgent call came through from the control tower: 'All B-52 aircraft, stop taxiing! Earth tremor in progress! The island experiences occasional earthquakes due to its location on the western edge of the Pacific Plate and near the Philippine Sea Plate.

'For this mission' recalls Captain Jacober 'crews pre-flighted the bombs and equipment a little bit more thoroughly, followed the checklist a little more closely, imagining what it would be like and would you panic. Everyone was offered extra ·38 ammo; only our gunner took more. He took two extra boxes. We still don't know what he was going to do with all that ammo.'

'The planning was complete, the briefings were finally over and we arrived at the aircraft to pre-flight the bombs and equipment' wrote Hendsley Conner. 'Wave II was scheduled to begin taking off at 1900. Every ninety seconds after the first takeoff another fully loaded B-52 would roil down the runway. Anyone who has ever witnessed such an event can never forget it.'

On the night of Monday 18/19 December seventy-five B-52Ds and fifty-four B-52Gs - 129 in all - were ready for take-off from Guam and Thailand. Every part of Andersen AFB was full to the brim with aircraft and personnel and the numbers of men needed to maintain and fly the

B-52s were enormous. There was a long line of B-52s nose to tail along the narrow taxiway, waiting their turn to use the two miles long runway oriented west to east. At 1451 local time Major William F. Stocker's crew from McCoy AFB, Florida who had been involved in the raid on Hảiphòng earlier in the year led the procession of bombers down the uneven runway in 'Rose 01'. Stocker had graduated from pilot training school in 1966, had been a member of an ICBM crew in SAC and had flown as an F-4C back-seater. Already he had logged 300 B-52 combat sorties. Stocker recalled that President Nixon had ordered that there would be no civilian casualties and no PoW casualties and demanded Air Force generals 'guarantee' these criteria would not be violated. The B-52s' engines were boosted with water-injection for take-off and as he took off he left eight wakes of smoke in the sky behind. After a number of B-52s had taken off the sky was full of smoke as there was not enough wind to clear it away. Every ninety seconds another fully loaded B-52 rolled down the runway. A Russian trawler counted the bombers as they took off and broadcast the information to North Việtnam. The runway had a 150 feet dip and rise from the middle to the end of Andersen's swaybacked runway and the most dangerous part of the mission was watching the last 1,000 feet of runway approach as the pilot tried to get a 480,000lb aircraft into the air. Each B-52 cleared the cliff which loomed after take-off and then made a precipitous drop of several hundred feet into the ocean as if falling into the sea. Onlookers watched aircraft struggle to become airborne just before reaching the visible rim of the island, only to drop out of sight momentarily and then climb away immediately beyond the edge of the island.

Major Locker eased back on the control column and 'Rose 01' took off. Twenty-six D's and G's of Wave I followed in quick succession. 'Charcoal 01' however, lost four engines on one side soon after take-off. Its pilot, Captain Jerre Goodman, managed to land safely. Lieutenant Colonel Don Rissi in 'Charcoal 02' now became the leading aircraft in 'Charcoal' cell and assumed the codename 'Charcoal 01'. Another B-52 suffered a refuelling system failure outbound. One crew, which lost an engine were told to push up the power, stay with the formation and pick up extra fuel on the return leg.

From his position Lieutenant Colonel George Allison, a master navigator who had flown a

B-52Gs taking off from Andersen AFB in Guam. In Operation 'Desert Storm' in 1991B-52G-125-BW 59-2582, now Grim Reaper II in the 2nd Bomb Wing at Barksdale AFB, Louisiana, took part in Operation 'Secret Squirrel' (call sign 'Doom 33'). 59-2582 was scrapped at AMARC in 1999.

twelve-hour interdiction mission near Quang Tri the night of the 17th, the only portion of most of the taxiing force which was visible was the vertical stabilizers. 'They could be seen moving along the line of revetments, an assembly line of aircraft tails' he wrote. 'The similarity of these to the moving targets in a shooting gallery stuck in my mind. I didn't like the analogy but it was too vivid to dismiss. They would move forward, ever so slowly but the line seemed never to stop... When would the line end? We don't have that many B-52s on the whole island, which can be the sensation when you've lost count! Finally, around midnight, they were all airborne and the ensuing silence was as thunderous and the hours of launches.'

During a one hour and 43 minute period 87 B-52s departed Andersen. These aircraft were joined by approximately forty bombers from U-Tapao. The Guam based B-52D/G units were to attack forty-eight targets in the Hànôi area in three waves in four-to-five hour intervals between each wave. The long time lapses between waves was designed to keep Hànôi's population awake throughout the night but it would also enable SA-2 crews a chance to engage the first attack and then re-arm their missile launchers to meet the next two raids. Because of their shorter endurance the 'Wild Weasels' and other support aircraft could stay in the target area for only about an hour so the support packages had to be split into three groups rather than operating as one large force. The first wave of forty-eight B-52D/Gs would arrive just after dark, the second wave of thirty aircraft striking at midnight and fifty-one aircraft of the third wave attacking Hànôi at 0400 hours on the morning of the 19th. The U-Tapao-based B-52Ds of the 307th Strategic Wing were tasked to suppress the MiG-21 'Fishbed' bases at Hòa Lac, Kép and Phú Yên. Half an hour before the first Buffs arrived over the targets F-111As were to hit the MiG-21 airfields and F-4s would sow two Chaff corridors to screen strikes on the Kinh Nỗ storage complex and Yên Viên rail yards north of Hànôi. Air Force and Navy ECM aircraft and SAM hunter-killer fighter-bombers also supported the strikes. Supporting the first wave were 19 countermeasures aircraft: three EB-66s for standoff jamming, eight chaff-dispensing F-4s and eight 'Wild Weasels' for radar suppression. 1st Lieutenant Nick Holoviak, an F-4 Weapons Systems Officer at Korat recalled: 'They told us we're going downtown; we're going to take the Buffs down with us... Because the Buffs were relatively vulnerable in that they had to keep on for the bomb run, they had to be on a relatively straight line as they would come into the target and drop the bombs for that finite period of time... It also made it really easy for a MiG to come up and tap them because they could see the contrails and they would just follow the contrail and at the end of the contrail, there's a big airplane...'

The second wave received the same countermeasures support, but as the third wave arrived, four Navy A-7s replaced the eight 'Wild Weasels' and five EA-3Bs joined the EB-66s, their Air Force counterparts, in long-range jamming. Unfortunately, at altitude a 100-knot wind blowing from the northwest dispersed the Chaff before the B-52s arrived and caused much soul searching at Andersen. The decision was made to continue with their part in the mission but the mission time was increased from fourteen hours to eighteen hours and as a consequence tanking assembly points had to be repositioned and schedules altered.

Captain Robert P. Jacober recalled. 'Crossing the pond westbound was the usual boredom. But spirits were high. There was some kidding. The gunner was bragging how he was going to get a MiG. The return trip was going to be more subdued, introspective.'

'After we levelled off' wrote Hendsley Conner 'I tried to get some sleep. I had gotten very little the night before because of the many problems that had come up during mission planning. I slept about three hours before the co-pilot woke me up for our flight refuelling. Since the mission was scheduled to last over fourteen hours, refuelling was necessary in order to complete the mission and land back at Guam. When the refuelling was over, I tuned in the radio to hear how the lead wave was doing. They should then be in the target area and we should be able to hear how the enemy was reacting.' The first report he heard was when Colonel Thomas F. Rew the 50-year old commander of the 72nd Strategic Wing (P) made his call-in after they exited the target area. [7]

'They had had a tough experience. One airplane was known to be shot down by SAMs, two were presently not accounted for and one had received heavy battle damage. He initially estimated that the North Viêtnamese had fired over 200 SAMs at them. There were reports of MiG fighter attacks. The anti-aircraft artillery was heavy, but well below their flight level. For us, the worst part was now they knew we were coming and things probably would be even worse when we got there.'

In Hànôi General Võ Nguyên Giáp learned that B-52s had taken off from Guam and Thailand; the latter detected flying northward along the Mekong. The bombers from Andersen flew over the Pacific and into South Viêtnam then through Laos where they joined Thailand based B-52s and formed into one long line of aircraft in groups of three. With up to ten minutes between each three-aircraft cell the B-52s stretched over seventy miles of sky. The procession proceeded north towards the Chinese border before turning east into North Viêtnam. Then they headed southeast down the Tam Đào mountain range, known to US pilots as 'Thud Ridge' to Hànôi. Crews, who were unfamiliar with flying in large formations at night, were under orders to manoeuvre as little as possible to avoid collisions and the stream of three-aircraft cells was compressed to help preserve the mutual ECM protection and keep the B-52s within the Chaff corridors that were laid in the Hànôi area to interfere with enemy radar frequencies. If the SA-2 Guideline's 'Spoon Rest' long-range target acquisition radar or the 'Fan Song' shorter-range missile guidance system locked on to a B-52 the American crews were to break off their attacks and head for a secondary target. But this and other factors limited the approach and exit routes available to the B-52s. The southeast target approach was to take advantage of the 100-knot jet stream tailwind blowing from the northwest but the winds to a large extent dispersed the chaff. In any case, the North Viêtnamese tactic of firing a proportion of the SA-2 missiles without guidance meant that the effectiveness of the chaff was limited. The reliable but unsophisticated SA-2 system used vacuum tubes and slow, mechanical computers. It had been used throughout the war but had achieved mixed success against highly maneuverable US fighters and the 'Fan Song' guidance radar had proved vulnerable to various types of electronic jamming. The much-feared 'Wild Weasels' specially configured with electronics and the anti-radiation Shrike and Standard ARM missiles could home in on the SA-2's 'Fan Song' radar.

Only about 57 of the 98 Guam-based B-52Gs had received the 'Rivet Rambler' updates to their ECM equipment and yet all the B-52Ds had. While the 'Arc Light' B-52Ds had been refitted with the most up-to-date ECM jammers to counter Hànôi's highly sophisticated air defence system, there had not been time to do the same with the Gs when they were rushed into the war during the 1972 Easter Offensive. The 207 B-52s in Southeast Asia carried an impressive array of countermeasures equipment that included the ALT-22 jamming transmitter, used against the Fan Song track-while-scan beacon and the ALT-28, which could either reinforce the ALT-22 or engage in down-link jamming. By mid-December all B-52s serving in this area mounted four ALT-28s and three ALT-22s, except for 41 of the 98 G models on Guam that carried older, less powerful ALT-6Bs instead of the ALT-22s. Electronic warfare officers in the bombers usually directed two ALT-28s and two ALT-22s or ALT-6s against Fan Song and used the other pair of ALT-28s to jam the SAM guidance beacon. With the remaining ALT-22 or ALT-6, he usually attacked height-finder radars.

EWOs in single B-52s could operate their countermeasures to defeat single missiles but they were hard pressed to identify and individually jam missiles fired at the bomber stream in a shotgun pattern, as they often were. The Viêtnamese simply tripped off salvoes of six missiles from each site. The lighter structure of the B-52G, which contributed to its outstanding long-range performance and in turn reduced the need for aerial refuelling, meant that the aircraft was more vulnerable to battle damage. The B-52s were especially vulnerable just prior to bomb release (the radar signature of the B-52 increased significantly when the bomb doors were opened) and after when they were to swing in wide turns to the west and head back over Laos, which, it was hoped, would take them out of SAM range as soon as possible. Conventional B-

52 bombing techniques in Việtnam were identical to the procedures laid down in training for nuclear strikes whereby SAC crews executed a 45° banked turn known as the 'post target turn' or PTT to escape a nuclear blast. The Stratofortresses sought to minimize exposure to the SAMs by getting out of missile range as rapidly as possible, even though steeply banked turns of 113 to 160 degrees were required. The officers who approved these tactics realized that such a turn was 'a characteristically vulnerable position' because the 'effects of both TWS and beacon jamming were minimized as these steep turns blanked out the jamming antennas on the undersides of the B-52s and also turned the B-52s into 100-knot headwinds that kept the aircraft within range of the SAM operators for longer periods. They believed, however, that the greater speed in leaving the target area would more than offset the loss of jamming coverage. Requests by Eighth Air Force to allow B-52 crews to flatten out the turn to 15° of bank had fallen on deaf ears at SAC.

As the bombers closed in on their targets the North Việtnamese defences began to react. F-111A 67-099 piloted by Lieutenant Colonel Ronald Jack Ward and Major James R. McElvain were forced to ditch in the Gulf of Tonkin near the coastline at Hoành Đông . It was suspected that these two airmen may have ejected but they remain MIA. The greatest danger however, was from SAMs. That night the enemy fired 164 missiles. Captain Robert E. Wolf, the pilot of one of the B-52s operating from Guam, recalled: From the beginning of the bomb run to the target, my gunner counted 32 SAMs fired at or at least passing close to our aircraft.' Captain Robert P. Jacober adds: 'My first real sense of combat was not the flashes ahead - that would prove to be the SAMs detonating - but the sound of multiple 'beepers'; the emergency locator radio beacons that are activated by a parachute opening after an ejection. So many going off at once could only signify that a 'Buff' had been shot, down. The only advice I could remember was: 'If you can keep a SAM moving across your windscreen, it is not going to hit you.' Captain D. D. McCrabbe, a EWO on one of the bombers felt that the SAM crews were 'a little confused' at first, but the confusion ended as soon as the raiders had dropped their bombs. 'We started doing our post-target turn and just all hell broke loose,' the captain related. 'They just started throwing everything at us.' In Hànôi General Võ Nguyên Giáp was informed that a B-52 had been shot down by a unit of the 261st Missile Regiment.

In the first wave of forty-eight aircraft were nine cells from Guam that stretched for thirty miles as the strike force crossed over South Việtnam and headed northwest to Laos, where it was supposed to compress into a nine-mile-long bomber stream. 'As we approached the point where we were to bunch up', recalls Bob Certain on 'Charcoal 01' 'the two cells behind us discovered that they were to be at the rendezvous point at exactly the same time and altitude, rather than spaced out at three-minute intervals and had to some dog-legging to avoid midair collisions.'

B-52D 56-0678, Call Sign 'Lilac 03' of the 43rd Strategic Wing piloted by Major David O'Neil was hit near the left side of the cockpit by a SAM explosion which punctured most of the fuel tanks, knocked out the instruments and electrical power and damaged the bomb-release system. A fragment penetrated the pilot's side window and passed directly across the cockpit, shattering the co-pilot's side window before it spent itself. O'Neil had been hit by small pieces of shrapnel in his eye and arms and Joe Grega, the co-pilot, was hit in both arms. In the rear of the aircraft gunner Joe Smart's compartment had been hit heavily and all his oxygen lines were cut. There was a large hole the size of a small plate in the back of his seat but miraculously Smart was uninjured in the blast. With the loss of fuel in the drop tank the B-52D began rolling rapidly to the right before both pilots got it under control. 'Lilac 03' diverted to U-Tapao leaking fuel and with all radios and the interphone out. Unbeknown to the crew the bleed air duct in the bomb bay had ruptured and was pouring 800-degree bled air from the engines onto the full load of 750lb bombs still in the bomb bay. Grega managed to put 'Lilac 03' down at U-Tapao where the bombs were too hot to touch with bare hands and ground crew stopped counting after the damage to the aircraft reached 350 external holes and 24 areas requiring kits - work that would take 60,000 man hours!

Staff Sergeant Samuel O. Turner, tail gunner, B-52D 56-0676 'Brown 03' in the 307th Bomb Wing receives the Silver Star for shooting down a NVAF MiG-21 on 18 December from General John C. Meyer, Commander of SAC. B-52, 55-0676, is now on display at Fairchild AFB, Spokane, Washington.
Another tail gunner, 18-year old Airman 1st Class Albert E. Moore, a 307th Bomb Wing tail gunner on B-52D 55-0083 *Diamond Lil* call-sign 'Ruby 03' was also awarded the Silver Star for destroying a MiG-21, on Christmas Eve. It was the last victory by a tail gunner in wartime using machine guns.

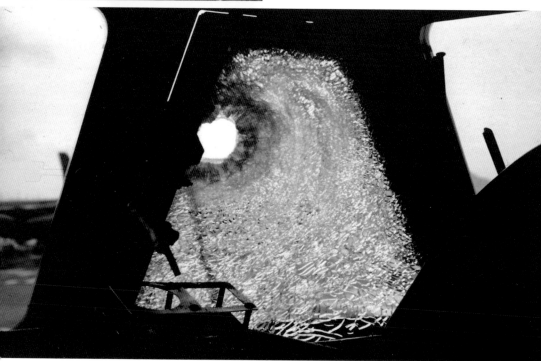

A fragment from the SAM explosion penetrated the pilot's side window and passed directly across the cockpit, shattering the co-pilot's side window before it spent itself. Major David O'Neil was hit by small pieces of shrapnel in his eye and arms and 1st Lieutenant Joseph Vincent Grega, the co-pilot of Dunmore, Pennsylvania, was hit in both arms, who nevertheless managed to put 'Lilac 03' down at U-Tapao and he was awarded the Purple Heart (right).

B-52D 56-0678 Call Sign 'Lilac 03' (pictured at MASDC in 1978) of the 43rd Strategic Wing which landed at U-Tapao on 19 December 1972 with 350 external holes and 24 areas requiring kits .

The Abuha Missile Control Station (pictured)operated by the 77th Battalion, 257th Air Defence Regiment (Hero Unit) which claimed four B-52s during December 1972. In their un-air-conditioned command van, each about the size of an 18-wheeler, whose noisy diesel engines to provide power to the radar, were a battalion commander, connected by phone to the regimental HQ, sat in front of the 'Spoon Rest' radar scope, where he watched the raids come in while waiting for orders assigning the battalion a target; a fire control officer in front of a 'Fan Song' radar scope that he used to locate and track the target; three guidance officers, one each responsible for elevation, azimuth and range of the missile, with radar scopes with large control wheels beneath them to keep crosshairs on the target's radar return; a plotter, also connected by phone to HQ; and a missile technical officer, responsible for monitoring the status panels of each of the six launchers and their missiles. When assigned a target the plotter tracked the raid manually on the plotting board. The van was tightly sealed to keep out light so the operators could focus on their radar scopes, below and the only sound other than the voices of the crew was that of loud cooling fans, necessary to control the temperature of the vacuum tubes in the relatively primitive electronics of the SA-2 system. The NVA sometimes placed the radars away from the missiles to make the site harder to destroy.

A typical SA-2 site had six missiles on launchers, control and command support vans, 'Spoon Rest' acquisition radar that detected incoming aircraft as far as 70 miles, providing location data to the system computer and 'Fan Song' target acquisition and guidance radar, which got its name from its horizontal and vertical fan scanning antennas and its distinctive sounding emissions that could be picked up by the B-52's warning equipment. 'Fan Song' could acquire as many as four targets before firing up to three SA-2s against one target.

The Initial Point-to-Target axis of attack took Don Rissi's crew over the most closely grouped SAM sites defending Hànôi and their aircraft was one of those on Guam that had not received the ECM equipment upgrades. B-52 bombing computers required an absolutely straight and level approach and crews had to maintain that approach for at least four minutes before dropping their bombs. If radar navigators were not entirely sure of their targets at this point they were instructed to abort their drop. Bob Certain in the lower deck crew compartment was as confident as any 25-year-old that he was not going to die but recalled that 'It had been a bad day - nothing had gone right from the mission briefing on Guam. As we turned eastbound out of Laos to enter North Viêtnam for the bomb run, we were all focused on making this the best, most accurate mission we had ever flown. We would be in lethal range of SAMs for about twenty minutes, but we couldn't be distracted by the threats. The radar navigator and I turned off our exterior radios so we could concentrate only on our checklists and crew coordination. We had been ordered to take no evasive action from the initial aiming point to the bomb release point. Those orders seemed to become increasingly suicidal as we heard multiple SAM calls from the B-52s from U-Tapao that had entered the target zone thirty minutes ahead of us.[8] Major Richard Johnson, the radar navigator and I had suppressed all emotion to concentrate on this critical phase of the mission. Fifteen seconds before bombs away we opened the doors and five seconds later I restarted my stopwatch as a backup to the drop should anything go wrong. Almost immediately it did.

At 0003 local time just after dark when 'Charcoal 01' ran in on the Yên Viên rail yards the radar signature of the B-52 increased significantly as the bomb doors opened and the aircraft suffered a near-direct SAM hit that same instant. Bob Certain recalled: 'We were exactly on target when the SAM from below kissed us on the cheek and we lost the plane and half the crew. The radar screens went blank and other instruments lost power. My first thought was that the copilot, Bobby Thomas had accidentally knocked the generators off line but before I could speak Bobby was shouting over the interphone, 'They got the pilot! They got the pilot!'

Looking at the clock on his console Bob Certain noted that the SAM exploded at 1313 Greenwich Mean Time. A few seconds later another SAM exploded nearby but later Captain Tom Simpson could not confirm a second SAM hit. He was also shouting: 'Is anybody there? Gunner! Gunner!' But Ferguson was dead. He could see the gunner's helmet in the glow of electrical panels that were exploding and sending showers of blue sparks bouncing off the cabin walls. Bob Certain looked over his left shoulder and saw fire in the forward wheel well through the porthole in the door behind him. 'My first thought was of the twenty-seven 750lb bombs in the bomb bay right behind the fire and I turned to the RN and yelled, 'Drop those damn bombs!'

Johnson safetied them because he did not know where they would land. 'I tried to hit the salvo button but I don't think we got rid of the bombs. I never did feel them go' he said later.

Bob Certain however, thought that 'they all seemed to drop away from our now-crippled B-52.' His next thought was that the fire was also directly below the main mid-body fuel tank, loaded with 10,000lbs of JP-4. Then aircraft commander Don Rissi's voice came weakly over the interphone. 'Pilot's still alive.'

'Figuring it was time to get out of here I called: 'Co-pilot, this is the nav; escape heading is 290.'

'It was now about ten seconds after the first of two SAMs hit the plane and I heard the call, 'EW's leaving!' as Tom Simpson ejected. I heard the explosion of his hatch above me and the boom from his seat as it rocketed up and out, but felt no decompression. I looked at the RN. Our eyes met and we both started preparing for ejection. I threw my flight case as far to the rear of the cockpit as I could, grabbed the ejection handle, looked at the RN again and then turned to face forward. I saw the ejection light come on showing the pilot ejected and pulled the handle. The seat failed. At least, that's what I thought. The ballistic activators were supposed to blow the hatch below my seat and fire me out of the bottom of the plane in one-tenth of a second, but I was so scared that the panels in front of me seemed to be barely moving at first, then to move

26

Right: Lieutenant Colonel Donald Louis Rissi, pilot of 'Charcoal 01'. (via Steve Rissi)

Below:1st Lieutenant Robert J. 'Bobby' Thomas, the subsitute co-pilot of 'Charcoal 01'.

Below right - Major 'Dick' Johnson, navigator is paraded through the streets of Hànôi following capture after ejecting from 'Charcoal 01'.

up in slow motion. Before I knew what had happened I was tumbling in the cold air of the stratosphere, thinking, 'That was a dumb thing to do. I'll bet the plane was still flyable. Where is it? Maybe I can crawl back in. OK God, it's you and me. If I'm going to die down there, don't even let my 'chute open. Just take me now.' But I felt the parachute opening. 'I checked for a good chute and then looked down for the first time. Between my boots, I saw the inferno that made up the three targets that we had hit over the last twenty minutes. As I watched, I saw a series of explosions walk though the target, another string of 27 bombs finding pay-dirt. Then, [just ahead on the ground] I caught another series of explosions - right in line with my drift. Oh God, now what? There shouldn't be another target over there; that was our escape route. As I looked down, I realized that this fire was shaped like an arrow - our B-52 had ploughed in flames into a village. Now panic was beginning to replace concern. Where were the ******* clouds that had covered the ground when I first bailed out? I was hurtling through the night sky over enemy territory with little or no chance of rescue. With the full moon I could see the ground clearly all around and the white panels in the canopy and my white helmet were not going to be assets as I slowly descended to the ground no more than ten kilometers north of Hànôi. The Holy Spirit was with me that night and never left me throughout the next hundred and one days' I was to spend as a prisoner.'

Certain's wife Robbie was looking forward to celebrating Christmas with her husband in Blytheville when an officer from the base accompanied by an Air Force chaplain knocked on her door and informed her that Certain was 'missing in action' over North Việtnam. Ironically, his brother, Captain John Certain, a KC-135 tanker pilot had been orbiting a refueling track called 'Purple Anchor' over the Gulf of Tonkin on the night of 18 December and he had seen a B-52 get hit over Hànôi and go down in flames. He was later informed that it had been his brother's bomber.

Shortly after his capture Bob Certain was shown the body of his commander, Don Rissi who had apparently died from wounds sustained during the SAM strike. On 23 August 1978 the remains of Rissi, Thomas and Ferguson were returned by the North Việtnamese and were identified by pathologists at the Armed Forces Identification Laboratory in Honolulu on 11 September. 'Bobby' Thomas the substitute co-pilot had been killed as the aircraft exploded in a ball of fire. After landing Dick Johnson was paraded through the streets of Hànôi for propaganda value on the world's TV news bulletins. Tom Simpson had received multiple fragment wounds on both arms and legs but had also landed safely. Certain and his cellmate, Major Fernando Alexander, who was from the second B-52 shot down had to move to another cell when the concussions from a strike on gun positions near the Hỏa Lò prison blew the cell door off its hinges one afternoon. They were moved to a two-man cell in a section of the prison they called 'Heartbreak Hotel. Before a week was out Certain and Alexander were moved into another cell with seven other PoWs. All were members of various B-52 crews that had gone down during the 'Eleven-Day War.'

'We never doubted that we would be out soon and expected every day to hear about the signing of the treaty which would end the longest war we had ever known. We knew our people wanted the end; we knew the President wanted the end; and we knew that God would answer our prayers. Before long we were holding regular Sunday church services - Catholics, Baptists, Mormons - everybody joined in. Then, it happened: PEACE. And the countdown started - only sixty days to go. Always long, each day seemed like a week; but we made it, thanks to the ever-present help of the Holy Spirit with us in answer to the prayers of millions of our fellow Americans.' [9]

On 'Peach 02' Hendsley Conner thought he knew what was in store for them - he had flown over 200 missions in B-57s - but he had never seen so many SAMs. 'They made white streaks of light as they climbed into the night sky. As they left the ground, they would move slowly, pick up speed as they climbed and end their flight, finally, in a cascade of sparkles. There were so many of them it reminded me of a Fourth of July fireworks display; a beautiful sight to watch if I hadn't known how lethal they could be. I did not feel nearly as secure in the big, lumbering bomber as I had in my B-57 Canberra that could manoeuvre much better.

'Just before we started our bomb run we checked our emergency gear to make sure everything was all right in case we were hit. We would be most vulnerable on the bomb run, since we would be within lethal range of the SAMs and would be flying straight and level. We had been briefed not to make any evasive manoeuvres on the bomb run so that the radar navigator would be positive he was aiming at the right target. If he was not absolutely sure he had the right target, we were to withhold our bombs and then jettison them into the ocean on our way back to Guam. We did not want to hit anything but military targets. Precision bombing was the object of our mission. The crew were briefed this way and they followed their instructions.

'About half way down the bomb run, the EWO on our crew began to call over the interphone that SAMs had been fired at us. One, two, three, now four missiles had been fired. We flew straight and level.

'How far out from the target are we radar?'

'We're ten seconds out. Five. Four. Three. Two. One. BOMBS AWAY! Start your turn, pilot.'

'We began a right turn to exit the target area.'

'KABOOM! We were hit.

'It felt like we had been in the centre of a clap of thunder. The noise was deafening. Everything went really bright for an instant, then dark again. I could smell ozone from burnt powder and had felt a slight jerk on my right shoulder.

'I quickly checked the flight instruments and over the interphone said, 'Pilot, we're still flying. Are you OK?'

'Yes, I'm fine but the airplane is in bad shape. Let's check it over and see if we can keep it airborne. Everybody check in and let me know how they are.'

'Navigator and radar are OK. We don't have any equipment operating, but I'll give you a heading to Thailand any time you want it.'

'EWO is OK but the gunner has been hit. We have about two more minutes in lethal SAM range, so continue to make manoeuvres if you can.'

'Gunner is OK. I have some shrapnel in my right arm, but nothing bad. The left side of the airplane is full of holes.'

'I called the lead aircraft to let them know we had been hit. He said he could tell we had been hit because our left wing was on fire and we were slowing down. I asked him to call some escort fighters for us.

'The airplane continued to fly all right, so the pilot resumed making evasive manoeuvres. We flew out of range of the missiles, finally and began to take stock of the airplane.

'The SAM had exploded right off our left wing. The fuel tank on that wing was missing along with part of the wing tip. We had lost #1 and #2 engines. Fire was streaming out of the wreckage they had left. Fuel was coming out of holes all throughout the left wing. Most of our flight instruments were not working. We had lost cabin pressurization. We were at 33,000 feet altitude. Our oxygen supply must have been hit because the quantity gauge was slowly decreasing. I took out two walk-around bottles for the pilot and co-pilot. If we ran out, they at least would have enough emergency oxygen to get us down to an altitude where we could breathe.

'We turned to a heading that would take us to U-Tapao, Thailand. I called again for the fighter escort to take us toward friendly territory.

'We're here, buddy.'

'Two F-4s had joined us and would stay with us as long as they were needed. One stayed high and the other stayed out on our wing as we descended to a lower altitude and to oxygen. They called to alert rescue service in case we had to abandon the aircraft. Our first concern was to get out of North Việtnam and Laos. We did not want to end up as PoWs. We knew they did not take many prisoners in Laos. Thailand locked beautiful when we finally crossed the border. Since Thailand was not subject to bombing attacks, they still had their lights on at night. We flew for about thirty minutes after we had descended to a lower altitude and began to think we would be able to get the airplane on the ground safely. The fire in the left pod was still burning but it didn't seem to be getting any worse. One F-4 left us. The other one said he would take one more close-look at us before he too would have to leave. His fuel reserve was running low. He flew down and joined on our left wing.

'I'd better stay with you friend. The fire is getting worse and I don't think you'll make it.'

'I unfastened my lap belt and leaned over between the pilot and co-pilot to take another look at the fire. It had now spread to the fuel leaking out of the wing and the whole left wing was burning. It was a wall of red flame starting just outside the cockpit and as high as I could see.

'I said, 'I think I'll head downstairs.'

'Good idea' said the pilot.

'The six crewmembers in the B-52G have ejection seats that they fire to abandon the aircraft. Anyone else on board has to go down to the lower compartment and manually bail out of the hole the navigator or radar navigator leaves when their seat is ejected. I quickly climbed down the ladder and started to plug in my interphone cord to see what our situation was.

'The red Abandon light came on.

'BAM! The navigator fired his ejection seat and was gone.

'The radar turned toward me and pointed to the hole the navigator had left and motioned for me to jump. I climbed over some debris and stood on the edge of the hole. I looked at the ground far below. Did I want to jump? The airplane began to shudder and shake and I heard another louder blast. The wing was exploding. Yes, I wanted to jump! I rolled through the opening and as soon as I thought I was free of the airplane, I pulled the ripcord on my parachute. I felt a sharp jerk and looked to see the parachute canopy open above me. The opening shock felt good even though it had hurt more than I had expected. Everything was quiet and eerie. There was a full moon, the weather was clear and I could see things very well. I looked for other parachutes. One, two, three; that's all I saw. Then I saw the airplane. It was flying in a descending turn to the left and the whole fuselage was now burning and parts of the left wing had left the airplane. It was exploding as it hit the ground.

'I saw I was getting close to the ground, so I got ready to land. I was floating backwards but I could see I was going to land in a little village. I raised my legs to keep from going into a hootch. I certainly didn't want to land in someone's bedroom. I got my feet down, hit the ground and rolled over on my backside. I got up on one knee and began to feel around to see if it was all right. Everything seemed to be fine. There was a little blood on my right shoulder from where a piece of shrapnel had hit, but otherwise, just bruises. It felt good to be alive.

'About twenty or twenty-five Thai villagers came out of their homes and stood watching me. They were very quiet and friendly and brought water for me to drink. None of them spoke English, so we spent our time waiting for rescue, trying to communicate with sign language. They kept pointing to the sky and showing what must have been an airplane crashing and burning. I tried to describe a helicopter to let them know one would be coming soon t6o pick me up. I hoped.

'In about twenty minutes a Marine helicopter did and I was picked up. We had bailed out near the Marine base at Nam Phong. All six of the crew had already been rescued and none had serious injuries. We were flown to U-Tapao and then on back to Guam the next day. Our particular ordeal in the bombing raids was over. The crew had performed well; I was proud of them. The reason I had decided to fly with them on the mission was because I thought they were one of my most professional crews. The outstanding way they handled our emergency showed how competent and courageous they were. They, along with survivors from other aircraft were flown back to the States for rest and leave. They were short of squadron commanders on Guam so I had to stay and help prepare other raids that were continuing each night.'

At the third wave's briefing at U-Tapao Lieutenant Colonel John Harry 'Yuma' Yuill, born in Boswell, Indiana, the oldest of six children, had sat 'looking around and thinking, you know, some of us probably have about three or four more hours to live. This is probably it for some of us. And I've never been in a situation in my life before... like that. Where you knew there was a pretty good possibility that at least some of the people in that room weren't coming back alive that night.'

Yuill had enlisted in the Air Force in February 1954, completed navigator training and was commissioned in April 1955. He attended pilot training and graduated in June 1959, being assigned to F-86s at Perrin AFB, Texas before flying B-52s at Altus AFB, Oklahoma. He then flew F-102s at Perrin for a short time before going to Grissom AFB, Indiana to fly the B-58 'Hustler'. This enjoyable assignment lasted from March 1967 until February 1970. During this time he flew as a pilot and CCTS instructor pilot. Next assignment was to 'CCK' (Ching Chuang Kang Air Base) on Taiwan for a tour in C-130s as a pilot and instructor pilot from May 1970 to July 1971 and most of this time was spent flying out of Sàigòn. He then went to Carswell AFB, Texas and B-52s once again. Yuill left Carswell TDY for Guam and Thailand in April 1972 flying missions over Việtnam. When 'Linebacker II' kicked off his crew was chosen to be wave lead on the last wave from U-T. He left the briefing when the crews from the first wave came in. 'They didn't say a word, but looking at their eyes I knew it must have been a bad day at the office.'

Captain David Ian Drummond, Yuill's 25-year old co-pilot, was born in Preston, England in 1947 and emigrated to the United States in 1951 and later set up home in Westwood, New Jersey with his wife Jill. In December 1970 he deployed to South East Asia and served as a C-7A pilot in the 535th Tactical Airlift Squadron at Cam Ranh Bay and for a short time as a KC-135 Stratotanker pilot in the 7th Air Refuelling Squadron at Carswell AFB, Texas before attending B-52 Combat Crew Training. Lieutenant Colonel Louis Henry Bernasconi, the 41-year-old radar/navigator from Napa, California served three tours in Vietnam and flew B-36s in the fifties and B-47s and C-123s in the sixties. 1st Lieutenant (later Colonel) William Thomas Mayall the 24-year old navigator from Levittown, New York had been flying overseas for about five weeks when the December eighteenth bombing raids began. Technical Sergeant Gary Lee Morgan the 26-year old gunner was a Texan from Abilene. He had taken part in 23 B-52 missions thus far. Thirty-seven-year old Lieutenant Colonel William Conlee from Galesburg, Illinois was the EWO: 'After the general briefing crews split up into specialties to discuss mission tactics, late intelligence and bombing information, Excitement ran high and the general feeling was 'At last - let's do it!'

Having lost the element of surprise the 51 B-52s of 'Wave III', which arrived five hours after the second wave to attack the Kinh Nỗ Complex, the Hànôi railroad repair shops at Giá Lam and the main radio station on the outskirts of Hànôi, was met with a formidable defensive array of sixty-one SAMs fired, heavy AAA fire and MiG-21s attempting interceptions. Six unmodified B-52Gs had been recalled from 'Wave II' but the twelve unmodified B-52Gs in 'Wave III', which were to strike the Kinh Nỗ Complex, an extensive area which contained four key targets, were not recalled. Seven B-52D cells of the 307th Strategic Wing flying in from almost due west came within range of eleven SAM sites. B-52D 56-0608, Call Sign 'Rose 01', piloted by Captain Hal K. 'Red' Wilson and co-pilot Captain Charles A. Brown Jr., whose crew was deployed from the 99th Bomb Wing at Westover AFB, Massachusetts was the lead aircraft in the last cell to bomb the radio station. Wilson, who was from Hamburg, New York, was flying his 251st combat mission over Southeast Asia in his four tours of duty. He recalled that SAMs were 'wall to wall'. 'Rose 01' was almost downed on its post-target turn by a SAM which went between the wing and the stabiliser. A second SAM detonated at the B-52's height of 38,000 feet and knocked out the Nos. 3 and 4 engines. In the ensuing fire, there was no time for orderly bailout as 'Rose 01' hurtled down in the vicinity of Hànôi. Wilson and co-pilot Captain Charles A. Brown Jr., both ejected. The radar navigator, Major Fernando Alexander looked through a large hole on the left side of the aircraft at the external bomb rack and saw the No.3 engine on fire. He had joined the

Air Force in 1952 and had been a navigator on B-29s and B-47s prior to converting to the B-52. Alexander too ejected. Captain Henry 'Hank' C. Barrows became the fourth member of the crew to be taken prisoner. A German whose family had emigrated to the USA in 1958, Barrows had previously flown 120 missions during a tour on the AC-130 Hercules gun-ship at Ubon. Later examination of radio tapes seemed to indicate that all six crewmen safely ejected and the aircraft damage report indicated that all were prisoners. Radio Hànôi announced in news broadcasts between 19 and 22 December that the six crewmen had been captured but when the war ended, only four of the crew returned from North Viêtnamese prisons. Hànôi remained silent about the fate of Sergeant Charlie Sherman Poole, the 40-year old tail gunner of Gibsland, Louisiana and Captain Richard Waller Cooper Jr., the 30-year old navigator of Salisbury, Maryland who had a 2½-year-old daughter and another on the way.[10] His brother said many years later that he was starting to question the war. 'He tried to be tough and macho on the surface, but he tended to be sensitive and felt things deeply.'

'We had already been warned that MiGs had launched and were heading our way' continues Captain Robert P. Jacober. 'The EWO alerted us that SAM radars were following us. There was a cloud layer beneath us, so when I saw the first SAM ignite on the launcher, the plume was diffused like a match seen through a fog. But it quickly focused into a sharp flame and the SAM looked like someone was throwing a candle at us. Seven were launched at us during the bomb run, four on our inbound run and three over the city. We could determine that only one was guided. It came at us from our 12 o'clock position. The EWO said 'Uplink' about the time I saw it come up through the clouds. No matter what the pilot did, we could not get it to move on the windscreen. It passed just off of our nose and exploded several thousand feet above us. If they had had our altitude right, we probably would have been hit. The bomb run itself went as briefed. Our post target turn took us among the four SAM sites that were in

Left: Captain Hal K. 'Red' Wilson, pilot, B-52D 56-0608, Call Sign 'Rose 01'.

Right; Sergeant Charlie Sherman Poole, tail gunner, 'Rose 01'.

Left; Captain Richard Waller Cooper Jr., navigator, 'Rose 01'.

Right; Captain Charles A. Brown Jr., co-pilot, 'Rose 01'.

downtown Hànôi. During the turn, the pilot had rolled into about 70° of bank. We lost several thousand feet. Since I was looking almost straight down, I had a good view of the three SAMs that launched. Fortunately none came close and the return flight to Guam was quiet.'

Seventeen SAMs had been fired at the first wave. Forty-five B-52s had bombed successfully. Over Hànôi 30-year old Staff Sergeant Samuel O. Turner of Atlanta, Georgia, tail gunner on B-52D 56-0676 'Brown 03' in the 307th Bomb Wing claimed the first Stratofortress victory of the war. He recalled, 'As we drew nearer to the target the intensity of the SAMs picked up. They were lightening up the sky. They seemed to be everywhere. We released our bombs over the target and had just proceeded outbound from the target when we learned that there were MiG aircraft airborne near a particular reference point...before long we learned the enemy fighter had us on its radar. As he closed on us I also picked him up on my radar when he was a few miles from our aircraft...A few seconds later, the fighter locked on to us. As the MiG closed in, I also locked on to him. He came in low in a rapid climb…As the attacking MiG came into firing range, I fired a burst. There was a gigantic explosion to the rear of the aircraft.'[11] Turner's claim was later confirmed as a MiG-21.

In all, the city's defences fired 164 SAMs and thousands of rounds of anti-aircraft ammunition, shooting down three B-52s and damaging three others. All the hits occurred as the B-52s were turning into wind of at least 71 knots and struggling to get out of SAM range. In the cold light of day senior staff officers had seriously underestimated the strength of the air defences and the tactics used so well on 'Arc Light' missions were no defence in the heavily defended airspace over Hànôi and Hải̇phòng. Thirty-six year old Richard J. Smith a a grizzled EWO who spent approximately ten years of his military career on TDY in Việtnam and was credited with 506 'Arc Light'/'Linebacker' combat missions flying out of U-Tapao, says: 'So, you're jamming the radar that's tracking you, but there's four other missiles that are coming up that aren't being tracked... And so that was the biggest though, was, how many do they have? How many are they going to fire at you or me?' The wide spacing of the waves created considerable problems for the SAM-suppression and Chaff-sowing aircraft and equally the long pause between attacks allowed the enemy air defences too much time to recover before the next wave. After releasing their bombs B-52 pilots had helped the defenders by making steep banked turns into the fierce headwinds, hampering their withdrawal and ECM patterns and enabling the SAM radars to pick them out more easily. Obviously, more Chaff corridors were needed to screen each wave in high tailwinds.

For Lieutenant Colonel Bill Conlee launch and join up was no problem and the mission had gone routinely until entry into North Việtnam, where a high level of radar activity was immediately apparent, 'Electronic countermeasures were applied. We proceeded to the IP and completed our bomb run without incident except for obvious SAM radar engagement attempts. We released our weapons and started our post release turn when SAM launches were detected, visually and electronically. From the time we started our turn until about forty miles southwest of Hànôi we came under heavy SAM attack employing evasive action turns to avoid SA-2s. During this seeming eternity of time we counted approximately forty SAMs launched in our general direction or in the vicinity of our cell. On the return route to U-T we were unable to contact 'Rose 01' and someone reported they were down near Hànôi. After landing, the debriefers were incredulous at the large number of SAMs which had been fired during the mission.'

In the 'Hànôi Hilton' there was no doubt in the minds of the prisoners that now the B-52 raids were hitting the Hải̇phòng-Hànôi area it could only hasten their release. Colonel Robinson Risner, who spent seven and half years in captivity said: 'On 18 December there was never such joy seen in our camp before. There were people jumping up and down and putting their arms around each other and there were tears running down our faces. We knew they were B-52s and President Nixon was keeping his word and that the Communists were getting the message. We saw reaction in the Việtnamese that we had never seen under the attacks from fighters. They at last knew that we had some weapons they had not felt and that President Nixon was willing to use those weapons in order to get us out of Việtnam.' The Senior PoW, Colonel (later Lieutenant General) John P. 'Sky' Flynn of the 388th TFW who was shot down flying an F-105 on 17 October 1967, agreed: 'When I heard the B-52 bombs go off I sent a message to our people. It said, 'Pack your bags - I don't know when we're going home - but we're going home.'

General John C. Meyer, Commander of SAC, considered the three losses sustained on 18/19 December to be an acceptable figure[12] and tactics remained largely unchanged. Dr. John F. Guilmartin Jr., a Professor of History at Ohio State University, Columbus and a Việtnam War veteran, having flown over 120 combat missions, said: 'I think it's very clear that General Meyer and his staff at Omaha were babes in the woods tactically about what the North Việtnamese defences could and would do to us.' When asked about the 'stupid' tactics 'and why?' the briefers told the pilots: 'The planning is being done at Omaha's SAC HQ and the common routes, altitudes and trail formations are used for ease of planning.' Lieutenant General Gerald W. Johnson Commanding 8th Air Force during 'Linebacker II' recalled: 'The thing you're really asking, you know, is... knowing all of this and now you're about to launch the next night's missions, what did you do to try to assure that it won't happen again the next night. Well, it turned out that SAC had already decided that the next night was going to be the same damned way it was the first night. Same routing and the same separations. And that same horrible turn right after bomb release.'

On 19 December President Nixon extended the 'Linebacker' campaign indefinitely. That night because of the long distances involved in operating from Guam, it had been necessary to order the ninety-three B-52D and Gs launched even before all the Day One aircraft returned. Colonel McCarthy flew the mission aboard 'White 01' piloted by Major Tom Lebar from Dyess AFB, Texas. The last cells of Day One were landing while the B-52s of Day Two were starting engines. The targets around Hànôi would again be hit in three waves and the approach route remained unchanged. The three B-52s lost the first night had been flying at 34,000 feet, 38,000 feet and 38,500 feet and indication that the lowest and highest aircraft in the bomber streams had not received adequate chaff protection. As a result, base altitudes of 34,500 and 35,000 feet were established for the bomber cells, keeping all the aircraft closer to the centre of a corridor sown from 36,000 feet. And, in order to give the B-52s room to avoid approaching SAMs, the interval between cells was doubled to four minutes. This increased interval allowed the enemy more time for passive radar tracking, but the increased chaff coverage, plus the jamming barrage from the bomber cells were expected to offset this advantage. No really drastic revision of B-52 tactics seemed necessary. As one of the aircraft commanders later pointed out, there really was no reason to change tactics at this point.' The Stratofortresses, after all, had used the same basic procedures over Hàiphòng on 15 April and suffered no losses. 'Sure,' he admitted, 'we lost some aircraft on the first day [of Linebacker II], but the area we flew in was better defended.' [13]

'About this timer there was a call from a cell back in the wave reporting MiGs and requesting MiGCAP. At one minute prior to bombs away, the EWO's scope became saturated with strong SAM lock-on signals. It was also at this point in the run that the bomb bay doors were opened. There had been and would continue to be, quite a bit of discussion by the staff and crews as to whether opening of the bomb doors, exposing the mass of bombs to reflect energy to the SAM sites, gave the enemy an even brighter target to shoot at.

'At about ten seconds prior to bombs away, when the EWO was reporting the strongest signals, we observed a Shrike being fired, low and forward of our nose. Five seconds later, several SAM signals dropped off the air and the EWO reported they were no longer a threat to our aircraft.

'The Buff began a slight shudder as the bombs left the racks. The aircraft, being relieved of nearly 22 tons of ordnance, wanted to rise rapidly and it took a double handful of stick and throttles to keep it straight and level. After the release was complete and the bomb doors closed, Tom Lebar put the aircraft in a steep turn to the right. The turn had saved us, but the gunner and co-pilot reported more SAMs on the way.

'It seemed like the turn was going to last forever and the co-pilot reported the SAMs tracking the aircraft and getting closer. It was now a race to see if we could complete the turn before the SAMs reached our altitude. Once the turn was completed we would be free to make small manoeuvres, because the other aircraft in our cell would still be in the turn... It is strange what goes through your mind at a time like this. My thoughts were: 'What the hell am I doing here?' With a lung full of what eventually turned into double pneumonia and no ejection seat I wasn't exactly an ideal insurance risk.

'We completed the turn and started our manoeuvre as the SAMs reached our altitude but they did not explode. One on the left and another on the right seemed to form an arch over the aircraft. As they approached each other at the apex of the arch they exploded.

'We saw another Shrike missile launched and again some of the threat signals disappeared. Those F-105 'Wild Weasel' troops from the 388th Tactical Fighter Wing were earning their pay tonight. I made a mental note to write their wing commander, Colonel Mele Vojvodich and congratulate his crews on their outstanding work. Mele and I had served together at Korat.

'As we egressed the target area the SAM signals dropped off. Now our problem was to get the wave back together and assess our battle damage, plus collect strike reports. It was the duty of the ABC to collect this information and then pass it through encoded HF radio communications to the 8th Air Force command post. If any aircraft were damaged, it was also up to the ABC to make the decision as to where the aircraft would go. If it was only minor battle damage, then the aircraft would normally be instructed to return to Andersen with the rest of the bomber stream. We needed every airframe we could get our hands on for the following day's sorties.'

Twelve B-52Ds carrying 42 750lb M117 bombs internally and 24 500lb Mk.82 bombs on the underwing pylons and nine B-52Gs from Andersen carrying an internal load of 27 M117s of Wave I headed for the Kinh Nỗ rail yard and storage area and other targets singled out for attention by two successive waves. These included the Bắc Giáng transhipment point, Colonel McCarthy recalled: 'The frag order called for our fighter escort to rendezvous with us approximately fifteen minutes prior to the IP for the bomb run. Due to weather in their own refuelling area, they were delayed so that they were unable to join up until just prior to the IP. This complicated communications and aircraft positioning, but they got there. As we turned over the IP the EWO detected the first SAM lock-on. At this time we were northwest of Hànôi, heading for the city in a south-easterly direction. Suddenly, the gunner broke in on interphone to report that he had two SAMs low heading right for us. The EWO confirmed that they were tracking toward us. The co-pilot then reported four missiles coming our way on the right side. Added to the pyrotechnics were Shrike anti-radiation missile firings, which would give us momentary concern until we identified them. Then it was nice to watch something bright streaking the other way - our guys had their own bag of tricks. The pilot then reported two missiles coming up on his side. The nav team downstairs was busy trying to complete their checklist fort the bomb run. Other aircraft and 'Red Crown' [the US Navy cruiser USS *Truxtun* stationed in the northern Gulf of Tonkin, which provided radar surveillance and other logistical support during missions] were also calling SAM warnings and antiaircraft fire. The primary radio frequency quickly became saturated.

'As we approached Hànôi we could see other SAMs being fired. As one fired on the ground, an area about the size of a city block would be lit up by the flash. It looked as if a whole city block had suddenly caught fire. This area was magnified by the light cloud undercast over Hànôi at the time. As the missile broke through the clouds, the large lighted area was replaced by a ring of silver fire that appeared to be the size of a basketball. This was the exhaust of the rocket motor that would grow brighter as the missile approached the aircraft. The rocket exhaust of a missile that was fired at you from the front quarter would take on the appearance of a lighted silver doughnut. Some crews nicknamed them the 'deadly doughnuts.'

'The silver doughnuts that maintained their shape and same relative position on the cockpit windows were the ones you worried about the most because that meant they were tracking your aircraft. Three of the SAMs exploded at our altitude, but in this case were too far away to cause any damage. Two others passed close to the aircraft, but exploded above us.

'At about 120 seconds prior to bombs away, the SAMs were replaced by AAA fire. There were two types. Of most concern were the large ugly black explosions that came from the big 100mm guns. Then there would be smaller multicoloured flak at lower altitudes, almost a pleasure to watch by contrast. There would be a silver-coloured explosion, followed by several orange explosions clustered around the first silver burst. About sixty seconds before bombs away, the flak was again replaced by SAMs. This time there were more of them and they exploded closer to the aircraft. There was no doubt about it - they were getting our range.

Hànôi radio station and the Thái Nguyên thermal power plant, 40 miles north of Hànôi, the target for nine cells of Wave III. The three cells in Wave III which attacked the Yên Viên Complex went in five hours after the attack by Wave II and retaliation was light. Lieutenant Colonel 'Yuma' Yuill's crew were again selected to fly wave lead as 'Green 01; against the power plant. Bill Conlee wrote: 'This mission went very smoothly despite some high altitude AAA fire and sporadic SAM firings, which were wild and not effective against our wave. No losses were incurred despite SAM radar engagement.'

Only fifteen minutes from the Kinh Nỗ rail yard Captain Charles Core's crew from Westover AFB, Massachusetts, flying as 'Rose 03' in Wave I found ways of relieving the tension:

Co-pilot: Well, there goes our nice clear night.
Pilot: But it's undercast for us.
Co-pilot: Rog. No biggy. You don't get to see much.
Nav: But how do you like the suspense?
Pilot: Pretty good.
'Red Crown': SAM threat! SAM threat! Vicinity Hànôi.
Nav: 'A taste of things to come'.

Several minutes later, nearing the IP, as the activity directed at 'White' and 'Amber' Cells just ahead became intense:

Pilot: 'It's triple A.'
'Red Crown': SAM, SAM, vicinity Hànôi!
Pilot: 'Boy, they're really puttin' it up!'
Co-pilot: 'Chesus! They're doin' a good job of it.'
Nav: 'I don't blame 'em.'
Co-pilot: 'I feel sorry for the guys down there with it.'
Nav: 'I feel sorry for us, too.'
Co-pilot: 'Eh, that's true.'
Pilot: 'OK guys, cut out the chatter.'
On the bomb run the crew got on with the work in hand:
Radar: 'OK pilot, I'm on the target.'
Nav: 'That checks.'
Pilot: 'I've got a SAM!'
EW: 'And EW has an Uplink.'
'Rose 1': 'Rose', Uplink, 'Rose', Uplink!'
Pilot: 'OK - you have an Uplink?'
EW: 'That's right - OK, he's back down.'
Pilot: 'Got another SAM.'
Co-pilot: 'SAM - have a visual SAM!'
Pilot: 'Holy Christ.'
EW: 'Four o'clock, comin' at us.'
Co-pilot: 'Rose 3' has visual SAM.'

'Rose 1': SAM Uplink, one o'clock.
'Red Crown': SAM launch, SAM launch, Hànôi!
Pilot: 'Here come some more - could be Shrikes - keep 'em in sight.'
Co-pilot: 'Three, two visuals.'
Red Crown: SAM launch, SAM launch, vicinity Hànôi!' [14]

One hundred and eighty SA-2s were fired at the B-52s. Two aircraft in the second wave were damaged by SAM near misses but they were not brought down. B-52G 'Hazel 03' in the lead cell flying directly toward Hànôi from the west-northwest had strayed from formation sustained minor damage and lost ECM transmitters but completed the mission and returned to Guam. Three cells behind 'Hazel' B-52D 56-0592 'Ivory 01' with a Westover crew was hit as the pilot, Captain John Dalton, who was leading six B-52Ds against Radio Hànôi; rolled the giant bomber into its post target turn and the B-52D slowed rapidly in the jet stream. The SAM when it hit almost seemed to stop the B-52 in mid air. 'You could feel the concussion,' Dalton told writer Marshall Michel[15] 'then you heard it. I never realized you could hear them explode like that… you get static electricity raising the hair on your arms …' No. 6 engine was set on fire and No.5 engine in the same pod flamed out. An alternator was running away and over-speeding and the cables for the rudder and right elevator were severed. Both tip tanks were holed and fuel streamed out of them. For 45 nerve-wracking minutes the B-52 staggered toward the Marine Corps base at Nam Phong in Thailand but as Dalton lined up on the narrow runway and lowered the gear the damaged bomber lost its electrical power, went dark and lost the stabiliser trim as the aircraft began to flare. A normal landing was out so Dalton made a hard landing that blew out two of the tyres but he managed to stop the B-52 going off the runway. Major Dalton was awarded the Silver Star for his actions. The Marines at 'The Rose Garden' as Nam Phong was known in USMC language later zapped the B-52 with the USMC insignia and a note, *'To the Boys in the Air Force From the Men in the Marines.'*

About thirty seconds from release on Radio Hànôi, 'Copper 02's electronic warfare officer (EWO) called, 'SAM Uplink, 2 o'clock!' A missile had them wired and the EWO could see on his equipment scope the guidance signal of a SAM coming toward them. Then the co-pilot yelled, 'Visual SAM at 2 o'clock, I have the airplane!' The pilot threw the big bomber into a hard, shuddering, right turn at a steep bank angle. Almost immediately there was a bright flash, and there was a bright flash inside the crew compartment.

'We heard a muffled explosion and felt an additional 'bump', as if driving over a speed bump' says Captain Wilton Strickland, the radar navigator. An ex-B-47E maintenance crew chief at Lincoln AFB in the late fifties, he flew 5,000 hours as navigator-bombardier in B-52s, including 72 'Arc Light' and six 'Linebacker II' missions.

'At the same time, EWO warned: 'SAM Uplink, 9 o'clock! Immediately, the pilot confirmed: 'Visual SAM to left, I have the airplane!'

'We suddenly went into a hard, shuddering (shuddering caused by tips of the wings in a high-speed buffet/stalling situation) turn to the left; again at a very steep bank angle' continues Strickland. 'About halfway through the roll from hard right to hard left, I got a peek at my aiming point [on the Câu Long Biên cantilever road and rail bridge across the Red River on the outskirts of Hànôi] on the radarscope. Worried that the steep bank angles may cause the gyros in the bombing and navigation system stabilization unit to 'tumble', I was surprised and pleased to find my cross hairs remaining where I had placed them. I reported, 'Still on the aiming point!' Again, there was a bright flash in the crew compartment, a muffled explosion, followed immediately by the slight bump or lurch of the aircraft flying through the exploding missile's blast wave. I knew we were very close to the release point, but in a hard left turn going way off the required heading. I directed the pilot, 'Roll it out, centre the PDI!' (Pilot's Data Indicator, a repeat of one of my instruments, showing direction to turn left or right to fly to the release point). As the aircraft rolled out with the needle centred, I reported again, 'Still on the point!'

'At the same time nav', reading the time to go (TG) meter said, with his voice getting high

and squeaky, 'ten seconds!' (Elapsed time was more than twenty seconds from the beginning of these manoeuvres because of the turns away from the release point.)

'Meanwhile, EWO was warning 'Two SAM Uplinks 12 o'clock!' (Two SAM's launched directly in front of us and coming toward us.)

'Co-pilot confirmed, 'Two visual SAM's, 12 o'clock!'

'I glanced at the TG meter, saw that it indicated eight seconds to go and ordered 'Hold it straight and level!'

'The pilots were watching the two missiles coming while keeping the PDI centred; EWO was watching the guidance signals on his scope as the missiles approached; nav' was watching the TG meter with his face shield on his helmet down and locked and his hands on his ejection trigger ring; I was watching the TG meter while keeping my radar cross-hairs on the aiming point. The needle seemed to take forever to come off the eight second mark. I watched it quiver slightly, I checked a couple of other indicators to make sure we were really going toward the release point and not around it. Again I ordered, 'Hold it straight and level!' The needle continued to quiver and creep downward -7-6, at five seconds, I hit the door-open switch; it took another eternity for the needle to pass 4 and 3. I continued to monitor my cross-hair placement; the needle continued to quiver ever so slowly downward -2 -1. At 0, as I felt the aircraft shudder slightly, indicating that the bombs were being released, I simultaneously operated a set of 'back up' switches to ensure that the bomb bay doors were fully open and sent an additional release signal manually to all bomb racks. At the same time my left foot had the interphone button depressed and I was yelling, 'Turn! Let's get the hell out of here!' The pilot yanked the aircraft into another shuddering, hard, right turn while I closed the bomb bay doors and brought the radar antenna up to look for other aircraft, rejoin the other two B-52s in our 'cell' of three and head back… continuing the evasive zigzag for another five minutes or so as more SAMs were fired at us from the rear… all was quiet on the aircraft except for the very loud scream of the slipstream and the eight jet engines. It was very hard for us to believe what we had just flown through.

'After a few minutes, the pilot quietly said to me 'Wilt - you will never guess where those two missiles went.'

'No, where?'

'You know where the auxiliary power unit sits on the ramp?'

'Oh, no, you have to be kidding!'

'Yep, that's where they went - just to the left of the fuselage in front of the left wing. Just as the nose of the aircraft moved to the right in that post-release turn, both missiles zipped past just to the left. If we had not turned at just the right moment, the missiles likely would have scored a direct hit on my crew position.' We all agreed that we had, indeed, had our 'lucky day.'

For their actions, all six crewmen received the Distinguished Flying Cross. [16]

The twelve cells in the Third Wave bombed the Thái Nguyên thermal power plant and Yên Viên storage area, again without loss. In all, ninety out of the ninety-three B-52s had bombed Hànôi successfully. One B-52 performed an evasion manoeuvre and bombed four seconds late and hit Giá Lam airport. The planning of these operations, which appear strangely reminiscent of the thinking behind some of the great air offensives in WW2, reveals how painful lessons learned in previous wars had gone unheeded. Only prohibitive losses could force a change in strategy and tactics but SAC was under the microscope. If B-52s could not successfully bomb North Viêtnam it could hardly be expected to destroy targets in the Soviet Union. Many in SAC also feared that if the raids were discontinued it would be difficult if not impossible to start them again.

Partly because there were no losses and because of long lead time from planning to execution, SAC HQ made the decision to continue with the same game plan on the night of 20/21 December, the third night of 'Linebacker II' operations, when ninety-nine B-52D/Gs in thirty-three cells in Thailand and Guam were detailed for Hànôi again. The targets for the eleven

Above: Captain Thomas J. Klomann, substitute navigator, 'Orange 03'.

Below: Major Randolph Allen Perry Jr., radar navigator, 'Orange 03'.

Below: Major John Franklin Stuart, pilot, of B-52D-80-BO 56-0622'Orange 03'.

cells in the first wave were the Yên Viên rail centre, Ai Mo warehouses and the Giá Lam railhead. The second wave cells were allocated the Thái Nguyên thermal power plant and Bắc Giáng and Giá Lam rail and trans-shipment centres while the eleven cells in the third wave was to strike at the Kinh Nỗ complex and Giá Lam rail centre.

At Offutt AFB, Omaha, Nebraska SAC appeared more than satisfied about the results of the previous two nights and saw no reason to change tactics. General Johnson and his senior officers on Guam felt that the second night the majority of B-52s had been lucky. The aircrews voiced concerns about the post-target turns where most of their aircraft had been hit. Some suggested that on the third night of operations the missions continue on out of Hànôi heading south towards the Gulf of Tonkin just five minutes away. This would avoid the precarious post-target turn into the headwinds and if any of them were in trouble they could at least eject over the sea where they had a better chance of rescue. Eighth Air Force HQ agreed. SAC however saw no reason to change direction - literally - though it altered the attack patterns and decided to send the B-52s along a much narrower cone than on the previous two nights, which only made it easier for the North Việtnamese to track the formations!

Crew morale however remained very high. 'This was brought home to us on the night of 20 December' wrote Lieutenant Colonel Bill Conlee 'when our crew pulled #1 standby crew. This meant we waited all night in a spare B-52D for any crew to abort so that we could fly, but nobody aborted. All bomber cells launched like clockwork.'

However, all the luck enjoyed by most of the B-52 aircrews had now been used up.

As the last B-52G in 'Cinnamon' cell was touching down at Andersen in the early afternoon of 20 December, 'Quilt' Cell was starting engines. Of the eleven cells which made up Wave I, nine were tasked against the Yên Viên rail yards and adjacent Ai Mo Warehouse area. 'Quilt' cell led the attack At Yên Viên there had been light retaliation the night before; next came Gold' and 'Wine' and then Brass' and 'Snow' and 'Grape' and 'Orange' cells flying B-52Ds. Four hours after Wave I had bombed, the nine cells in the 72nd Strategic Wing in Wave II arrived over the Thái Nguyên Thermal Power Plant and two cells, the Bắc Giang Trans-shipment Point. Of the 27 Wave II bombers, twelve were B-52Gs. While six of these Gs had some updated jamming equipment, the other six did not and so SAC recalled the half dozen unmodified Gs which left five cells of B-52Ds in the 43rd Strategic Wing and four cells of B-52Ds in the 307th Strategic Wing to continue to the Hànôi area. EWO 'Dick' Smith who flew seven of the eleven nights of 'Linebacker II' hacked into the North Việtnamese ground control intercept network, took out his 'lucky' whistle and let fly with a blast over Guard frequency - followed by an angry shout: 'Time out!' There was a lull in the

SAM launches and Smith, an only child who had grown up in Compton/Long Beach, California, and his crew successfully completed their bomb run. No aircraft were hit and all six Gs and fifteen Ds unloaded on their targets.

Captain Rolland A. Scott was TDY (temporary duty) to the 72nd Bomb Wing from Barksdale and flew in 'Gold 02' with another crew as a substitute pilot. 'The time, track and target location were nearly the same as my mission on the 18th. Shortly after takeoff, we lost one engine and flew the mission on seven. That wasn't too serious a problem in the 'G' model but I would have felt better if it hadn't happened. On the northbound leg over NVN we heard a good deal of fighter activity and numerous sightings were made of aircraft with lights on, presumably friendly fighters. There appeared to be no SAM activity. On the southeast leg approaching the IP my co-pilot stated that he saw a MiG-21 on the right wing of our aircraft. In mild disbelief, I stretched to see out his window and sure enough, a MiG-21 with lights off was flying tight formation with us. I believe we could actually see the pilot. The approach of the fighter had not been detected by onboard systems. Shortly, two or three minutes, the co-pilot reported the MiG had departed. Almost immediately I saw the same or another enemy aircraft flying formation on the left side of us. After a brief period, less than a minute, it departed.

'Our sighs of relief were short-lived and we quickly learned what the MiG had been up to. We visually detected missiles approaching from our eleven and one o'clock positions. Several pairs of missiles were simultaneously launched from these directions. I was extremely worried that missiles were also approaching from our rear that we could not see. The EWO reported no Uplink or Downlink signals with the missiles this mission as were reported on the night of the 18th. [17] However, these missiles appeared to be a lot more accurate than on the 18th. They seemed to readjust their track as I made small turns. I waited for each to get as close as I dare and then would make a hard, although relatively small, manoeuvre in hopes of avoiding them. They arrived in pairs, just a few seconds apart. Some, as they passed, would explode - a few close enough to shake my aircraft. In fact, one exploded so close and caused such a loud noise and violent shock that I stated to the crew that I thought we had been hit. In a very few seconds, after assessing engine instruments and control responses and having received an OK from downstairs, I determined that we had not been hit, or were at least under normal control and we continued the bomb run. Apparently the MiG-21 we saw was flying with us to report heading, altitude and airspeed to the missiles sites.

'The missiles were no longer directed toward us in the latter half of the bomb run; however, I could see SAM activity ahead in the vicinity of the target. In fact, while on the run we saw a large ball of fire erupt some few miles ahead of us and slowly turn to the right and descend. I thought it was a Buff and was sure no one would survive what was apparently a direct hit. I later learned that what I saw was 'Quilt 03' going down in flames.'

As 'Quilt' cell approached the Yên Viên rail centre through a narrow corridor to the northwest of Hànôi it started receiving SAM launch indications. The crew of B-52D-80-BO 56-0622 'Orange 03' captained by the 29-year old pilot Major John Franklin Stuart had deployed with the 346th Bomb Squadron in the 99th Bomb Wing at Westover AFB, Massachusetts. As 'Orange 03' started the bomb run on Yên Viên the crew heard the ghastliest sound imaginable - the wailing AHH-WAAH! AHH-WAAH! AHH-WAAH! from several emergency locator beacons from the crew of 'Quilt 03', commanded by 26-year old Captain Terry Mercer Geloneck of Decatur, Alabama and crew who were deployed from the 456th Bomb Wing at Beale AFB, California. An unmodified 'G', 'Quilt 03' had lost two ECM transmitters. Geloneck recalled: '… Captain Warren Richard Spencer [the 29-year old radar navigator of La Crescenta, Los Angeles] got on and he said, 'The same offsets are in here that were in here from day one.' I guess the plane... had flown day one. 'What that tells me is that we're coming in on the same routing, the same turn points, the same setup that the guys on day one had.' And he said, 'That's probably not good.'

Approaching the initial point where the bombing run was to begin, about thirty seconds to target, Captain Craig Allan Paul the 26-year old EWO reported three or four SAM signals but the crew could do nothing but watch their progress until the 'bombs away' was called and evasive action could be taken. As Geloneck rolled the wings level to stabilise the B-52G for the bomb run the aircraft was rocked by an exploding SAM missile. All twenty-seven 750lb bombs were dropped and as soon as the bomb bay doors were closed Geloneck rolled the B-52G into a steep post-target turn. The aircraft had been in its hard turn about ten seconds when the loud metallic bank of an exploding SAM hit them, accompanied by a bright white flash. One of two SAMs that had been fired at them had hit the EW and gunner's compartment. 1st Lieutenant Michael Robert Martini the 26-year old navigator reported that he and 1st Lieutenant William Y. Arcuri the 25-year old co-pilot from Satellite Beach, Florida and Spencer were okay, but that they had sustained a fuel leak in the left main fuel tank and that cabin pressurization was lost. Shrapnel wounded Captain Craig Paul and he was bleeding heavily. There were four six-inch holes in the fuselage next to Tech Sergeant Roy Madden Jr., the gunner from Hayward, California who was three days short of his 35th birthday and his leg was shattered. 'Quilt 03' fell almost

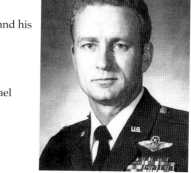

Left: Captain Terry Mercer Geloneck, pilot, 'Quilt 03' and his crew.

Right: 1st Lieutenant Michael Robert Martini, navigator.

Left: 1st Lieutenant William Y. Arcuri, co-pilot.

Right: Captain Craig Allan Paul, EWO.

Left: Captain Warren Richard Spencer, radar navigator.

Right: Tech Sergeant Roy Madden Jr., gunner.

vertically out of the sky. With his hydraulics out and the aircraft descending fast Geloneck hit the abandon light. He and Arcuri, Martini and Madden successfully ejected from the aircraft and were captured immediately. It is not known whether Spencer and Paul ejected.[18]

'Gold' and 'Wine' cells made it through safely but after completing the bomb run and in the middle of their post-target right turn 'Gold 02' again became an item of interest to the missiles, as Captain Rolland Scott recalls. 'From our left and below were at least three missiles, perhaps four, approaching rapidly. I felt I had no chance to avoid them by either maintaining or rolling out of the right turn, so I increased the planned bank angle drastically... and lowered the nose. The SAMs passed above us from our left. I lost some altitude in the manoeuvre and in the attempt to climb and accelerate on seven engines I lagged behind lead and somewhat out of position. There were no further SAMs directed at our aircraft; however, there was apparently a lot of enemy fighter activity on our withdrawal, according to radio transmissions. We could see numerous fighters with lights on and the gunner reported numerous targets on radar, one of which appeared to follow us, but not in the cone of fire. We saw no aircraft which appeared to be hostile, nor any hostile manoeuvres.

'As we passed east of NKP (Nakhon Phanom, Thailand) on a southerly heading, we heard what was apparently a B-52 crew abandoning their aircraft over friendly territory. In the distance, toward NKP, we soon saw a fireball which we assumed to be a Buff impacting on the ground. It must have been 'Brass 02' and Captain John Ettinger and his [Loring AFB, Maine] crew were mighty lucky.'

'Brass 02' had three jammers out of action so to keep the radar signature to a minimum Ettinger did not open his bomb bay doors until just fifteen seconds before the target but he could do nothing when two SAMs were fired as they were on their right post-target-turn near Yên Viên. The first SAM exploded off 'Brass 02's right wing and the second detonated just off the right side. The explosions knocked out the B-52G's electrical power damaged the controls and put the No.4 engine on the right side out of action. Ettinger and his co-pilot, Captain Lawrence A. Casazza nursed the crippled bomber to Thailand where they and Major Charles E. Archie the radar navigator, 1st Lieutenant Robert A. Clement, navigator, Captain Silvero A. Barroqueiro, EWO and Tech Sergeant George H. Schryer, gunner ejected safely at around 10,000 feet near Nakhon Phanom.

Just seconds before bomb release, 'Orange 03' was attacked by a MiG-21 resulting in damage and a small fire in the forward wheel well. Between fifteen and twenty SAMs were fired at 'Orange' cell while in the target area and a volley of three SAMs was fired at 56-0622 at 35,500 feet about five miles north of Hànôi. While the rest of the cell was on its post-target-turn the B-52 received at least one direct hit in the bomb bay just before bombing and went into a flat spin with its starboard wing on fire. Pieces fell off, the cabin depressurised and the electrical power failed so Major John Stuart ordered the crew to abandon the aircraft, which then crashed in Yên Thường village and exploded in a ball of fire. Smoke and flames could be seen eighty miles away over the Gulf of Tonkin by the crew of a RC-135. Stuart, Master Sergeant Arthur Vincent McLaughlin the 38-year old rear gunner born in Boston, Suffolk County, Massachusetts; Captain Irwin Stuart Lerner the 31-year old EWO from Stratford, Connecticut and Major Randolph Allen Perry Jr., the 35-year old radar navigator from Troy, Lincoln County, Missouri were killed. Incredibly, Captain Thomas J. Klomann, born in Chicago, Illinois in December 1945, who was flying as a substitute navigator after flying two missions with his old crew and 1st Lieutenant Paul Louis Granger, co-pilot survived the explosion and they managed to eject. Klomann was seriously injured and remained semi-conscious for two weeks but was nursed back to health by his fellow PoWs.

'Apparently, after free falling 20,000 feet without my parachute deploying, I was unconscious when I landed. I was taken to a North Viêtnamese hospital. I didn't regain consciousness for about a week and remained semi-conscious for another two weeks. The delirium resulted in the nickname 'Spaceman' as I could not even state my own name. The other

Above: Lieutenant Colonel James Yoshikazu Nagahiro, pilot, 'Olive 01'.

Below: Lieutenant Colonel Keith R. Heggen, the deputy airborne mission commander (ABC) aboard 'Olive 01'.

Below: Captain Donovan K. Walters, co-pilot, 'Olive 01'.

PoWs had asked the Viêtnamese to feed me intravenously, which they did and also take care of a large bed sores which had developed on my tailbone and feet. They also gave me leg splints to keep my feet from dropping. I spent a little less than two months in Hànôi and was among the first to be returned. I entered the States on 16 February 1973.' Granger was released on 29 March 1973.

In all, the North Viêtnamese fired over 220 SAMs at the three waves on the night of 20/21 December. Three B-52s in Wave III with three of its four targets in and around Hànôi were downed by SAMs. First to go down was B-52D 'Straw 02' the fifth aircraft in, commanded by Captain Vincent F. Russo, on detachment from the 306th Bomb Wing at McCoy AFB, Florida. 'Straw 02' took four very near misses from SAMs probably fired by VN 549 during the bomb run on the Giá Lam railway repair shops just east of Hànôi, which was attacked by three cells. No one was injured but 'Straw 02' lost two ECM transmitters. After bombs away and about two seconds into 'Straw 02's post-target run, a SAM most probably fired by SAM site VN-549 exploded in the front lower part of the B-52D seriously wounding Captain Deverl H. Johnson the 33-year old navigator.[19] Two engines caught fire and the electrical power failed. Co-pilot 1st Lieutenant James T. Farmer opened his side window and tried to send a Mayday call by using his survival radio as the aircraft slowly began descending, streaming fuel. The crew was unable to transfer fuel from one side of the aircraft to the other and it became difficult to control. Thirty minutes after it was hit and just after the aircraft crossed the North Viêtnam-Laos border the aircraft became uncontrollable and 'Straw 02's engines flamed out and the crew abandoned the B-52D about ten miles northeast of the Ban Ban Valley in Laos. All crew members except Major Frank Alton Gould the 39-year old radar navigator from New York who was injured when the SAM struck the Stratofortress and was not thought to have escaped from the aircraft, ejected safely.[20] At 15,000 feet Russo exited the plane and watched as the aircraft turned into a fireball as it impacted a hillside. After landing in a tree, Russo waited twenty minutes for first light before lowering himself to the ground. After a few minutes, he used his survival radio to transmit a Mayday call. An F-4 crew responded, telling him help was on the way. At first light A-1J Skyraiders contacted the crew and a USAF HH-53 of the 40th ARRS at Nakhon Phanom eventually located them and hoisted Deverl Johnson, Jim Farmer, Captain Paul J. Fairbanks the EWO and the gunner, Tech Sergeant James R. Barclift to safety. This was the first B-52D from Andersen to be shot down during the 'Linebacker' raids.

Eight minutes behind the raid on Giá Lam, 'Olive 01', an unmodified G, led a raid on Kinh Nỗ by four cells of aircraft from Guam just as dawn was beginning to break. The pilot, Honolulu, Hawaii-born Lieutenant Colonel James Yoshikazu Nagahiro had started his flying career as a navigator in C-124

The notorious Hỏa Lò Prison was used by the French colonists in Vietnam for political prisoners and later by North Vietnam for USAF prisoners of war when it was sarcastically known as the 'Hànôi Hilton'. The 'Little Vegas' area built for American PoWs in 1967 is shown in a final inspection in 1973 shortly before the Americans' release. The Hỏa Lò Prison was demolished during the 1990s, though the gatehouse remains as a museum.

transports before pilot training and conversion to the B-47 and B-52. Captain Donovan K. Walters the 27-year old co-pilot was from Lebanon in Red Willow County, New England. Captain Robert Ray Lynn, the 32-year old EWO came from Jacksonville in Morgan County, Illinois and Captain Lyn Richard Beens the 26-year old navigator born in Michigan, Detroit was now living in Salt Lake City, Utah. Major Edward Harvey Johnson the 40-year old radar operator was from Newburg, Oregon. Staff Sergeant Charles James Bebus the 21-year old gunner was from Osseo in Hennepin County, Minnesota. He and John A. Beier met at the base gym where the crews were waiting to be issued their in-flight meals for the evening. They were classmates going through the B-52 Gunnery School at Castle AFB and had not seen each other again until that night. 'While waiting for our respective crew in-flight meals to be prepared, 'Chuck' and I spent about ten minutes catching up how each of us had been doing. We then picked up the crew meals and proceeded to our respective aircraft.'

In addition to the normal crew who were on deployment from the 92nd Bomb Wing at Fairchild AFB in Washington, Lieutenant Colonel Keith R. Heggen, the 41-year old deputy airborne mission commander (ABC) born in Hardy and now of Renwick, both in Humboldt County, Iowa took his place on the IP seat. 'Olive 01's young crew chief, Sergeant Ed Bredbenner knew only Keith Heggen on the crew. 'He was TDY from the same base I was from [Blytheville AFB Arkansas, often referred to as 'Hooterville' by flyers there and renamed Eaker AFB in 1988]. Prior to engine start we stood in front of my Buff and reflected a little on why we were there and of course talked about home and going back soon. I kneeled under the fuselage, looking up into the cockpit at the crew just before closing the entrance hatch (the crewmembers looking down at me), Lieutenant Colonel Nagahiro telling me to disconnect my ground interphone and pull the chocks. He thanked me for a great launch, said he would buy me some beer when he got back and saluted after marshalling them out of the parking spot.'

'Olive 01' was hit by a SAM in the tail section at 35,000 feet two miles west of Hànôi moments after it had dropped its bombs and was turning on its course for the return flight. On

Above, L-R: Captain Randall 'Tom' Craddock, pilot, 'Tan 03'. 1st Lieutenant Charles Edward Darr, navigator, 'Tan 03'. Captain Ronald Dwight Perry, EWO, 'Tan 03'.

Left: Captain George Barry Lockhart, co-pilot, 'Tan 03'.

Right: Staff Sergeant James Leon Lollar, gunner, 'Tan 03'.

a B-52D ahead of 'Olive 01' the tail gunner reported that 'Olive 01' took a direct missile hit and descended. It burst into a fireball about 10,000 feet below the formation. 'Olive 02' captained by Captain Green who exited after bombing the rail yards at Kinh Nỗ at 35,000 feet went through a thin cloud over target area and did not see 'Olive 01' hit or go down. They tried to contact 'Olive 01' for about forty minutes before they determined from other aircraft that 'Olive 01' had been hit. 'Olive 02' said they saw lots of missiles - about 25. They were scared. 'Olive 03' only reported three missiles.

Having no ejection seat Keith Heggen had to descend to the navigators' hatch hole and he bailed out before the aircraft crashed in flames. Nagahiro saw Captain Donovan Walters eject and heard Lynn, 'Chuck' Bebus, Heggen and Beens go out from behind him. Beens stated later that he saw Walters' identification card in a stack of cards on a desk at the 'Hànôi Hilton' and Nagahiro saw Harvey Johnson's name written on a pad at the prison. Heggen died of his injuries in a NVA hospital a week later. Though the Việtnamese returned his remains on 13 March 1974 they consistently denied knowledge of Edward Johnson, Walters, Lynn and Bebus.[21] When Sergeant (later Lieutenant Colonel) Ed Bredbenner returned the next night and was told they were shot down, he was devastated. 'The realization that we were fighting a war where people were dying hit me like a bucket of ice water.'

'For the Blytheville crews, the whole 'Linebacker II' experience became very personal, because a total of 19 individual crew members were shot down' recalled Dick Rynearson, a native of Ohio, who served a tour in Việtnam as a C-7A aircraft commander/instructor pilot and two tours on Guam as a B-52G aircraft commander, flying three of the eleven nights of the campaign. 'The war became very personal at that point.'

Two cells behind 'Olive' cell was 'Tan' cell, also headed for Kinh Nỗ. Twenty-six year old Captain Randall 'Tom' Craddock commanded 'Tan 03', an unmodified B-52G which had suffered a complete failure of its bombing and navigation radar. Standard procedure called for the lead Fire Control Operator of the three-ship cell to use his radar to keep 'Tan 03' lined up behind the cell and direct the other aircraft to the target area. Staff Sergeant James Leon Lollar

46

the 27-year old gunner began directing the cell using his Fire Control System but the procedure broke down. 'Tan 03' drifted off to the left and while bereft of jamming support was hit by the first of two SAMs about eight miles northwest of Hànôi. Lollar, from Kilmichael Mississippi, who had previously served a double-tour at Phan Rang AB, first in aircraft armament and then as a door-gunner on the AC-47, recalled: 'We were all injured... everybody on the crew [from the 97th Bomb Wing based at Blytheville AFB, Arkansas]... took shrapnel on that first SAM. I know the EW [28-year old Captain Ronald Dwight Perry, who was from Gallatin, Sumner County, Tennessee] sitting right beside me was injured, I was injured and I could see over my shoulder the pilot and co-pilot [25-year old Captain George Barry Lockhart of Sulpher Springs, Texas] ... both acknowledged they were hit. The pilot recovered the aircraft and then we got hit with two SAMs and the pilot said, 'Fire on the left wing; bail out' so I pulled the trigger.'

Multiple emergency beepers were heard by aircraft in the area indicating that several of the crew members had safely bailed out of the crippled aircraft but whose radios beeped in distress from the ground is unknown. Lollar ejected successfully but the US did not know he had been captured. He was released on 29 March 1973. The remains of Captain Perry were returned by the Viêtnamese on 21 December 1975, three years to the day of his death, but it was not until 15 December 1988 that remains subsequently identified as belonging to Craddock, Lockhart, 1st Lieutenant Charles Edward Darr the 28-year old navigator from Little Rock and Major Bobby Alexander Kirby the 41-year old radar navigator from Fulton County, Atlanta were returned.

Shortly after 'Tan 03' went down the three cells of B-52Ds of the 43rd Strategic Wing bombed the Hànôi petroleum storage area. A SAM detonated close to B-52D 'Brick 02' commanded by 32-year old Captain John Davis Mize of Shreveport, Louisiana and his crew from Ellsworth AFB, South Dakota, as he completed his post-target-turn but it was not enough to bring the bomber down and Mize continued home to Thailand.[22] Mize landed at U-Tapao with nineteen holes in the aircraft and a large piece of shrapnel had entered the EWO station at head level. If the EWO had not been leaning forward over his jammers at the time he would have been decapitated. Mize received the award of the Distinguished Flying Cross for this action.

In 'Aqua' cell Captain Chris Quill and his crew from Barksdale AFB, Louisiana were on the same routing as 'Olive' and 'Tan' cells and they came under intense attack as Major Dick Parrish, the RN recalls:

'As we made out turn north of 'Thud Ridge' both the pilot and co-pilot saw a burning aircraft [most likely 'Straw 02'] at a lower altitude heading back to the northwest. We were an item of interest to the SAMs at the time and were having problems enough of our own. However, they were able to look at the burning plane long enough to be satisfied that it was a Buff. As we pressed on, I heard Chris and Joe Grinder our co-pilot exchange the following remarks:

'Good Lord, what was that?

'Must have been a direct hit.'

'My God what a fireball. [It was most probably 'Tan 03']

'I couldn't worry with the EWO's threats, or fireballs, or anything else. I had only one job - to get the bombs on the target with no mistakes. I had half-seriously told Bill Stillwell earlier that if he sat over there in the navigator's position and let me forget to open the doors, I'd kill him. He didn't forget and neither did I. I wasn't about to be on a crew of six people, going all the way up there and risking our lives, only to not get the bombs out. We made it through release and the big turn back to the west. After we had rolled out, Chris was considering putting the aircraft back on autopilot because it had become so quiet around us. This procedure would allow both pilots more time to concentrate outside the aircraft. Both he and Joe decided to take one more good-look beforehand, though. As Chris looked as far back and down to the left as he could, he spotted two white streaks coming at us. The next thing I knew, we were in a steep, descending right turn. Almost instantly, Leo Languirand saw two traces come onto his gunnery scope. While we continued to manoeuvre, the traces continued to climb and were closing. Then the two blips disappeared. We did a little mental gymnastics and figured they went off just about where we would have been.

F-111A 67-068 'Jackal 33' of the 429th Tactical Fighter Squadron at Takhli Royal Thai AFB was shot down over North Vietnam on 22 December 1972 flying a typical F-111 tactical mission when they were hit flying at supersonic speed only a few hundred feet altitude. At a point 53 miles west of Hànôi, Captain Robert D. 'Bob' Sponeybarger [right] and his Weapons Systems Officer, 1st Lieutenant William Wallace 'Bill' Wilson ejected. On the third day after the ejection, Sponeybarger was captured by NVN Army troops. Wilson was finally captured after Christmas.

'It got quieter as we headed for Laos. Then, as we were nearing the border, Chris and Joe saw a large explosion on the ground out ahead of us. If it was an airplane, which they were sure it was. It had to have been a big one. [This could possibly be another sighting of 'Straw 02'.]

'All of the sightings the pilots had made, plus what we had experienced on our own sort of got to us, I think. As we headed on down-country and towards the water I tried to break the ice with some weak joke. Dick Engkjer our EWO had been staring at all that wild stuff on his scope and he didn't think I was very funny. He promptly chewed on me for trying to act happy at a time like that. I understood how he was feeling. But then I got to thinking and said, 'What the heck. We did the job and we're out in one piece. I think there's plenty to be happy about.' The flight back home went better for me after that.'

'Brick' cell was the last cell to cross the immediate Hànôi area to attack the Petroleum Products Storage Area. After bomb release a proximity SAM detonation was not enough to bring the aircraft down and it safely reached U-Tapao. Four Gs and two Ds had been destroyed with a third D damaged. All the missing Gs were unmodified. In the course of nine hours, 220 SAMs had been fired at the Stratofortresses - 39 more than had been fired on the 19th - and six of the B-52s despatched - four of them unmodified B-52Gs - were lost to SA-2 strikes, with seventeen men killed or MIA and nine taken prisoner. The North Viêtnamese SAM crews had shot down three of the B-52s in less than ten minutes using just 35 missiles. In three days over 300 sorties had been flown and nine aircraft lost. Statistically, the overall loss rate of three per cent was acceptable but the losses on 20/21 December were nine per cent for the night. At SAC General John C. Meyer and his senior officers were stunned at the news. Quite simply if the casualties sustained on 20/21 December persisted; 'Linebacker II' would have ground to an abrupt halt.

The tactics that worked on the second night failed on the third. 'Just watching all the SAM's,' said Captain Bruce Kordenbrock 'was like watching a show until you realized they were starting to shoot at you.' To Captain D. W. Jamieson, the enemy seemed to be 'just salvoing off like six SAM's at a time,' of which 'maybe one or two would be tracking.' Other B-52 crewmen, such as Major L. M. Sweet, reported hectic radar activity on the night of the 20th, with as many as three Fan Song radars simultaneously tracking a single plane. A tail gunner saw three missiles, obviously guided from the ground, pursue his bomber through a hard left turn and explode within 750 feet of him.

Below the bomber stream, Captain Kordenbrock saw a stratum of antiaircraft shells bursting so close together that 'you could get out and walk on it.' The scene reminded him of 'all the war movies you've ever heard about. Tech Sergeant C. M. O'Quinn, the tail gunner whose B-52 had been chased by three missiles, believed 'they were sending up triple A and SAMs together... hoping we'd dive to avoid the SAMs and fly through the flak.' Although the B-52s remained above 34,500 feet and escaped flak damage, missiles downed six bombers and damaged a seventh. After this costly night the unmodified B-52Gs were not sent on raids over Hànôi again.

On Guam and at U-Tapao the losses were only part of the problem. A high loss rate and the increased operational turnaround leading to crew fatigue and maintenance problems cannot be sustained indefinitely. Crews were on duty sixteen hours at a stretch. By the end of the third night of operations morale among the B-52 crews was at very low ebb indeed. According to Charles R. Schaefer the author of *The Final Conflict - The End of Innocence'*, the first days were an absolute disaster for the whole force... and to go the same route, the same altitude, the same headings for four nights in a row is probably the worst planning that I think that's ever been done in the world of strategic bombing. I think the SAC planning staff had no idea of how to go against a high-threat area like the tactical people had; that had been doing it for seven years.' [23]

When word of the losses arrived at U-Tapao Brigadier General Glenn R. Sullivan the commander of the 17th Air Division (P) called the operational commanders, Colonel Don Davis and Colonel Bill Brown and told them 'to get a bunch of the experienced guys together as soon as they landed and give me some changes to go to SAC with' he recalls. 'I was opposed to the single-file 'bomber stream' concept, every night at the same altitude and the other dumb tactics. These guys came up with a bunch of smart changes and put them in a message. Early that morning I signed the message out directly to General John C. Meyer CINCSAC and sent an information copy to my boss at Eighth Air Force, General Jerry Johnson. I wanted it to get to SAC right away. Some of the people were afraid I would get in trouble for sending it to Meyer directly, but we had to do something.' (Sullivan was denied a second star and retired two years later.) One of the most serious problems was the B-52's vulnerability to SAMs on turns after their withdrawal from the target - Sullivan later described the post-target turn as 'the murder point' - so pilots were authorised to make shallow post-target turns and to withdraw with maximum speed, flying a straight-ahead 'feet-wet' exit out to the Gulf of Tonkin. There was an urgent need to vary the inbound routes and altitudes and greater compression of the bomber stream, within which random spacing and altitudes would hopefully serve to confuse the air defences. The bomb run no-evasion order issued by an Andersen wing commander that aircrews had repeatedly ignored on Days One and Two, without affecting bombing results, was quietly rescinded and pilots were allowed more freedom to carry out evasive tactics. Sullivan's Eighth Air Force commanders sent a 'we agree' message to Meyer but approach angles, bombing altitudes and timing between cells and waves could not be streamed in until Day Five, though the PTT was eliminated on Day Four[24] when SAC decided that to minimise losses the raid on Hànôi would be flown by just thirty Stratofortresses and these would exclusively be B-52Ds from U-Tapao. It meant that some crewmembers in the 307th Strategic Wing would be flying to Hànôi four nights in a row but at least it allowed maintenance on Guam to catch up after three days of sixteen-hour missions. 'It was all we could do to keep airplanes in the air' recalled Ed Wildeboor a B-52G co-pilot during 'Linebacker II', flying from Andersen AFB. 'I mean, it was just a full-out effort for eleven days, absolutely... The guys in maintenance and putting gas in the planes - bomb loaders... I don't know when they slept, if at all. You know, I don't know how they did it. It's just amazing...'

The two tactical wing commanders spent the morning of 21 December along with their executive officers and the chaplains, personally meeting with the missing crewmembers' wives who were on Guam at the time. A decision had already been made after the B-52G losses and

U-T's significantly shorter mission length that B-52Ds would provide the weight of effort on Day 4 while Andersen committed 30 B-52Gs to support of the war in South Việtnam. The planned sortie rate at U-T for Day 4 (and 5 and 7) was reduced to just thirty aircraft per day. Of the ten cells dispatched on the night of 21/22 December, six were to hit Quảng Tế airfield, twelve the Bạch Maï/ Hànôi storage area and twelve the Văn Điển warehouse complex. About 75 ECM, fighter and tactical strike aircraft flew in support of the attack, which began a little after 0330 hours local time and ended about fifteen minutes later. Those B-52s striking Quảng Tế and Văn Điển escaped unscathed, despite encountering many SAMs but this was not the case at Bạch Maï. Immediately after departing the IP B-52D 55-0061 'Scarlet 01' in the first cell inbound to Bạch Maï lost its bombing and navigation radar in the turn southeast towards Hànôi and the pilot, 28-year old Captain Peter J. Giroux was forced to move away to allow the other two aircraft in the cell to pass. Giroux, born in Ithaca, New York then dropped back behind the two other B-52Ds where he could bomb using another B-52 gunner's radar. While 'Scarlet 1' carried out the complicated manoeuvre Giroux's 37-year old gunner Senior Master Sergeant Louie E. LeBlanc detected an aircraft approaching from the rear and thinking it might be a MiG-21 he warned the crew. LeBlanc, born 15 October 1935 in Woonsocket, Rhode Island, had been a B-36 Peacemaker ECM Operator and ECM Repairman and a B-66 Destroyer Defensive Fire Control Systems Operator. From June 1968 to June 1969 he flew 'Arc Light' bombing missions as a B-52 gunner. Giroux began to weave back and forth while LeBlanc fired at the enemy aircraft. At the same time and when the B-52D was approximately fifty miles northwest of Hànôi and two minutes from its bomb release point four SAMs were fired at the harried Stratofortress. The first two SA-2s missed but the second pair detonated under 'Scarlet 01's right wing. Giroux reported they had been hit and he had numerous fire warning lights. Captain Thomas Waring 'Buddy' Bennett Jr., the 30-year old co-pilot from Natchez, Mississippi sent the mayday call shortly after they completed the bomb run. At 0345 hours, approximately three minutes after bombs away and roughly 45 miles after target, the aircraft's condition rapidly deteriorated and Giroux determined it would not remain in the air much longer. His interphone was inoperative so he turned on the abandon light thereby issuing the bail-out order to his crew. Likewise, he immediately heard ejection seats fire. Giroux's oxygen system was damaged by shrapnel and he was rendered unconscious when the aircraft decompressed. After the B-52D descended substantially, Giroux regained consciousness long enough to realize he was hanging upside down in his seat harness and reached down to pull his emergency ejection seat handle. He next awoke in the morning to find himself surrounded by North Việtnamese civilians while getting a rough haircut with a pair of garden shears. He also discovered he had a broken arm and dislocated elbow to contend with.

The flaming B-52D went down slowly at first before the burning wing folded over the top of the aircraft and plunged to earth near Bạch Maï. The 28-year old EWO, Captain Peter Paul Camerota of Gibbstown, New Jersey ejected successfully. Camerota landed in a rice paddy. After hearing loud voices nearby, he took only his emergency radio with him when he began to run along the levees. He stopped a couple times while he attempted to establish contact with other members of his crew or with any other aircraft operating in the area, but to no avail. In the predawn hours he continued moving toward a thick group of trees, but as he approached them, he saw that it was actually a hill 700 to 800 feet high. Upon reaching the base of the hill, Peter Camerota found a cave at ground level that he hid in for the next three days. He ventured out only at night to attempt to establish radio contact. Unfortunately, he was unsuccessful in these attempts so he decided to climb higher up the hill. He found another cave about halfway up along with a trickle of water to drink from where he remained for the next four days. Again he tried to make contact with other Americans at night, but still had no luck in doing so. He then decided his only chance was to go to the top of the hill. On the morning of 30 December Camerota finally established two-way communication with a pilot from the crest of the hill who marked his position before departing the area. About three hours later he made contact with another pilot.

With Buddha Mountain in the background, a Thai Marine watches a B-52D land at U-Tapao as a KC-135 taxis for takeoff.

However, because the downed EWO was in a heavily populated and fortified area, he could do nothing more than the first pilot did. On the afternoon of 3 January 1973 - and after successfully evading capture deep in enemy held territory, nearly dead from exposure, Peter Camerota finally had no choice but to submit to capture due to extreme exhaustion. He signalled to some of the villagers who were returning from their work in the fields. They, in turn, turned him over to North Viêtnamese regulars who took him to the infamous 'Hànôi Hilton'.

Louis E. LeBlanc was also captured by civilians a short time after reaching the ground and was immediately turned over to the military. He believed that he was one of the last of the crew to bail out of the damaged Stratofortress because as he descended in his parachute, he observed the fully deployed parachutes of the other five crewmen but Major Gerry William Alley the 38-year old radar navigator from Pocatello Idaho, Captain 'Buddy' Bennett and 1st Lieutenant Joseph B. Copack Jr., the 25-year old navigator from Chicago, Illinois were killed.

About four minutes after 'Scarlet 01' had been hit two SAMs stuck B-52D 55-0050 'Blue 01' commanded by Lieutenant Colonel 'Yuma' Yuill, whose crew were flying their third mission in four days over Hànôi. Lieutenant Colonel Bill Conlee his EWO wrote: 'Our target was again Bạch Maï with a release time of 0347 local time on the 22nd. This mission was routine until we reached the IP for our bomb run. At this time the co-pilot, 25-year old Captain Dave Drummond remarked: 'It looks like we'll walk on SAMs tonight,' as he could see numerous SAM firings ahead of us. This comment proved only too true. Between IP and bomb release point, ten SAMs were fired in the vicinity of 'Blue' cell. At 'Bombs Away' we were bracketed by two SAMs; one going off below us and to the left, the second exploding above us and to the right. Shrapnel cracked the pilot's outer window glass, started fires in the left wing and wounded Yuill, Bernasconi, Mayall and myself. We also experienced a rapid decompression and loss of electrical power. Shortly after this with the fire worsening Yuill gave the emergency bailout signal via the alarm light and I ejected from the aircraft.

'During free-fall two more SAMs passed me and I attempted to look for our aircraft, but was unable to see it. I was also unable to see any other chutes in the darkness. I realized after my chute had opened at preset altitude that my left arm was numb and that I had lost my glove from my left hand during ejection. I also realized that I was bleeding profusely from my face and arm due to shrapnel wounds. I deployed the survival kit with my right hand and prepared for landing. I steered for an open field, just missing going into a large river and believed that I would land undetected.

'About 200 to 300 feet from touchdown, my illusions were shattered when small arms fire was directed at me. I ignored the firing and concentrated on making a good landing. I touched

down, dumped my chute and took off my helmet and at once was set upon by a mob of North Viêtnamese, both civilian and military. They immediately took my gun, my watch and my boots. They then stripped me at gun point to my underwear and forced me to run for approximately a mile through a gauntlet of people with farm implements, clubs and bamboo poles. During this wild scene, several of their blows succeeded in

Main Picture: Senior Master Sergeant Louis E. LeBlanc, gunner, 'Scarlet 01' is captured by militiamen in Hà Tây Province, northwest of Hànôi, on 22 December 1972. (Texas Tech University Vietnam Archive)

Left: Major Gerry William Alley, radar navigator, 'Scarlet 01'.
Top right: Captain Thomas Waring 'Buddy' Bennett Jr., co-pilot 'Scarlet 01'.
Right: Captain Peter Paul Camerota, EWO, 'Scarlet 01'.

breaking ribs and badly damaging my right knee. The mob scene ended when they halted me in front of a Russian truck, which was used to transport me to Hànôi. During the ride they kept me face down, which allowed me to staunch the flow of blood from my face and arm. The ride itself seemed to last less than an hour. They stopped in front of an old French building of large size and allowed me to sit up in the early morning twilight. I was then unceremoniously pushed off the truck flatbed, falling about six feet to the pavement, where I suffered a shoulder separation. I was unable to move from where I had landed and was then dragged by two soldiers into the prison yard of what I was do discover was the 'Hànôi Hilton.'

'I was placed in a small solitary room in a section of the 'Hilton' known as 'Heartbreak Hotel'. Because of spinal compression and other injuries, I was unable to move for the first three days of my stay in solitary. On Christmas Day I was unable to sit in an upright position and with great effort to stand for a minute or two before getting woozy. During this period I was subjected to several minor beatings and kicking sessions by them. They just have realized the futility of their efforts, for these sessions stopped just before I was able to sit and then stand. I was unable to eat a Christmas meal, but drank the pot of tea which accompanied the meal. I

stayed there until 31 December. I was then placed in a cell with seven others and here I stayed until 19 January 1973 when we all were moved to the Zoo.' [25]

Dave Drummond had used his upward ejection seat to escape the doomed aircraft. Down in the navigators' 'Black Hole' Lou Bernasconi and 1st Lieutenant Bill Mayall fired their downward ejection seats also. Mayall recalled that 'the missiles impacted the aircraft in the belly just in front of where the navigators sit. The plane, although still flying, was burning badly. With the impact of the second missile, we had lost our interphone and were unable to communicate with each other. After approximately thirty seconds the red bail out light came on and the ejection sequence was started. Lou gave me a thumbs-up signalling me to go. I pulled my ejection handle but unfortunately my ejection seat malfunctioned and would not

Top right: Lieutenant Colonel Louis Henry Bernasconi, radar navigator, 'Blue 01'.
Right: 1st Lieutenant (later Colonel) William Thomas Mayall navigator, 'Blue 01'.
Below, left: Captain David Ian Drummond, old co-pilot, 'Blue 01'.
Below, centre: Lieutenant Colonel William Conlee, EWO, 'Blue 01'.
Below, right: Lieutenant Colonel John Harry 'Yuma' Yuill, pilot, 'Blue 01'.

work. After several moments of frantic pulling, Lou, realizing what had happened, proceeded to eject, thus affording me an alternate means of escape. I saw him eject and then I disengaged myself from my seat and proceeded to make a manual bailout out the navigator's hatch. Upon hitting the slip-stream, I was violently tossed about in the air. I had my fists clenched and my gloves were ripped off down to my finger nails. I had the sensation of a doll being flailed about in a strong a wind. I remember fighting to obtain a good body position so as to be prepared for the initial shock of my parachute opening. I was still struggling when suddenly I heard a loud pop and I was under my chute. The ride down was a long one. I couldn't see the ground or where I was going to land because of dense cloud coverage. I finally broke through the clouds about ten seconds before I hit the ground. I landed in a rice paddy and within moments the North Viêtnamese had arrived with their rifles blazing and effected my capture. The time was 0400. By mid-afternoon I was in an isolation cell in the 'Hànôi Hilton'. The interrogation began almost immediately. I remained in isolation five days and was then moved into a larger cell with seven other B-52 prisoners. Fortunately I was only held captive a comparatively short time. Ninety-seven and a half days to be exact.'

Technical Sergeant Gary Morgan pulled the handle to fire four explosive bolts holding his rear turret in position and the entire back end of the B-52 was blown out into space. The tough Texan dived out of the hole created when the gun turret was jettisoned. That quick decision by the pilot saved the entire crew because the B-52 blew up only a minute or two after Yuill was the last man to leave. 'Our captors became very excited when they realized they had captured an entire B-52 crew intact, especially with so many Lieutenant Colonels on it. We were heavily interrogated as a result. I was threatened many times that my crew would be a 'show case' crew and tried as war criminals.' Yuill's crew were the only crew shot down during 'Linebacker II' to survive intact.[26] In 1973 he and his crew were released. Lou Bernasconi - a happy Californian - returned home 26lbs lighter from his ordeal in the prison camps.[27]

Endnotes for Chapter One

1   Uplink was a Command guidance signal transmitted from a ground radar site to a launched SAM, which when detected the EWO would attempt to jam the signal. Downlink was a Beacon signal transmitted from a SAM missile to the command guidance radar site.
2   *Linebacker II; A View From the Rock.*
3   *The Christmas Bombing* by Marshall Michel, *Air & Space Magazine,* January 2001.
4   He flew with Standardization Crew SO-4 from March AFB, California. His crew flew three of the eleven nights of Linebacker II. John served as Chief of the Tactical Evaluation Branch of the 43rd SW.
5   *The Cadre Papers; The Art of Wing Leadership and Aircrew Morale in Combat* by Lieutenant Colonel John J. Zentner USAF (College of Aerospace Doctrine, Research and Education).
6   With over 9,200 hours in the B-52 alone, Major Mizner holds the record for flight time in a B-52. He retired with over 11,000 hours' total flying time in military aircraft.
7   He was promoted major general on 6 February 1976.
8   *The Christmas Bombing* by Marshall Michel, *Air & Space Magazine,* January 2001.
9   Simpson suffered massive infection in his left arm and hand due to lack of medical attention during captivity prior to the peace agreement, but was afforded treatment at the time of the peace signing. Certain, Simpson and Johnson were held prisoner in Hànôi until 29 March 1973 when they were released in Operation 'Homecoming'. Six years later, the bodies of Rissi, Thomas and Ferguson were returned to US control by the Viêtnamese. After completing his degrees the Reverend Dr. Certain went on to become a Chaplain in the Air Force. He officiated the memorial services for President Gerald Ford. He has authored a book about his life journey, Unchained Eagle and collaborated with C. K.

McCusker on *Yankee Air Pirates*, a fictional account of Linebacker II.

10 Cooper's daughter, Jennifer was born five months after her father was declared missing. In 1997 US investigators of the Joint PoW/MIA Accounting Command found items that were determined to be the B-52 wreckage. Cooper's Captain's insignia near the wreckage led investigators to identify Cooper; DNA samples were used to identify Poole. The identifications were confirmed in 2003.

11 B-52D 56-0676 'Brown 03' is now displayed at Fairchild AFB, Spokane, Washington. Samuel Turner died on 12 April 1985.

12 In addition, apart from 56-0678 'Lilac 3' which landed at U-Tapao with 350 external holes and 24 areas requiring kits; 56-0583 had ten external holes and several dents and gouges and was returned to service on 20 December after three repairs totalling 53 man hours; 56-0592 landed at Nam Phong, Thailand with external holes estimated to take 2,000 man hours; 58-0254 landed at Andersen with 30 to 50 holes.

13 On the second night, 19 December, no B-52s were lost, though two suffered damage, which seemed to confirm these views.

14 *Linebacker II: A View From The Rock.*

15 Marshall L. Michel III flew more than 321 combat missions in F-4s and RF-4s. He is the author of *The Eleven Days of Christmas - America's Last Vietnam Battle and Clashes: Air Combat over North Vietnam, 1965-1972.*

16 *The Christmas Bombing* by Marshall Michel, Air & Space Magazine, January 2001.

17 As a supplement to the jammers which hid the attacking force, additional jammers were employed to disrupt communications between the SAM site and its launched missile. The controlling ground radar emitted s command guidance signal (Uplink) to which the in-flight missile responded with a beacon signal (Downlink). Desirably, both were jammed by the penetrating aircraft.

18 When they were released on 12 February 1973 Madden, Arcuri and Geloneck were all injured but Martini had to wait until 29 March for his release. Madden's leg was still in dangerous condition and he was brought home on a litter. The leg was later amputated as a result of his injuries and the effects of gangrene. The remains of Paul and Spencer were handed over by the Việtnamese on 30 September 1977 despite earlier protestations that they knew nothing about them.

19 On 24 August 1984 Deverl Johnson was flying as co-pilot of a West Wings Beechcraft C-99 commuter aircraft and was among those killed in the crash after a mid air collision with a light aircraft over San Luis Obispo, California.

20 Conflicting information exists that suggests that Major Gould did escape and may have been captured. Several live sightings of Major Gould in Laos were claimed in the early 1990s together with other information from Laotian villagers giving fresh but ultimately false hope to his family.

21 In 1976 the Secretary of the Air Force approved presumptive findings of death for the four crewmen listed as Missing in Action. In October 1988 the Việtnamese returned the remains of Bebus, Johnson, Lynn and Walters to US control.

22 Captain Mize served as a B-52 pilot with the 77th Bomb Squadron of the 28th Bomb Wing at Ellsworth AFB, South Dakota, from December 1967 to February 1973 and during this time he participated in 'Arc Light' and Linebacker I and II bombing missions in Southeast Asia from January to July 1968, September 1969 to February 1970, February to July 1972 and August to December 1972.

23 Charles R. Schaefer retired from the USAF as a Lieutenant Colonel with over 5,000 hours of flying time, about 2,500 of them in the B-52. He was a B-52 instructor pilot and became the B-52 Training Officer for the 15th Air Force. He also worked at SAC headquarters on the Joint Strategic, Targeting and Planning Staff and in the Pentagon in Strategic Force Planning, XOXFS, before his retirement.

24 *Flying From The Black Hole: The B-52 Navigator-Bombardiers of Vietnam* by Robert O. Harder (Naval Institute Press 2009).

25 He was moved around in the Zoo until freed on 29 March 1973.

26 John's son Mike - one of seven children - became a pilot and flew B-52s. In 1991 at Randolph AFB John had his Freedom Flight, flying #3 with his son flying #4. In 1996 he was a B-1 pilot. John Yuill retired from the US Air Force as a Lieutenant Colonel in April 1979. He and his wife Rose reside in Texas.

27 After leaving the Air Force, Dave Drummond served as a Flight Test Engineer for Bell Helicopters and then retired after a career flying airliners for American Airlines. He also later was trapped and survived the Dupont Plaza Hotel Fire in San Juan, Puerto Rico, on 31 December 1986.

Chapter Two

A War That Nobody Won

'Holy Christ! A SAM!'

The targets chosen for the night of Friday 22 / Saturday 23 December when again only thirty B-52Ds from U-Tapao were to be used, were Petroleum Products Storage (PPS) and rail support structure in Hảiphòng. (Andersen sent 22 B-52Gs and six Ds against targets in South Việtnam). This time the change in tactics was used in full. For the first time, the approach and egress routes were both over the water. Sixty-five 'Iron Hand' and 'Wild Weasel' aircraft of Seventh Air Force were involved and some would lay a chaff blanket thirty miles by twelve miles before the B-52s arrived. In addition Navy aircraft would make attacks on all seven SAM sites in the Hảiphòng area. 'Snow' cell led 'Gold', 'Yellow', 'Ebony', 'Amber', 'Walnut', 'Rust', 'Red' and 'Ivory' in for the attack. The bomber stream, which flew in from the Gulf of Tonkin feinted towards Hànôi and then turned towards Hảiphòng before dividing into three different tracks. By the time they were about sixty miles south of the targets they occupied the whole southern quadrant. At this point, the split force abruptly altered course along six different tracks, which were staggered in time and distance to provide TOT (time over target) spacing. None of these tracks was aimed directly at the Hảiphòng complex. Three of them feinted into the coastline as though to pass well to the south of the port city. Hànôi looked a possible target for them. Then, when thirty miles or less from their intended release points every cell again abruptly zeroed in on Hảiphòng to further confuse the defences. It worked. The increased support package limited the number of SAMs fired at the B-52Ds to forty-three and none of the bombers was lost.

On the sixth night, Saturday 23 / Sunday 24 December, the support package was increased

A B-52G lands at Andersen AFB with B-52D-80-BO 56-0624 of the 28th BW at Ellsworth in the foreground, which was scrapped at AMARC in 1978.

to seventy aircraft as twelve B-52Ds on Guam and eighteen B-52Ds at U-Tapao were despatched to North Viêtnam. Twenty-four of the B-52Ds bombed the rail yards and repair shops in deep canyons near Lang Đàng 45 miles north of Hảiphòng. Six B-52Ds singled out the SAM sites VN 537, 563 and 660 thirty miles northeast of Hànôi. The routes were varied with random changes of height (31,000-38,000 feet), speed and direction and even though the support aircraft fell behind schedule (only the F-111As, which did not need air refuelling arrived on schedule) none of the Stratofortresses was lost or even damaged. Only forty SAMs were fired at the bombers and just four MiG-21s were available to intercept the bombers. Enemy fighters fired about four K-13 'Atoll' infrared guided air to air missiles at 'Topaz' and 'Copper' cells but none found their mark.

The first week of 'Linebacker II' raids ended on Christmas Eve when thirty B-52Ds of 307th Strategic Wing at U-Tapao supported by sixty-nine ECM aircraft and fighter-bombers and 763 refuelling sorties by 194 KC-135As were sent to bomb the rail yards at Thái Nguyên and Kép north of Hànôi. The Buffs were routed to their targets from Laos, flying close to the border with China before turning south into the target areas. Once again the Seventh Air Force chaffers

BDA photo of Bạch Maï/Hànôi issued on 22 December after the bombing on 21 December.

BDA photo of the damage to the Hảiphòng area.

sowed a very effective chaff blanket and for the first time the B-52s dropped chaff during their shallow post-target-turns to further disrupt the enemy defences. Nineteen SAMs were fired at the B-52s but none scored any hits. Eighteen-year old Airman 1st Class Albert E. Moore, from San Bernadino, California, a 307th Bomb Wing tail gunner on B-52D 55-0083 *Diamond Lil* call-sign 'Ruby 03' picked up a MiG-21 on his radarscope at 4,000 yards and he told his pilot to fire flares and chaff.

'I observed a target in my radar scope 8:30 o'clock, low at eight miles,' Moore wrote six days later in his statement of claim for enemy aircraft destroyed. 'I immediately notified the crew and the 'bogie' started closing rapidly. It stabilized at 4,000 yards, 6:30 o'clock. I called the pilot for evasive action and [the electronic warfare officer] for chaff and flares. When the target got to 2,000 yards, I notified the crew that I was firing. I fired at the bandit until it ballooned to three times in intensity then suddenly disappeared from my radar scope at approximately 1,200 yards, 6:30 low. I expended 800 rounds in three bursts.'

A gunner aboard another B-52, Technical Sergeant Clarence Chute, verified Moore's kill in his report. 'I went visual and saw the 'bandit' on fire and falling away,' Chute wrote. 'Several pieces of the aircraft exploded and the fireball disappeared in the under-cast at my 6:30 position.' Moore's kill is one of only two confirmed kills by a B-52D in the Việtnam War and the last confirmed kill by a tail gunner in wartime using machine guns. Following the MiG kill, Moore, who was awarded the Silver Star, wrote, 'On the way home I wasn't sure whether I should be happy or sad. You know, there was a guy in that MiG. I'm sure he would have wanted to fly home, too. But it was a case of him or my crew. I'm glad it turned out the way it did. Yes, I'd go again. Do I want another MiG? No, but given the same set of circumstances, yes, I'd go for another one.'[28]

One of the B-52Ds that attacked the Thái Nguyên rail yard was 'Ash 02' B-52D 56-0599,

B-52Ds and B-52Gs of the 72nd Strategic Wing (P) on Guam. B-52G-120-BW 59-2572 flew 14 missions in 'Desert Storm' in 1991 from Diego Garcia and was sent to AMARC on 11 January 1994.

commanded by Captain John Mize whose aircraft had already been hit by enemy fire on two previous sorties. 'Ash 02' was damaged when a 100mm anti aircraft shell exploded just below the aircraft in front of the tail, wounding everyone on board and severely damaging some of the B-52D's systems. One engine was put out of action and the stabilizer trim was damaged while fuel was trapped in some of the fuel tanks, all of which meant that Mize was unable to raise the nose high enough to land back at U-Tapao unless remedial action was used. A KC-135A tanker was summoned and transferred enough fuel to the stricken B-52D to alter the aircraft's centre of gravity so that Mize could land. Despite Mize's wounds and severely damaged aircraft, he somehow manhandled the doomed bomber into Laos, electing to stay with it until his entire crew had successfully bailed out before ejecting. The navigator, Lieutenant William Robinson suffered an ejection seat malfunction and bailed out manually. All crew members were picked up by rescue helicopters. For his heroism, Mize was awarded the Air Force Cross, the first such award to a SAC pilot in South East Asia.

Hànôi claimed heavy damage and destruction of densely populated civilian areas in Hànôi, Håiphòng and their suburbs. The bombing reportedly resulted in the deaths of 1,318 in Hànôi.

President Nixon ordered the JCS to take a thirty-six hour bombing halt for Christmas and B-52 operations were not due to resume again until the night of 26/27 December when the missions were planned by the Eighth Air Force using the ideas developed by General Sullivan and the combat crews. The bombing pause gave the North Viêtnamese a window of opportunity which they exploited to the full, moving some missile battalions to the northeast and southwest of Hànôi while two additional battalions were added to increase the number protecting Hànôi to twelve. The capital was now completely ringed by SAM sites, which could challenge the B-52s in any direction they might care to take. Seven highly compressed waves of 120 B-52D/Gs preceded by 113 Seventh Air Force and Navy support aircraft were sent to bomb 120 individual targets in ten concentrations in Hànôi and Håiphòng. The total Andersen force would be 45 B-52Gs and 33 B-52Ds. The plan of attack was for the B-52Ds from both Andersen and U-Tapao to strike Hànôi with four different waves from four different directions at once.

Major Bill Stocker, who had led the first B-52D wave on the first night, was again selected for Wave I lead as 'Snow 01'. Colonel James McCarthy would fly on Stocker's aircraft as Airborne Commander. Behind 'Snow' cell were 'Slate' followed by 'Cream', 'Lilac' and 'Pinto' with 'Cobalt' bringing up the rear. Wave I would come in from the northeast striking the Giá Lam rail yards and the PPS Area at Giá Thượng. This wave, which faced 100-knot headwinds, would be exposed to SAMs around Hànôi for the longest time of any strike forces during the entire campaign. All seven Waves had the same initial TOT. The separation between targets of Waves I and V was three miles. The same separation between applied to the targets being hit by the strike force coming in from the southeast and southwest. Waves II's B-52Gs would be led by Major Louis Falk from Blytheville AFB in 'Opal' cell and would be joined by one cell of B-52Ds from U-T over northern Laos, from where they would swing across and hit the Thái Nguyên rail yards. Major Tom Lebar who had led Wave I on the second night was selected to lead Wave III. Led by 'Rust' cell this wave would come in off the Gulf and hit SAM site VN 549 and the Văn Điền vehicle depot from the southeast. Wave IV B-52Ds from U-T led by 'Pink' cell would hit the Giáp Nhi rail yards on Hànôi's south side from the southwest. Wave V, more B-52Ds from U-Tapao led by 'Black' cell, was to bomb the Dục Nội rail yards and the Kinh Nỗ complex from the northwest. Wave V would have a tailwind of 100 knots, giving the B-52s a groundspeed of over nine miles a minute and a twenty-second overfly of the target that would put a B-52 on a near-collision course with a bomber coming in from the northeast. The flight plan separation between the northern and southern bomber streams was only seven miles. B-52Gs of Wave VI led by Major 'Woody' O'Donnell from Blytheville AFB in 'Paint' cell and Wave VII led by Major Glenn Robertson from Barksdale AFB in 'Maple' cell would carry out a double strike on the Håiphòng rail yards and transformer station from the northeast and the southeast.

The air crews stationed at U-Tapao had been flying every night. Because of this several crews were transferred from Guam to U-T to provide relief. Twenty-seven-year old Captain Bob Morris Junior's crew in the 307th Bomb Wing on TDY from Kincheloe AFB, Michigan was one of these. They probably arrived from U-T on Christmas Day. On the morning of the 26th Lieutenant Colonel Wilton W. Strickland ran into the Morris crew at breakfast in the officer's club. They had a great time reminiscing because they had all been stationed together in Michigan. The Morris crew brought the latest news from the States and asked the colonel for tips on flying over Hànôi. They had flown one mission to North Việtnam. While having breakfast the Morris crew was notified that they would be flying that night. On the breakfast table was a Bangkok English language newspaper showing pictures of bomber crew members that had been lost a few nights before. As the men left the club, Morris and Wimbrow told the colonel they were going to stop by the barber shop and get haircuts so they would 'look good on Hànôi TV and in the papers tomorrow.' The colonel told them 'so-long' and 'good luck.'

Morris, who was from St. Charles, Missouri and his crew were assigned B-52D 56-0674 'Ebony 02'. It is probable that they had been accustomed to flying the B-52G, which carried a much lighter payload of conventional bombs because it had been modified to carry nuclear weapons so Morris and 1st Lieutenant Robert M. Hudson his co-pilot were probably flying a much heavier aircraft (with 21 tons of bombs in the fuselage and another twelve tons slung from pylons under the wings) than they were accustomed to. In the 'Black Hole' sat Captain Michael Harold LaBeau the 27-year-old radar-navigator of Lincoln Park Michigan and 1st Lieutenant Duane P. Vavroch, navigator born in 1947 in Tama, Iowa. Captain Nutter Jerome Wimbrow III, the 33-year old EWO on 'Ebony 02' had been raised in the Whaleyville area of Worcester County,

Maryland. While in elementary school his father had moved the family from Berlin to reside with his grandparents who were in failing health and needed assistance. His father had owned the original Style Guide clothing store on Main Street in Berlin. His grandfather, along with two brothers were business partners in a tomato canning and a sawmill business. He and one brother operated a general store in Whaleyville for sixty years.

Six B-52Ds allotted to Wave 4 aborted on the ground and only two spares were available so four of the cells comprised just two aircraft each. 'Ebony 02' also suffered a set-back, as Bob Hudson recalls: 'As we taxied out our gunner got ill. I called for a replacement and I was told I would get one once we reached the hammerhead. At our takeoff time a truck pulled up and a guy [Senior Master Sergeant James Raymond Cook, from Wilmington North Carolina] ran to the back of the plane. He comes over the interphone and says 'I am ready' and we launched. We never got a chance to introduce ourselves nor get his name.'

Master Sergeant Philip Edmund Lebadie, Jr. a B-52D gunner in the 379th Bomb Wing who flew over 100 combat missions recalled: 'According to our briefing officer it was the biggest bomb raid in the history of the world.'

Just before he scrambled up the crew entry hatch on Stocker's B-52 Colonel James McCarthy looked at the serial number painted on the side of the nose - #680. 'This particular aircraft had been manufactured in 1955. It had flown a lot of missions and was plainly showing its age. Seventeen years of hard flying leave indelible marks on an aircraft that the trained eye of a crewmember can easily detect. I had seen my first D model when I was checking out in B-52s in 1960 as a junior captain. When we went out to fly our B-52G one day there was a B-52D from another base parked next to our aircraft. The pilot happened to be there and I asked him to show my crew and me through his airplane. After we had completed inspecting the aircraft, I remember remarking to my crew, 'I'm sure glad we're flying the G models and not those tired old D's.' (Flying the B-52D has been compared to driving an 18-wheel truck without power steering, air brakes or automatic transmission in downtown Washington during the rush hour).

Soviet 'advisors' inspect the wreckage of a B-52 on 23 December.

Little did I realize then that twelve and a half years later I would be riding one of these old D models into combat.'

At 1618 local time, the first B-52s rolled down the runway at Guam. As Stocker took off he was treated to the sight of one of the most awesome armadas ever assembled. As far as he could see there were B-52s lined up nose-to-tail. 'It's difficult to describe the feeling of leading such an array of power' he said. Two hours and 29 minutes after 'Opal 01' started its take-off roll, the last of the aircraft was airborne. The Soviet trawler that continually maintained a position off the end of the runway also observed the launch of this strike force. His radio message would reach Hànôi long before the bombers.

Of the seventy-eight B-52s from Guam forty-five of the more vulnerable B-52Gs were assigned the Thái Nguyên rail yards and Hàiphòng leaving the forty-two B-52Ds to head for Hànôi. All bombs were to be released within a fifteen-minute time period instead of the fifty minutes required on earlier 'Linebacker II' strikes. A massive U-shaped 'Chaff' blanket would be laid by sixteen F-4s just north of Hànôi and five minutes later eight more F-4s would do the same north of Hàiphòng. (This greatly aided protection despite 100-knot headwinds which only served to blow the chaff together to form a huge, dense blanket over Hànôi and Hàiphòng).

The common routing into the compression box, followed by a movement of a substantial portion of the force north towards the Gulf of Tonkin, created a memorable night as one crewmen recalled; 'I never fully realized just how many of us there were up there, or how close together we all were until we headed north over the Gulf. It looked like a highway at night - nothing but a stream of upper rotating beacons as far as I could see. It was sort of eerie too once we went into radio silence procedures. Nothing was said but each aircraft was flashing an 'I'm here' to his buddies. Then it occurred to me that we would be meeting a whole bunch more of the force which was coming up using a route over the land mass. As many of us there were, the U-T troops were also going to be there in strength. At that moment, it dawned on me just how special this night was.'

Colonel McCarthy continues:

'As we headed north over the Gulf of Tonkin I heard Tom Lebar call in that his wave was at the join-up point on time and that the wave was compressed. They had done one hell of a fine job. When we crossed the 17th parallel we were committed. That was the last point at which I or higher headquarters could recall the forces. From here until the target area we would be using radio silence procedures. The only radio call allowed would be if you got jumped by a MiG and you needed MiGCAP support.

'As Hàiphòng passed off our left wing we could see that the Navy support forces were really working over the SAM and AAA sites. The whole area was lit up like a Christmas tree. We could hear 'Red Crown' issuing SAM and MiG warnings to the friendly aircraft over Hàiphòng. We hoped that this activity would divert their attention from our G model bombers, who would soon be arriving. Even though they weren't going to downtown Hànôi anymore, they were headed for the port city. As we all knew, that was plenty tough duty.

'We coasted in northeast of Hàiphòng and headed for our IP, where we would turn southwest toward Hànôi. The IP turned out to be in the same area that Marty Fulcher[29] had led the Buffs on the 23rd against the SAM sites that had the reputation of being such lousy shots.

'The flak started coming up when we made our first landfall. Once again, we were most vividly aware of the heavy, black, ugly explosions which characterized the 100mm. Even at night, the black smoke from these explosions is visible. Since we were at a lower altitude than we had flown before, our wave would be more vulnerable to this AAA than on most previous missions. Close to the IP the flak became more intense and the explosions were closer to the aircraft.'

Before turning IP inbound for the Giáp Nhi rail complex 'Ebony 02' suffered a fire in No.7 engine. After putting out the fire Captain Morris deliberated whether to continue to the target or not. If they aborted, 'Ebony 01', the other aircraft in the cell, would have to continue to the target alone. Morris decided to press on, cutting back the second engine in the pod to sixty per cent power.

Colonel McCarthy in 'Snow 01' again:

'As we turned over the IP we picked up the first SAM signals. We could see them lift off, but their guidance seemed erratic. The SAMs exploded far above us and at a considerable distance from the formation. It appeared that 'F Troop' was still in business and their aim was as bad as it had always been.[30] However, inbound to the target the SAM signals became stronger. Captain Don Redmon, the EWO, reported three very strong signals tracking the aircraft. Bill Stocker ordered the cell to start their SAM threat maneouvre. The navigator, Major Bill Francis, reported that we had picked up the predicted 100 knot headwinds. Then the SAMs really started coming. It was apparent that this was no 'F Troop' doing the aiming. The missiles lifted off and headed for the aircraft. As we had long ago learned to do, we fixed our attention on those which maintained their same relative position even as we manoeuvred. All of the first six missiles fired appeared to maintain their same relative position in the windshield. Then A1C Ken Schell reported from the tail that he had three more SAMs at 6 o'clock heading for us. The next few minutes were going to be interesting.

'Now that the whole force was committed and we were on the bomb run, I had nothing to do until after bombs away, so I decided to count the SAMs launched against us. Out the co-pilot's window, 1st Lieutenant Ron Thomas reported four more coming up on the right side and two at his 1 o'clock position. Bill reported three more on the left side as the first six started exploding. Some were close - too close for comfort.

'Listening to the navigation team on interphone downstairs, you would have thought they were making a practice bomb run back in the States. The checklist was unhurried. Captain Joe Gangwish, the RN, calmly discussed the identification of the aiming point that they were using for this bomb run with his teammate, Major Francis.

'About 100 seconds prior to bombs away, the cockpit lit up like it was daylight. The light came from the rocket exhaust of a SAM that had come up right under the nose. The EWO had reported an extremely strong signal and he was right. It's hard to judge miss distance at night, but that one looked like it missed us by less than fifty feet. The proximity fuse should have detonated the warhead but it didn't. Somebody upstairs was looking after us that night.

'After 26 SAMs I quit counting. They were coming up too fast to count. It appeared in the cockpit as if they were now barraging SAMs in order to make the lead element of the wave turn from its intended course.

'Just prior to bombs away, the formation stopped manoeuvering to provide the required gyro stabilization to the bombing computers. Regardless of how close the SAMs appeared, the bomber had to remain straight and level.

'At bombs away it looked like we were right in the middle of a fireworks factory that was in the process of blowing up. The radio was completely saturated with SAM calls and MiG warnings. As the bomb doors closed, several SAMs exploded nearby. Others could be seen arcing over and starting a descent, then detonating. If the proximity fuse didn't find a target, SA-2s were set to self-destruct at the end of a predetermined time interval. Our computer's bombs away signal went to the bomb bay right on the time hack. Despite the SAMs and the 100 knot headwinds, the nav team had dropped their bombs on target at the exact second called for in the frag order.'

Between 10.30 and 10.45pm local time 120 B-52s converged on ten targets in Hànôi and Hảiphòng from four directions. Aircraft attacking Hảiphòng approached from the northeast and southeast. Two streams attacked Hànôi from the northwest, flying in from Laos and out over the Gulf of Tonkin. Another two approached on a reverse course, from the northeast and southeast over the Gulf, flying away through Laos.

'Over the Hànôi railway yards' recalled Philip Lebadie Jr., 'we had our bomb bay doors open and a pilot said 'crew we have two at one o'clock.' He was [saying] there were two surface-to-air missiles heading directly for our aircraft. Nobody said a thing. Then a few seconds later, he says, 'gunner, they're under our belly.' And I immediately grabbed for the ejection panel because I had the only manual bail out position on the aircraft. I knew if we were hit I had to get out immediately because I had to eject some of the gunnery system off the back-end of the aircraft so I could jump out. And when I looked up those two missiles passed my cabin off the horizontal stabilizer and banked up over top of me when they both went off in directions away from me. And if those missiles had come back up mid-wing alongside our fuselage, it would have separated both of our wings and we would have been immediately down. That was the most harrowing event that I've ever experienced on a B-52.'

Approaching landfall and heading for Hànôi, 'Lilac 02' a 306th Bomb Wing B-52G from McCoy AFB, Florida picked up communications from 'Red Crown':

SAM Threat! SAM threat southwest Hànôi! All stations, this is net; Red Crown showing negative bandits, negative, negative bandits.

Pilot: 'Is 03 turning with us Guns?'

'Yeah, sure is. It's one mile back.'

Pilot to co-pilot: 'AAA over there about 11 o'clock.'

Co-pilot: 'Roger that'.

Navigator: 'Hảiphòng's about 70 miles at 10 o'clock'.

'Stand by 'Indigo'.'

Indigo: *Roger Indigo, copy. Copy 'Red Crown'?... Bulls-eye again please.*

Navigator to pilot: 'IP in five minutes. Are we over land yet?'

'Negative.'

'Roger that.'

Pilot: 'First bombs are hittin'. 130 miles from Bulls-eye; you copy?'

(Radar navigator and navigator perform bombing checklist).

'Lights on. Lights on.'

Navigator (to radar navigator) 'Roger, all we gotta do is get the aim point and RCD and we'll be all set.'

'Roger that.'

Pilot: 'Crew, they got a lot of AAA out there and lots of it at our altitude, so you can be prepared for maybe getting some of that.'

'Copper', all checked in?'

'That's affirmative.'

'Roger.'

'Radio check, loud and clear?'

'Roger.'

'... 'Lilac'... 281.'

'Lilac 02', copy 281.'

'Lilac 03'...

Navigator (to pilot): 'IP'

Co-pilot: 'Roger.'

Pilot: 'Wha'd you say, nav?'

'India Papa'.

'Okay.'

Pilot (to 'Red Crown'): 'Mark you position on Bulls-eye for list.'

'Stand by.'

'Confirmed.'

Co-pilot: 'Lilac' right. What heading nav?'

'280'

Co-pilot to pilot: 'Stand by. We got company. I got a visual SAM at 11 o'clock. Far away. Two of 'em.' Got 'em both... There's another one.'

'Roger that.'

'And another one.

'Roger that, got 'em both.'

SAM launch, SAM launch, vicinity Hànôi.

Pilot: 'Okay, got four of 'em.'

'Roger'.

SAM, SAM Nam Dinh.

'Keep your eyes on that one.'

SAM launch Hànôi; SAM launch Hànôi.

'Where they coming from?'

'Eleven o'clock'.

SAM launch Hảiphòng; SAM launch Hảiphòng.

'Roger 'Red'. Request you call your position from bulls-eye so I can move up and join.'

'Roger'.

Gunner (to pilot): 'I got two SAMs out there. 'Just one left. There's another one just coming up.'

SAM launch Hảiphòng.

'Roger that.'

150 miles Bulls-eye... SAM launch Hànôi.

'There's another SAM. Turning left.'

SAM 3 o'clock.'

'SAM, 10 o'clock low.'

Pilot (to gunner): 'What's it like back there gunner?'

'Looks all right.'

'Red Crown': *Multiple SAMs. Multiple SAMs.*

'I got it'.

'Red' is 150 zero, sixty miles bull's-eye.'

SAM launch Hảiphòng. SAM launch Hảiphòng.

'There's four.'

'Two minutes.'

'SAM 3 o'clock.

'SAM 10 o'clock low.'

Navigator: 'Pilot, keep your eye on 01. He'll be turning soon.'

'Roger that.'

'Left turn, Left turn. SAM 9 o'clock.'

Co-pilot (to pilot): 'You ready to take it off autopilot anytime?'

'Nah, I'm not gonna take it off right now.'

'Does it look like we're getting anything at that turn point?'

Gunner (to pilot): 'Does it look like we're getting anything at that turn point?'

Co-pilot (to navigator): 'Lilac's left. (Negative).

'Lilac's turning.'

Navigator: 'Roger, let's go 251.'

'251.'

'That SAM's at 2 o'clock'.'

Navigator (to EWO): 'Mostly 'Triple A' Dub.'

'I'd say. Hey, can you turn the heat down a little bit?'

SAM launch, 9 o'clock possible.

Co-pilot (to pilot): 'My God look at that secondary over there.'

'Secondary?'

'All lit up.'

'Okay possible SAM.'

SAM launch Hànôi; SAM launch Hànôi.

Co-pilot (to pilot): 'Got AAA right here, 1 o'clock.

Gunner: 'Two SAMs, 9 o'clock, visual low'.

'Roger. I got it. Autopilot's off now.'

EWO: 'Okay, no Uplink, no Uplink.'

Gunner: Two SAMs, 9 o'clock, visual low.

'SAM 8 o'clock.'

Radar navigator (to navigator. centring the target): '... in the crosshairs; Crosshairs centred.'

'PDI centred.' [Pilot's Deflection Indicator; a needle monitored by the pilot and the radar navigator, indicating the nose of the aircraft relative to the bombing crosshairs to ensure that the aircraft remain on course during the bomb run].

'SAM 10 o'clock.'

Check your position.

'Okay, two visuals on our right, 9 o'clock.'

'Here comes another one.'

'No Uplink. No Uplink.'

'Visual SAM, 12 o'clock low.'

SAM launch; SAM launch.

'Two right.'

Continuous bell rings fill the flight deck. The TG - To Go, or Time to Go, a metre that displayed the time to bomb release automatically based on flying conditions, gave a reading.

'We're on the inside of 90 seconds now' (navigator)... Okay we got TG problems.'

'Get a 60-second call from 01.'

'Lilac 01, gimmie a 60-second call'.

'Copy'.

'Can you get him on target?'

'He's working it.'

Co-pilot: 'Keep your eye out there, pilot, 1 o'clock. I mean 11.'

'All right I'm lookin'.'

'Centred PDI.'

'Possible SAM 3 o'clock'.

Radar navigator: 'We're back synchronous all the way, now.'

Navigator: 'Roger, we got it back.'

'Doesn't look right.'

B-52D at U-Tapao, Thailand and (next page) the scene on the beach during operations (*Stars & Stripes*).

23577

'It's right, it's right. I'm offset 1 on the bridge.

'Okay, it's coming across now.'

Lilac 01, 60 seconds, ready, ready... now.

'Lookin' good.'

EWO (to pilot): I got a weak Uplink. Weak Uplink.'

'What clock?'

'...I'll break you off the manoeuvre.

'What clock position?' *'Get my doors Mac.*

'You got it Co?' *Doors comin' open.*

'No I don't. Where is it?'

'I don't know; it's weak though.'

'I got the RCD connecting light on the bomb doors... 30 seconds.'

'Okay, Uplink off the air, off the air.'

'Okay'.

Navigator to co-pilot: 'We're slightly left of the other airplanes.'

'No sweat.

'Looking good. Inside of 30 seconds, centred inbound.'

Navigator: 'Standby release'.

'Co-pilot (to pilot): 'I got a SAM right here at 1 o'clock.'

'Roger'.

'You see it?'

Negative.'

'There they are, right there, you got 'em?

'Negative, I gotta get behind this other one.'

'They're there right in front of us,'

Gunner: 'Visual SAM, 3 o'clock low!'

'I got it.'

'Real close!'

'I got it"

Bombs Away!

Precisely at 2330 hours all lead aircraft in each wave released their bombs. In just fifteen minutes 4,000 tons of bombs rained down on all the targets. Eighty-five per cent of the B-52s were inside the chaff cloud when they dropped their bombs and made their post-target turns and 'Iron Hand' and 'Wild Weasel' aircraft dealt with thirty SAM sites.

Gunner (to pilot): 'SAMs are coming, 3 o'clock low!'

'I know, got 'em both.'

Co-pilot (to pilot): 'Break left... Break left.'

'I gotta go right. Behind this other... Okay I see 'em.'

'Okay, got room?'

'Roger.'

Gunner: 'Two visuals, 6 o'clock!'

I got the other airplane.

Co-pilot (to pilot, giving altitude as 33,000 feet): 'We got 33 even.'

'Roger that.'

'Red Crown': All stations, *'No Bandit activity, Negative bandit activity... (Warning klaxon sounds on Lilac 02's flight deck).*

'Holy Christ! A SAM!'

'Thank you gunner.'

AHH-WAAH! AHH-WAAH! AHH-WAAH! Wailing parachute beepers sound on the flight deck.

Co-pilot: 'That one blew up.'

Pilot (to co-pilot): 'He sure did.'

'Roger that.'

'With unmistakable finality, 'Ebony 02' flipped over on its back and began to break apart. The co-pilot gave the bail-out order and the crew started punching out. Moments later the B-52 turned supernova and the North Viêtnamese sky lit up for a hundred miles in every direction. Thousands of gallons of burning JP-4 hung as if suspended in the sky, while shattered remnants of the great ship slowly fluttered to earth like dead leaves.'

Above: Captain Nutter Jerome Wimbrow III, EWO, 'Ebony 02'. Below: 1st Lieutenant Duane P. Vavroch, navigator, 'Ebony 02'

It was some minutes after bombs away, as they were departing the immediate Hànôi area when Bill Stocker's crew and Colonel McCarthy in 'Snow 01' saw the 'brilliant explosion' off to their left rear. 'It lit up the whole sky for miles around' wrote McCarthy later. 'Momentarily, the radios went silent. Everyone was listening for the emergency beepers that are automatically activated when a parachute opens. We could make out two, or possibly three, different beepers going off.'

'Ebony 02' may correspond to a claim by Pham Tuan of the 921st Sao Dao Fighter Regiment 'Red Star' based at Nôi Bài who fired two K-13 (AA-2 'Atoll') AAMs and may also be the first B-52 claimed as MiG-21 air-to-air victory. As Captain Bob Morris rolled out to stabilize 'Ebony 02' on the bomb run at the Giáp Nhi rail complex the first of a salvo of four SAMs fired at 'Ebony 01' missed but the second missile detonated in front of 'Ebony 02's cockpit, blowing away the radome and radar and dislodging part of the hydraulic panel, which hit Bob Morris killing him. Bob Hudson recalls: 'When we got hit by the second SAM and after we got the bombs off - all 108 of them and on target I might add - I gave the order to bail out. The nose of the airplane pitched violently down, so I assumed our gunner had jumped.' But Jim Cook had remained on board because communication was cut off from the forward compartment and the 'Abandon' signal had not flashed in the tail. Cook rode the aircraft down until a third SAM hit the aircraft and blew him from the aircraft. The B-52's left wing flipped the mighty bomber onto its back. Later, an A-6 driver told Bob Hudson he was slightly behind and below the 'Buff'

Senior Master Sergeant James Raymond Cook, gunner, 'Ebony 02'.'

Captain Bob Morris Junior, pilot, 'Ebony 02' and below, with his family in happier times.

that was going down when it exploded in mid air. He said he had never seen such a violent explosion. The remains of the bomber crashed near Giáp Nhi. Bob Hudson suffered a broken left arm, facial injuries and multiple puncture wounds from glass and flying debris.

It was assumed that 'Nut' Wimbrow was killed in the ejection when the second SAM had hit. Weeks and then months passed with no word as to the status of the missing EWO. Because of his time in grade and training the family was notified that 'Nut' had been promoted to the rank of major. The family arranged a funeral ceremony in the Whaleyville Methodist Church with their son absent. Cook and Hudson, Michael LaBeau and Duane Vavroch survived to become PoWs. During the early winter evening hours of 27 December the Wimbrow family was just sitting down to dinner when the phone rang. The call was from a US Air Force official representing the wing commander of Kincheloe AFB in Michigan. He informed the family that Captain Wimbrow's B-52 had been shot down near Hànôi. They were advised that he was officially being listed as Missing in Action.

On 'Lilac 02' meanwhile the crew heard the bleepers emitted by the bail out of the surviving crew members of 'Ebony 02' sound continuously as conversation on interphone began again.

'Pilot to navigator: 'Hey nav', confirm we're supposed to be at 33,500?'

'33 even.'

'Gotcha, 33 even.'

'Correction, correction, 33,500, you're right.'

'Yeah, okay. That's where I am, 33,500.'

'Roger that.'

'What's our heading?'

'280'.

'Roger.'

Gunner: 'Visual SAM, 5.30.'

'Keep your eye on it J.P.'

'Visual SAM, 5.30, another one, low.'

'Roger'.

Gunner: 'I can't see.'

'I'm watchin' 'em.

Navigator to pilot: 'We turn in about a minute.'

'Roger'.

'I can't see that SAM anymore.'

Pilot to co-pilot: 'We'll have to manoeuvre and see if it's underneath us.'

'Maybe it just went off.'

'Take a look out the left.'

'Your right J.P.

'See it?'

'Where, where is it? I don't see it anymore. Okay, I thought I saw it go off. Yeah, it just went off; I just saw one go off.'

'Is 03 still behind us?'

'He sure is.'

Navigator to pilot: 'Inside a minute to the turn'.

'Roger.'

Navigator: 'Inside a minute to the turn.'

'Red Crown': You missing one of your chicks?

'Negative'.

Pilot: 'On autopilot again.'

Navigator (to pilot): 'Okay, let's go now: Turn 257.'

'Lilac' left. 'Lilac 02.'

Radar navigator: '01 may be over-running another airplane here shortly.'

'We got 'im. 'Lilac 03'.'

'Okay get on your 33,500, pilot.'

'I'm on it nav.'

'Okay.'

EWO to co-pilot: 'Look out the right. There's two SAM sites out there. Be aware.'

'Roger that.'

Pilot (to navigator): 'You're reading about a 200-foot difference than I nav.'

'Okay buddy.'

'SAM Uplink, 7 o'clock low, 'Lilac' cell.'

Pilot (to gunner): 'Got it J. P.?'

'Visual SAM, 6 o'clock low.'

'Okay.'

'...coming this way, two of 'em, 6 o'clock low.'

'Okay, just keep watchin' it.'

EWO: 'I have no Uplink.'

Gunner: 'Okay, 6.30 low, now. Don't turn back your way pilot.'

'I'm not.'

This is 'Lilac 1 - come right.

Gunner (to pilot): 'Visual SAM, 7 o'clock low, two

An SA-2 after launch.

'Ebony 02' is hit by SAMs on the night of 26/27 December.

Wreckage from 'Ebony 02' goes down after the SAM hits.

of 'em.'

'Roger.'

'Three of 'em... Detonation.'

'How many detonated?'

'Two.'

'Got the other one?'

'I got two more... We're all clear now. We're all right.'

'What heading nav?'

'257, you're looking good. You're right on 01's front.'

'Don't go left 'till he goes left.'

'Don't worry nav.'

Copper, 'Lilac', let's slow ten knots through.

Radar navigator: 'Coming within a mile of 01... About to run over these guys in front of us.'

Gunner: 'When we gonna be out of this shit?'

Navigator: 'About another five, J.P.'

'Lilac 01's coming back left. 'Lilac 02'. 'Lilac 03.'

Five minutes away. Five minutes away.

Pilot: 'What's our range on 01?'

Navigator: 'Gettin' close, about a mile.'

'Okay, no sweat.'

Shot gun, Shot gun.

Co-pilot: 'I got him.'

Pilot: 'Yeah, I got a good visual on him. I just wanted to know how far back we are.'

...Lilac 01: roll out 250. Lilac 02. Lilac 03, 250.'

Radar navigator: 'Coming within a mile of 01.'

Pilot: 'We got him, got him good.'

Co-pilot: 'About four minutes on this heading.'

'We're on hard auto pilot once more.'

...Gunner: 'Okay, visual SAM 7 o'clock.

'Roger'

Two SAMs, 7 o'clock low.'

EWO: 'I have no Uplink, no Uplink.'

Pilot: 'How's it look, gunner? Is he a real threat to us?'

'The SAMs?'

'Roger.'

'I can't tell from here.'

Navigator (to EWO): 'Should be out of it, eh Dub?'

'It's hard to say.'

Co-pilot: 'Keep an eye on the son of a bitches.'

Gunner: 'Okay, they just detonated. One of 'em did.'

('Red Crown' comes on the air to talk to Snow cell, the lead B-52D cell led by 'Snow 01' carrying Mission Airborne Commander Colonel James R. McCarthy.

Go ahead'

Roger, Snow; are you with three?

Affirmative, Snow Cell out with three. Say again Red Crown:

Do you have anything on the rest of the aircraft in your

Above: 1st Lieutenant Bob Hymel, co-pilot, 'Ash 01'.

Below: Major Lawrence Jay Marshall, navigator, 'Ash 01'.

General John C. Meyer, Commander-in-Chief, SAC, presents the Air Force Cross to Colonel James R. McCarthy, Commander, 43rd Strategic Wing for his participation in the historic mission of 26 December 1972.

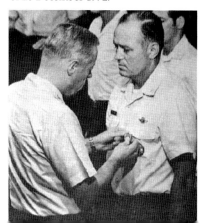

wave?

Negative.)

Gunner (to pilot): 'The second one just detonated. We're okay now.'

'Copy.'

Gunner: 'Okay, another visual SAM, 7 o'clock.'

SAM launch, west of Hànôi;'SAM launch, west of Hànôi. Bogey 2 o'clock.

Lilac 03: SAM low, 7 o'clock. There's one. SAM at 1.

Lilac 01: let's go left.

'Lilac 02' is going left'.

'J. P.? What's it doing Guns?'

'Well, I got two more at 6.30 now.'

SAM launch Hànôi; SAM launch Hànôi...

'What's the range on it...?'

EWO: 'I have no Uplink. I have no Uplink.'

Gunner: 'You can see him back there, pilot if you look back.'

'I'm going the other way. Okay, I see 'em, yeah. They're far off.'

SAM launch Hàiphòng; SAM launch Hàiphòng.

Co-pilot (to navigator): 'He said Lilac right. What's heading nav?'

'Still on 257.'

'Slow it down, slow it down.'

'¾ of a mile.'

'Rog, I got him good. Tucked right in there.'

'We'll be turning 219 shortly.'

Co-pilot: 'They just detonate, J. P.?'...

Gunner: 'How we doing on COA [Confirmed Operating Area]?'

Navigator: 'We're about out of it J. P.'

EWO: 'Yeah, we should be out of the COA as far as we know': 'Lilac... 'Lilac 02'.'

'All right just keep your eyes open.'

'Say again'.

'Roll out 250 then.'

'Lilac 02 copies 250.'

Lilac 03, three miles.

'Roger 3'.

'Lilac 01': 'Lilac left, 22-niner, now.'

Radar navigator: 'Roll out this turn; Co, you'll be at the gate.'

Gunner: 'Is that the gate or the fence?' [Over the fence - beyond reach of enemy fire; having exited the threat zones.]

'The fence.'

'Fuckin' wall.'

Pilot: 'Some traffic there about 3:30 low - got it.'

Gunner: 'Okay, another visual SAM at 7 o'clock. Okay.'

SAM launch Hànôi; SAM launch Hànôi.

EWO: 'Have no Uplink.'

Co-pilot: 'I don't believe that one can reach us.'

Navigator: 'He's shootin' at those guys behind us.'

Gunner: 'I hope not... There's another one... Go left'.

Co-pilot: 'Get the hell out of here.'

Radar navigator: 'Laos border, one minute.'

Roger, what's the position?

'Ah...'

Lilac 01, Red Crown's calling. Go ahead Red Crown.

SAM detonation, no threat. SAM detonation, Lilac.
Hello Red Crown, this is Lilac 01, go.
Roger Lilac 01. You out with 3?
'Roger, Lilac 01's over the fence with 3.
Roger Lilac 01, do you have anything on Cream or Slate?
... Negative at this time...
'Ash 01 is hit!'
Lilac 01, 'Red Crown', Lilac has visual on Cream just out
in front of us.
...SAM launch, Hảiphòng; SAM Launch, Hảiphòng...
Understand Ash 01 is still flying?
'Ash 01 is still flying.
Roger, give me his position please.
Pilot to co-pilot: '... AAA out there.' Rings sound
repeatedly.
Ash 01, 050 at 30 miles.
Roger.
Gunner: 'What's our position?'
Radar navigator: '...south of the Laos border now.'
Navigator: '... 2,255 for 100 off my bulls-eye.'
'Okay.'
Co-pilot: 'Listen up the radios a minute. Somebody
has smoke in the cockpit. 'Ash 01 got hit, I think.'
Pilot: 'Who's that?...'
I have no contact with Brown 2.
Co-pilot: 'You didn't hear any beepers did you?'
Pilot: 'Nope, he's still flying.'
'Who got hit?'
'Ash 01'.'
In the leading 'Snow' cell Bill Stocker's crew and
Colonel McCarthy also heard the distress calls:
'There was a call from another aircraft stating that
he had been hit and was heading for the water. The pilot
reported that he was losing altitude and he was having
difficulty controlling the aircraft. 'Red Crown' started
vectoring F-4s to escort the crippled bomber to safety.
The crew actually saw a SAM that was going to hit them
when they were only seconds away from bomb release.
The co-pilot calmly announced the impending impact
to the crew over interphone. The aircraft dropped its
bombs on target and was hit moments later. That's what
I call 'guts football.'
B-52D 56-0584 'Ash 01' was hit by two SAMs,
eleven nautical miles left of its planned track, having
possibly been taken off course by attacking MiGs prior
to bomb release. Two of the three 307th Strategic Wing
cells attacking at Kinh Nỗ had just two B-52s in the cell
and with limited jamming the SAMs found their mark.
'Ash 01' from the 28th Bomb Squadron, 19th Bomb
Wing, Robins AFB, Georgia was commanded by 30-year
old Captain James Mack Turner of Athens, Georgia. His

Above: Major Donald O. Aldridge, 43rd
Strategic Wing assistant deputy
commander for operations and the
Deputy ABC on B-52D 'Green 01'.

Below: Captain John Davis Mize, pilot
'Ash 02'.

Below: General James R. McCarthy.

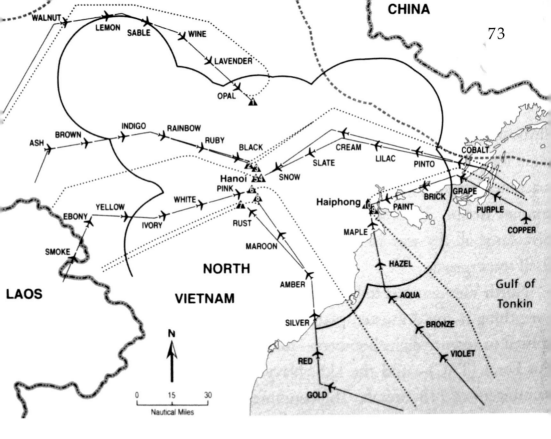

Plan of Attack for Linebacker II at 2230 hours local time on 26 December 1972.

LEGEND

- - - - - - - -	CHINESE BUFFER ZONE
————	APPROXIMATE SAM COVERAGE
▲	TARGETS
—→-	BOMBER ROUTE IN
··············	BOMBER ROUTE OUT
COLOR	CALL SIGN OF CELL

TARGETS

1	THAI NGUYEN	18
2	KINH NO COMPLEX	9
3	DUC NOI RAILROAD	9
4	HANOI RAILROAD	9
5	HANOI PETROLEUM STORAGE	9
6	GIAP NHI RAILROAD	18
7	SAM VN 549	3
8	VAN DIEN VEHICLE	15
9	HAIPHONG RAILROAD	15
10	HAIPHONG TRANSFORMER	15
		120

113 SUPPORT AIRCRAFT

EB-66, EA-3A & EA-6B (NAVY), EA-6A (MARINE) ECM
F-4 CHAFF
F-4 CHAFF ESCORT
F-4 (AF & NAVY) MIG CAP
F-4, B-52 ESCORT
F-105 & A-7 (NAVY) IRON HAND
F-4 HUNTER/KILLER

B-52 CELLS/TARGET TIMES

'D' GUAM		'G' GUAM		'D' U-TAPAO	
SNOW	2230	OPAL	2230	BLACK	2230
SLATE	2232	LAVENDER	2232	RUBY	2232
CREAM	2236	WINE	2235	RAINBOW	2235
LILAC	2238	SABLE	2238	INDIGO	2237
PINTO	2242	LEMON	2241	BROWN	2240
COBALT	2245			ASH	2244
		PAINT	2230		
RUST	2230	BRICK	2233	PINK	2230
MAROON	2232	GRAPE	2236	WHITE	2232
AMBER	2235	PURPLE	2239	IVORY	2235
SILVER	2238	COPPER	2242	YELLOW	2238
RED	2241			EBONY	2242
		MAPLE	2230	SMOKE	2245
		HAZEL	2233		
		AQUA	2236	GOLD	2245
		BRONZE	2239		
		VIOLET	2242	WALNUT	2245

co-pilot, 26-year old 1st Lieutenant Bob Hymel, born in New Orleans, had felt uneasy at briefing at U-Tapao. 'It was extremely tense for everyone. We were concerned about the Christmas bombing halt; afraid that the North Viêtnamese had used the halt to restock and repair their SAM facilities.'

'Ash 01' dropped its bombs and turned off target. Technical Sergeant Spencer Grippin the 40-year old rear gunner of Great Barrington, an affluent town in Berkshire County, Massachusetts called, 'two SAMs coming up'. Despite evasive action the missiles exploded just to the right of the bomber, wounding Grippin in the leg and groin, setting the Nos. 7 and 8 engines on fire and causing major fuel leaks and undetermined structural damage. Turning his head, Hymel saw the two SAMs coming up side by side, turn directly toward the B-52 and explode along the plane's right side. 'It felt as though we had been kicked in the pants,' he said. Two engines had been knocked out, fuel was leaking and the gunner was wounded. Turner shut down the number seven engine and pulled number eight to idle. With the right wing leaking fuel, he headed for an emergency landing at Đà Nẵng and then decided that, with several refuellings, they could make it back to their base at U-Tapao. The wounded gunner would have better medical treatment there.

'As we withdrew farther from the target area' continues Colonel McCarthy, 'the gunner reported an additional barrage of SAMs headed our way. Bill gave the order to the formation to again start their manoeuvres. It seemed like an eternity before the gunner reported that they had gone over the top of the aircraft and had exploded. That was our last encounter with SAMs that night.

'Now came an equally hard part - sweating out the time until the entire bomber stream had dropped their bombs and the cell leaders reported their losses. From the congestion on the radios it was apparent that the NVN had loaded up plenty of missiles and were using them.

'Suddenly, one of the cells in our wave reported MiGs closing in and requested fighter support. 'Red Crown', who had been working with 'Ash 01', started vectoring other F-4s to the Buff under possible attack. I gave the command for all upper rotating beacons and all tail lights to be turned off. As the F-4s approached, the MiG apparently broke off his attack because the fighters couldn't locate him and the target disappeared from the gunner's radars. This appeared to be another one of those cases where the MiGs were pacing the B-52s for the SAM gunners. It was speculated that if, while doing this, they thought they saw a chance for a one-pass quick kill, they would try to sneak within range and fire off a missile. Either that or make one screaming pass through the formation and then disappear. It was apparent that they didn't want to mix it up with our F-4 escort.

'Finally, the last cell had exited the threat zones and reported in.'

Except for the violent loss of 'Ebony 02' and the problems 'Ash 01' was still having, the rest of the force was intact. Considering what had just happened their successive reports of 'out with three' were heart lifting. 'Cream 01' and '02' had the dubious honour of both being damaged by the same SA-2 detonation, but it was minor in both cases and they were headed for the Rock.[33] As we turned south we could overhear 'Ash 01's' conversations. He had made it to the water OK and was now heading south.'

Further back in the pecking order behind 'Snow', 'Slate' and 'Cream' 'Lilac 02' flew on; interphone conversation by now almost casual as thoughts turned to home and reflections on the mission thus far.

Gunner: 'Are we gonna be driving into Thailand?'

Radar navigator: 'Rog'.

'Lemme know when we get into Thailand will you please?'

'Roger that.'

Lilac 01; Lilac, let's go back to frag airspeed [standard mission airspeed according to fragmentary operations order or frag.]

'Lilac 02', 'Lilac 03', let's go back to frag airspeed.

Pilot to co-pilot: 'I've never seen such a....'

'I haven't either.'

'You got any MiG calls at all there, Co?'

'Negative, negative.'

'Okay.'

Pilot: 'I've never seen so much AAA. I was just as worried about that.'

Co-pilot: 'Boy, ain't that the truth.'

Gunner: 'That one SAM that exploded in front of us?'

'Roger.'

'That son of a bitch was close to us, I'll tell you that, dude.'

Co-pilot: 'I got news for you. Those ones you were calling at 3 o'clock were right out my window here.'

Pilot to co-pilot: When we were in the right turn?'

'Damn right. That's when I said don't turn right. Those were damn close.'

'Seems like; we passed right between two of 'em.'

'Exactly right. I think we did, I swear to God. Because I said, don't go right and you said I gotta go right.'

EWO: 'Pretty good shootin' for no Uplinks.'

Gunner: 'Pretty fuckin' close, I'll tell you that.'

Co-pilot: 'Yeah, that was weird. I don't understand that, how there was no Uplinks... Hey pilot, did you see when I said 'what a secondary' did you see that glow over there about 1 o'clock?'

'Yeah, I saw it over your windscreen there. I couldn't see the actual centre of it.'

Co-pilot to pilot: 'My God, they must've hit a POL [Petroleum, Oils and Lubricants; a storage facility for such and a popular bombing target]. I never thought the sun was coming up.'

On 27 December B-52D 55-0062 'Cream 01' and B-52D 55-0090 'Cream 02' landed at Andersen. Following 'Dash 3' repairs they returned to service on 27 and 28 December respectively. B-52D 56-0629 'Black 03' (pictured at the Barksdale Global Power Museum, Barksdale AFB, Louisiana) landed at U-Tapao needing 63 man hours to repair fourteen external holes plus three dents and returned to service on 31 December. (author)

'Yeah, it was pretty bright...'

Shortly after midnight, 'Ash 01' started a straight-in approach to the Thai base. Captain Brent O. Diefenbach, a B-52 aircraft commander who had just returned from a mission in the North, sat in a crew bus, waiting to cross the end of the runway as Turner's battle-damaged B-52D neared the runway lights. The approach did not look or sound right. Suddenly, the aircraft veered to the left and the engines roared as power was added for a go-around. Diefenbach watched, horrified, as the big bomber pitched up, plunged to earth about a mile beyond the runway and exploded in a ball of fire killing Turner, Major Lawrence Jay Marshall, the 43-year old navigator of Manchester, New Hampshire, Lieutenant Colonel Donald Arrington Joyner the 41-year old radar navigator of Henderson, North Carolina who left behind four children and a widow, and 31-year old Captain Roy Tom Tabler, EWO of Crossett in Ashley County, Arizona. Spencer Grippin escaped when the tail section broke free on impact. Diefenbach later remembered the compulsive thought that he had to get to the crash site. 'It appeared obvious to me that no one was alive, but something kept drawing me to go.' He knew he had to get there fast. Jumping off the bus, he went out an entrance gate and climbed aboard a Thai bus that was headed in the direction of the crash. When the driver refused to go further, Diefenbach ran down the road toward the burning B-52 until he spotted a path in the tall grass that seemed to lead to the aircraft. For a second Diefenbach thought, 'Why go on? No one is alive in that inferno.' But again he felt impelled, almost against his will. He approached the wreckage, shouting to see if anyone was alive. To his surprise, he heard a voice inside the bomber calling for help. Rolling down the sleeves of his flight suit for protection against the heat, he entered the burning plane amidst a fusillade of exploding ammunition and pressure lines. There was no way of knowing if bombs were still aboard. Diefenbach followed the cries - the only sign of life - through a pall of smoke to find copilot Bob Hymel badly injured, crumpled in a position that prevented him from unbuckling his seat harness and with one fractured leg trapped in the wreckage. He had collapsed lungs and a crushed arm and was administered last rites. Diefenbach remembers accusing Hymel of not helping and of falling asleep - 'anything to keep him conscious.'

In desperation, Hymel told his rescuer to cut off the leg if he had to. Finally, working together for what seemed an eternity, they were able to free the injured man. 'By that time, the explosions [and] the heat were nearer than I care to think about.' Diefenbach dragged Hymel out of the fuselage and carried him away from the blazing wreck just as a helicopter and fire trucks arrived. The rescue crew was unable to approach the B-52, now engulfed in flames. Hymel was air-evacuated to Clark Air Base in the Philippines and then to a hospital in the States where he eventually recovered from multiple fractures and lacerations. His wife Beatriz 'Pat' said his doctors were astonished at his recovery and attributed it to the fact that he wanted to meet his daughter Natalie, then two months old. After Diefenbach had reported details of the rescue to the wing commander and his staff, he was taken to the base hospital 'for some minor repairs and bandages.' Sometime later, he discovered there were 'a lot of thank you's in order for the Chief Pilot in the Sky.' He had extricated the co-pilot from an armed ejection seat. That it had not fired in the struggle to free Hymel was a miracle within a miraculous and heroic rescue, for which the Commander in Chief of Strategic Air Command, General John C. Meyer presented Diefenbach with the Airman's Medal.[32]

After Colonel McCarthy had given his ABC summary report to 8th Air Force over HF radio he noticed he was having difficulty breathing. 'Although we were supposed to still be at combat pressurization at this point, I couldn't stand the pain any longer. Before takeoff the flight surgeon had put a stethoscope to my lungs and said the pneumonia, which was diagnosed a week earlier, had settled in both lungs. He went away shaking his head, muttering something about idiots and pilots who fly with pneumonia. With normal cabin pressurization, 100 per cent oxygen and pressurized oxygen flow, the pain subsided to tolerable levels. It would take me six months to get over the effects of pneumonia.

'As we headed towards Okinawa and our post-strike refuelling, made necessary by the extraordinary length of this mission, we received a piece of bad news from our tankers. The weather had deteriorated in the refuelling area. Visibility was dropping and there was moderate turbulence at refuelling altitude. By this time it had been about sixteen hours since the crews had reported for duty. They had just flown one of the most difficult and dangerous missions of their careers and now they would have to conduct a night refuelling in weather conditions which were very hazardous. If we had planned it, we couldn't have come up with a situation that would more severely challenge the ultimate flying abilities of these combat crews. However, despite visibility that sometimes blotted out the view of the tanker's wings and the refuelling lights and turbulence that made the instrument panel hard to read, all refuelling was completed as briefed.[33]

'As the lead airplane touched down safely at Guam in the warm sunshine I felt proud and humbled to have been their commander. The record mission was executed flawlessly and the crews met every challenge thrown at them. When the history of Air Power in Southeast Asia is finally written, the raid flown on 26 December 1972 by the B-52s and their support forces will, I suspect, be judge as one of the most successful bombing missions of the war. The credit for this outstanding achievement belongs not only to the magnificent flight crews, but to all the support and maintenance troops as well. It was truly an outstanding team effort.'

In Hànôi the walls in the 'Hànôi Hilton' had shook with the proximity of the B-52 bombing, which was of great encouragement to Bill Conlee. 'It was immediately obvious that SAMs were being fired from several sites located right outside the prison walls. I could also hear AAA fire coming from the roof of the 'Hilton', using the prison as a sanctuary from attack. The next morning a large group of ashen-faced Viêtnamese came into my room and asked how close the bombs were and what airplanes were dropping them. I said, 'Very close and you know already' and smiled. This proved to be a mistake as I was quickly subjected to a rough beating, the worst I received during captivity. From this experience I concluded that the North Viêtnamese were genuinely terrified about the B-52 bombing and were striking out in fear and frustration at an available target - me. After licking my wounds for a couple more days, I was then moved to a larger room in what was known to PoWs as 'Heartbreak Annex'.[34]

This raid was the climax of 'Linebacker II' and the most concentrated bomber attack in history. It took total B-52 losses to thirteen but the raids were having the desired effect on the enemy. 'Even the Viêtnamese were hard pressed to keep a straight face while spinning many of their propaganda yarns' wrote Bill Conlee. 'We responded with laughs to daily lies from our captors about vast numbers of B-52s shot down...'

On the afternoon of 27 December Hànôi indicated it wanted to restart peace talks on 8 January. President Nixon promised that all bombing north of the 20th Parallel would cease within thirty-six hours of the Communists agreement.

On the ninth night, 27/28 December, sixty bombers - 39 B-52Ds and 21 Gs, thirty of which came from U-Tapao supported by 101 USAF and USN aircraft were sent in six waves to bomb seven targets close to Hànôi. Andersen also flew thirty additional sorties - six in South Viêtnam, plus 24 in other parts of North Viêtnam. Seven cells were allocated Lang Đàng rail yards and three cells targeted Dục Nội, while four cells were given Trung Quảng rail centre and two cells, the Văn Diệm supply complex. One cell each was given SAM sites VN 234, 243 and 549, which US intelligence wrongly credited with having downed six B-52s. A new tactic used this night was to split the wave coming in from the northeast into three smaller streams attacking separate targets and then reform into one wave after the PTT. The wave coming in from the southeast used identical pre-and post-strike tactics, except that it split into two streams from the IP inbound. The entire force was to drop its bombs in ten minutes instead of the fifteen minutes planned for the night before.

The launch went like clockwork. The weather was good in the refuelling area and the support aircraft were 'blistering' the defences or were in position to escort the B-52s. The mission was flown as briefed. This was the third mission flown by Lieutenant Colonel Phil Blaufuss the RN on Captain Dick Martin's crew on TDY from Barksdale.

'Our ability to work smoothly as a crew was what made the difference between having a good tour or a so-so one and it was a key to our success on 27 December, my third mission as a RN during the campaign. In many ways it was the toughest. That might sound surprising, considering that we had less thrown at us in the way of defences that night. However, my job was to bomb. Worrying about defences was, from my downstairs position, an evil I had to ignore. I can't think of anything more useless than to worry about missiles when you're a RN or nav, stuck in the belly of an airplane with no windows to see all the hell that's breaking loose, no guns to shoot, no ECM equipment to jam with and no control column or throttles to manoeuvre the plane. Talk about a waste of time; worrying about enemy defences is sure one of them under those conditions.

'The toughness of this mission came from the target we were fragged against. We were leading 'Opal' cell in the middle of a wave of Gs, all headed for the Lang Đàng rail yards. The marshalling yards and rolling stock were important targets but Lang Đàng is up in the hill country northeast of Hànôi. That's in the boondocks and our radar aiming points were some of the toughest I ever had to use. If the mission was going to be a success, I simply had to put my full attention to my own special job. That was to make sure the checklist for releasing armed bombs was completed with no omissions, to make sure the equipment was working properly to solve the bombing problem and to make sure that I was on the aiming point. Anything else would have detracted from that and that's where Dick Martin showed one of the many talents he had. Dick kept the crew informed. No theatrics - just good, solid information. He reacted to a SAM launch with a quiet running advisory on where it was and what it meant to us. He was relaxed and self-disciplined and it rubbed off on the whole crew. Each one knew his job, kept the rest of the crew advised - if they needed to know - and we all calmly went about our business. I counted it a pleasure to fly with them.

The remains of B52D 56-0584 'Ash 01' which crashed at U-Tapao on 27 December.

A pre-packed clip assembly of Mk.82 500lb bombs for easier loading. In practice bombs were often loaded individually using a device known as a 'stuffer'.

'We did have a situation that night which wasn't in the frag order and caused us some aggravation. After we had coasted in off the Gulf we temporarily became a four-ship cell. At least that's what the guys in 'Grey' cell behind us observed. It seems that a MiG had decided to come up and play tag-along by flying loose formation off our wing. It was probably another case of being up there as a traffic cop for the SAM batteries. Anyhow, somebody called for MiGCAP and when the F-4s headed our way I'm told that our fourth aircraft left the scene about as urgently as anybody had ever seen before.'

Lieutenant Colonel Gerald Wickline a B-52D pilot in the 307th Strategic Wing at U-Tapao, who was flying his first sortie over Hànôi later recalled: 'You can't believe how bad it was. Our target was a rail yard on the north side of Hànôi. We saw well over 100 SAMs fired and more than thirty of them came within one mile of our airplane, with at least half of those missing us by less than 200 feet. My mouth was so full of cotton I could barely talk and the whole time I thought I would be dead the next second. There was no way to outmanoeuvre them and several times I was blinded by a near-missile detonation or from the brilliant glare of their rocket trail as they went past me. The mission was a nightmare that I would not soon forget. I found out on that sortie that I was not a coward. I begged for an excuse to turn that airplane around and not fly through those missiles but I was more afraid of being branded a coward than I was of dying.'

Altogether, 120 SAMs were launched and they succeeded in hitting two Stratofortresses. Forty-year old Major Donald O. Aldridge, who flew 35 B-52 combat missions in Southeast Asia, was the 43rd Strategic Wing assistant deputy commander for operations and the Deputy ABC on B-52D 'Green 01'. He wrote:

'Started to see AAA around the IP or slightly before. Most of it was around 20-25,000 fee but fairly heavy. MiG activity west of Hànôi but were being engaged by F-4Cs. TAC kept them busy and off of us. Started seeing SAM firings around the IP. Lots of low AAA, some 122mm unguided rockets. SAMs becoming more frequent and apparently aimed at the cell. F-4 escort flying either side of cell in opposite direction - rotating beacons on.

'TTR manoeuvre was commenced...[35] Gunner reports two and three tucked in and cell moving as one aircraft. SAMs getting pretty thick but most missing by at least one-half mile. Gunner reported one SAM very close to 'Green 03'. Three okay. 120 seconds to go - six SAMs obviously aimed at 'Green' cell - the cell continues to manoeuvre. The two SAMs at 1 o'clock are well off target - exploded high about one-half mile horizontal range; the two at 10-11 o'clock are not going to be a factor. Pilot reports that the two at 9 o'clock are staying in one spot on the side window and appear to be tracking 'Green 01'. TTR continued but altitude variation increased. SAMs are now visible to me, out of my seat so I can see. Looked close to me! At what appears to the uninitiated to be very close, the pilot starts a small rapid descent - SAMs go over the aircraft - I can see the exhaust - they both explode above the aircraft. Height unknown but the concussion can be felt slightly and the co-pilot reports he could hear the explosion. Back on altitude immediately and TTR continued. Actually, the pilot never ceased the 'book' TTR bank angle for the entire time except for the final moments of the bomb run... then straight and level, on bomb run heading!

'Bombs away, back into the TTR. 'Ash 02' is hit!' 'Ash 01' reports he is heading for the fence. 'Ash 02' has two engines shut down and a few moments later is down to four engines and losing altitude fast - down to 19,000 and still in North Việtnam.'

For Captain John Mize, commander of B-52D 56-0599 'Ash 02', who was to bomb the SAM site at VN 243, it was third time unlucky. Mize stood 'Ash 02' almost on its wing during the post-target turn as a salvo of SAMs were fired at the formation. One hit the B-52 in the left wing and knocked out all four engines on that side and two were on fire. Despite being wounded by shrapnel in his left leg Mize managed to keep the aircraft aloft for almost an hour before the bomb bay doors fell open and one of the landing gear began to cycle, lowering then retracting. Mize knew that he was losing his hydraulic system and the B-52's descent steepened with the sudden increase in drag. Major Donald Aldridge noted: 'Ash 02' is nearing time to punch out.' Mize saw the lights of Nakhon Phanom and told the crew to eject. Captain Bill North the radar navigator, Captain Dennis Anderson the EWO and the gunner, Tech Sergeant Peter E. Whalen ejected safely but navigator Lieutenant Bill Robinson's ejection seat failed and he was forced to unstrap and bail out through the hole left by the radar navigator's seat. Then the co-pilot, Terrence Gruters and lastly, Mize, ejected.

Major Donald Aldridge continued making his notes: 'Looks like the aircraft crashed about 20-25 miles from NKP [Nakhon Phanom]. Can hear Rescue talking to pilot and radar navigator but cannot hear their reply. Later confirmed - all out and okay...' Mize was awarded the Air Force Cross.

'31 SAMs were fired at 'Green' cell. I was writing down data on damaged aircraft and probably missed several, but none of them were exceptionally close. At 1608Z (11.08pm) there was a gigantic explosion on the ground. The entire landscape was illuminated through the thin undercast. 'Cobalt 02' reports he thinks he is now a flight of two - lead has taken a hit! Confirms 'Cobalt 01' is going down - beepers heard - in target area. 'Red Crown' notified. Apparently hit immediately at or after the BRL.'[36]

B-52D 56-0605 'Cobalt 01' in the 7th Bomb Wing, 43rd Strategic Wing was deployed from the the 441st Bomb Squadron, 320th Bomb Wing at Mather AFB, California. At the controls were 28-year old Captain Frank Douglas Lewis of Fort Wayne Indiana and his 26-year old co-pilot, Captain Samuel Bolden Cusimano of Birmingham, Alabama. Lewis received the Distinguished Flying Cross for extraordinary achievement while an F-4D Weapons System Operator on 22 September 1970 when he led a tactical combat mission in marginal weather conditions against three companies of highly defended hostile troops. Cusimano had flown 155 combat missions, mostly night recce forward air controller and flare missions, over Laos between December 1969 and December 1970 before being assigned to fly B-52s at March AFB, California. One minute before bomb release on the railway yards at Trung Quảng 'Cobalt 01' was locked onto by two SAMs at 25,000 feet. Lewis and Cusimano evaded these but they were not able to dodge a third missile that hit between the forward wheel-well and the right wing root, as the B-52 was in a

Main picture: Wreckage from Cobalt 01', shot down by the 72nd Battalion, 285th Air Defence Missile (Hero Unit) on 27 December can still be seen on the surface of Huu Tiep Lake at Ngọc Hà, Ba Đình district, Hànôi. The North Viêtnamese keep it that way as a reminder of a war that nobody won.

Top left: 1st Lieutenant Bennie Lamar Fryer, radar navigator.
Centre: Major James Carroll Condon, substitute radar navigator.
Top Right: Captain Frank Douglas Lewis, pilot.

Left: Senior Master Sergeant James Wayne Gough, gunner.

Right: Captain Samuel Bolden Cusimano, co-pilot, 'Cobalt 01' receiving the Bronze Star with Valour for his service as a PoW in North Vietnam.

Lieutenant Vũ Xuân Thiều of the 921th Sao Sao Fighter Regiment 'Red Star' who took off in his MiG 21 from Cẩm Thủy, Thanh Hòa at 2141 hours might have shot down 'Cobalt 01'. Born in 1945, the seventh in the family of ten children, in 1968 he successfully completed flight training in the USSR. At 2152 hours Akatsuki control had commanded him to fly 360° to a target 15 kilometres distant but he was unable to successfully intercept due to heavy radar interference. Trần Xuân Mão, an experienced radar operator, found among the opaque background noise white dots, which he confirmed that the B-52 had changed direction, flying back towards Son La and then up to Hànôi. HQ immediately ordered Vũ Xuân Thiều to fly 90° to Sâm Nua to chase the B-52. At 2158 Vũ Xuân Thiều detected his quarry but the sky was dark and he was experiencing very serious radar interference, making it difficult to judge distances. He estimated the distance to his target and fired both K-13 (AA-2 Atoll) AAMs but they did not hit the B-52. According to Việtnamese documents Vũ Xuân Thiều then accelerated and crashed into the debris of the B-52, which was on fire. A US investigation determined that the MiG-21 was either destroyed by the resulting explosion or was shot down by three AIM-7 Sparrows fired from a USAF F-4D flown by Major Harry McKee and Captain John Dubler before it could reach the B-52.

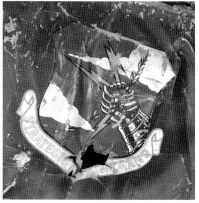

Right: Crumpled remains of a downed B-52 in the museum grounds in Hànôi.

tight turn. The wings caught fire, the fuel tanks were ruptured and the electrical system failed. All the crew were injured to some extent by the explosion and 1st Lieutenant Bennie Lamar Fryer the 27-year old radar navigator of Stockton, California was killed. Forty seconds after being hit and unable to release his bombs, Lewis gave the order to abandon the aircraft. Four of the crew ejected before the aircraft crashed near Hànôi. Thirty-four year old Senior Master Sergeant James Wayne Gough the rear gunner of Fresno, California who flew as a gunner in the B-26 Invader during the Korean War could not hear the ejection order, but knew that he would soon have to bail out. The flames from the burning aircraft extended back on both sides of the B-52 to the gunner's turret and he decided to wait for a better chance as long as the aircraft was still in level flight. By then the other crew members who were able to eject had departed the plane. When he saw that the aircraft was descending into the low undercast, he knew he had to leave then or lose his chance. When he jumped, he went through burning debris of the disintegrating engines and wings and had numerous pieces of wiring and metal fragments embedded in his body. Luckily, Gough was able to deploy his parachute. He was captured soon after he landed on the ground.

Captain Lewis was lucky to be captured alive after he landed in a rice paddy. A North Việtnamese peasant took Lewis' revolver and would have killed him on the spot if the gun had been loaded. As the click, click of the empty pistol sounded, NVA troops approached and captured Lewis alive, taking him from the custody of the peasant. He and Major James Carroll Condon, 38, a substitute radar navigator from Versailles, Ohio, who had heard three ejection seats going above him before he ejected were reunited soon after they were captured. Major Allen Louis Johnson the 36-year old EWO from Tuscumbia, Alabama had only enough time to call out 'They've got us!' before the violent detonation near the forward wing root. He was thought to have ejected from the aircraft but the Vietnamese denied knowledge of him. A North

Viêtnamese interrogator told Lewis that he knew that his EWO was a black man, a fact not revealed by any of the crew in interrogation, indicating either that he had been captured or that his body had been found. It was not until 4 December 1985 that Johnson's remains were returned. The positive identification of these remains was announced publicly in June 1986.

Lewis was subjected to harassment and torture by his captors. After a month in solitary he was moved to the 'Zoo', - a staging/collection point for the repatriation of the fourth and final increment of PoWs - in the southwest suburbs of Hànôi where he was reunited with Gough, Condon and Cusimano.[37] Together, they reconstructed the shoot down. Jim Condon said that Bennie Fryer was apparently killed in the SAM explosion, as he collapsed forward on the nav table and was bleeding profusely. His seat was the closest of any crew member to the point of impact of the SAM. Condon himself was wounded in the leg by shrapnel and tried shaking Fryer and yelling at him to arouse him, but got no response. On 30 September 1977 the Vietnamese 'discovered' and returned Bennie Fryer's remains. Bennie adored airplanes and had constructed many models as a boy, which still hang from the ceiling of his bedroom at his parents' home in Stockton, California - just where he had placed them.[38]

Major Donald Aldridge concluded: 'Cinnamon' cell reports three aircraft out and that accounts for the B-52G wave within radio range. 'Green', 'Topaz' and 'Ivory' report out with three. Gunner reports SAM low at 4.30 position - time 1620Z. Suspect it was a flare or rocket - no known or suspected site in this area. Return trip to Andersen - long. Co-pilot (Captain Tom Brown Jr.) executed perfect penetration, approach and landing. Flying time - 15.5 hours. A thoroughly professional crew, AC (Captain Glenn Schaumberg) and RN (Captain Arthur Matson) are superb. These two among the best I have ever seen.'[39]

'Cobalt 01' was the 15th and final loss of the 'Linebacker II' bombing campaign. The four survivors of 'Cobalt 01' were all released on 29 March 1973. For Phạm Thị Quy, a former member of the Ngọc Hà, Ba Đình district, Hànôi self-defence platoon, the image of the falling B-52 shot down by the 72nd Battalion, 285 Air Defence Missile (Hero) Regiment on the morning of 27 December 1972 never fades from her mind. 'We experienced a mixture of feelings when the plane was shot down. Some villagers were killed during the shooting down. Bombs scattered around the village but did not explode. Our air defence soldiers managed to shoot down the plane before the bombs were dropped. On that day, sappers were sent to help the villagers in bomb disposal. Then, General Võ Nguyên Giáp visited the village and encouraged the villagers to keep their fighting spirit. Those are unforgettable memories to me'.

Another villager, Ân Việt Mỹ never forgets the village's great pride and happiness at seeing the B-52 shot down right in their midst. 'That night, the whole village was sleepless. Every villager was eager to see how 'the American Flying Fortress' [sic] was destroyed. Mỹ recalls: 'The plane burst into flames and looked like a torch. It fell into the lake and killed many fish. Some of the villagers emerged from their shelters to look at the fallen plane. The village became quiet following the fierce air attacks. We had never been so happy before and cheered the moment. The village spent a sleepless night'.

One of the oldest witnesses in the village, Nguyên Trọng Hiên feels proud that he took part in the fierce fight to protect Hànôi. In the late 1960s, Hiên fought in many battles in Quảng Tri and Cambodia. He was sent back to defend Hànôi. His wife also joined the self-defence forces of Ngọc Hà village to be close to her husband. 'This task was important to me to come back to defend the capital city of Hànôi, my homeland. Though my battle station was only 1 kilometre from the shelter, I could not be with my children because the fighting was so fierce. Fortunately, one day I managed to visit my family while marching to the other side of the Red River, but I didn't see any family member. I was very worried, but the villagers told me my wife was helping with bomb clearance. Then I felt relieved enough to return to my unit and continue fighting'.

The 'Linebacker II' attacks for Day 10 called for sixty B-52s, 15 each D's and Gs from Andersen and thirty Ds from U-Tapao supported by ninety-nine tactical aircraft. On the night of 28/29 December they formed into six waves attacking five targets. Four waves and their four

A B-52D refuelling from a KC-135 tanker.

targets were in the immediate Hànôi area, while the other two waves attacked the Lang Đàng rail yards. Of the four targets around Hànôi, two were again SAM sites - VN 158 and 266 plus a SA-2 storage area near Hànôi.

Only twenty-seven SAMs were fired and every target was successfully attacked without loss. Everyone took pleasure hearing the last of the airborne commander's exit roll call:

'Orange' cell out with three.'

'Quilt' out with three.'

'Violet' out with three.'

As the Day Ten aircraft were returning to Guam (Andersen had also sent 28 B-52s to attack targets in southern North Việtnam, Laos, Cambodia and northern South Việtnam) the last of the aircraft for Day Eleven were being uploaded with bombs. What had been 12-hour shifts, six days a week had become a back-breaking seven day a week task and preliminaries for Day Twelve were in hand. But Friday the 29th of December would be the final day of 'Linebacker II' for General Jerry Johnson was notified later in the day that all bombing operations north of 20 degrees latitude would cease following the mission of the 29th. Sixty B-52s - thirty from U-T and twelve G models and eighteen Ds from Andersen - in three waves of three cells each, would strike two large SAM storage and support areas at Trại Cá forty miles north of Hànôi and Phú Yên northwest of the capital and the Lang Đàng rail yards again. (Andersen also dispatched thirty B-52Gs on 'Arc Light' strikes in southern VN and South Việtnam). Colonel McCarthy who gave the last briefing could sense the crews rising level of confidence as they filed into the briefing room.

'We were closing in for the final finale and they knew it. The rumour had started floating around that this might be the last day of the big raids and they wanted to be part of it. I had crews who had just landed hours earlier from the previous night's mission ask to be put in the line-up. Crews who had been designated as spares argued emphatically as to why they should be designated as primary crews rather than spare. One crew even went so far as to file an Inspector General complaint. Their argument was that they, being a less experienced crew, needed the mission for crew proficiency more than the older heads. With morale like that I knew I had the best outfit in the US Air Force. I knew how they felt. I had asked General Andrew B. Anderson Jr., commanding 57 Air Division to let me fly as the ABC but he turned me down emphatically. I think the Flight Surgeon had said a few words to him in private. His compromise was to allow me the final briefing.'

The tactics for the final curtain were complex. The release time of each cell exactly matched those of the other cells in the other two waves. After bombing the post-target routing, which had two of the waves crossing tracks, separated only by altitude. A combination of chaff sown by the F-4s, mutual ECM support provided by nine B-52s in close proximity, a consolidated point attack from three widely separated axes of attack and the post target routing produced maximum ordnance on target in minimum exposure time.

'The launch went flawlessly' wrote Colonel McCarthy. 'By now the launch of a 30-plane mission had become a rather routine affair but there was something about them that always drew a crowd. For this launch, there must have been at least 8,000 spectators along the flight line and gathered at vantage points on buildings. Sensing the end, offices all over the base closed down to let their people see it.'

On 29/30 December SAM firings declined dramatically, as the combination of bombing and blockade had prevented fresh supplies reaching the North Viêtnamese.[40] The SAMs had been Hànôi's first line of defence; deprived of their air bases, the North Viêtnamese were able

A 'cell' of three B-52Ds in formation.

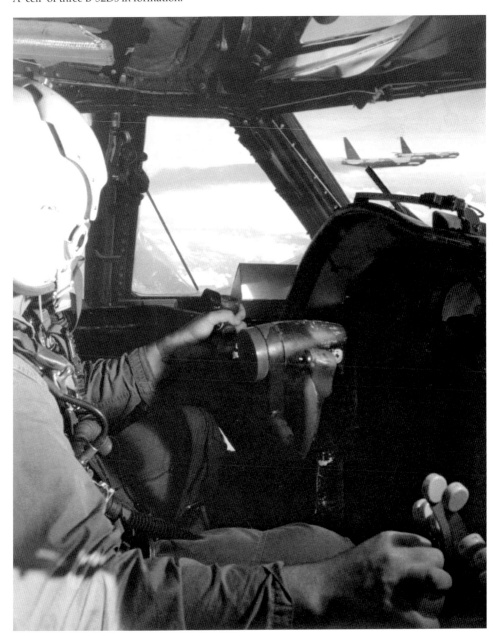

to deploy only about thirty MiGs in the defence of Hànôi-Hảiphòng, eight of which were shot down. Support aircraft flew 102 sorties, only one MiG pilot unsuccessfully made a half hearted attempt to attack 'Aqua' cell and no B-52s were lost but 'Grey 03', the last B-52 in the last wave, which evaded nine SAMs, was peppered with 119 shrapnel holes. 'Wine 03' had to return early with refuelling problems and the other two 'Wine' aircraft attached themselves to 'Walnut' cell just ahead and hit Phú Yen as a five-ship cell. The other fifty-four B-52s also bombed successfully. The bomb-train from 'Grey 03' hit the Trại Cá SAM storage area 17 minutes before midnight. The final bombs dropped by B-52s had fallen north of the 20th parallel. While the raid was in progress, the North Viêtnamese signalled the White House that they were ready to return to the Paris peace table. In the space of eleven days B-52s flew 729 sorties against 34 targets in North Viêtnam above the 20th parallel, the last of which ceased at midnight, 'Arc Light' missions continued however.

On the evening of the 3/4 January B-52D 'Ruby 02' commanded by Lieutenant Colonel Gerald Wickline who had suffered such a traumatic flight on Day Nine, took off from U-Tapao AB at 0243 and proceeded to the target area (SAM sites at Vinh, North Viêtnam about 150 miles north of the DMZ). On approach to the target Captain William E. Fergason, the 27-year old EWO notified the pilot of threat radars. Just prior to bomb release he notified him of missile launch. Since it was still early morning and dark, he confirmed the missile launch visually. Just after bomb release, Wickline and Captain William 'Bill' F. Milcarek, co-pilot and Tech Sergeant Carlos S. 'Chuck' Kilgore, gunner reported missiles passing on both sides of the aircraft. While the crew were releasing their 500lb bombs at 30,000 feet, a SAM was reported on a collision heading with the bomber, which still had its bomb bay doors open. 'At about 40 seconds TTG (time to target) four missiles were fired at us, off our left wing recalled Gerald Wickline. 'I manoeuvred to avoid No.1 and No.2 with No.1 going past our nose (really close) and detonating just above us (going up). No.2 SAM missed our tail by an estimated fifty feet and also detonated just above us. I had

B-52D-20-BW 55-0067 on finals at Okinawa. This aircraft is now displayed at the Pima Air & Space Museum, adjacent to Davis-Monthan AFB in Tucson, Arizona. It is marked as '067 *The Lone Star Lady*' and was operated by the 7th BW at Carswell AFB and withdrawn from service on 5 November 1982.

Maintenance work being carried out on the J57 engines of a B-52.

lost sight of Nos. 3 and 4 and we were close to TTG zero so I rolled level and simultaneously with bombs away, there was a tremendous explosion directly below our nose. Three windows on my side of the airplane shattered, showering us with broken bits of plexiglas. The No.1 engine fire light came on and a blazing fire was burning in the No.1 pod. All of my flight instruments, including airspeed and altitude, were inoperative. Most of the engine instruments on both sides of the cockpit were inoperative, the glass having been shattered in most of them. All hydraulic power to the left wing was out and all fuel gauges on the left wing were either spinning or stuck.

'I polled the crew and everyone answered but the tail gunner. No one was hurt at this time but a couple of minutes later Captain Myles McTernan the navigator called in a fuel leak that had just developed above his head and JP- 4 fuel was pouring in right on top of him and Major Roger A. Klingbeil the radar navigator. Shortly McTernan started screaming from the pain of the fuel burning him - these were chemical burns. The lower deck was literally floating in fuel. We tried continuously to contact the gunner but to no avail. We started a descent over the South China Sea. Soon after level off we felt a thump and heard a parachute beeper go off. Our gunner had bailed out all on his own as flames from a fire in the belly began licking around his turret.'

When the missile exploded below the aircraft Bill Fergason observed sparks and shrapnel flying about inside the aircraft cabin. 'The pilot immediately put out the word that we were hit and started to descend. Our flight path to and from the target area was east bound toward the sea. We continued east as the pilot descended to approximately 10,000 feet and tried to slow the airspeed to a safer bailout speed. Most of this was done with the help of one of our 'cell' mates flying with us and reporting on altitude and speed (the explosion and concussion of the missile caused the instruments to malfunction including shattering the pilot's windows to the point they could not clearly see out.) When it was confirmed we were in an area safe for bailout (over water with Navy assets in the area for pickup), the pilot ordered a controlled bailout sequence.'

'The airplane was barely controllable. Every time we would attempt to slow down it would start a roll to the right and we could only straighten it out by gaining airspeed. By this time we were abeam Đà Nẵng, so I turned eastbound (away from land). When he was satisfied that the entire crew had ejected, he followed, first trimming the aircraft nose down on the southerly course, about ten miles off the coast and heading toward Đà Nẵng. We were almost sure that when the first ejection seat was fired we would become a fireball but thank God that didn't happen. I heard two thumps which I assumed was the navigator and RN ejection seats firing, followed a few seconds later by a third, which was the EWO. I told the co-pilot to go and he squeezed the trigger. I was temporarily blinded by flying debris. After I got my eyes cleared and looked, he was gone. I made a call on interphone to see if anyone was still on board, waited a few seconds and then pulled the throttles to idle, assumed the position and squeezed the trigger. I felt a tremendous kick in the seat of my pants, a great blast of cold air, severe tumbling, a extremely sharp jolt tearing the ejection seat from my hands and a loud 'pop, followed by the most intense silence I have ever heard. I could hardly believe my good fortune when I looked up and saw that beautiful big orange and white canopy of the parachute above my head. About that time I felt extremely nauseous, so I pulled my oxygen mask from my face and barfed into the Gulf Of Tonkin. I saw a fireball on the horizon. Our B-52 had hit the water and exploded.'

Unknown to Wickline, Myles McTernan was still aboard. His seat, which ejected downward, was jammed, probably as a result of the SAM explosion. A partial ejection left him in a position where he could not be seen by other crew members, nor could he reach up to the foot-operated microphone switch on the floor of his compartment. After what seemed an eternity, McTernan

BDA photo of rail targets in Hànôi taken on 31 December.

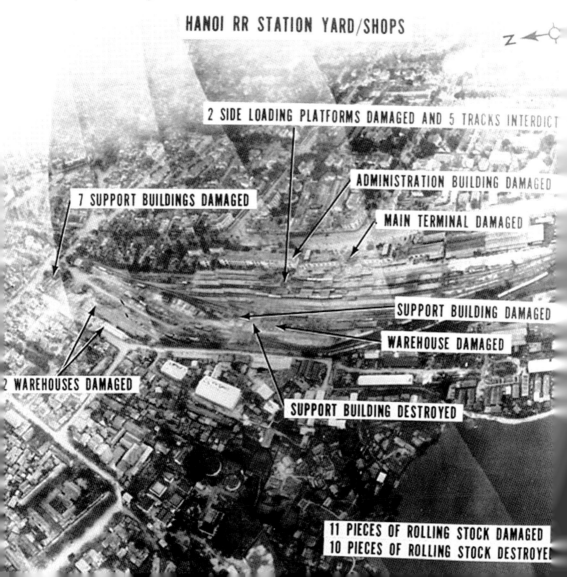

managed to struggle out of the ejection seat, forced to leave his survival kit behind. He was unable to find a soft-pack survival kit that contained a life raft. Only his survival vest remained to keep him afloat if he survived to reach the water. McTernan bailed out through an open escape hatch into the pitch-black night and the turbulence created by the diving aircraft. He suffered deep lacerations of his face, hands and arms and a fractured bone on the side of his face. Because he was in a semiconscious state, he did not remember pulling his rip cord or landing in waves that were from 8 to 10 feet high. It was some time later and daylight before he regained full consciousness.

Meanwhile the other crew members had been rescued. None of them suffered serious injuries, except Wickline, who was painfully injured in ejecting. All members believed that McTernan had bailed out and should be in the general area where they had been rescued. A search for him would continue. McTernan knew that the chance of his being rescued was slim. He had left the aircraft many miles from the rest of the crew, landing in high seas in which the tiny dot of orange that was his life preserver would be extremely difficult to see from above. He was to be blessed by good fortune, however. After several hours, a search plane scanning the general area where the others had landed reached bingo fuel and was forced to turn back to its base. In one magic moment, a member of the search crew spotted McTernan as he was at the top of a wave and briefly visible. His rescue was a multiservice affair. The Navy directed the search from USS *Saratoga*. He was spotted by an Air Force search aircraft, picked up by a Marine helicopter and flown to the Đà Nẵng Army hospital, where his injuries were treated. McTernan, born on 9 March 1948 in Cambridge, Massachusetts had enlisted to avoid the draft and having to serve in foxholes and get shot did not have good enough eyesight to be a pilot so it was off to Navigator School for him. Based on his experiences his advice would be 'stay under the radar'.

Bill Fergason's ejection sequence had worked perfectly, just as it was supposed to (canopy jettisoned, seat ejected and separated from him, parachute deployed as did the seat gear with inflated raft dangling below on descent). But on encountering the airstream his helmet face visor burst and temporarily damaged his left eye. His lower chin experienced a slight cut that required several stitches. This injury was the result of the parachute harnessing gear striking his face. 'As I descended, I immediately checked that I had a good chute, inflated my underarm LPUs and checked that all my seat gear was still with me. The only problem was with my hand-held radio. After I climbed in the raft, I tried to establish contact with rescue crews. I could hear the rescue crews in the area but they could not hear me. I had a problem with transmitting. As a result it took approximately three hours before I was found and picked up. Major Roger Klingbeil and I were picked up by the USS *Inchon*, a Marine Helicopter rescue flattop. We were both in the ship's hospital quarters while they spent another four or five hours searching for the navigator.

'After all was said and done the gunner made his exit from the aircraft and landed near an aircraft carrier and was picked up almost immediately. The pilot and co-pilot were picked up by helicopters out of Đà Nẵng and flown directly back there. Since the navigator had to make a manual bailout (getting out of his malfunctioning ejection seat and actually falling out of the radar navigator's open hatch), he was knocked unconscious by hitting the bottom of the aircraft in the wind stream. He obviously had his hand on the 'D' ring of the parachute because it did open and he was found in the water semiconscious with his parachute still attached and floating on only one side of his underarm LPU (one side did not inflate). He was 'extremely' lucky!'[41]

Peace talks were resumed on 8 January and on the 27th a cease-fire agreement came into effect. Captain Don Becker's Dyess AFB crew in 'Brass 03' at U-Tapao who had a Stars and Stripes reporter on board, who wrote an article about the mission, dropped the last bombs in Việtnam from a B-52. Release time was 23:00:52Z. A cell from Guam was scheduled to drop one hour later but they aborted. The cease-fire continued in Laos until mid-April and in Cambodia until mid-August, when Congress cut off funds for the air war.

The 'Linebacker II' offensive was the heaviest of the war and no fewer than 729 B-52D and Gs made it to their targets - 340 from U-Tapao and 389 from Guam - of which 703 were considered 'effective', dropping 15,000 tons of bombs on fifty-four targets. The cost was fifteen B-52s (nine B-52Ds and six B-52Gs) which were shot down by, or crashed as a result of, being hit by SAMs. Three B-52s (two Ds and one G) were seriously damaged and six had minor damage.[42] Reports indicated that no fewer than 1,242 SAMs had been fired at the B-52s during the eleven-day campaign. Of the 92 crewmembers aboard, 52 were killed; thirty-three bailed out and became PoWs while Air Force rescue teams recovered another twenty-six men in post-strike operations. Four crewmen died in a crash landing and twenty-nine were killed. Over 13,000 tons of bombs had hit thirty-four targets, targets, killing 1,318 civilians in Hànôi and 305 in Hàiphòng.

The 'Linebacker' campaign undoubtedly was instrumental in forcing the North Viêtnamese back to the peace table. In all 1,600 military structures had been damaged or destroyed, three million gallons of petroleum destroyed and roughly eighty per cent of North Viêtnam's electrical generating capacity had been put out of action. Peace talks were resumed on 8 January 1973. The B-52s continued to bomb targets in North Viêtnam below the 20th Parallel until the bombing was halted on 15 January but 'Arc Light' operations in South Viêtnam continued until 27 January, when a cease-fire agreement came into effect. The cease-fire continued in Laos until mid-April

BDA photo of Hànôi/Bạch Maï airfield.

and in Cambodia until mid-August, when Congress cut off funds for the air war. Inevitably, the South soon collapsed and on 12 April 1975 the American Embassy in Sàigòn was evacuated and 287 staff flown to carriers offshore. On 29 April a further 900 Americans were airlifted by the Navy to five carriers. Next day Sàigòn was in Communist hands and the South was now under the control of North Viêtnam. In May 1975 the USN airlifted US nationals and personnel from Sàigòn in Operation 'Frequent Wind'.

During twelve years of war the Viêtnam conflict had cost the Americans 58,022 dead. On 12 February 1972 the first of 651 American PoWs released by the North were flown home from Hànôi. In the period June 1965 to 15 August 1973 of 126,663 B-52 sorties scheduled, 126,615 B-52 sorties were flown, 9,800 of them against North Viêtnam. Of these 124 499 reached their targets with 124,532 B-52s successfully dropping their bombs. In all, 2,633.035 tons of bombs were dropped. Fifty-five per cent of the sorties flown were against targets on South Viêtnam, twenty-seven per cent against targets in Laos, twelve per cent in Cambodia and six per cent in North

Left: Captain Myles McTernan, navigator, 'Ruby 02'.

The crew of 'Ruby 02', taken the day after the six were rescued. From left to right: Roger Klingbeil; Bill Milcarek; Gerry Wickline (arm in sling); Bill Fergason (eye patch) and Chuck Kilgore. Not pictured is Myles McTernan - who had not been discharged from the hospital (the building the five are standing in front of in the picture). On ejection and encountering the airstream Bill's helmet face visor burst and temporarily damaged his left eye. His lower chin experienced a slight cut that required several stitches. It was concluded this jury was the result of the parachute harnessing gear striking his face. (via Kelly DeSoto and Bill Fergason)

'Operation Homecoming', a series of diplomatic negotiations, made possible the return of 591 American prisoners of war held by North Việtnam in January 1973. On 12 February 1973 three C-141 transports flew to Hànôi and one C-9A aircraft was sent to Saigon to pick up released prisoners of war. The first flight of 40 US prisoners of war left Hànôi in a C-141A, later known as the 'Hanoi Taxi'. From 12 February to 4 April there were 54 C-141 missions flying out of Hànôi, bringing the former POWs home.

Việtnam. During the war in South East Asia twenty-six B-52s, including two B-52Fs and two B-52Ds in collisions, were lost.

In the spring of 1973 591 Americans were released in Operation 'Homecoming' from prisons in and around Hànôi. One of them was 31-year old Senior Master Sergeant James Raymond Cook who on 26/27 December when 'Ebony 02' exploded came down head first because his legs got tangled in the chute risers and later discovered that both his legs were shattered below the knee. His back had been fractured and his right shoulder and elbow were broken. He was interrogated for twenty-four hours by the PAVN who broke five of his ribs in the process. Exactly thirty days later on 27 January 1973 North Việtnam and America signed a peace agreement and all hostilities ended between the two countries. Jim Cook was one of the first American PoWs to be released, on 11 February 1973, because of his injuries and an infection, which reduced his weight from 175lbs to 90lbs. After release both of his legs were amputated below the knee.

Nearly 2,500 Americans remained 'missing'. In June 1974 three representatives of the air force showed up at the Wimbrow home in Whaleyville, Maryland. They had brought a photograph of 'Nut' Winbrow with them. The parents made a positive identification of their son's body in the photo. He had been shot through the facial part of his head with a small calibre bullet. Major Wimbrow was officially pronounced 'Killed In Action'. In September 1977 the Việtnamese announced that they 'had discovered' the remains of Nutter Wimbrow and his pilot, Captain Bob Morris. Their bodies were returned to America. At the time the US Congress heard testimony that the Việtnamese 'stockpiled' the remains of many Americans in caskets to return at politically advantageous times. The Wimbrow family and military authorities arranged a second funeral with full military honours. Major Nutter Wimbrow was awarded The Purple Heart, The Distinguished Flying Cross and a Bronze Star as well as other campaign theatre ribbons. An American patriot was home at last.

Endnotes for Chapter Two

28 Moore died in 2009 at age 55.

29 Colonel Martin C. Fulcher was the Vice Commander of the 57th Air Division on Guam and had previously flown a tour in fighters over NVN.

30 Originally a US television series depicting the inept life and actions of a bumbling group of post Civil War cavalrymen.

31 *Flying From The Black Hole: The B-52 Navigator-Bombardiers of Vietnam* by Robert O. Harder (Naval Institute Press, Maryland 2009).

32 *Miracle at U-Tapao* by John L. Frisbee, Contributing Editor (Air Force Association, August 1983, Vol. 66, No. 8. On 11 September 2001 Lieutenant Colonel Hymel USAF Retired was sitting at his desk as a Defense Intelligence Agency analyst in the Pentagon. He was one of the thousands of Americans killed that day.

33 From Kadena AFB on Okinawa 95 KC-135 sorties by the 376th Air Refuelling Wing provided a record 156 post-strike refuellings. SAC tankers from U-Tapao, Takhli and Clark AFB in the Philippines recorded 607 air refuellings solely for TACAIR aircraft, the largest number provided during the eleven days. This total of 763 refuelling sorties to support one mission was the largest such undertaking of the war. The 376th had come to the rescue on Day One when some B-52s reported lower than specified fuel reserves and KC-135 tankers available in Thailand were already committed to pre- and post-strike refuelling of F-4s, F-5s and EB-66s that were supporting the bomber mission. This meant that the 14-hour mission became an 18-hour one for some of the B-52 crews who had to fly close to Kadena.

34 Quoted in *Linebacker II; A View From The Rock* by Brigadier General James R. McCarthy and Lieutenant Colonel George B. Allison (USAF Southeast Asia Monograph Series Volume VI, Monograph 8, Office of Air Force History USAF 1985).

35 Target tracking radar; used to identify the manoeuvre flown to counter the threat and deny tracking information to the hostile radar.

36 Bomb release line, imaginary or theoretical line around a target area at which a bomber releases its first bomb.

37 After spending 91 days in captivity, they were released during Operation 'Homecoming' on 29 March 1973.

38 Lieutenant Fryer's remains were returned by the North Viêtnamese on 30 September 1977 and Major Johnson's were returned on 4 December 1985 and formally identified the following June.

39 Promoted Lieutenant General in 1988, Donald O. Aldridge became vice commander in chief, Headquarters Strategic Air Command Offutt Air Base, Nebraska.

40 Linebacker II SAM Firings: 18 December, 164 (2 B-52Gs and 1 B-52D lost): 19 December 182: 20 December 221 (4 B-52Gs, 2 B-52Ds lost); 21 December 40 (2 B-52Ds lost): 22 December 43: 23 December 4: 24 December 16: 26 December 68 (2 B-52Ds lost): 27 December 73 (2 B-52Ds lost): 28 December 48: 29 December 23: Total 882 (6 B-52Gs, 9 B-52Ds lost). Tactics & Techniques in the Air War Against North Vietnam 1965-1973 by Bernard C. Nalty (Office of Air Force History).

41 Sincere thanks are due to Kelly DeSoto and *Project Get Out and Walk* and her father Captain Bill Fergason USAF retired.

42 The total number of B-52s lost in combat was 17 plus eight B-52s were lost while en route to a combat area. On 14 January B-52D 55-0116 landed at Đà Nẵng with over 200 holes. The left wing section 21 and the left drop tank needed replacing but there was not enough time before the cease-fire to salvage the aircraft so it was scraped. And, B-52D 55-0058 landed at U-Tapao with over 120 holes, having taken hits from two of six SA-2s fired just prior to drop and from one of 3 more SAMs on exit.

Chapter Three

Raging Storms

'The first time in history that a field army had been defeated by air power.'
'General Merrill A. 'Tony' McPeak, USAF Chief of Staff.

Not since the Việtnam War had America needed to deploy its vast and impressive Navy in a full-scale war; but in the early 1980s the 6th Fleet in the Mediterranean, in particular, proved a very efficient avenger and then deterrent, in the fight against international terrorism. An uneasy peace existed between Libya and the United States and in 1981 Colonel Gadaffi, President of Libya, threw down the gauntlet when he announced that, contrary to all international maritime law, Libyan territorial waters were to be extended to nearly 300 miles, incorporating the Gulf of Sidra. In response, the nuclear-powered aircraft carrier *Nimitz*, which had left its US east coast home port on 3 August, headed to the Mediterranean with its support vessels to join up with the *Forrestal* for training exercises which would culminate in a live missile firing in a test zone which would include part of the Gulf of Sidra area. On 18 August the two battle groups were probed on several occasions by sections of Libyan fighters. On 19 August while flying combat air patrol (CAP) from the *Nimitz* to cover aircraft engaged in a missile exercise, a pair of F-14As from VF-41 'Black Aces' detected two Libyan Sukhoi Su-22 'Fitter-Js' taking off from Ghurdabiyah Air Base near the city of Sirte. 'Fast Eagle 102' crewed by Commander Henry 'Hank' Kleeman (CO of VF-41) and NFO Lieutenant Dave 'DJ' Venlet and 'Fast Eagle 107' crewed by Lieutenant Larry 'Music' Muczynski and Lieutenant (jg) James 'Amos' Anderson set up for an intercept as the contacts headed north-east in tight formation about 500 feet apart towards them. Kleeman picked them up at eight miles range. He intended to come alongside the Su-22s so that he could warn them off but with his Tomcat about 500 feet above the leading Su-22 and about 1,000 feet apart the Sukhoi fired an AA-2 'Atoll' heat-seeking missile. Both Tomcat pilots saw the firing and broke hard left, the missile passing right under Kleeman's wing. Muczynski then turned inside the lead Sukhoi and came in behind. At this instant the second 'Fitter' broke hard right and started to climb so Kleeman reversed his turn to the left and followed his target round until he was flying almost directly into sun. The Libyan fighter continued to pull round to the right and, as soon as his target was clear of the glare and flying south-east, Kleeman launched an AIM-9L Sidewinder which hit the 'Fitter' in the rear fuselage seconds before the pilot ejected. By this time Muczynski had turned inside his target and came out high and behind as the Su-22 continued on a northerly heading before coming round to the right toward the sun. Before he reached the safety of the glare the No.2 Tomcat had fired a Sidewinder which homed on the Su-22, swept straight up the tailpipe and blew the back off the fuselage. The pilot ejected but his parachute failed. The engagement had taken place about fifty miles from the Libyan coast and was notable as the first engagement between variable-geometry aircraft.

Prior to the ejections, a US electronic surveillance plane monitoring the event recorded the lead Libyan pilot report to his ground controller that he had fired a missile at one of the US fighters and gave no indication that the missile shot was unintended. The official United States

F-14 Tomcat '102' which was flown on 18 August 1981 by Commander Henry 'Hank' Kleeman (CO of VF-41) (left) and NFO Lieutenant Dave 'DJ' Venlet who destroyed two Libyan Air Force Su-22s in the Gulf of Sidra.

VF-41 'Black Aces' crews who shot down two Su-22s on 18 August 1981. Far left: Lead RIO Lieutenant Dave 'DJ' Venlet; Lead pilot Commander Henry 'Hank' Martin Kleeman, CO VF-41 (second from left); Wing pilot Lieutenant Larry 'Music' Muczynski (second from right) and Wing RIO Lieutenant Jim Anderson (far right).

Navy report states that both Libyan pilots ejected and were safely recovered, but in the official audio recording of the incident taken from USS Biddle, one of the Tomcat pilots stated that he saw a Libyan pilot eject, but his parachute failed to open. Less than an hour later, while the Libyans were conducting a search and rescue operation of their downed pilots, two fully armed MiG-25s entered the airspace over the Gulf and headed towards the US carriers at Mach 1.5 and conducted a mock attack in the direction of USS Nimitz. Two VF-41 Tomcats headed towards the Libyans, which then turned around. The Tomcats turned home, but had to turn around again when the Libyans headed towards the US carriers once more. After being tracked by the F-14s' radars, the MiGs finally headed home. One more Libyan formation ventured out into the

The USS *John F. Kennedy* on patrol
in the Mediterranean in 1982.

Gulf towards the US forces later that day. [43]

In October 1983 the 82,000-ton *John F. Kennedy* (CV-67), the 'Big John' or 'Slack Jack' as it was known was diverted to Beirut, Lebanon from her planned Indian Ocean deployment, after the Beirut barracks bombing killed 241 US military personnel taking part in the multi-national peacekeeping force in Lebanon. On 4 December the peacekeeping force - including 800 US Marines - was threatened by both Lebanese military groups and Syrian forces. Two VF-102 F-14s from USS *America* that were orbiting in international air space on a CAP station were fired upon by SA-5 missiles. A-7s operating from Saratoga responded by firing the first AGM-88 HARM missiles used in combat. Next day ten A-6 aircraft of CVW-3 on board the *Kennedy*[44] and A-6 and A-7 aircraft from USS *Independence* took part in retaliatory missions and VF-11 'Red Rippers' and VF-31 Tomcatters F-14As came under fire from Syrian Surface-to-Air missiles and

On 5 December 1983 two of the 28-strong strike package
were shot down, one A-7E from USS *Independence* (CV-62)
and an A-6 of VA-85 'Black Falcons' from the *Kennedy*
during a retaliatory strike against Syrian AAA sites. The A-
6 pilot, Lieutenant Mark Lange, was killed. The back-seater,
Lieutenant Robert 'Bobby' Goodman (pictured), ejected
safely and was captured by the Syrians and taken to
Damascus. The A-7E pilot was picked up by a fishing boat.
'Bobby' Goodman was released on 3 January 1984.

Two Libyan MiG-23s in formation.

AAA. One of the VF-11 aircrews recalled: 'I engaged eight MiGs over Lebanon. I was the CAP for this mission and flew 3,000 feet above the TARPS F-14 on the run over Lebanon. My section engaged four MiGs. I locked on and prepared to shoot. Four MiGs did a split S and ran for Syria. Four more MiGs came in to shoot us but blew through without engaging.' None of the F-14s were lost or damaged, but the Syrians' aggressive action resulted in air strikes against Syrian positions near Hammana. A-6E Intruders from the Kennedy attacked Syrian positions in the Bekaa Valley of Lebanon. Two of the twenty-eight strong strike package were shot down, one A-7E from USS *Independence* (CV-62) and an A-6 of VA-85 'Black Falcons' from the *Kennedy* during a retaliatory strike against Syrian AAA sites. The A-6 was hit by an infrared homing missile (SA-7 or SA-9) into the engine nozzle upon dropping its bomb-load, while still in a dive through 1,800 feet AGL. The fuselage and a wing were immediately engulfed in flames and then the right side engine erupted. Lieutenant Mark Lange tried to control the aircraft in order to safely eject his B/N, Lieutenant Robert 'Bobby' Goodman. After a rapid, low-level descent, the Intruder was seen to pull up and likely stalled, resulting in a crash on a 1,000 foot hill above a village surrounded by Syrian Anti-aircraft artillery positions. Lange ejected both himself and Goodman in the final moment, but his parachute failed to properly deploy by the time he hit the ground. Lange's left leg was severely injured and he died shortly after capture by Syrian troops and Lebanese civilians. Goodman, rendered unconscious, broke three ribs, injured a shoulder and a knee during the landing, but was otherwise stable. He was captured and awakened by the Syrians and taken to Damascus. The A-7E pilot was picked up by a fishing boat. 'Bobby' Goodman was released on 3 January 1984.

On 7 October 1985 the Italian cruise liner *Achille Lauro* was hijacked by terrorists from the Palestine Liberation Organisation (PLO) in an attempt to free political prisoners and terrorists by putting pressure on the Israeli government. During the hijacking of the cruise liner, the terrorists murdered the American Leon Klinghoffer. Therefore, after the end of the hijacking, the US government decided to get hold of the terrorists. US intelligence uncovered the plans of the PLO terrorists and then US President Ronald Reagan ordered the 6th Fleet in the Mediterranean to take action against the flight of the terrorists from Egypt to Libya. What followed was condemned by many as an act of 'airborne piracy', but it was in fact a well planned precision operation by carrier aircraft launched from USS *Saratoga* (CV-60) and intelligence aircraft from the USAF: No less than seven F-14As from VF-74 'Bedevilers' and VF-103 'Jolly Rogers' were launched, four to undertake the interception of the Boeing 737 plus three to fly

Two F-111Fs of the 48th TFW over the Mediterranean in 1991. The 'Liberty Wing' carried out daring precision-bombing attacks at night against Libyan targets in 1986 and against Iraqi bunkers, vehicles and buildings in 'Desert Storm'. (USAFE)

top cover for the unlikely event that Libyan fighters would take aggressive action against the US aircraft. Additionally, an E-2C, four KA-6D tankers, EA-6B Prowlers, EA-3B Skywarriors and a RC-135 electronic intelligence aircraft participated in the operation. Once on its way to Libya, the Egypt Air Boeing 737 with the terrorists on board was located by an E-2C Hawkeye which vectored the Tomcats into position to perform the interception. The Tomcats approached the 737 with all lights extinguished in total radio silence, only using modern data link facilities between the participating aircraft. The Tomcats positioned themselves ahead, to the rear and on each side of the airliner. Once in position, the F-14s switched on position lights and made a call to the 737 pilot to follow. Without another choice the airliner was escorted to NAS Sigonella in Italy, where a Navy SEAL (Sea-Air-Land) team surrounded the airliner and captured the terrorists.

On 27 December 1985 terrorists attacked the El-Al check-in counter at airports in Rome and Vienna, killing fourteen people, including an 11-year-old American girl and injuring fifty others. The attack was thought to be Libyan-backed. In late January 1986 Gadaffi established his so-called 'line of death' in the Gulf of Sidra from a point just south of Tripoli across to Benghazi and warned that any American aircraft or surface vessels entering it would be destroyed. America's patience was exhausted and in February 1986 Operation 'Prairie Fire' was launched to provoke Libya into a direct military confrontation. Three carrier battle groups crossed the 'line of death' and on 24 March two SA-5 'Gammon' missiles were fired at the 6th Fleet but both missed their targets. Later that day two F-14A Tomcats chased off a pair of MiG-25 'Foxbat-A' interceptors and tension increased as more missiles were fired at the carrier groups. Two Grumman A-6F Intruders sank a Libyan Nanutchka-class missile patrol boat with AGM-84A Harpoon anti-ship missiles and Rockeye cluster bombs. Vought A-7E Corsairs badly damaged a shore installation with AGM-88A High-Speed Anti-Radiation (HARM) missiles and further attacks on Libyan targets were carried out by more A-6Es and A-7Es. A total of four Libyan vessels had been destroyed or damaged and one or two SAM sites knocked out.

Regrettably, terrorist action continued on 5 April 1986 when a bomb left by a Palestinian terrorist exploded in the La Belle disco in West Berlin, frequented by hundreds of off-duty US

A F-111F in the 48th TFW at RAF Lakenheath is prepared for take-off for Libya on 14 April 1986.

personnel. A US Army sergeant and a Turkish woman were killed and 230 people were injured, including seventy-nine US servicemen. The Libyan regime clearly backed the attack. More bomb plots were uncovered by intelligence sources, aimed at US military targets around the world, with ten planned for Berlin alone. Certainly, swift action was needed to deter the terrorists and their Libyan paymasters. President Ronald Reagan kept a five-year-old promise to the American people to meet terrorism with 'swift and effective retribution' and the decision was taken to bomb terrorist-related targets at Tripoli and Benghazi, using air force squadrons on mainland Europe and carrier-borne aircraft of the US Navy in the Mediterranean. NATO countries would not allow US aircraft stationed in its countries to use European bases or overfly their airspace for attacks on Libya. Britain's Prime Minister, Margaret Thatcher, placed no restrictions on strike aircraft based in eastern England. This allowed the US planners the option of using F-111F tactical strike bombers based in East Anglia for a retaliatory strike against Tripoli, the Libyan capital, while US Navy A-6E Intruder carrier borne attack planes bombed Benghazi. The F-111s were given three targets in Tripoli, while attack planes from the America and Coral Sea were to carry out strikes against the Al Jumahiriya barracks in Benghazi and Benina airport outside the city.

At the time, over 150 F-111E/Fs were based in Britain for NATO duty. The F-111E equipped the 20th TFW at Upper Heyford in Oxfordshire while the 48th TFW, 'The Liberty Wing' based at RAF Lakenheath in Suffolk, was equipped with four squadrons of F-111Fs. The F-111F was equipped with the Ford Aerospace AVQ-26 Pave Tack infrared target acquisition and laser-

A F-111F in the 48th TFW taking off from RAF Lakenheath for Libya on 14 April 1986.

Above: The destroyed barracks at Bab al
Aziziya during Operation 'El Dorado Canyon'.

Right: An Il-76 destroyed during Operation 'El
Dorado Canyon'.

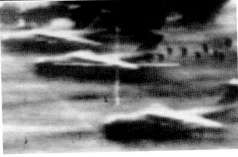

designating pod mounted under the fuselage centreline. Armed with laser-guided bombs, the FB-111F could be particularly effective for bombing by night. The WSO operates an IR scope in the cockpit to lock the designator pod onto the target and a thin laser beam keeps the target 'spotted' for laser-guided Paveway bombs to follow the beam transmission directly onto the target no matter what manoeuvres the pilot puts the bomber through. Despite this incredibly accurate method of bombing, crews were briefed not to launch their bombs unless they also gained a positive radar identification. Civilian casualties had to be avoided where possible.

At around 1815 hours on 14 April 1986, Lakenheath dispatched 24 F-111Fs while nearby, RAF Mildenhall had earlier sent off six KC-135 Stratotankers followed by a KC-135 A and two KC-10As and finally ten KC-10A Extender refuellers. A further seven KC-l0As and two KC-135 As left RAF Fairford for Libya. 'Operation 'El Dorado Canyon' as it was code-

A Grumman/General Dynamics EF-111A (nearest the camera) and a F-111F in formation. Five EF-111A Raven ECM aircraft of the 42nd Electronic Combat Squadron in the 20th TFW at Upper Heyford in Oxfordshire were first used operationally during the 'El Dorado Canyon' operation of 14/15 April 1986. Ravens were also used in 'Desert Storm'.

named marked the first operational use of the Grumman/General Dynamics EF-111A Raven ECM aircraft. Five Ravens of the 42nd Electronic Combat Squadron of the 20th TFW took off from their home base at Upper Heyford and flew to Fairford to escort the F-111Fs. Off the northwest coast of Spain, the KC-10s took on fuel from other KC-10s. Shortly afterwards, between 2030 and 2130 hours, six F-111Fs acting as spares, returned to Lakenheath and one of the EF-111As also returned to base, leaving the second spare Raven to continue to the target area as an airborne reserve. The F-111Fs each carried free-fall and laser-guided bombs which meant there was no room for external fuel tanks. Three 'silent' in-flight refuelling operations were therefore carried out off Portugal, south of Spain (after passing through the Straits of Gibraltar) and near Sicily.

Meanwhile, the USS *America* and USS *Coral Sea* were at their positions off Libya ready to strike at military targets in Benghazi. At 2220 hours the first of eight A-6E Intruders of VA-55 'War Horses' and six F/A-18A Hornets from CVW-13 were launched from the deck of the *Coral Sea*. Starting at 2245 and ending at 2315 six A-6Es of VA-34 'Blue Blasters' and six Vought A-7E Corsair IIs from CVW-1 were catapulted off the deck of the *America*. F-14A Tomcats took off to

Left: Captain Paul F. Lorence, WSO of F-111F call sign 'Karma 52' in the 48th TFW.

Right" Captain Fernando L. Ribas-Dominicci, pilot of F-111F call sign 'Karma 52' in the 48th TFW which was involved in the attack on the barracks at Bab al Aziziya where Gadaffi resided, crashed and exploded as they re-crossed the coast. Both crew were killed.

An A-6E Intruder taking off during Operation 'El Dorado Canyon' in April 1986. Twenty-four Intruders operated from the aircraft carriers, USS *America* VA-34 ('Blue Blasters') and *Coral Sea* (VA-55 'Warhorses') during the bombing of Libya and F/A-18 Hornets launched from aircraft carriers bombed radar and antiaircraft sites in Benghazi before bombing the Benina and Jamahiriya barracks. Six A-6Es launched from the *America* and eight from the *Coral Sea* acquired their targets with AN/APQ-148 multimode radars and then zoomed in with AN/AAS-33 TRAM infra-red vision turrets using its laser for precise ranging to release unguided 1,000lb demolition bombs and 500lb CBUs; the latter used extensively at Benina. F/A-18A Hornets operated from the USS *Coral Sea* in the top cover MiGCAP and defence suppression role in company with F-14s and in the more active defence suppression role with A-7s of VA-72.

A flight deck crewman checks an LTV A-7E of VA-72 'Blue Hawks' aboard the USS *America* (CV-66) during flight operations off the coast of Libya on 17 April 1986. The aircraft is armed with an AIM-9L Sidewinder missile on the fuselage station, a Mk.20 Rockeye II bomb on the middle wing pylon and an AGM-45 Shrike missile on the outside wing pylon. Defence suppression was provided by 6 A-7Es on the America and 6 F-18As on the *Coral Sea* which approached the coastline as the F-111s and A-6s neared their targets but unlike the bombers at 200 feet they popped up to several hundred feet of altitude a few miles from the target zones to allow the Libyan air defence radars to detect them to allow their Shrike and HARM anti-radiation missiles to lock on. Over a dozen Shrikes and about 30 HARMs that were fired effectively suppressed the acquisition radars associated with the Soviet supplied SAM systems in Tripoli and Benghazi.

Aircraft assigned to Carrier Air Wing 1 (CVW-1) aboard the USS *America* (CV-66) in the Mediterranean during attacks on Libya on 15 April in Operation 'El Dorado Canyon', the bombing of Libya. Visible are (front to back): a F-14A Tomcat of the VF-102 'Diamondbacks', a LTV A-7E Corsair II of VA-46 'Clansmen' armed with AGM-88 HARM missiles and a EA-6B Prowler radar and communications jammer of VMAQ-2 Det.Y 'Playboys' equipped with the ALQ-99 jamming system similar to that in the EF-111.

fly top-cover for the attack forces while E-2C Hawkeyes carried out their AEW tasks and KA-6Ds carried out in-flight refuelling. EA-6B Prowlers began their ECM jamming of Libyan radars while the A-7Es and F/A-18As on TARCAP (target combat air patrol) blasted the SAM and radar installations with SHRIKE and AGM-88 HARM air-to-surface missiles at Libyan air defence sites along the coast and in and around 750lb bombs began at 0001, simultaneously with the USAF strikes on Tripoli.

Near Tripoli, the three EF-111A Ravens began their ECM jamming of Libyan radars at 2354, while the Navy's A-7E Corsair IIs and F/A-18A Hornets blasted the SAM and radar installations around Benghazi with anti-radiation missiles. USAF and US Navy bombing runs started simultaneously at 0001. The eighteen F-111Fs of the 48th TFW roared in 200 feet below the Libyan radar sites on the coast and headed for the brightly lit streets of the capital. Nearing the city, the force split into three cells of six aircraft. Two cells headed for the Terrorist Training camp at Sidi Bilal naval base and the barracks at Bab al Aziziya where Gadaffi resided. The third cell flew on to the south before swinging round to bomb the military airport.

Pilots had been briefed to bomb only if they had positive radar and IR scope target acquisition. Four F-111Fs in the naval base and barracks attack and one in the attack on Tripoli, did not bomb after experiencing problems with their equipment or failing to obtain the necessary electronic validation of their targets. The eight remaining bombers in the raid on the naval base and barracks made low-level single-pass attacks and each toss-bombed four 2,000lb laser-guided bombs onto the targets before climbing away to a height of 250 feet at 518 mph for their rendezvous point over the Mediterranean. F-111F call sign 'Karma 52', flown by 33-year old Captain Fernando L. Ribas-Dominicci of Utuado, Puerto Rico and 31-year old Californian WSO Captain Paul F. Lorence, which had been involved in the attack on the barracks, crashed and exploded as they re-crossed the coast. A long sea search was mounted but no trace of the crew was found.

The third group of six F-111Fs attacked the military airport with 500lb Mk 82 low-drag retarded bombs, although one bomber was forced to carry its bombs home after a systems

BDA photo of Benina airfield taken by a High-altitude reconnaissance SR-71A aircraft following the strike by US Navy A-6E Intruders who destroyed at least four MiG-23s, a Fokker F-27 and two Mil Mi-8/Hip helicopters during Operation 'El Dorado Canyon'. The information the SR-71As gathered, along with that from other reconnaissance platforms such as the RC-135Ws operating from Hellenikon confirmed that all five assigned targets had been hit and considerable damage and destruction caused.

malfunction. US Navy A-6E Intruders destroyed at least four MiG-23s, a Fokker F-27 and two Mil Mi-8 helicopters at Benina airfield. Crews began landing back on their carriers while the F-111Fs headed for their tankers and the long flight back to Britain. One F-111F was forced to land at Rota in Spain suffering problems from engine overheating. Despite the limitations of crossing international boundaries and the loss of one fighter-bomber, 'El Dorado Canyon' had been a great success. Two days after the attacks, post-strike reconnaissance by two Lockheed SR-71As from Mildenhall confirmed that all five targets had been well hit.

When the F-111F crews of the 48th TFW began touching down at Lakenheath at 0630 on 15

Libyan air defences open up on F-111Fs low over Tripoli during Operation 'El Dorado Canyon'.

April, few could have imagined how important their experience had been and that they would be heading back over the Mediterranean only four years later to participate in another series of pin-point bombing missions at night.

During Operation 'Praying Mantis' 18-19 April 1988 A-6Es of VA-95 'Green Lizards' from CVW-11 on board *Enterprise* in the Arabian Gulf sank an Iranian Boghammar speedboat and damaged another with Rockeye cluster bombs. Later, after evading SAMs fired by the Iranian frigate *Sahand,* two VA-95 crews severely damaged *Sahand* with Harpoon missiles and Skipper laser-guided bombs. After taking another Harpoon hit from a US destroyer, *Sahand* almost sank when fires reached her magazines. Later, *Sahand* drew fire from VA-95 after the ship fired a SAM at the Intruders. One A-6E hit *Sahand* with laser-guided bombs, leaving the ship dead in the water; the ship was taken under tow with its stern submerged.

In late 1988 tensions between Washington and Tripoli raised again. The United States government accused Libya of building a chemical weapons plant near the town of Rabta and once again Gaddafi warned the US against interfering in Libyan affairs, reiterating the threat of military actions. In response, the USS *John F. Kennedy* and its battle group were dispatched to conduct a 'freedom of navigation' exercise off the Libyan coast. On the morning of 4 January 1989 the *Kennedy* battle group was operating just north of Libya, with a group of A-6 Intruders on exercise south of Crete, escorted by two pairs of F-14As from VF-14 'Tophatters' and VF-32 'Swordsmen' and as well as an E-2C 'Hawkeye' from VAW-126 'Sea Hawks'. Later that morning the southernmost Combat Air Patrol station was taken by two F-14As of VF-32: Commanders Joseph Bernard Connelly and Leo F. Enwright ('Gipsy 207') and Lieutenant Hermon C. Cook III and Lieutenant Commander Steven Patrick Collins ('Gipsy 202'). The officers had been specially briefed for this mission due to the high tensions regarding the carrier group's presence and were advised to expect some kind of hostilities. Their aircraft were each armed with four Sparrows and two Sidewinders. After being refuelled by a KA-6D Intruder, the two F-14As with Gipsy 207 leading the section, returned to their CAP station, when at 11:50 am the Hawkeye, call sign 'Closeout', warned them that two Libyan MiG-23 'Floggers' had taken off from Al Bumbah airfield, near Tobruk. The F-14As from VF-32 turned towards the first two MiG-23s and at a distance of about 72 miles acquired them on radar, while the Tomcats from VF-14 stayed with the A-6 group. This procedure was aimed at alerting the Libyan fighters that they were monitored by armed F-14s. The Tomcats used their Television Camera System (TCS) to verify that the MiGs were armed. At the time the Floggers were 72 nautical miles away at 10,000 feet and heading directly towards the Tomcats and carrier. The F-14s turned away from the head-on approach to indicate that they were not attempting to engage. The 'Floggers' changed course to intercept at a closing speed of about 870 knots. The F-14As descended to 3,000 feet to give them a clear radar picture of the 'Floggers' against the sky and leave the 'Floggers' with sea clutter to contend with. Four more times the F-14As turned away from the approaching MiGs. Each time the Libyan aircraft turned in to continue to close. At 11:59 Leo Enwright in the lead Tomcat ordered the arming of the AIM-9 Sidewinder and AIM-7 Sparrow missiles it was carrying. The E-2C had given the F-14A crews authority to fire if threatened; the Tomcat crews did not have to wait until after the Libyans opened fire.

At almost 12:01 Enwright said that 'Bogeys have jinked back at me again for the fifth time. They're on my nose now, inside of 20 miles', followed shortly by 'Master arm on' as he ordered arming of the weapons. At a range of 14 nautical miles Enwright fired the first AIM-7M Sparrow; he surprised his pilot, who did not expect to see a missile accelerate away from his Tomcat. The RIO reported 'Fox 1. Fox 1.' The Sparrow failed to track because of a wrong switch-setting. At ten nautical miles he launched a second Sparrow missile, but it also failed to track its target. The 'Floggers' accelerated and continued to approach. At six nautical miles the Tomcats split and the 'Floggers' followed the wingman while the lead Tomcat circled to get a tail angle on them. Steven Collins fired a third Sparrow from five nautical miles and downed one of the Libyan aircraft. The lead Tomcat by now had gained the rear quadrant on the final 'Flogger'. After closing to 1.5 nautical miles Joe Connelly fired a Sidewinder, which hit its target. At 12:02:36 Connelly reported to the E-2C that they had 'splashed two 'Floggers' and that there were two good 'chutes in the air'. The Libyan pilots were both seen to successfully eject and parachute into the sea, but the Libyan Air Force was unable to recover them.

In August 1990 conflict in the Persian Gulf began after talks between the representatives from Iraq and Kuwait did not resolve grievances over oil pricing. On 2 August 1990 President Saddam Hussein of Iraq massed seven divisions and 2,000 tanks along the Iraq-Kuwait border and invaded Kuwait in the early hours of the morning. On 7 August, after Saddam Hussein refused to remove his troops from Kuwait, President Bush had ordered the start of 'Desert Shield', the US contingency commitment, ordering warplanes and ground forces to Saudi Arabia, stating that the country faced the 'imminent threat' of an Iraqi attack. On 8 August Saddam Hussein announced that Kuwait was the 19th province of Iraq. President George Bush immediately put Iraq under a US economic embargo. The United Nations Security Council quickly followed suit.

More than 55,000 Air Force personnel would be ultimately dispatched to the Gulf, including more than 180 aircraft and 5,400 personnel assigned to USAFE units. The US Central Command HQ, which would direct the coalition of allied forces against Iraq under the command of Army General H. Norman Schwarzkopf, immediately set pre-planned preparations in motion. CENTCOM's function was to co-ordinate US force deployment to the Gulf region to help defend Saudi Arabia and provide security to other Arab states. Lieutenant General Charles A. Horner, USAF, the allied coalition's supreme air commander, began co-ordinating all air actions related to the build-up and within days, established Central Command Air Forces (Forward) HQ in Saudi Arabia. From his HQ, the air actions that would bring an end to the war were put into operation. Five fighter squadrons, a contingent of AWACS and part of the 82nd Airborne Division moved into theatre within five days. In total, 25 fighter squadrons flew non-stop to the Gulf. Some 256 KC-135s and 46 KC-10 refuellers were deployed to the Gulf and 4,967 tanker sorties were flown during 'Desert Shield'. Within 35 days, the USAF deployed a fighter force that numerically equalled Iraq's fighter capability. In late August, President Bush signed an order authorizing members of the armed forces reserves to be called up for active duty. Throughout the campaign, Air Force Reserve and Air National Guard members flew and maintained aircraft for strategic and tactical airlift, fighter and reconnaissance operations, as well as tanker support.

On 4 August *Saratoga* deployed with CVW-17 on board and in September *Midway*, with CVW-5 on board, left its home port of Yokosuka, Japan, for the Indian Ocean, where it replaced *Independence* (CV-62). 'Indy', with CVW-14 on board had been the first carrier to 'take station' off the Gulf and she returned to home port San Diego. On 27 November the *America* (CV-66) and *Theodore Roosevelt* were ordered forward-deployed from Norfolk, Virginia with Carrier Air Wing One (CVW-1) and Carrier Air Wing Eight (CVW-8) respectively, onboard. Each of the carriers could support up to nine squadrons, which normally included two F-14A fighter, one A-6E medium attack, two F/A-18 light attack squadrons, an S-3A and an SH-3H squadron for ASW, an EA-6B electronic warfare (EW) squadron and an E-2C AEW squadron. On 8 December the *Ranger* sailed from California with CVW-2 on board and was followed on 28 December by the *America* and the *Theodore Roosevelt*. *America* replaced the *Eisenhower* in the Red Sea before war operations commenced. *Roosevelt* arrived just in time to transit from an initial position in the Red Sea to the Gulf station. In the Persian Gulf *America*, *Midway*, *Ranger* and *Theodore Roosevelt* became what were known as Battle Force Zulu while the *John F. Kennedy* (which had been re-deployed to the Mediterranean in August) with CVW-3 on board remained in the Red Sea.[45] *America* became the only carrier to operate in both the Persian Gulf and the Red Sea.[46]

Efforts to find a peaceful resolution with Iraq proved futile. On the morning of 15 January 1991, an eleventh-hour appeal by the Council for Iraq to withdraw from Kuwait drew only silence and at twelve noon the deadline for peace passed. Next day, at approximately 7pm

A Libyan Air Force Sukhoi Su-22.

Eastern Standard Time, Operation 'Desert Storm' began as Allied forces answered Iraq's silence with attacks by strike aircraft based in Saudi Arabia and Turkey[47] and by naval aircraft units and missiles at sea, against Saddam Hussein's forces. The war began during the night of 17 January with the launching of 52 Raytheon BGM-109 Tomahawk land-attack missiles (TLAM) from the battleship *Wisconsin* and other surface ships, against a variety of Iraqi targets. On this date, two pilots, Lieutenant Commander Mark Fox and Lieutenant Nick Mongillo of VFA-81 'Sunliners' on the USS *Saratoga* scored the Navy's only fixed-wing aerial victories of the war and the first ever kills for the Hornet, when they shot down two Iraqi MiG-21s while en route to a target. This they also successfully bombed before returning to their carrier. The *Saratoga's* Air Wing lost an F-14A (Plus) and an F/A-18C over western Iraq during the second week and they are thought to have been downed by SAMs.

While conventional cruise missile attacks launched from ships hundreds of miles away were an important element of the first phase of the operations, they did not have the long-term impact of sustained naval air operations. 'Desert Storm' had already passed through two distinct phases by the power, based largely, from mid-February, upon six carrier-based air wings operating in the Arabian Gulf and Red Sea, had accounted for one third of all air sorties, despite adverse flight ranges of typically 450 to 650 miles from the carriers, which required most aircraft to perform at least one aerial refuelling from USAF and USN KA-6D tanker aircraft each mission and navigational restrictions imposed by the area of these waters. The six aircraft carriers operating in mid-February consisted of the *America, Saratoga* and *John F. Kennedy* operating in the Red Sea; and the *Theodore Roosevelt, Ranger* and *Midway* operating in the Arabian Gulf.[48] The flight operations of the carriers in the Red Sea were concentrated in the western area, while the carriers in the Gulf concentrated strike missions in the south and southeast area of Iraq. This had some similarities to the 'route package' system used during operations over North Việtnam, but was largely based on aircraft strike range from the carriers. Strike ranges were typically 450-650 miles from the carriers, requiring most aircraft to perform at least one aerial refuelling from KC-10A, KC-135/-135R, or KA-6D aircraft each mission. The tempo of USN air operations was above that flown during the Việtnam War, averaging 125-150 sorties per day per aircraft carrier (weather permitting).[49] Operations were flown by day and night with about half the sorties being strike missions flown by F/A-18, A-7E and A-6E TRAM-equipped[50] attack aircraft. As during the Việtnam operations, one carrier 'on the line' was usually engaged in support functions, such as at-sea refuelling or munitions and logistic replenishment, at any given time, with the carrier's flight schedule reduced accordingly.

The air campaign commenced when three USAF MH-53J Pave Low special operations helicopters leading nine Army AH-64 Apache attack helicopters, destroyed two early warning radar sites in Iraq with 30mm cannon and AGM-114 Hellfire missiles. Meanwhile, TLAMs (Tomahawk Land Attack Missiles) launched from US ships in the Gulf and the Red Sea, struck targets in Baghdad. F-117A stealth fighter-bombers of the 37th TFW, which because of their construction are almost invisible to radar, flew deep into Iraq, hitting 34 targets, including hardened command and control bunkers, communications sites and chemical, biological and nuclear production and storage facilities.

The 4th TFW F-15E Eagles, equipped for the night precision-bombing role, (which were used against Scud missile sites) and B-52s also joined the attack. The first air-air kills of the war occurred when two USAF F-15Cs shot down two Iraqi MiG-29s. Later that same night, an F-15C scored a double-kill against two Mirages with AIM-7 missiles. His wingman scored another kill on a third Mirage F1, for a total of three kills in the dogfight. Two F/A-18s of VFA-81 were flying outside of Baghdad when two Iraqi MiG-25PDs interceptors from the 96th Squadron engaged them. In the beyond-visual-range (BVR) kill, one of the Iraqi MiGs piloted by Lieutenant Colonel Zuhair Dawood fired an R-40 missile, which impacted 33-year old Lieutenant Michael Scott Speicher's jet head-on when he was travelling Mach 0.92. The impact sent the aircraft spiralling downwards. Speicher probably died on the impact of the missile. He was the first American combat casualty of the war. His remains were not recovered until 2 August 2009; his fate had not been known until then. Two other F/A-18s from VFA-81 shot down two MiG-21s, one with an AIM-7 Sparrow missile and one with an AIM-9 Sidewinder missile, in a brief dogfight with their bombs still latched on. Two MiG-29s attempted to engage a flight of F-15Es. One of the MiGs crashed while flying at low altitude but the other MiG pressed on. One of the F-15Es fired an AIM-9 Sidewinder when the MiG locked him up but missed. Several other F-15Es simultaneously tried to engage the lone MiG-29 but were unable to get the kill. One F-15E was actually flying past the Iraqi jet and manoeuvred in for the kill but the pilot hesitated to take the shot because he was unsure of his wingmen's location and because he did not get a good tone with the Sidewinder missile. Two IRAF MiG-25s fired missiles at a group of F-15Cs escorting a bombing run in Iraq (which were evaded by the F-15s). The F-15Cs gave chase, but were forced to give up when the MiGs outran them. A total of ten missiles were fired at the MiGs.

Before the night ended virtually every aircraft in the USAF inventory had participated in the massive air strike. Captain Brent Brandon flying a EF-111 'Spark Vark' on an electronic warfare mission ahead of a group of jets on a bombing run was attacked by one of several IRAF Dassault Mirage F1s. Brandon executed a tight turn and launched chaff to avoid the missiles being fired by the Mirage. An F-15 piloted by Robert Graeter trying to protect the EF-111 went after the Mirage. The Mirage launched a missile which the Raven avoided by launching chaff. Captain Brandon hit the deck to try to evade his pursuer. As he went down he pulled up to avoid the ground, the Mirage followed him through, though the Mirage went straight into the ground. An unarmed EF-111 thus scored an air-air victory against a Dassault Mirage F1, although Graeter was credited with a kill. The EF-111A pilots were awarded the DFC.

Of 668 aircraft in the assault, 530 were USAF, ninety were USMC and Navy, 24 were RAF, twelve were French and twelve were Saudi Arabian. F-16Cs of the 401st TFW based at Doha attacked Ali Salem airfield in Kuwait and Tallil airfield in Iraq, while F-16Cs of the 50th TFW attacked Al Taqaddum airfield near Baghdad. Fifty-five F-111Fs of the 48th TFW attacked Iraqi airfields and chemical storage bunkers in a dozen attack cells each of four to six aircraft. Each cell was supported by ten US Navy A-7E Corsair SAM suppression aircraft equipped with AGM-88A HARM missiles and three EA-6B Prowlers for ECM jamming while four F-14C Tomcats flew top cover. For these first strikes, the F-111Fs carried 2,500lb Rockwell GBU-15 electro-optical glide bombs fitted with imaging infrared guidance specially developed for night bombing, 2,000lb GBU-24A/B laser-guided bombs (LGBs) and CBU-89 mines for cratering runways. Royal Saudi Air Force Tornadoes also attacked the runways with JP233 cratering bombs.

As befits a crack specialist unit, the 48th TFW commanded by Colonel Tom Lennon, was the first wing in the USAFE to be deployed to the Middle East as part of 'Desert Shield'. 'Having

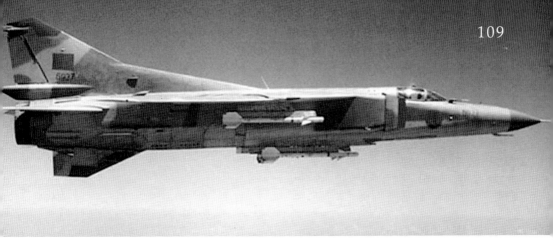

The second Gulf of Sidra incident occurred on 4 January 1989 when two F-14A Tomcats of VF-32 'Swordsmen' from the USS *John F. Kennedy* shot down two Libyan MiG-23 Floggers (like the one pictured) that appeared to have been attempting to engage them, as had happened in the first Gulf of Sidra incident in 1981.

so long to prepare for combat was great. It allowed us to practise operations with very large packages of aircraft. It allowed us to convince the Saudis that we needed to do business differently on their airfields, with mass night comms-out [radio-silent] launches, mass rejoins on the tankers, things that we don't practise in peace time.' On 25 August 1990 the wing deployed eighteen F-111Fs of the 493rd TFS each carrying four LGBs or four EOGBs and supported by KC-135 tankers flew non-stop to the Royal Saudi Air Force base at Taif near Mecca in Saudi Arabia. By the time the war started, the 48th TFW had deployed 66 of its seventy F-111Fs to Taif. 'It was a maximum effort' recalled Tom Lennon: 'we launched 54 F-111Fs out of 64 and 53 of them went into action that night.[51] If I had had sixty planes available, I would have sent all sixty.'

The aircraft were split into forces of four to six planes and delivered attacks on the chemical weapons storage bunkers at H-3, Salman Pak and Ad Diwaniyah and on the airfields at Balad and Jalibah in Iraq and Ali Al Salem and Al Jaber in Kuwait. The attacking F-111Fs received fighter and SAM-suppression support at their target areas, but they were on their own while en route to and from their targets. F-111Fs making for the same target flew singly at low altitude in trail, with a spacing of about a minute (about 8½ miles) between each. Tom Lennon led the deepest penetration by the Wing that night; a six-plane strike on Balad airfield north of Baghdad. Designated buildings in the maintenance complex were attacked with EOGBs and then the remaining F-111Fs dropped area-denial mines across the ends of each of the runways and among the hardened aircraft shelters to prevent the movement of Iraqi aircraft until the mines could be cleared.

Colonel Dennis R. Ertler of the 48th TFW earned the Silver Star, the third-highest American combat award, for his actions this first night of the war. After Iraqi defensive fire forced half the attack force to turn back he continued with the remaining aircraft on an attack against a HAS near Ali Al Salem airfield, Kuwait. He also out-manoeuvred a SAM on the way to the target. During delivery of a GBU-24A/B and in the centre of intense defensive fire, Colonel Ertler again avoided a SAM while his WSO, Captain Keith Zuegel, marked the target with his laser and scored a direct hit, destroying the HAS. As their aircraft departed the target area north of Kuwait City, Colonel Ertler released chaff and used other escape tactics to avoid a third SAM. Ertler recounts:

'We were getting AAA, radar warnings and SAM activity so I set the jet on automatic terrain following radar when I saw the first launch of a SAM on the left side of the aircraft. The TFR seemed to be flying us directly into the path of climbing AAA. I was forced to fly the jet manually at low-level because of that... [During the weapons release, Ertler received a second warning of a SAM closing in on his aircraft]. 'I saw it coming at us at the same time we were trying to put our weapons through the door of the shelter, but that second SAM forced me to pull off at the last second. I released some chaff and the SAM blew up right behind us. Our bombs were still on target and they hit dead centre.' The Iraqis threw everything they had into the night sky. Ertler continues: They still had all their defence capabilities and used them. We read about avoiding SAMs in our training manual but when you see a missile with your name on it coming your way, you don't really have time to think about it. You just do what you're trained to do.'

During the second night of the war, on 17/18 January, the 48th TFW sent 35 F-111Fs to several other targets. Four F-11Fs carrying EOGBs attacked and destroyed Saddam Hussein's summer palace at Tikrit, which served as one of his command centres. En route to the target the last F-111F in the formation was tailed by a MiG-29 'Fulcrum' but the American pilot folded back his aircraft's wings and accelerated to maximum speed at low altitude and continued for more than seventy miles before the Iraqi pilot gave up the chase. At Mudaysis airfield a six-plane striking force attacked Hardened Air Shelters with LGBs from around 20,000 feet. Each aircraft carried out four separate runs, aiming a single 2,000 pounder at an individual HAS on each run. Captain Brad Seipel, a WSO in the 492nd TFS, 48th TFW, recalled: 'It was awesome. After you released your bomb (from medium altitude] it was in the air for nearly a minute. While you marked your own target with the laser, on the Pave Tack video screen you saw this shelter blow up, then you saw that shelter blow up, then you saw another one blow up. Then the one that you had your laser on blew up.' By the time the F-111Fs departed they had knocked out no less than 23 HAS's.

The raids were a great success and despite their worst fears there were no losses and only two F-111Fs received minor battle damage. Thereafter, senior officers felt confident in replacing the 'small' strike units with larger formations of up to 24 F-111Fs against one airfield at a time as Tom Lennon recalled: 'After the first night we didn't do anything with six aircraft. When we went after something, we would go after it big time. We would put twenty to 24 airplanes on one airfield at one time. If we had to hit a target, we hit it with everything we had; all at once and got out of there.'

During the night of 20/21 January twenty F-111Fs delivered a set-piece attack on Balad airfield. By now the threat from Iraqi fighters and long-range SAMs was adjudged to have been contained and even when crossing the most heavily defended areas the F-111Fs could fly at medium level and attack from altitudes of between 12,000 and 20,000 feet, beyond the range of most of the Triple A sites. Over the airfield the F-111Fs launched individual 2,000lb LGBs at strategic points on the runways and taxiways, penetrating the concrete surface before detonating to produce large craters. As the last F-111F was leaving Balad a MiG-29 closed in to attack it and locked on its radar. Captain Jerry Hanna, the WSO, recalled: 'We immediately initiated a high-speed combat descent, the pilot got the wings back and we went screaming downhill. Puking Chaff, we went from 19,000 to about 4,000 feet in a heartbeat! The adrenalin was really pumping. Jim [the pilot] was busy trying get the plane close to the ground, I was on radio hollering at the AWACS that we had been jumped by a MiG and to get the F-18s coming back in our direction.' Hanna set up the terrain-following radar so that it would take automatic control of the F-111 as soon the latter got close to the ground. By following the contours closely at maximum speed, the F-111F made a very difficult target. Before that happened, however, the MiG suddenly broke away.

Lieutenant Colonel Tommy Crawford, the 48th TFW's Assistant Deputy Commander for Operations, was of the opinion that Iraqi Triple A was ineffective against high-flying night raiders: 'They fired lots of SAMs. At first there were cases of the guys on the ground holding the radar lock-on throughout an engagement. But with the HARM firers ['Wild Weasel' aircraft firing High Speed Anti-Radiation Missiles at the radars] supporting us they didn't survive long if they did that. Then the SAM batteries changed their tactics. The radar would come on. They would lock on and fire their missile and then shut down the radar. They would send the missile up ballistically and hope that we didn't turn or anything. We could see them coming, so it was

F-14B of VF-143 'Pukin' Dogs' over burning oil wells in Kuwait in 1990.

pretty easy to avoid them.'

Shortly after midnight on 17/18 January 'Proven Force' carried out its first combat operations in support of 'Desert Storm', with attacks on four radar sites in northern Iraq by 20th TFW F-111s carrying 500lb bombs. Air cover was furnished by F-15Cs of the 525th TFS, while F-4G 'Wild Weasels' of the 52nd TFW carried HARM anti-radiation missiles and EF-111 Ravens of the 42nd ECS provided ECM support. Complementing the Ravens were EC-130 Compass Call aircraft which monitored radar emissions from the radar sites about to be attacked. Of the eight radars in the Iraqi radar complex, seven were destroyed in the attack. The USAF lost its first aircraft when an F-15E Strike Eagle in the 335th Squadron in the 4th Tactical Fighter Wing flown by 37-year old Major Thomas F. Koritz the wing's flight surgeon and the 42-year old weapons/systems operator, Major Donnie R. Holland was shot down near Basra. Both men were killed. Holland had been in the Air Force for 17 years, but this was the first combat mission he had flown.

On 19 January two F-15Cs destroyed two Mirage F1s with AIM-7 missiles. In a brief dogfight, two other F-15Cs engaged and shot down two Iraqi MiG-25s attempting to engage them, both using AIM-7 missiles. One was destroyed by Captain Rick Tuleni and the second by Captain Larry Pitts. Two F-15Cs, piloted by Captains Craig Underhill and Cesar Rodriguez gave chase to a pair of MiG-29s detected by AWACS. The Iraqi aircraft, one piloted by Captain Jameel Sayhood, promptly turned and engaged the two American fighters and one of the most dramatic dogfights of the Persian Gulf War ensued. The two MiGs and F-15s flew straight at each other, each attempting to visually identify the other. Underhill was facing Sayhood's wingman, while Sayhood was facing Rodriguez. Underhill fired an AIM-7 at Sayhood's wingman, scoring a head-on hit and killing the opposing pilot instantly. Simultaneously, Sayhood gained a lock on Rodriguez, throwing him onto the defensive. Rodriguez dived to low altitude in order to clutter Sayhood's radar and break the lock-on and dropped flares to counter his adversary's infra-red search-and-track. However, after seeing his wingman shot down, Sayhood disengaged and fled to the north. Considering the engagement over, Rodriguez and Underhill turned south to rendezvous with a KC-135 tanker in order to refuel, but Sayhood reversed course and set off after them, prompting them to reengage. With the now lone MiG-29 closing head-on with the pair of F-15s, Underhill gained radar lock-on, but did not fire due to a glitch in his IFF interrogator system keeping him from being certain he wasn't about to shoot down a Coalition aircraft. Sayhood sliced into the American formation, causing a classic merge. Underhill kept Sayhood locked-on and climbed, while Rodriguez committed to the merge in order to visually identify the opposing aircraft as hostile. As they passed head-on, Rodriguez identified it as an Iraqi and each pilot turned left to engage the other. Sayhood was relying on his MiG's better turning radius to get into a firing position on Rodriguez' tail. Both aircraft lost altitude through the sustained hard turning, bringing them perilously close to the ground. Fearing that Rodriguez would obtain infra-red lock-on and shoot him down with an AIM-9, Sayhood attempted to disengage using a split-s. Rodriguez didn't match Sayhood's manoeuvre and observed him eject just prior to his MiG impacting the ground - he'd commenced his escape maneuver too low. It was reported decades later by Iraqi sources that the Captain was rescued by some farmers after he broke his leg and evacuated to a local hospital.

Early in the Gulf War, the Eagles were assigned mainly Scud missile targets while the stealth fighter-bombers were tasked to hit selected targets in highly defended areas. During Operations 'Desert Shield' and 'Desert Storm', 120 F-15Cs and Ds deployed to the Gulf and flew more than 5,900 sorties. Every Iraqi fixed-wing aircraft destroyed in air-to-air combat, including five Soviet-made MiG-29 'Fulcrums', were shot down by F-15Cs. Forty-eight F-15Es were deployed to the Gulf and flew more than 2,200 sorties. They were used to hunt Scud missiles and launchers at night, employed laser systems to hit hard targets and attacked armoured vehicles, tanks and artillery. Primary targets included command and control centres, armour, electrical facilities and Scuds as well as carrying out road interdiction. The F-15Es used the LANTIRN navigation and targeting pods with spectacular results. The first air-to-air kills by F-15Cs took place on 17 January when three MiG-29s and three Mirage F.1EQs were downed using AIM-7s. Two nights later, six Iraqi MiGs and Mirages were brought down in air-to-air combat with the Eagles.

That day, Captain Michael V. McKelvey and his WSO, Captain Mark A. Chance, became the next members in the 48th TFW to receive the Silver Star for their actions during the attack on the heavily defended Al Habbaniyah airfield, 35 miles west of Baghdad. They were in a fourteen aircraft package which included F-111Fs, EF-111As, F-4G 'Wild Weasels' and F-15C Eagles. During the pre-strike air refuelling, the lead and deputy lead F-111Fs aborted with avionics malfunctions. Captain McKelvey assumed command of the attack group. The Chance-McKelvey team encountered radar warnings of an air-to-air missile launch to their right. McKelvey dispensed chaff and initiated a 5 g turn causing the missile to overshoot and explode in the clouds overhead. Chance guided his bombs onto the target and they severely cratered the runway, effectively stopping take-offs and landings at the MiG-29 airfield. On the way out, heavy defences and a confirmed air-to-air threat forced them down to 200 feet using terrain following radar.

In an attack on the Kirkuk research facility, pilots reported a 'brilliant flash' about a minute after F-111s of the 20th TFW had attacked, 'with a fireball reaching to at least 15,000 feet'. Four

F-111F of the 48th TFW being prepared for a mission at its desert base during Operation 'Desert Storm' in the Gulf War in 1991. The 48th TFW was the first wing in the USAFE to be deployed to the Middle East as part of 'Desert Shield'. By the time the Gulf War started, the 48th TFW had deployed 66 of its seventy F-111Fs to the Royal Saudi Air Force base at Taif near Mecca in Saudi Arabia. During early missions the a few F-111F crews encountered Iraqi MiG-29 Fulcrums and escape was made by fully sweeping the F-111's wing and accelerating to high Mach numbers, then descending to 200 feet using terrain-following radar.

F-111F *Miss Liberty* of the 48th TFW over the desert during Operation 'Desert Storm'. The 'Liberty Wing' destroyed 245 HASs or two-thirds of the total destroyed during the Gulf War. No less than 920 tanks and armoured vehicles were destroyed in the Gulf War by the 48th TFW. (USAFE)

aircraft were lost. The crew of an F-4G 'Wild Weasel' were recovered but the crews of two F-16Cs and an F-15E were taken prisoner by the Iraqis. By the third day of 'Desert Storm', more than 7,000 coalition sorties had been flown and ten aircraft lost. Iraqi aircraft loses totalled fifteen. The Iraqis had lost eight aircraft in air-to-air combat on the first day of 'Desert Storm' and 35 more would follow before the end of the war.

On 23 January, attacks were made by F-117A stealth fighters and F-16s on the Tuwaitha Nuclear Research Facility on the outskirts of Baghdad. The facility was the focal point of Iraq's nuclear research programme and was described by the US Defence Intelligence Agency as 'the most heavily defended facility in the Middle East'. Originally it had been bombed by the Israeli Air Force in 1981. In all, nineteen SAM systems and more than 200 anti-aircraft guns could be brought to bear on attacking aircraft. No significant damage was caused to the plant and on 24 January an F-l6 and its pilot were lost over the target area, shot down by Iraqi defences. The pilot was later recovered.

Also on 23 January, Lieutenant General Charles 'Chuck' Horner, commander of all Central Command's air forces, ordered attacks on hardened aircraft shelters (HAS) by F-117s and F-111s. At the start of the war, Iraq had an estimated 594 HASs. Pilots of the 48th TFW reported 'sending hardened penetrating laser guided-bombs into shelter after shelter'. Bombing accuracy remained good enough to justify the change of tactics, although manoeuvrability suffered, especially for the F-111. One pilot likened flying the F-111 at 25,000 feet to trying to get 'a drunken elephant on ice skates to dance'. But aircrews adjusted and found that higher altitudes in the F-111 'gave an ever better look at targets on the Pave Tack system and allowed for even higher success rates'. Three days later, approximately 137 Iraqi aircraft flew to Iran, apparently seeking to escape the shelter attacks.

During the night of 26/27 January Captain Michael Russell and his WSO, Captain Brad Seipel of the 492nd TFS in 72-1446 'Charger 32', the controlling aircraft, were responsible for one of the most famous bombing missions of the Gulf War when GBU-15(V)-2/B electro-optical-guided bombs were toss-launched into the two pumping stations at Al Almadi in occupied Kuwait which were dumping millions of gallons of crude oil into the Persian Gulf. Five F-111Fs (including two reserve aircraft) took off for the mission, each carrying two 2,000lb EOGBs and a data-link pod. One F-111F suffered a technical malfunction and aborted, but the rest of the mission was entirely successful. Flying supersonic at 20,000 feet, F-111F 72-1452 'Charger 35' flown by Major Sammy Samson and his WSO Captain Steve Williams in the 493rd TFS, successfully lobbed two GBU-15(V)-2/B from 15,000 feet in supersonic speed to two different pumping stations from more than twenty miles away. The aircraft then entered a sharp diving turn and left the area at high speed. 'Charger 32', flying a race-track pattern more than fifty miles offshore parallel to the coast on a north-westerly heading and beyond the reach of the defences using AN/AXQ-14 data-link took control of the bomb and guided it throughout the rest of its flight.[52] Bradley Seipel observed the video picture transmitted from the camera in the nose of the missile and steered the weapon in for a direct hit on the first pumping station. Captain Michael Russell then turned 'Charger 32' through 180 degrees and flew south-east, parallel to the coast, as 'Charger 35', a second F-111F, lobbed an EOGB in the direction of the second pumping station. Again Seipel took control of the EOGB in flight and guided the weapon to score a direct hit. The raid cut the oil spill off at its source.

The next night, 29/30 January, the 48th TFW opened its campaign against bridges along the Iraqi supply routes into Kuwait using GBU-24 laser-guided bombs and GBU-15s. The first such attack was on bridges over the Hawr Al Hammar Lake north-west of Basrah and in the days that followed the unit mounted a systematic campaign against bridges over the Tigris and Euphrates rivers. One of the most difficult such targets proved to be the twin highway bridges over the River Tigris near Basrah, which required three separate attacks before they were put out of action. Lieutenant Dave Giachetti, a WSO, recalled: 'With precision-guided munitions, hitting the bridge was not a problem. The problem was hitting it at a weak part, a point where the weapon would cause structural damage and drop a span. If you didn't hit it exactly on the abutment at either end, or where the supports were, the bomb would often go through the pavement, leaving a neat round hole that they could easily repair.'[53]

When the campaign finished the 48th TFW had scored 160 hits, destroyed twelve bridges and damaging 52 more. The 48th TFW proved equally adept at destroying Iraqi tanks and armoured vehicles at night; a role carried out in daylight hours by A-10s and F-16s. The Pave Tack pods of the F-111Fs easily picked up the heat signatures left in the soil during the day by the tracks of the enemy tanks and armour, now dug in for the night. Called 'tank plinking', the forward looking infrared equipment paved the way for 500lb laser-guided bombs and more accurate assessment of numbers of Iraqi tanks destroyed. The 48th TFW scored 920 hits on tanks and armour and a further 252 strikes on artillery pieces, using GBU-12s in single-bomb attacks, all at night. The greatest success occurred on the night of 13/14 February when 46 F-111Fs, each carrying four GBU-12s, scored hits on 132 tanks and armoured vehicles from 184 bombs dropped. One EF-111 Raven was lost.

Planners had divided Kuwait into 'kill boxes' in which aircraft like the F-111s, F-16Cs and A-10As concentrated their fire. F-16C pilots in the 401st TFW reported: Flying in the area of the Republican Guard was a fighter pilot's dream-come-true. There were revetments full of tanks, APCs, ammunition, AAA and artillery as far as the eye could see. To destroy the Republican Guard, the BA1 (battlefield air interdiction) campaign would have to be tank by tank, one at a time and the F-16 was just the aircraft to do that.'

By mid-February, Central Command was estimating that 35 per cent of Iraq's tanks, 31 per cent of its armoured vehicles and 40 per cent of its artillery had been destroyed. The US Air Force's 249 F-16Cs flew more than 13,450 sorties - more than any other aircraft in the war. The Air Force sent 144 A-10A Warthogs to the theatre. While flying only 30 per cent of the USAF's total sorties, these aircraft achieved more than half of the confirmed Iraqi equipment losses and fired 90 per cent of the precision-guided AGM-65 Maverick missiles launched during 'Desert Storm'. They demonstrated versatility as daytime Scud hunters in Iraq and even recorded two helicopter kills with their 30mm cannon. Although A-10As flew more than 8,000 sorties in 'Desert Storm', only five were lost in combat. The first occurred on 2 February when Captain Richard D. Storr was made a PoW.

On 4 February, eighteen F-111Fs of the 48th TFW led by Lieutenant Colonel James F. Slaton and supported by four F-15Cs, four F-4Gs and two EF-111Fs, attacked the Tuwaitha Nuclear Research Facility. As Slaton and his WSO, Captain John F. Daughtry approached the target their F-111F was engulfed by triple-A fire. There were so many missile launches by the Iraqis that the F-4Gs had to fire all their HARMs within the first few moments of the attack. The fire was so intense that only three aircraft reached their targets. Slaton led the remaining aircraft below the cloud cover into the heart of the AAA where they destroyed three of the critical nuclear component buildings. Despite having a weapons system problem which forced Daughtry to an extremely difficult manual back-up delivery mode, the Slaton-Daughtry team hit and destroyed their target. Slaton recalls: 'The clouds were too thick for our equipment, so we had to fly lower to get a good look at our targets. The only problem was, this put us within the heart of their defences.' To add to the excitement, their Pave Tack pod malfunctioned. Daughtry recalls: 'Luckily, after going through three or four backup modes, it came back up just in time for the weapons release.'

Slaton recalled: 'Bear (Captain Daughtry's call-sign) guided the bombs directly on target and we got out of there. By that time the whole sky was lit up; at least that's how it looked to me.' Daughtry confirmed that 'it was a pretty awesome light show'. Slaton added: 'The Tuwaitha Nuclear Research Facility's primary purpose wasn't supplying electricity to Baghdad. It was for building nuclear weapons. We put a stop to that.' The weapon used in the attack was the GBU-24A/B 2,000lb laser-guided bomb. Slaton describes the weapon: 'It has steep impact angles and a long cruise range, so we could release the bomb several miles from the target. During peace we train to get into precise parameters but during the war you're getting shot at and dodging SAMs and AAA. These hi-tech weapons make the difference.' Slaton and Daughtry were awarded the Silver Star for their actions on the night of 4 February.

During the night of 5/6 February Tom Lennon and Tommy Crawford in the 48th TFW each in an F-111F carrying four 500lb LGBs attacked a Republican Guard unit in the desert. Flying at medium altitude so that the bombs would impact at a steep angle to achieve maximum destructive effect they released each weapon one at a time and guided it to impact on an individual vehicle and scored hits on seven Iraqi vehicles. On the night of 13/14 February 46 F-111Fs attacked dug-in vehicles and crews were credited with scoring hits on no fewer than 132 tanks and armoured vehicles.

On 7 February the opening round of Phase III operations, largely against stationary ground forces dug in during the previous six months, began with shelling of the Iraqi and Kuwaiti coast by the *Missouri* and *Wisconsin*.[54] The McDonnell Douglas Standoff' Land Attack Missile (SLAM) was used for the first time from the *John F. Kennedy* in late-February.[55] The strike involved

Colonel Tom Lennon who commanded the 48th TFW during the Gulf War led the deepest penetration by the Wing on the first night of the Gulf War, on 25 August 1990; a six-plane strike on Balad airfield north of Baghdad.

On 28 January 1991 Captain Brad Seipel of the 493rd TFS, 48th TFW flew 70-2390, *Miss Liberty II* from which two GBU-15 bombs were accurately guided onto the Al Almadi pumping station in occupied Kuwait on 28 January 1991 thus halting the flow of oil into the Gulf.

116

coordinated use of A-6Es armed with two SLAMs and an A-7E used as the missile control/target designation aircraft.[56] The first target was an Iraqi power plant, which is understood to have had a reinforced concrete embankment wall to protect the main control building from bomb attacks. The first missile was used to puncture the protective external wall, with the second SLAM missile directed into the blown portion to make a direct hit on the interior of the power plant building. A small number of SLAMS were reported to have been available on board *Saratoga*.

On 24 February, almost 270,000 troops of the Coalition ground forces made an all-out ground assault on the Iraqi border preceded by 900 aircraft sorties. The 101st Air Assault Division carried out the largest helicopter assault in history when 300 helicopters transported a brigade fifty miles into Iraq. Coalition air forces flew a record 3,159 sorties, of which 1,997 were direct combat support missions. Coalition air strikes turned the road leading out of Kuwait City into a 'Highway of Death' for hundreds of Iraqi vehicles and armour and their occupants. US losses totalled four killed and 21 wounded in the first two days of the operation. On 27 February Captain William F. Andrews of the 10th TFS (from the 50th TFW, Hahn Air Base, Germany) in the 363rd TFW(P) was lost over Iraq. Andrews ejected from his F-16C Fighting Falcon and landed in the middle of a Republican Guard infantry unit. Despite a broken leg and imminent capture, he radioed to warn his wing-man of a SAM launch. 'When they were ten metres away, I saw an IR [infrared] SAM fired at my wingman. I grabbed my radio off the ground and called for a 'break right with flares.' It was a beautiful sight when the missile bit off the flares and went wide. The soldiers opened fire on me and blew my radio apart as I dropped it like a hot potato.'

Shortly thereafter, he was in radio contact with NAIL 51, an OA-10 in the area and twice directed the pilot to break and expend decoy flares when he saw missile launches. In both cases, the pilots indicated that they would have suffered direct hits from enemy infrared seeking missiles had Andrews not made the threat calls from the ground. Captain Andrews provided the support despite having just suffered a broken leg and could not move, was exposed in the open and was being fired upon by enemy forces. One rescue effort for Andrews failed. An Air Force search and rescue team was flown in by helicopter. Onboard the aircraft was its crew, the search team and a flight surgeon, Major Rhonda Cornum. The helicopter was shot down and five bodies were located. According to some news sources, three individuals remained missing from the aircraft. When darkness fell, Andrews was to hide and wait for morning rescue. When morning came, Andrews could not be found. On 6 March 1991 Andrews, Cornum and Troy

An EF-111A of the 366th TFS and a F-111F at a desert base during 'Desert Storm'.

F-117A Nighthawk stealth fighter-bomber of the 37th TFW in flight over mountains in Nevada in 2002. During the Gulf War in 1991 the F-117A flew approximately 1,300 sorties and scored direct hits on 1,600 high-value targets in Iraq over 6,905 flight hours.

Dunlap, who had been on the helicopter, were released by the Iraqis. Cornum and Andrews were injured, Cornum with two possible broken arms. Andrews received the AFC for his actions.

The most incredible weapon dropped during the Gulf War was probably the 4,700lb GBU 28/B 'Deep Throat' 'bunker buster' bomb invented by a Lockheed engineer who hit on the idea of encasing 650lb of molten Tritonal explosive in lengths of used 8-inch barrels from self-propelled howitzers and fitted with slightly reprogrammed GBU-27 laser guidance systems. The bombs were delivered to the 48th TFW only seventeen days after 'Desert Storm' officials requested a more powerful weapon than the 2,000lb BLU-109 bomb which was being used against Iraqi hardened aircraft shelters. The USAF needed a weapon that would penetrate deeper for use against Iraq's underground command and control facilities built about 100 feet below the surface. During a test at the Tonapah Test Range in Nevada, a GBU-28 penetrated over 100 feet of earth and in a sled test at Holloman AFB, New Mexico one penetrated almost 25 feet of reinforced concrete. The F-111F was chosen as the delivery system after it beat the F-15E in a fly-off competition. On 27 February the two GBU-28 bombs were delivered to the 48th TFW base at Taif by a C-141 Starlifter. Within five hours of arrival, just before dusk, two F-111Fs took off to destroy the underground command centre at Al Taji airbase, north of Baghdad. Lieutenant Colonel Ken Combs, commander of the 495th TFS, call sign Cardinal 7-1', the flight leader, recalls:

'We were notified about the mission two days before we were supposed to fly. Naturally, we were excited about flying this mission because it was the first time this bomb was to be dropped other than during testing. It was an unknown munition. We didn't have any delivery parameters and didn't know any of its characteristics. We had to wait to get all the preliminary data from the contractors to even begin planning what we were going to do. The profile we flew was pretty much what we'd been flying all along. We took off just before dusk and flew at high altitude to a tanker for pre-strike refuelling. Then we headed up north, staying at high altitude: The delivery altitude and air speed for this mission were different than what we had used in other missions, so once we got into Iraq, we did a step-climb to get to release altitude.

Major Jerry Hust, Combs' WSO adds: 'What we were aiming for was basically a piece of dirt. I thought I had the reticule on the target so we released the bombs. As we got closer to the target I realised we were off to the left.'

The second F-111F (70-2391) call sign 'Cardinal 7-2' was piloted by Lieutenant Colonel Dave White, the 492nd TFS operations officer, with Captain Tom Himes as his WSO. White recalls: 'We were concerned about making the target on time because we were delayed on the ground. It was the maintainers who loaded the bombs that made it possible to take off as soon as we did. They only had 45 minutes notice and did an outstanding job getting the bombs loaded so we could meet our target time.' White and Himes were about 45 minutes late taking off, but caught up to the lead aircraft at the refuelling tanker. White continues: 'Colonel Combs turned the tanker towards us so that we could get on the boom as soon as possible. Actually, we left the tanker at the no-later-than time. So, by turning the tanker when he did, he saved us a lot of time because we just flew behind it and got our fuel.'

The original plans called for White and Himes to hit a second target. However, they were instructed to take the lead and drop on the primary target again. White explains:

'Captain Himes was set on hitting another target and when we were instructed to go for the target again, he had to focus back to the other one and make some adjustments. Basically, all I was trying to do was keep the air speed steady and keep the aircraft on course. I think that what made the mission so successful is that Tommy Himes wanted to hit the target. He made it happen.' The bombs hit the command centre, causing a secondary explosion. It was the final mission of the Gulf War.

When the cease-fire came into effect on 3 March, the Allied air forces had flown 110,000 sorties with devastating effect on the Iraqi military forces. The conflict confirmed the 48th TFW's remarkable reputation for night attack missions, earned over Libya four years before. During the Gulf War, its F-111Fs flew 2,500 sorties and dropped 5,500 bombs, scoring hits on 920 tanks and armoured vehicles, 252 artillery pieces, 245 HAS's as well as 113 bunkers, thirteen runways, twelve bridges (with another 52 seriously damaged) and 158 buildings. In addition, 284 other targets were also hit, including eleven Scud launchers and 25 SAM/AAA sites. Some 321 secondary targets were also knocked out by the hard-hitting 'Liberty Wing' and only one aircraft was damaged by enemy air defences. The F-117A stealth fighters flew almost 1,300 sorties, dropped more than 2,000 tons of bombs and flew more than 6,900 hours during 'Desert Storm'. They were the only aircraft to bomb strategic targets such as aircraft shelters and bunkers in Baghdad and did so using 2,000lb GBU-27 laser-guided bombs with unprecedented accuracy. Without stealth, a typical strike mission required 32 aircraft with bombs, sixteen fighter escorts, eight 'Wild Weasel' aircraft to suppress enemy radar, four aircraft to electronically jam enemy radar and fifteen tankers to refuel the group. With stealth technology the same mission could be accomplished with only eight F-117s and two tankers to refuel them.

The Iraqis lost 43 divisions, 3,700 tanks, 2,400 armoured vehicles and 2,600 artillery pieces and 112 aircraft, 40 of them in air-to-air combat, including 35 to the USAF. US Air Force F-15Cs accounted for 33 of these using radar-guided AIM-7 Sparrows and heat-seeking AIM-9 Sidewinders and A-10s destroyed two helicopters with their GAU-8 30mm cannon. In addition, six Iraqi aircraft were lost in accidents and sixteen were captured or destroyed by Coalition ground forces. About 375 aircraft shelters were destroyed and it is estimated that 141 aircraft were lost inside these shelters. Another 137 aircraft were flown to Iran. Coalition air forces lost 75 aircraft, including 33 in accidents. Included in these figures are nineteen USAF aircraft lost, including three non-combat losses. Eleven US pilots, including eight Air Force pilots, were made prisoners of war.

Endnotes for Chapter 3

43 Jim Anderson was later killed in a skiing accident. Hank Kleeman was killed on 3 December 1985 when he flipped an F/A-18 while taxiing. Larry Muczynski later became an airline pilot. Dave Venlet became a pilot and ultimately rose to the rank of Vice Admiral and headed the Naval Air Systems Command.

44 In an experiment, the two usual LTV A-7E squadrons were replaced with a second Intruder squadron and this resulted in VA-75, VA-85 and VA-176 (which had flown combat sorties over Grenada in October 1983) being embarked aboard.

45 VA-46 'Clansmen' and VA-72 'Blue Hawks' A-7Es were on their last operational deployment before the Corsair II was replaced by F/A-18s.

46 Maritime reconnaissance in the Gulf was carried out by P-3C Orions possibly based at Masirah Island (Oman) and carrier-based S-3 Vikings, while tactical air reconnaissance missions were flown from the carriers by TARPs (tactical air reconnaissance pod system)-equipped F-14s (normally three Tomcats in each squadron per carrier). ELINT/SIGINT support missions were flown by EP-3Qs in conjunction with EC-130Es and two E-8 Joint-STARS aircraft.

47 On 26 December, Joint Task Force 'Proven Force' had been formed at Incirlik in Turkey and by 16 January, four F-111Es of the 79th TFS, 20th TFW were redeployed there with fourteen F-15Cs of the 525th TFS, 36th TFW and six EF-111As of the 42nd Electronic Combat Squadron, 66th ECW, plus three EC-130s of the 43rd ECS, 66th ECW and five F-15Cs of the 32nd TFG as well as eleven F-16Cs and thirteen F-4G 'Wild Weasels' from the 23rd TFS, 52nd TFW, all from bases in England, Holland and Germany. 'Proven Force' had to wait for Turkish parliamen¬tary approval and as a result joined the war one day after it started.

48 The *Independence* returned to home port San Diego prior to the outbreak of war, being replaced in the Gulf by the *Midway*. From the East Coast the America replaced the *Eisenhower* in the Red Sea before war operations commenced; the *Theodore Roosevelt* arrived just in time to transit from an initial position in the Red Sea to the Gulf station.

49 As during the Viêtnam operations, one carrier 'on the line' was usually engaged in support functions at any given time, ie at sea refuelling, munitions and logistic replenishment etc, with the ship's flight schedule reduced accordingly.

50 Target Recognition Attack Multi-sensor. This, added to the standard A-6E a Hughes turreted optronic package of FLIR and laser detection equipment, integrated with the Norden radar; CAINS (Carrier Airborne Inertial Navigation System) provides the capability for automatic landings on carrier decks; and provision for autonomous and laser-guided air-to-surface weapons.

51 F-111F 70-2384 collided with a KC-135 and was damaged.

52 When it operated with this weapon, the F-111F had a special data-link pod mounted under the rear fuselage. The EOGB was aimed and released in the same way as a normal free-fall bomb and was controlled only during the final part of its trajectory. The weapon was fitted with a TV-type camera in the nose, whose picture was relayed by radio link to the controlling aircraft (which might or might not be the one that released the weapon). The picture seen from the nose of the bomb was viewed in the cockpit of the controlling aircraft on a screen in front of the WSO and the latter operated a hand controller to send steering signals to correct the missile's flight path during the final fifteen seconds or so to impact.

53 Quoted in *Sky Battles: Dramatic Air Warfare Actions* by Alfred Price (Cassell 1998).

54 Targets for the heavy guns included defensive positions on Faylakah and Bubiyan islands and around Al Faw; As Salimiyah beach area east of Kuwait City; beach areas off Mina Su'ud (Saud), Umm Qasabah, Qulayat Al Ahrar and Al Funaytis, including defensive positions, artillery sites and defensive barriers surrounding these potential landing beaches. Coalition air force aircraft, including USAF B-52s and B-1Bs, carried out widespread attacks against Iraqi Republican Guard positions and other ground forces in SE Iraq and Kuwait, preparatory to the ground offensive.

55 SLAM is essentially an air-launched Harpoon missile but 25.5 inches longer. SLAM uses a AGM-65 Maverick imaging IR seeker, a single-channel global positioning system (GPS) and a Walleye video data linking control system. Once launched, SLAM navigates to the target using the onboard GPS. With a range of around 60nm and a 500lb penetrator or standard HE warhead, the missile offers significant range increase over the Air Force's GBU-15 or -130 standoff glide bomb systems and sufficient hitting power to take out bunkers, hangarettes etc. SLAM was first delivered in prototype form to the Navy in November 1988.

56 Because of tanking requirements under 'Desert Storm' operating conditions, A-6Es could carry only two SLAMS, although they had the potential to carry four missiles.

Chapter Four

The Falklands Air War

Flight Lieutenant David H. S. 'Mog' Morgan, thirty-five years-old, married with two children, had been in the services since 1966, flying helicopters as well as Harrier jump-jets. Beginning in 1982 he began an exchange tour with the Royal Navy, found a house, started the conversion of the Sea Harrier and was one third of the way through this when, one Friday morning, he went into work and found everyone sitting around. Morgan walked in and said 'Hey! have you guys heard? The bloody Argentineans have invaded the Falklands.' And, to a man, they looked at their watches and said, 'Where have you been for the last four hours?' They'd all been called out at four o'clock in the morning but as I'd only been based there a short time my name wasn't on the call list.'

In 1976 a coup in Argentina placed the South American country under military rule and in 1981 the Junta in charge changed when General and President Leopoldo Galtieri took over. He was in the thrall of Admiral Anaya, a man who, thanks to time spent in the UK, literally hated the British. He wished to conquer the Falkland Islands and possibly all British interests in the region. Brigadier Lami Dozo commanded the Fuerza Aérea Argentina or Argentinean Air Force. In 1982 Argentina was in the midst of a devastating economic crisis and large-scale civil unrest against the repressive military junta. In desperate need of a morale boosting, nation uniting event which would distract from their economic failures and numerous human rights abuses Galtieri thought that by launching what it thought would be a quick and easy war to reclaim the Falkland Islands, it would re-kindle national pride and popular support. Britain and Argentina generally enjoyed

HMS *Hermes* leaving Portsmouth for the Falklands on 5 April 1982 with ten of the eleven of 800 Squadron Sea Harrier FRS.1s on board. A twelfth joined the carrier in the English Channel. (Flight Lieutenant D. H. S. Morgan RAF)

good relations, although controversy over the islands' sovereignty had been the cause of some tension. In December 1981 planning for the conquest of the Falkland Islands went ahead. By March 1982 the plan called for Argentina's biggest warships, 3,000 marines, Special Forces and heavy air support, aiming at a mid-May to June attack. There was a second plan, to capture the British dependency of South Georgia, which is 700 miles from the Falklands. On 19 March 1982 fifty Argentine scrap metal merchants raised the Argentine flag on South Georgia. The Royal Navy ice patrol vessel HMS *Endurance* was dispatched from Port Stanley to South Georgia in response, subsequently leading to the invasion of South Georgia by Argentine forces on 3 April.

The Argentine military junta, suspecting that the UK would reinforce its South Atlantic Forces, ordered the invasion of the Falkland Islands (Operation 'Rosario') to be brought forward and on 28 March, Task Force 40 headed to the islands. Instead of the original plan, it consisted of 900 marines and the Buzo Tactico special forces and a small naval force. On 2 April they landed, quickly seizing the islands from the small population and even smaller British garrison. Despite facing armed opposition, the Argentine troops were ordered not to kill any British civilians. The Falkland's governor, Rex Hunt, had been informed by the intelligence services that the attack was imminent and he organised a defence with what he had: 68 marines, 25 Local Defence Force men and eleven sailors. The defenders caused damage but ran short of ammunition, were surrounded by heavier weapons and were ordered to surrender. The exact death toll is uncertain, but around twenty-five Argentineans may have been killed. Nearby island groups were also seized and the captured British troops were quickly deported back to the mainland, while a governor was put in charge of the civilian population. By the end of the month a 10,000 strong force was in place. However, three quarters were conscripts with poor training.

Britain was initially taken by surprise by the Argentine attack on the South Atlantic islands, despite repeated warnings by Royal Navy captain Nicholas Barker and others. During a crisis meeting headed by the Prime Minister Margaret Thatcher, the Chief of the Naval Staff Admiral Sir Henry Leach, advised them that 'Britain could and should send a task force if the islands are invaded'. Following the invasion on 2 April, after an emergency meeting of the cabinet, approval was given for the formation of a task force to retake the islands, code-named Operation 'Corporate'. This was backed in an emergency session of the House of Commons the next day. The British government dispatched a naval task force to engage the Argentine Navy and Air Force and retake the islands by amphibious assault. The government had no contingency plan for an invasion of the islands and the task force was rapidly put together from whatever vessels were available. The nuclear submarine *Conqueror* set sail from France on 4 April, whilst the two aircraft carriers *Invincible* and *Hermes*, in the company of escort vessels, left Portsmouth only a day later.[57] Upon its return to Southampton from a world cruise on 7 April, the ocean liner SS *Canberra* was requisitioned and set sail two days later with 3 Commando Brigade aboard. The ocean liner RMS *Queen Elizabeth 2* was also requisitioned and left Southampton on 12 May with 5th Infantry Brigade on board. The whole task force eventually comprised 127 ships: forty-three Royal Navy vessels, twenty-two Royal Fleet Auxiliary ships and sixty-two merchant ships. Argentina refused to withdraw her forces from the Falklands and so British preparations for landings on the Falklands went ahead. The main British naval task force sailed for the mid-Atlantic British overseas territory of Ascension Island, 3,375 miles from the Falklands to prepare for active service before leaving for the Falklands on 16 April.

The retaking of the Falkland Islands was considered extremely difficult (the US Navy considered a successful counter-invasion by the British to be 'a military impossibility'): the main constraint being the disparity in deployable air cover. The only aircraft available was the Hawker Harrier but the Royal Navy had a total of just twenty-eight FRS.1 Sea Harriers and so 1 Squadron, 38 Group RAF was ordered to prepare for deployment to the South Atlantic with its fourteen Harrier GR.3s. Apart from some necessary modifications to the aircraft for carrier operations, this involved some hurried training in air combat techniques, for 1 Squadron was a ground attack unit and the Harriers had to be fitted with points for Sidewinder AIM-9L AAMs as well as IFF transponders. For all operational missions, the Sea Harrier and the RAF GR.3s (which joined *Hermes* in May) carried 100-Imperial gallon drop-tanks on the inboard wing pylons and two 30mm Aden cannon pods under the fuselage, leaving the outboard wing pylons and the centre-line pylon for bombs, rockets, or missiles. For ground attack missions these three pylons were generally used for 1,000lb GP bombs or Hunting BL.755 cluster weapons (single carriage in either case). The latter had been developed originally for anti-tank use, but also gave worthwhile effects over a large area against parked aircraft, radars and AAA.

Nine pilots and six Harrier GR.3s from 1(F) Squadron discovered that their new home had its drawbacks, as Flight Lieutenant Tony Harper, a GR.3 pilot recalled. 'Operating the Harriers from the deck of HMS *Hermes* (known as 'Mother' by the Fleet Air Arm pilots and as the 'Rat Infested Rust Bucket' by the RAF) was an adventure in itself, getting safely from the 'Ready Room' to the aircraft across a moving deck often humming with noise and activity. Entertainment was provided by the three cans of beer we were each rationed to daily, whilst listening to the Principle Warfare Officer (PWO) giving a summary of each day's actions over the evening 'pipe'. (Amusement was caused by watching the Lieutenant finish his game of bridge in the wardroom, so that one could erect one's camp bed and get some sleep on the wardroom floor.)

Flight Lieutenant David 'Mog' Morgan was about a third of the way through his course on the Sea Harrier when he was sent to the Falklands with 800 Naval Air Squadron on board *Hermes*. Initially he was told he would not be flying, but that he would go as a back-up ops man and then twelve hours later he was told that he would be a pilot after all.

`On the Sunday I jumped in an aeroplane at Yeovilton and landed on *Hermes* at Portsmouth and on the Monday she sailed. I said goodbye to my wife Carol and my children on Saturday. Then it was all delayed so I went back home again and said, 'I haven't really gone, but I'm going tomorrow.' I'd always explained to the kids, while we were in Germany, what might happen if ever there was a war. We'd taken them up to Berlin and showed them the other side of the Wall and said, you know, 'That's why we're here, to stop that happening to us. We wouldn't like that, would we?' They couldn't get any chips in East Berlin and the Coke tasted horrible. Communism was way-off! I'd always told Carol, if I actually had to go off to war, not to expect me back, because in Germany we were operating so close to the front that life expectancy would be pretty short because we would be prime targets. The kids, however, were rather confused that I was going off to war when we were back in England. I'd certainly resolved to do the best I could to stay alive but I didn't really expect to live through the campaign. There was every chance that I was going to get killed. In fact, while I was down south, Carol moved house and I came home to find all my belongings packed in boxes. But that's better than one chap I heard about whose wife said, 'Okay, he's not coming back,' sold their house, bought a smaller one, got rid of all his kit - and then he came back!

'When I said goodbye to the kids for the final time my son Charles who was five said, 'Don't worry, Daddy. You'll be all right. They've only got tatty old aeroplanes - you've got brand new ones!'

'The landing I made on *Hermes* was the only deck landing I'd ever done, apart from once in a helicopter. I didn't actually see England to say goodbye to it because by the time I got up on deck, we were out to sea and England had disappeared. All I saw was the overhead projector screen start to swing in the briefing room. So we rattled off down the Channel with helicopters bringing things on board all the way down.

`I was feeling a whole range of emotions,' he said, `I was very concerned on the one hand but on the other it was something I had been training for nearly twenty years. The Sea Harrier was very different from the RAF Harrier, which was more of a ground attack aircraft, so I had to learn about a whole new weapons system. It took us about three weeks to get to the Falklands so we had time to carefully devise our attacks using cluster bombs. You can never be one hundred per cent ready for something like that, but by the time we got to the Islands we were feeling very confident.

'There was a lot of discussion about what we were actually going to do. We considered ourselves basically as the big stick, the big threat that probably wasn't going to be used because there would be a political solution and I think a lot of people thought that until we got to Ascension Island. We were anchored off to re-store and bring on kit which had been flown down to us when one of the Royal Fleet Auxiliaries sighted a periscope, so we all upsticked and went very, very quickly and left the Sea Kings tracking this submarine. I don't know whose sub it was to this day, but it wasn't American; it wasn't Argentinean.

'While we were heading off south the Admiral came on to the intercom and said, 'Okay, we've actually left earlier than we anticipated. However, we're going now, we aren't going back and you can take it from me that we are going to war. So get settled down, sort out what you've got to do, get your house in order, as things are going to hot up from now on.' We'd already formed planning teams on the way down so we started doing quite a lot of fairly heavy training. There were some pretty heavy sessions for the next ten days or so, to make sure we'd got everything exactly right. A team of us sat down and looked at the ground-attack options. We worked out the best way to attack our first option, which was the airport at Port Stanley. We also discovered that Goose Green was being used, so we had to plan a secondary attack. Basically, we were trying to use all the aircraft on *Hermes* - we had twelve at the time - nine to attack the airfield and three in reserve to take the place of any which was unserviceable. If any two of those three were left at the end of the day, they would go and attack Goose Green. We decided early on never to send 'singletons' because that is a sure way of losing a guy.

'It worked itself up gradually, the pitch getting higher and people getting more and more finely-tuned. Our time from normal cruising to action stations went from about twenty-five minutes on the first try, down to a couple of minutes as we approached the zone, so things were getting pretty sharp. We started intercepting an Argentine Boeing 707 which was coming out and snooping around us and finally got clearance to fire at him if he came again. That obviously

Royal Marines line up for a weapons check in the hangar of HMS *Hermes* in the South Atlantic en route to the Falklands on 20 April. (PA)

got back through the Argentine channels because they never came again.

'In the four weeks that it had taken us to sail the 8,000 miles from Portsmouth the mood aboard the Flagship had changed dramatically. When we first set sail, a large percentage of the ship's company had thought that we were purely the big stick that would frighten the Argentines into giving up their illegal occupation of these far flung islands. As we pressed south, however, the mood gradually changed. The Sea Harrier force had always assumed that we would be called upon to show our mettle, an occasion that all fighter pilots anticipate with a peculiar mixture of eagerness and foreboding throughout their careers. We had, therefore, set about a daily round of planning and practice that would hone our already considerable skills to a razors edge before closing the enemy. We practiced ship attacks and Air Combat, dropped an example of every live weapon in the ship's magazines and planned assiduously for every conceivable contingency. By the third week in April, when it became obvious that a political solution was impossible, we were confident that we would give a good account of ourselves despite our ten to one disadvantage in the air.'

The Harrier force faced approximately 122 serviceable jet fighters in Argentina's air forces, of which about fifty were employed as air superiority fighters and the remainder as strike aircraft. The Falklands had only three airfields with the longest and only paved runway at the

Sea Harrier FRS.1 ZA191/18 tied down on Hermes while riding out a South Atlantic storm. On 16 May while being flown by Lieutenant Hargreaves, the Argentine supply vessel *Bahia Buen Suceso* was strafed as it lay alongside the pier at Fox Bay East. The aircraft was damaged in the tail area by Argentine gunfire during the attack. On 23 May Flight Lieutenant John Leeming accompanied by Flight Lieutenant 'Mog' Morgan strafed and destroyed a Agusta A-109A helicopter (AE-337) of Batallon de Aviacion de Combate 601 Ejercito, a special commando unit of the Argentinian Army near Shag Cove House, West Falkland.

A Harrier taking off from the ski jump on the crowded flight deck of *Hermes*.

capital, Stanley. Though the newly-designated 'Aerodromo Malvinas' was too short to support fast jets[58] IA-58 Pucará's (an Argentinean-built counter-insurgency aircraft) and lightly-loaded C-130 Hercules could operate from half the length of the Stanley runway.[59] Swift, decisive air strikes would deny its use to Argentine Mirages, A-4s and Super Etendards and thus keep them operating at the limit of their radius. Since it is practically impossible to make large craters in a runway built on solid rock it was never expected to close Stanley Airport completely but it was hoped that attacks on the airport would force the Argentines to disperse aircraft and supplies away from the main airhead by damaging parked aircraft and rendering the airport buildings unserviceable. Forced to launch their major strikes from the mainland, would severely hamper their efforts at forward staging, combat air patrols and close air support over the islands. The effective loiter time of incoming Argentine aircraft was low and they would be compelled to overfly British forces in any attempt to attack the islands. A decision therefore was taken to base Avro Vulcan B.2s modified to carry a war-load of 21 general purpose 1,000lb bombs instead of their normal load of low-level retarded bombs, on the US airfield at Wideawake on Ascension Island for raids on Stanley airfield.

When the Falklands crisis developed, the Vulcan force was being run down at a rapid rate; what remained of it was concentrated at Waddington on 44 and 50 Squadrons; two more units, 9 and 101 Squadrons, being on the point of disbanding. 44 Squadron was tasked with offensive operations over the Falklands, the most experienced crews being selected from all four squadrons and ten of the most airworthy Vulcans were selected from the aircraft pool. An air-to-air refuelling capability was restored on these, the necessary equipment being acquired from time-expired Vulcans at points throughout the UK and farther afield. A Carousel INS was fitted to help with long-range navigation. Later, the AN/ALQ-101D (Dash Ten) ECM pod was fitted to the Vulcans on the starboard underwing hard point that had originally existed for the carriage of the Skybolt missile. The port hardpoint was reserved for the carriage of the AS37 Martel anti-radar missile, but in the event the AGM-45A Shrike was used instead.[60]

Once the refuelling equipment had been installed, the Vulcan crews embarked on a three-

The 14,950 ton Cunard-owned roll-on, roll-off container ship SS *Atlantic Conveyor* en route to the TEZ (Total Exclusion Zone) from Ascension Island on 7 May with her forward deck crammed with containers and GR.3 and FRS.1 Harriers and Wessex and Chinook helicopters 'bagged' for corrosion protection.

week series of air refuelling exercises with the Victor K.2 tankers of the Marham Wing. Handley Page Victor K.Mk.2 tanker aircraft were essential for refuelling the Vulcans for the demanding trip to Stanley airfield. Squadron Leader Bob Tuxford, a Victor pilot on 55 Squadron, recalls. 'We did a number of work-up sorties before leaving for Ascension. We had an inclination of what was ahead, but I think it's fair to say no one expected to be launching eighteen-ship sorties and assisting a Vulcan to drop the hardware. It was a massive operation. We were taken aback with the logistical aspects. Air-to-air refuelling was our business, but normally escorting fighters around the world in much reduced numbers.'

While these preparations were under way, aircraft of 38 Group were busily flying stores and equipment into Wideawake. On 5 April two Nimrod MR.Is on 42 Squadron arrived with their ground crews to begin long-range patrols in support of the Task Force and on 12 April they were joined by detachments of 120, 201 and 206 Squadrons with better-equipped Nimrod MR.2s. On 18 April the advance party and five Victor K.2s on 55 and 57 Squadrons (one of which was fitted with cameras for the strategic reconnaissance role) left RAF Marham in Norfolk for Ascension Island. Next day four more Victors flew the 4,100 miles from Marham to Ascension and by the end of the month fourteen Victors were stationed at Wideawake with McDonnell Douglas

Phantom FGR.Mk.2 fighters to protect them.

Beginning on 20 April, Victors, supported by five more operating in the air refuelling mode, flew three maritime reconnaissance operations, each more than fourteen hours duration, to waters in the region of South Georgia. The first reconnaissance mission by a radar-mapping Victor was flown over South Georgia to pave the way for repossession of the island. The Nimrod force, unlike the Victors, did not have the unrefuelled range to operate as far south as the Falklands so Squadron Leader John Elliott and his crew on XL192 flew the first operational Victor sortie during Operation 'Corporate'. The primary purpose of the MMR (and two similar MMR sorties flown by Victors on 22/23 and 24/25 April) was to provide data on surface shipping and ice conditions etc to HMS *Antrim*, the ship leading the small naval Task Group responsible for recapturing South Georgia (Operation 'Paraquat'). Having reached its target area Elliott descended from its transit height to around 18,000 feet and for ninety minutes Squadron Leader A. I. B. 'Al' Beedie, who with Squadron Leader Tony Cowling formed the radar team aboard the Victor, carried out a radar sweep of 150,000 square miles of ocean. Nothing untoward was found and the information was made available to *Antrim*. The 7,000-

On arrival off San Carlos Water the GR.3s were flown off *Atlantic Conveyor* to HMS *Hermes* while the Sea Harriers were divided amongst the existing squadrons on *Hermes* and *Invincible*. Requisitioned by the MoD, *Atlantic Conveyor* was not fitted with either an active or a passive defence system. On 25 May the vessel was hit by two AM39 Air Launched Exocet missiles fired by two Argentine Navy Super Étendard jet fighters which killed the ship's master, Captain Ian North (who was posthumously awarded the Distinguished Service Cross), eleven crew and a Lynx, three Chinooks and six Wessex helicopters. *Atlantic Conveyor* finally sank whilst under tow on 28 May; the first British merchant vessel lost at sea to enemy fire since WWII.

Canberra B.62 B-101, one of ten operated by the Grupo 2 de Bombardeo, was deployed to Trelew, presumably in late April 1982, with later operational detachments to Rio Gallegos. The refurbished Canberras were delivered to Argentina in 1971 together with two T.64s.

mile sortie took fourteen hours forty-five minutes. It was the longest operational reconnaissance mission ever carried out. The Argentine forces on South Georgia finally surrendered without resistance on 26 April.

On 21 April the first airdrop to the Task Force was made by a C-130 and a Sea Harrier intercepted and turned away a Boeing 707-320B of the Argentine Air Force evidently carrying out a search for the Royal Naval Task Force. Several of these flights were intercepted by Sea Harriers outside the British-imposed exclusion zone; the unarmed 707s were not attacked because diplomatic moves were still in progress and the UK had not yet decided to commit itself to armed force. On 23 April a Brazilian commercial Douglas DC-10 from VARIG Airlines en route to South Africa was intercepted by Harriers who visually identified the civilian airliner.

On 29 April the first Vulcans were deployed to Ascension when B.2s XM598 and XM607 were tanked from Waddington to the island. The Victors air refuelled the Vulcans twice en route and the tankers required numerous fuel transfers of their own to complete the nine-hour flight. After their arrival the two Vulcans were loaded with twenty-one general purpose 1,000lb free-fall bombs for the 7,860-mile round trip to Stanley airfield on 30 April/1 May. They took off just after 2300 hours GMT on the evening of 30 April on an incident-filled, complex operation, which was code-named 'Black Buck I', supported by no less than ten Victors. Squadron Leader Bob Tuxford of 55 Squadron recalls.

'The tanking support for this mission took eighteen individual Victor sorties - a very complicated operation, but one we thought absolutely achievable. We had a fuel planning cell at 1 Group that looked after the tanker force. Mostly ex-navigators, their business was to produce fuel plans - 'Black Buck' was just a variation on a theme. We saw the plan for the very first time on the evening of 30 April, but it was our experience using formation procedures that allowed us to run with it quickly. Martin Withers has acknowledged that the plan was mind-boggling to him. He had Dick Russell [who had just turned fifty, an experienced Victor AAR instructor at Marham] with him in the cockpit to bring some air-to-air refuelling expertise into the Vulcan crews. [The Vulcan crews had just twelve days in which to hone their refuelling skills.] I flew over fourteen hours that night. I went through every emotion from excitement in the launch phase to worry in the early stages.'

'Al' Beedie recalls.

'At the start the primary Vulcan [XM598] aborted after its cabin could not be pressurized and the Victor fleet, too, suffered malfunctions. Victors refuelled Victors until only two remained with the reserve Vulcan [XM607], flown by Flight Lieutenant Martin Withers and Flight Lieutenant Dick Russell. Just before the fifth refuelling of the Vulcan one of the Victors [Squadron Leader Bob Tuxford flying XL189] attempted to refuel the other Victor in very

Right: B-52G-95-BW 58-0168 *Treasure Hunter* in the 379th Bomb Wing which operated from Fairford during the Gulf War in 1991.

Below: B-52G-85-BW 58-0170 *Special Delivery II* of the 416th Bomb Wing from Griffiss AFB, which operated in the 801st Bomb Wing (P) at Morón AB, Spain, during the Gulf War and flew 23 missions. It was sent to the AMARC on 10 November 1992. (USAF)

Above: B-52G-95-BW 58-0164 *SAC Time* in the 416th Bomb Wing at Jeddah.

Left: B-52G-95-BW 58-0173 *Let´s Make A Deal* in the 379th Bomb Wing.

Below left: B-52G-85-BW 57-6492 *Old Crow Express* in the 2nd Bomb Wing.

Below: B-52G-75-BW 57-6474 *Lone Wolf* in the 379th Bomb Wing attached to the 801st Bomb Wing (P) at Morón Air Base, Spain.

Above: In May 1992, two Russian Air Force Tu-95 Bear bombers and an An-124 Condor transport, along with 58 airmen, paid a reciprocal visit to Barksdale. It was the first time Russian bombers had landed in the United States. The Bears and the Condor shared the Barksdale ramp with a host of B-52H bombers, including one From the 5th Bomb Wing at Minot Air Force Base, North Dakota. The visit coincided with the annual 'Bomb Comp' at Barksdale. (2nd Bomb Wing History Office.)

Below: An F-22 being refuelled over Syria.

Above: Aviation ordnancemen assigned to VFA 136 'Knighthawks' download a GBU-38 JDAM satellite guided bomb on an F/A-18C Hornet on the flight deck of the nuclear-powered aircraft carrier USS *Enterprise* (CVN 65).

Left: A RAF Harrier GR.9 over Afghanistan in 2008.

Below: USAF F-16As, F-15C and Es overfly burning oilfields during 'Desert Storm'.

Above: An F/A-18E Super Hornet of VFA-97 'Warhawks' conducts a touch and go landing and take-off aboard the USS *Nimitz* on 30 October 2015.

Below: A RAF Tornado GR.4 landing at Kandahar Air Base in Afghanistan on 6 July 2011.

A F/A-18E Hornet of VFA-81 'Sunliners' takes off from the USS *Carl Vinson* (CVN-70). In 2014 the squadron was embarked with Carrier Air Wing 17 aboard USS *Carl Vinson* in support of Operation 'Inherent Resolve' and returned to its home port of Naval Air Station Oceana in 2015.

Below: A RAF Tornado in Cyprus following a raid on Islamic State targets in Iraq in 2014.

An AV-8B of VMA-211 'Wake Island Avengers' in Afghanistan in 2012. In April the 'Avengers' deployed in support of Operation 'Enduring Freedom', moving from Kandahar airfield to Camp Bastion in July. That September the Avengers experienced six Harriers destroyed and two severely damaged during a Taliban attack on the base described as 'arguably the worst day in USMC aviation history since the Tet Offensive of 1968.' Two Marines were killed, including squadron commander Lieutenant Colonel Christopher K. Raible. In September 2014 the 'Avengers' deployed to Bahrain to support the fight on terrorism in Iraq and Syria until April 2015.

Below: F/A-18E Super Hornets of VFA-136 'Knighthawks' and Grumman E2D Hawkeyes of VAW-125 'Tigertails' aboard the USS *Theodore Roosevelt* (CVN-71) on 20 November 2015. The other embarked squadrons were VFA-11 'Red Rippers' with F/A-18F Super Hornets, the similarly equipped VFA-211 'Fighting Checkmates' and VMFA-251 'Thunderbirds' with F/A-18C 'Legacy' Hornets.

Above: A F/A-18C of VFA-113 'Fighting Stingers' launching from the USS *Carl Vinson* on 3 March 2015. In August 2014 VFA-113 embarked aboard the carrier for a deployment of almost ten months to the Western Pacific and Middle East. The 'Stingers' took part in 'Inherent Resolve' supporting combat operations in Iraq and Syria.

Above: A Sukhoi Su-34 taking off from Beltyukov-1.

Right: A Russian ground technician at Latakia in Syria writes a message of support for the French after the ISIL terrorist bombings in Paris on 13 November 2015.

Below: A Su-24 'Fencer' operating from Latakia, Syria on 18 November 2015.

A B-52H from the 96th Bomb Squadron, Barksdale AFB, deployed to the 2nd Air Expeditionary Group, Naval Station Diego Garcia, drops away after air refuelling with a KC-135. The 96th Bomb Squadron and support personnel from the 2d Bomb Wing were deployed in support of 'Desert Thunder' 11 November-22 December 1998, a response to threats by Iraq's president Saddam Hussein to shoot down U-2 spy planes and violate the no-fly zone over his country.

The two RAF Tornado GR.4s at RAF Akrotiri, Cyprus being armed with the Paveway IV Laser Guided bomb for the first RAF raid on Syria on 18 December 2015.

turbulent conditions and the receiving Victor [XH669 flown by Flight Lieutenant Steve Biglands] had its probe broken during the transfer. The two Victors exchanged roles and the provider took back the fuel. Although dangerously low on fuel itself the Victor then transferred enough fuel to the Vulcan to allow it to make its attack, before heading back towards Ascension and calling for another tanker to meet it.'

Squadron Leader Bob Tuxford recalls. 'Much of the 'excitement' for me came in the sixth and seventh hours when I was refuelling one of the other tankers, Victor K.2 XH669 piloted by Steve Biglands, which broke its probe in my basket. That necessitated changing places and receiving back the fuel we'd just passed in pretty shocking weather. The degree of difficulty at that stage was as hard as anything I'd had to deal with before. Despite a shortage of fuel in the whole formation, I was able to give the final offload to the Vulcan, which then went onto the Falklands, albeit with less fuel reserves than hoped. As I 'turned the corner', it was seven hours back to Ascension and we had five hours worth of fuel. I didn't have any options to divert; there was no option but the South Atlantic. We were very focussed at that point, not sure if the Vulcan could finish the job. But once we'd intercepted the code word that indicated the job was done, we went from a subdued state to an elated one and then concentrated efforts on recovery, which would require another tanker. The original plan hadn't allowed for such a contingency so I was relying on their knowledge at Ascension on how the plan had gone and the fact the formation was short of fuel, so they would launch additional recovery aircraft, which indeed they did.'

Squadron Leader 'Al' Beedie continues: The last refuelling bracket took place 3,000 miles south of Ascension and Tuxford had to transfer more fuel than planned, which left XL189 with insufficient fuel to return to Wideawake. The need for radio silence meant that the Victor could not call Ascension and arrange for another tanker to meet him on the return. Tuxford and his crew could only pray that another tanker from Wideawake would intercept them before they ran out of fuel and had to ditch in the freezing South Atlantic when death would be almost instantaneous. 'Black Buck I' was the first time that a Vulcan had dropped bombs in anger in its twenty-five-year history.

Squadron Leader Bob Tuxford recalls. 'The Vulcan crews were not very familiar with air-to-air refuelling operations - the managers at the Vulcan bases did not have the best available information to them on the fuel consumption rates the aircraft would endure, especially fully laden and undertaking multiple formation changes. So, the figures were not as accurate, in retrospect, as we would have liked. A number of things also went significantly wrong, Steve Biglands' unfortunate breaking of the probe being the biggest. We were flying in towering cumulous clouds at night. Your visual references for formating on the aircraft in front are reduced. Therefore with the turbulence, the distracting lightning, St. Elmo's Fire all around the cockpit windows, the whole process of achieving a stable contact and maintaining it for long enough to get the fuel on becomes much more difficult. On approaching the Falklands, the whole formation had burnt a lot more fuel than had been planned. Unfortunately, that ended up with me, the final tanker, 20,000lbs short.

'There is a weak link on the front end of the probe that is designed to shear if too much lateral force is put upon it. One of two things can happen; the probe tip can lodge inside the coupling of the basket, which would render it useless, or the tip breaks off and falls into the sea, if it doesn't enter the engine intakes. At this point, I wasn't aware whether I would be able to use the centre HDU [Hose Drum Unit] again. But everything premised on my ability to change places with Steve Biglands and take back the fuel we had just given him. If I couldn't do that, then it didn't matter my hose may be damaged. So, I took back the fuel, so I had enough to go on with the mission. Then we had to decide if the hose would be satisfactory. We brought Withers' Vulcan behind, they visibly inspected it but that wasn't quite confirmatory enough, so we made a small additional transfer of about 5,000lbs. That demonstrated how flexible this whole refuelling plan was. We were effectively making it up as we went along. Once I knew he could take on fuel, we could then continue with the mission.

Above: Primer Teniente César Fernando Roman of Grupo 6 de Caza in front of Dagger C-412 which he flew on 1 May in the attack on *Alacrity*, *Arrow* and *Glamorgan* which were withdrawing from a bombardment of the Port Stanley area. The ship silhouette stencilled below the cockpit denotes a 'damaged' vessel in that action.

Above left: Wing Commander Peter Squire.

Right: Thirty-five -year old Capitán Gustavo García Cuerva of Grupo 8 de Caza whose Mirage IIIA (I-019) was damaged over West Falkland on 1 May by an AIM-9L fired from 801 Squadron Sea Harrier XZ453 of Lieutenant Stevie Thomas. Cuerva flew the aircraft to the environs of Port Stanley where it was brought down by Argentine AAA. Cuerva was killed in the crash.

Right: Primer Teniente Danilo 'Ruso' Bolzán of Grupo 5 de Caza in the cockpit of A-4B C-204. Bolzán was KIA in this Skyhawk on 8 June when he was shot down by an AIM-9L fired from XZ499, the 800 Squadron Sea Harrier flown by Lieutenant Dave Smith.

'If we hadn't been able to transfer to Withers, the mission would have been aborted. I had grounds for aborting the mission somewhat earlier, as I was prejudicing my own recovery, as I wasn't sure we could get another tanker on the way home. I hasten to add that I discussed the options available with my crew and each of the other four members came back and said. "Let's press on and get the job done'. That was in the full knowledge that we would be two hours short of fuel in getting back to Ascension, about 600 miles south.

'We gave the Vulcan sufficient time to effect the mission and my AO, [Airborne Electronic Officer] Flight Lieutenant Mick Beer, intercepted the code word 'Polo' designed to communicate the mission had been a success. I was then able to make arrangements for my own recovery. Two Victors were scrambled from Ascension. They were from the recovery wave of six tankers for the mission to bring the Vulcan back post-strike. The six aircraft were required to provide two Victors at the RV in case of problems. Fortunately, Group Captain Gerry Price, the Station Commander from RAF Marham who was running the Air Bridge at Ascension made the decision to divert two of the Victors to assist us. Another of our tanker crews, Flight Lieutenant Alan Skelton, had developed a fuel leak and also required assistance. They met us three hours south of Ascension when we had about an hour's fuel left.'

XM607 reached Stanley airport at 0745 GMT (0345 local time) on the morning of Saturday 1 May and Withers successfully dropped his twenty-one 1,000lb bombs by reference to the

Canberra B.62 B-110 was brought down over the South Atlantic about 150 miles north-northwest of Port Stanley on 1 May by an AIM-9L fired from 801 Squadron Sea Harrier XZ451 of Lieutenant William Alan Curtis. Teniente Eduardo de Ibáñez (25) and his navigator/bombardier Primer Teniente Mario Hipolito González ejected but they perished in the freezing cold sea. Another (B-108), whilst under escort by Mirage IIIs on 14 June, was downed by a Sea Dart SAM fired from HMS *Exeter* when on the way to attack British troops on Mount Kent. It crashed in the sea south of Fitzroy. The navigator did not eject and was killed but the pilot ejected successfully and was recovered by British forces.

Right: Armourers loading an AIM-9L
Sidewinder onto a Harrier.

Below: Harrier GR.3 and Sea Harriers
being rearmed on the deck of HMS
Hermes.

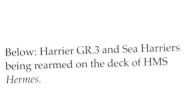

Vulcan's ground-mapping radar, in a single stick at approximately thirty degrees to the runway,
the classic line of attack to ensure at least one crater in its surface. One bomb hit the centre-line
of the runway and the remainder marched on toward the airport facilities and aircraft parking
area; the flashes of the explosions were clearly visible to the crew of the Vulcan and the shock
waves were felt through the aircraft structure. Stanley was defended by a mixture of surface-to-
air missile (SAM) systems (Franco-German Roland and British 'Tiger Cat') and Swiss-built
Oerlikon 35mm twin anti-aircraft cannons but there was no evidence of defensive fire and the
crew transmitted their code-name 'Superfuze' to the Task Force to indicate completion of the
strike as they began the long haul back to Ascension. The Vulcan was then refuelled a sixth time
and returned to Ascension, landing back at 1445 hours GMT after being airborne for fifteen
hours forty-five minutes. At the time it was the longest-range operational bombing operation
ever flown.

Squadron Leader Bob Tuxford concluded: 'I'm very proud, both for my crew and the whole
of the tanker force. Any one of those eighteen tankers failing would mean the mission failing.
Pretty much the whole of 1 Group's tanker force was on the island and it was thanks to some

pretty skilful flying from every pilot that enabled the whole plan to be accomplished. It was very much more than a simple bombing mission. The Argentines then knew we could attack them on the mainland.'[61]

The Vulcan's night attack was to be followed by a low level dawn strike against Stanley airfield and that at Goose Green by twelve Sea Harriers of 800 Squadron from the Task Force, which had closed in to a position ninety nautical miles east of the islands. For this first operation the RN established a line of SAR (search and rescue) helicopters out from the carriers, but thereafter this mission was left to the ASW Sea King screen with complete success. Nine Sea Harriers led by Lieutenant Commander Andy Auld were detailed to bomb Stanley airfield. No FAA (Fuerza Aérea Argentina (Argentine Air Force) combat jets could safely operate from Stanley's short runway so four (later six) Aeromacchi MB-339As of CANA's 1 Escuadrilla De Ataque were allocated a small, improvised parking area on the southern side of the runway and away from the congested main apron area for anti-shipping duties. Three other Sea Harriers led by Lieutenant Commander 'Fred' Frederiksen were detailed to hit Goose Green. Rodney Vincent Frederiksen was born in South Shields on 7 April 1947. His father was a wartime wireless officer in the Danish merchant navy who moved to England. Rodney was educated at St. Aidan's, joined the Royal Navy in 1966 and began his operational career as a Sea Vixen pilot in 893 Naval Air Squadron on *Hermes* in 1970. He flew the Phantom jet fighter-bomber in 899 NAS from the carrier *Eagle* in the early 1970s, attended the central flying school at RAF Little Rissington in 1973 and subsequently taught flying. In 1977 Frederiksen was selected for No 36 Fixed Wing Course at the ETPS and for the next five years, until the Falklands War broke out, he was a test pilot at Boscombe Down.

Flight Lieutenant David Morgan was 'Black 2' on the strike on Stanley airfield.

'The evening before 1 May we'd got everything sorted out and there was just the final briefings. Before dawn on 1 May the Vulcan went in and dropped a bomb in the middle of the runway and that was really the most damage they ever did with the Vulcan. We were to follow up just before eight o'clock with a raid of twelve Harriers and hit Stanley just as dawn was breaking. This was the first time we'd really been into action and everyone was very tense beforehand, very much introverted, very quiet, with the odd stupid joke at which everyone sort of cackled aimlessly and then went back into their shells again, everyone walking around, thinking very hard about what they were going to do. Having had a Vulcan through, the ground defences would be very alert.

'Grey fingers of dawn tentatively probed the eastern sky as the twelve of us made our way across the gently pitching deck towards the silent bulk of our fully armed Sea Harriers. We moved with the slightly shambling gait associated with the modern fighter pilot. All of us were weighed down with helmet, oxygen mask, anti-G suit, maps, immersion suit and layers of thick pile clothing to enable us to survive in the near-freezing water around the islands. HMS *Hermes*, the old lady of the Royal Navy, who had sailed millions of miles since her commissioning in 1959 and launched hundreds of thousands of aircraft sorties, was, in her twilight years, about to launch her first ever air strike against the enemy.

'It was now the first of May. In Somerset, my children would be celebrating the coming of spring with traditional dance and jollification. In the South Atlantic, the autumnal storms were gathering and the Sea Harrier force was about to show its mettle. The weeks of meticulous planning and practice were now coming to a head. Each pilot carried a Browning 9mm automatic pistol together with two loaded magazines, probably more of a psychological prop than any practical use, even for a passably good shot like myself. After a few half-hearted jokes, we had taken refuge in our private thoughts and most of us were happy to immerse ourselves in the well-practised and comforting routine of preparing to fly.

'My aircraft was lined up on the Flight Deck centre-line behind Andy Auld's with three 600lb cluster bombs hanging from the weapons pylons. Having carried out the initial safety checks in the cockpit, I walked slowly around the aircraft, checking that it was, in all respects, ready for flight. I also checked that both guns were loaded and connected, that all the arming leads and lanyards on the bombs were correctly fixed to the pylons and that all the safety pins had been removed. The bombs looked rather less warlike than the 1,000lb bombs, their thin skins being built more for aerodynamic function than to cause damage. I was under no illusions, however, that these weapons would wreak havoc once they were deployed against targets on the ground. Nick Taylor had carried out a very impressive practice drop of the bomb a few days previously and the resultant area of beaten water was a sobering sight. So too was the bomblet that detonated prematurely and sent a white-hot slug of copper whistling past his tail.

'I mentally ran through my part in the plan as I carried out an extremely thorough check of my Martin-Baker 'bang seat'. It was essential that everyone carried out his individual role as perfectly as possible to preserve the integrity of the attack. We had only allowed three seconds between aircraft over the target, so there was little room for error. As I strapped myself into the seat, I was acutely aware that the odds were very much against us all returning safely. The temptation was to look over at the others, as they settled into their cockpits, just to catch a final glimpse, to preserve a final picture of each of them as some sort of insurance against them not making it through the day. I double-checked all the armaments settings in the cockpit and set up the Head-Up Display aiming data, adding two chinagraph pencil marks on the sight glass in case I suffered a display failure. These marks coincided with the weapon aiming point; one seen from my normal sitting position and a further one seen from a position crouching down behind gunsight camera, where I suspected I might be during the final stages of the attack! The marks were calculated for a delivery at 480 knots (550 mph) and a height of two hundred feet.

'At 0640 the order came booming over the flight deck broadcast system 'Stand clear of jet pipes and intakes: start the Sea Harriers'. I held up five fingers to my Plane Captain, to show that my ejection seat was now live and he replied with the signal to start as I heard the other eleven Pegasus engines winding up around me. As my engine stabilised at ground idle, I began my post-start checks and after a few minutes the flashing anti-collision lights showed that all twelve fighters were ready to go. There was time for a quick glance at the en-route map before *Hermes* turned into the prevailing westerly wind and the chocks and chain lashings were removed leaving the aircraft ready for take-off.

'As the hands on my watch moved, oh so sluggishly, towards ten minutes to the hour, I

A-4B C-226 of Grupo 5 De Caza flown by Teniente Juan J. Arrarás during air-to-air refuelling with KC-130 TC-69 *Parca 1* en route to attacking British shipping in the Falklands. This aircraft was brought down over Choiseul Sound on 8 June by an AIM-9L fired from the 800 Squadron Sea Harrier ZA177 of Flight Lieutenant Dave Morgan. It fell into the sea off Philimore Island killing Teniente Arrarás. (Museo Malvinas Oliva).

inserted the ships heading into my inertial navigation kit, rechecked: Flaps down, Armament Master Switch live, Nozzle Stop set at 35 °, Trim 3° nose up and Ejection Seat live. Exactly on time, the red traffic light below the window of Flying Control turned green and Tony Hodgson dropped his green flag to launch Andy Auld ahead of me. My machine was buffeted violently by Andy's jet efflux and as the grey bulk of his aeroplane threw itself off the end of the ski-jump, I taxied quickly forward to the take-off point. Tony, braced against the jet wash, gave me the green flag and with a final nod, I slammed the throttle open. Within one second, the power of the engine started to drag the locked wheels across the deck and in two seconds the jet was accelerating at a terrific rate towards the ramp, driven by the ten tons of engine thrust. As the end of the deck disappeared below me, I rotated the nozzles and leapt into the air some seventy knots below conventional stalling speed, accelerating rapidly into forward flight. Within ten seconds of launch, the wheels were up and I was in a tight left hand turn to join up with the leader, as the other aircraft got airborne at five-second intervals behind us.

'As we carried out a lazy orbit I watched the other aircraft cut the corner to join us and by the time we over flew *Hermes*, we were all together and starting to take up our defensive formation for the transit to the islands, still well over the western horizon. As we set heading, Andy called to Mike Blissett, the number three, 'Three, you have the lead, my nav kit has dumped' Mike replied, 'Sorry Boss, so has mine!'

'Mike was the Senior Pilot of the squadron, an experienced ex-Buccaneer man who was dying to get to grips with the enemy. He had very fixed ideas as to how fighter pilots should behave and I had already been bollocked for not eating my cheese rind at dinner. To this I had replied that, in my view, fighter pilots could eat what the hell they liked. It must have been galling for him to have to turn down the lead on this, our first mission.

'Andy then asked me to take the lead, but my kit had also dumped as I left the ski-jump. Faced with such a catalogue of unserviceabilities, Andy decided to retain the lead and in fact, we all managed to realign our systems on the way into the islands.

'The initial transit went without incident and we soon settled down into a flexible formation, with everyone scouring the rapidly lightening sky for enemy aircraft. After ten minutes on a westerly heading, we turned south towards our planned landfall at Macbride Head, the most north-easterly point of East Falkland. Almost immediately I saw a couple of dark shapes, hugging the water and closing rapidly from the east. I shouted, 'Break port! Bogies left 10 o'clock level' and we all pulled our jets into a screaming left-hand turn, to face the threat. As we turned through about forty-five degrees, I realised that the sinister shapes were, in fact, our three spare aircraft, now on their way to attack the grass airfield at Goose Green. As 'Fred' Frederiksen

Sea Harrier FRS.1 in the hover near a Royal Fleet Auxiliary (RFA) vessel. The RFA *Fort Austin* and *Fort George* operated in South Atlantic waters during the Falklands conflict.

hopped his formation over ours, we regained our heading and with pulses racing, caught our first sight of the islands.

'The coastline crystallised slowly into a dark scar separating the restless sea from the layers of cloud stacked over the high ground to the south. My first impression was of its similarity to the Scottish coast, which made it quite difficult to believe that we were not on one of our more familiar exercises, rather than bent on an errand of destruction. There was little time to dwell on this, however, as we made our way down the coast towards our Initial Point near Volunteer Beach. I can remember being struck by the complete absence of trees, the beauty of the white sand beaches and the sight of a lone cow pausing in mid chew to watch, with a detached interest, as we swept past on our deadly mission.

'After a couple of minutes, my Radar Warning Receiver suddenly emitted a high-pitched rattle. This was an indication that I had been illuminated by a radar-laid gun but after half a second, it fell silent and I never found out the origin of the warning. The area seemed completely uninhabited and I saw no anti-aircraft fire.

'At Volunteer Point, some ten miles north of the target, Red section detached to the southeast, to set up for their Loft attack. Gordie, 'Oges', Neill Thomas and 'Spag'[62] accelerated and ran into the mouth of Port William, pulling up some three miles out and releasing their weapons in a forty-five degree climb before banking away hard to the left, diving back down to low level and running out to the east. This attack put nine airburst bombs in the air and three with delayed action fuses. The airburst weapons were fused to explode fifty feet above the target and produced a devastating cone of shrapnel over a wide area, together with a very impressive fireball. We had planned a one-minute interval between the impact of these weapons and the arrival of the low-level attack to ensure that no one caught a 1,000lb bomb in the back of the neck as they ran over the target. To make doubly sure, 'Spag' had been briefed to give a 'Bombs gone' call as soon as he had completed his delivery.'

'That morning' says Chief Petty Officer Alfredo Paniagua of 1 Escuadrilla De Ataque 'we were surprised with the sound of bombing and explosions. We were spending the night in a hangar with a Beaver seaplane. Before reaching our combat outpost there were 'red alerts'. Twice we had to run the truck to take cover from the Sea Harriers. Finally we reached our aircraft, which by the grace of God, were intact in two small hangars next to the airport tower. Suddenly there appeared, four Sea Harriers. Within seconds we took cover. A Sea Harrier, while toss-bombing, altered course slightly to the right. If the airplane followed its original course, the bombs would have been very near. We all looked and agreed it was the hand of God that had saved us.'[63]

'As we approached the northern shore of Berkeley Sound, with only ninety seconds to run to the airfield' continues 'Mog' Morgan, 'Black formation split into two sections. Mike Blissett, Ted Ball and Bertie Penfold detached to the right, in order to set themselves up to approach from the northwest whilst Andy Auld and myself headed for the east side of the pair of nine hundred feet high mountains to the north of Stanley. I was aware of the increase in tension as I urged my machine as low as I possibly could, towards the craggy outline of Mount Low. Right on cue, I heard 'Spag' shout, 'Bombs gone!' just before we passed abeam Cochon Island. Ten seconds later, to my amazement, Andy Auld suddenly pulled his aircraft into a tight right-hand orbit. This was the manoeuvre that we had briefed to ensure separation from the Loft bombs, should we not hear 'Spag's call. Andy was the only one not to have heard the call and as I followed him around the orbit, I saw to my horror that the rest of the formation was continuing with the attack. As the other three disappeared over the saddle between Mount Low and Beagle Ridge, I realised that this put me as the last aircraft across the target. The very place that I had not wanted to be!

'There was not much time to worry about this, however; the die was cast and I just had to press on and do the best I could. As we crossed the south shoreline of the sound, I was aware of intense concentration as my eyes flicked between engine instruments, the Head-Up Display and the inhospitable rock strewn tussock grass that whipped past at over five hundred mph, a scant fifty feet below my aircraft. I was flying lower than I had ever done before.

'As I rounded the eastern slopes of the mountain, tucked behind and slightly to the left of my leader, the target came into view. At first, I couldn't take in the sight that greeted me in the thin grey dawn light. The airfield and the entire peninsular on which it was built seemed to be alive with explosions. Anti-aircraft shells carpeted the sky over the runway up to a height of one thousand feet, so thick that it seemed impossible for anything to fly through unscathed. Missiles fired from the airfield and outside the town, streaked across my path, long wavering white fingers chasing the previous attackers out to the southeast. Tracer fire criss-crossed the sky and as I watched, a number of guns turned in my direction sending feelers of scarlet probing towards me. The tracer curved lazily down, rather like a firework display and not initially conveying much feeling of imminent danger. I was reminded, in a bizarre way, of Antoine de Saint Exupéry's description of anti-aircraft fire over Arras in 1944. It was almost beautiful in a peculiar detached way. As the tracer fire got closer, however, it suddenly seemed to accelerate and began whipping past my ears, bouncing off the grey sea all around me. My brain froze in horror for a fraction of a second, as I realised that this wasn't a game anymore and someone was actually trying to kill me! The years of training then took over and as I took evasive action, I realised that I was automatically flying even lower.

'In London, Antje was at her desk, with the all-important, slim volume safe in her handbag.
Hold hard to the dear thought, for courage less
This tenderness is but a dress worn thin
Against the cold.

'I hauled the aeroplane hard left and then right, to pass between and below the Tussock Islands and Kelly Rocks, themselves only thirty feet high. This gave me a few seconds of perceived safety before I was, once again, over the open sea and pressing on towards the airfield

What occurs when a Mirage is hit by a Sidewinder AAM.

Grupo 6 de Caza Dagger A's at San Julián in late April. C-404 of
IIº Escuadron Aeromovil, the nearest aircraft (inset), one of nine
Argentine aircraft lost in action on 21 May was brought down by
an AIM-9L fired by Lieutenant Stevie Thomas of 801 Squadron
piloting FRS.1 ZA190. Mayor Gustavo Piuma Justo ejected.
Thomas then shot down Dagger C-403 flown by Capitán
Guillermo Donadille, who ejected before the aircraft crashed
close to Piuma's Dagger off Green Hill Bridge. Lieutenant
Commander 'Sharkey' Ward destroyed Dagger C-407 flown by
Primer Teniente Jorge D. Senn (who ejected successfully).

below the level of the sand dunes.

Keep jinking; never be predictable, fly as low as you possibly can.

'Inspection of the gunsight film later in the day showed that we were all flying at a height of between five and fifteen feet as we approached the target!

'I became aware that a number of Argentine soldiers were firing down at me from the sand dunes on the northern edge of the airfield, their bullets kicking up the water all around me. I raised the guns safety catch on the side of the stick and squeezed the trigger hard, expecting to hear the roar of the 30mm cannon and see the eruptions of smoke and flame amongst the enemy on the near horizon. But the guns would not fire! I thought that they must have jammed but realised later that in the heat of the moment I had failed to select the gun master switches on; a salutary lesson!

'As I crossed over the beach, I yanked back on the stick, flattening the defenders on the dunes with my jet wash and levelled at one hundred and fifty feet, the minimum height required for my cluster bombs to fuse properly. In slow motion, I took in the damage caused by the rest of the formation, the airport buildings were billowing smoke and a number of aircraft were lolling at drunken angles, obviously badly damaged. The fuel dump to my right was a storm of orange flame, under a gathering pall of oily black smoke and huge lumps of debris were still falling from the sky from the explosions of the 1,000lb bombs. The dust cloud from Andy's cluster bombs was drifting slowly away to the east, although I was not aware of his aircraft at all. One aircraft, which seemed undamaged, was a small civilian Britten-Norman Islander. I quickly lined up my bombsight raised the safety catch and mashed the release button, dispatching my three cluster bombs. The first bomb separated from the port, outboard wing pylon and after a short safety delay, blew off two sections of skin to expose the one hundred and forty seven bomblets. These were, in turn, ejected to form a cloud of death, which rolled over the airfield. One third of a second after the first weapon had dropped, I felt the thump as the second bomb left the centreline pylon mounted under the fuselage and fell away towards the target.

'Suddenly there was a huge explosion and the aircraft started vibrating like a road drill. It was impossible to read any of the cockpit instruments to check for engine damage but the aircraft still seemed to be flying. I now had a dilemma; in the GR.3, if you interrupted the release sequence, you had to close and reopen the safety catch before the rest of the weapons would release. I wasn't sure of the logic in the Sea Harrier's Weapon Aiming Computer and just pressed

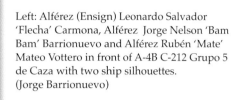

Left: Alférez (Ensign) Leonardo Salvador 'Flecha' Carmona, Alférez Jorge Nelson 'Bam Bam' Barrionuevo and Alférez Rubén 'Mate' Mateo Vottero in front of A-4B C-212 Grupo 5 de Caza with two ship silhouettes. (Jorge Barrionuevo)

Capitán Fassani, an IA.58A Pucará pilot and 34-year old Capitán Pablo Marcus Rafael 'Cruz' Carballo of Grupo 5, pilot of A-4B C-225 who on 21 May attacked HMS *Ardent* whilst lying in Falkland Sound. On 23 May Carballo was one of four A-4Bs in two waves that bombed the ill-fated HMS *Antelope* while on air defence duty at the entrance to San Carlos Water.

Left: On 21 May flying XZ455 'Fred' Frederiksen of 800 Squadron brought down Dagger C-409 with a AIM-9L fired from FRS.1 XZ455. Primer Teniente Héctor Luna ejected safely.

Right: On 6 May 39-year old Lieutenant Commander John Edward Eyton-Jones RN (pictured) and Lieutenant Alan Curtis on 801 Squadron flying a night patrol in two Sea Harriers from HMS *Invincible* were vectored to investigate a suspicious radar contact near the stricken hulk of HMS *Sheffield*. The weather was appalling, with rain, fog and low cloud. Both pilots failed to return.

the button and hoped. Instantly there was a very satisfying thump as the third bomb released and fell towards the aircraft on the concrete pan by the control tower. As soon as the last bomb had cleared the starboard wing pylon, I dived my machine for a large pall of smoke beside the Tower. I still have a very clear recollection of passing below the level of the tower windows as I entered the cloud of thick black smoke. When I returned to the airfield after the war was over, I discovered that the tower windows were only about twenty feet above the ground! I waited a short pause inside the smoke, with visibility absolutely zero and then pulled the aircraft into a maximum rate turn to the east. I was acutely aware that the ground rose gently to the south of the airfield and I didn't want to become a crater in the side of Canopus Hill.

'As I punched out of the smoke, my Radar Warning Receiver emitted a strident, high-pitched warbling note: I had been locked up by a radar-laid anti-aircraft gun! This was no time for gentle flying. I racked the aircraft into a bone-crushing six G break to the left through ninety degrees, to put the radar at right angles to my flight path and flicked out the airbrake to release a bundle of chaff into the airflow. Despite the Heath Robinson design, it did its job; the radar lost its lock and I was able to haul the vibrating aircraft back onto an easterly heading and run down the beach and out to sea and safety.

'As we cleared the target area, we changed radio frequency and checked in. To my amazement, everyone acknowledged the call. It seemed that we had all survived the attack, against all the odds and despite the last minute screw-up in the order of attack. I felt a wave of euphoria sweep over me and realised that I would have held myself personally responsible had any one died during the attack that was mainly of my own design. It suddenly struck me that I had been subconsciously studying each member of the formation, before we manned our aircraft, in an attempt to ascertain who would not be coming back.

'Once safely clear of land, I slowed down and climbed gently up to ten thousand feet; it was now time to pay some attention to my own predicament. I called *Hermes* and informed the Ops

Room that I might need a helicopter to pull me out of the water, if my damage was serious. I knew that there was a Sea King stationed about forty miles out from the carrier and he could be with me in a few minutes if the need arose. As I reduced speed, the vibration that had been shaking me so violently began to reduce to acceptable levels and I was able to check out the aircraft systems. I was amazed to find that everything appeared to be working correctly except a tiny gauge down by my left knee, which showed the position of the rudder trim. This, in itself was of no consequence to the operation of the aeroplane but gave me the first

Grupo 5 de Caza personnel with bombs painted with nicknames. (Atillo Maggi)

indication that damage had been done to the tail of the plane. On the way back to the ship, I carried out a low speed handling check, which proved to be normal and then began to consider my options.

'Once back in the overhead of *Hermes*, I circled at a height of five thousand feet whilst Ted Ball came up to inspect the damage. After a fruitless inspection of the left side of the aircraft, he swooped underneath the belly and formated on my right side. After a few seconds said 'Ah yes... you have got a bloody great hole in the tail'. I moved the control surfaces to and fro and he told me that they appeared to be working correctly but that there was a distinct possibility that the reaction controls, critical for vertical landing, might have taken some damage. This put me on the horns of a dilemma. It was obviously important to recover the aircraft if at all possible but if I could not control it in the hover, I might crash on the flight deck and cause an enormous amount of damage to both men and aircraft. I therefore decided to try a rolling vertical landing. This entails running the aircraft onto the deck with about fifty knots of forward speed. There is a distinct danger of running over the side into the sea! It does, however, reduce the reliance on the reaction controls and might give me the option to overshoot and try again if the controls jammed. Flyco accepted my decision and the Goofers prepared to watch the first ever RVL at sea.

'I waited until all the other Sea Harriers had landed safely and been lashed down securely, before starting my approach. I was feeling remarkably in control of the situation as I selected my undercarriage and flaps to the landing position, tightened my lap straps and set myself up for a straight-in approach to the back end of the ship. As I got closer, everyone on the flight deck started to creep forwards to get a better view of the impending arrival. This worried me somewhat as, if I lost control, I might take a lot of people with me. I pressed the transmit button and called 'Clear the deck, I'm coming in!' The flight deck crews soon got the message and headed rapidly for the comparative safety of the catwalks on either deck edge!

'I stabilised the speed at fifty knots and adjusted the power and nozzle angle to give me a gentle rate of descent towards the stern of the carrier. Slight adjustments were required to compensate for the rise and fall of the deck but I managed to achieve a good firm touchdown about fifty feet past the round down and braked cautiously to a halt before following the marshaller's signals to park at the base of the Ski-Jump. As the chain lashings were attached and I started my shutdown checks, I became aware that I was sweating profusely, despite the biting thirty-knot wind whipping in through the open cockpit canopy. The adrenalin flow also made it difficult to unstrap and undo the various connections to the ejection seat, before standing up on rather shaky legs to leave the cockpit. Outside, on the windswept and slippery deck stood a crowd of people staring at my tail. Having given a thumbs-up to Bernard Hesketh of the BBC, I walked a little unsteadily round the tail of the aircraft to inspect the damage. The hole was about six inches across and had obviously been caused by a 20mm shell, which had entered the left side of the fin at a grazing angle of about ten degrees and exploded, causing considerable damage to the right hand side of the fin and tail plane. After a little consideration, I realised that the shell had probably passed very close to my head and was actually only one of about forty per second coming from this particular gun. Lady Luck had certainly been on my side that morning.

'As we signed our aircraft back in, there was a mighty roar from outside on the flight deck, as Tartan section returned from Goose Green. After encountering us near Macbride Head, they had carried out a photographic reconnaissance run along San Carlos Water, before carrying out a low-level attack on the second airfield on East Falkland. They ran in so low that the defenders hardly had time to raise their weapons before they were past. One of the Argentine soldiers said that only madmen would fly so low and one of the pilots was surprised to come face-to-face with a horse as he ran in for the attack. The cluster bombs dropped by 'Fred' and Martin Hale destroyed one Pucara, killing the pilot and severely damaged at least two and possibly five others. Lieutenant Andy McHarg also dropped three 1,000lb retard bombs, one of which made a large crater in the grass runway.'

At Goose Green where a dozen IA-58 Pucarás were based, Lieutenant Commander 'Fred'

Frederiksen and the two other Sea Harriers, all armed with both retarded and cluster bombs, caught the Argentinean aircraft just as they were taxiing out for take-off. The Sea Harriers flew down Falkland Sound at wave-top height, past Fanning Head before turning southeast to climb over the peat plains of Lafonia for a perfectly-executed surprise attack which caught the defences completely unawares, a solitary burst from a machine-gun following the last Sea Harrier to leave. Pucará A-527 of III Air Brigade received a direct hit from a CBU and blew up, killing the pilot, 26-year old Teniente (Lieutenant) Daniel Antonio Jukic. Nine other Argentinean Air Force airmen were killed and fourteen seriously injured in the wake of the detonating bombs. Two more Pucarás were seriously damaged. The Falklands Government BN-2A Britten-Norman Islander light transport was damaged.[64] Bombs had hit the runways at both targets, but at Stanley they failed to penetrate the surface and were easily repaired. At Goose Green the craters were filled with earth and compacted.

'Thus ended the first sortie' concluded 'Mog' Morgan. We had flown a total of twelve Sea Harriers against two heavily defended airfields, delivered a total of thirty-six bombs, destroyed a large number of enemy aircraft, set light to a number of fuel storage sites and buildings and escaped almost unscathed. Euphoria now took over from the concern of the pre-dawn briefing. The first operational sortie, the most important in any pilot's life, was over. The rest would now be easier for everyone.'

Although no enemy-aircraft had been encountered, ground fire was intense. Short Tigercat SAMs were also launched, but without success. To quote one pilot: 'It was like Fireworks Night: they were hosing it around everywhere!' Lieutenant Commander Mike Blissett recalled; 'Nine aircraft hit the place, three sections of three. One section was toss-bombing with VT (variable time or delayed action) parachute-retarded bombs. One section went in on lay-down (level) attacks and one put down BL755 cluster bombs. We couldn't really hope to crater the runway, but we had a good go at the buildings and POL (petrol and oil supplies) and destroyed some aircraft on the ground.'

'That evening' concludes 'Mog' Morgan 'Brian Hanrahan sent his report of the raid back to the BBC, with a phrase that became famous:

A few hours after the Vulcan attack, it was Hermes' turn. At dawn, the Navy's Sea Harriers took off, each carrying three 1,000lb bombs. They wheeled in the sky before heading for the islands - at that stage just ninety miles away. Some of the planes went to create more havoc at Stanley, the others to a small airstrip called Goose Green, near Darwin, one hundred and twenty miles to the west. There they found and bombed a number of grounded aircraft mixed in with decoys. At Stanley, the planes went in low, just seconds apart. They glimpsed the bomb craters left by the Vulcan and they left behind them more fire and destruction. The pilots said there had been smoke and dust everywhere, punctuated by the flash of explosions. They faced a barrage of return fire, heavy but apparently ineffective. I'm not allowed to say how many planes joined the raid, but I counted them all out and I counted them all back.'

That same morning Flight Lieutenant Paul Barton RAF, who was attached to 801 Squadron, was flying CAP west of the task force with a second Sea Harrier flown by 39-year old Lieutenant Commander John Edward Eyton-Jones RN. They made contact with six Mirages, but the latter were at high altitude and had no intention of coming down to engage the Harriers in a sea-level combat. After a few minutes, both sides headed for their respective bases and it was left to two Royal Navy Sea Harrier pilots, Lieutenant Commander Nigel 'Sharkey' Ward and Lieutenant Mike Watson of 801 Squadron to fight an inconclusive action against the Argentines later in the morning. In the afternoon, however, keeping up the pressure on the Argentines, warships from the Task Force closed in and bombarded Stanley airport. This finally provoked retaliation from the Fuerza Aérea Argentina, which sent over a number of Mirage IIIEAs of Grupo 8 de Caza at high level. *Invincible* maintained two fighters airborne on CAP and two on deck alert. Presently Flight Lieutenant Paul Barton flying a Sea Harrier of 801 Squadron and his wingman, Lieutenant Steve Thomas RN, became involved in a series of inconclusive fights in and out of cloud with Mirages and Beech T-34C Turbo-Mentors of 4 Escuadrilla de Ataque.

The first major Argentine strike force comprised thirty-six aircraft (A-4Q Skyhawks, IAI Daggers, English Electric Canberras and Mirage III escorts) and was sent on 1 May, in the belief that the British invasion was imminent or landings had already taken place. Only a section of Grupo 6 de Caza (flying IAI Dagger aircraft) found ships, which were firing at Argentine defences near the islands. The Daggers managed to attack the ships and return safely. This greatly boosted morale of the Argentine pilots, who now knew they could survive an attack against modern warships, protected by radar ground clutter from the Islands and by using a late 'pop-up' profile.

By early afternoon, the Fuerza Aérea Argentina believed it knew where the carriers were operating and launched a series of strikes. Barton and Thomas were vectored onto one of the first 'inbounds' by the destroyer *Glamorgan*, finding two Mirages which were in trail, rather than battle formation over San Carlos Water. What followed was probably the closest thing to a traditional dogfight to be seen in the Falklands conflict. This engagement between two Sea Harriers and two Mirages flown by thirty-five-year old Capitán Gustavo García Cuerva and Primer Teniente (First Lieutenant) Carlos Eduardo Perona began virtually head-on, but the Harrier pilots were soon positioned behind the enemy aircraft. From five miles distance Steve Thomas saw what he thought was the failed launch of missiles from each Mirage but they could have been drop tanks being blown off. Thomas and Perona crossed very close to one another but as the Argentinean tried to follow visually, Barton, who was at 12,000 feet, got missile lock, fired an AIM-9L at a range of approximately one nautical mile (1850 metres) and saw the Sidewinder hit the rear fuselage of his Mirage IIIEA (1-015) and he claimed the first air-to-air kill of the conflict. It was the first victory in the air by a Royal Navy fighter since Lieutenant Peter Carmichael, flying a Hawker Sea Fury FB.11 from HMS *Ocean*, had shot down a Mikoyan-Gurevich MiG-15 'Fagot' fighter over North Korea in 1952. The Mirage burst into a ball of flame. Few pilots survived a strike by the AIM-9L but Perona was unhurt and managed to eject safely from his doomed aircraft. He dropped into the shallows north of Pebble Island and damaged both ankles as he struggled ashore and was rescued. Moments later Steve Thomas pulled high and right, passing about 100 feet over Cuerva's Mirage (I-019) which turned to port and dived, giving the Sea Harrier an AIM9 Sidewinder missile lock. Thomas fired and watched his missile pass close to the Mirage as it entered cloud. The Mirage's fuel tanks were ruptured and the control runs damaged when the missile detonated by proximity fuse close to the rear fuselage and Cuerva decided to divert to Port Stanley. As he approached the airfield he was shot down and killed by Argentine anti-aircraft fire.

As a result of this experience, Fuerza Aérea Argentina staff decided to employ A-4Q Skyhawks and Daggers only as strike units, the Canberras only during the night and Mirage IIIs (without air refuelling capability or any capable AAM) as decoys to lure away the British Sea Harriers. The decoying would be later extended with the formation of the Escuadrón Fénix ('Phoenix'), a squadron of civilian jets flying twenty-four-hours-a-day simulating strike aircraft preparing to attack the fleet.[65]

On that same afternoon two Argentine Dagger (Israeli-built Mirage IIICJ fighter-ground attack) fighter-bombers under radar control from an Argentine unit sited at Port Stanley attempted to attack Royal Navy forces which had been bombarding Port Stanley airfield. Two Sea Harriers on 800 Squadron on CAP flown by Flight Lieutenant 'Bertie' Penfold and his wingman, Lieutenant Martin Hale RN engaged them. The Daggers carried out a head-on attack, diving from 35,000 feet towards the Sea Harriers at 20,000 feet. At five miles the Daggers fired two old-model Sidewinder AIM-9Bs, one of which locked and began to home onto Martin Hale's aircraft. He broke downwards and dived for the cloud cover 15,000 feet below but saw the missile fall away clear of him. The Daggers had not seen the second Sea Harrier, however and 'Bertie' Penfold lined up behind one which had unsuccessfully fired at his wingman. It was C-433 of Grupo 6 de Caza flown by twenty-seven-year old Primer Teniente José Leónidas 'Pepe' Ardiles, a cousin of 'Ossie' Ardiles the Tottenham Hotspur and Argentine footballer, who turned gently across 'Bertie' Penfold's nose. With re-heat selected, Penfold fired at three miles against the fast-disappearing targets. Once again, the characteristic growl in the headphones from the locked-on AIM-9L - a flight time of three or four seconds - and a large explosion. He had hit Ardiles' Dagger, which exploded. No trace was found of the unfortunate pilot of C-433. The other Dagger, piloted by Capitán Carlos Alberto Rohde broke off and flew off for home.

Throughout the afternoon and evening, CAPs continued to be vectored onto radar contacts. HMS *Brilliant* reported a flight of three Canberras of Grupo 2 de Bombardeo from 'Almirante Zar' in Trelew, Chubut, that were attempting to attack the British ships carrying out a bombardment. Led by Capitán Alberto Baigorri, the flight approached at medium level and then descended to low altitude. As they descended to lower level the Canberras were positively identified by the fighter controller in *Invincible* who vectored two 801 Squadron Sea Harriers towards the enemy formation. Lieutenant Commander Mike Broadwater and his wingman, thirty-five-year old Lieutenant William Alan Curtis intercepted the Canberras at low level, Curtis firing at B-110, the left-hand wingman at a range of about 2,000 yards. The Sidewinder hit the Canberra, setting its engine and wing on fire and briefly continued to fly straight and level before it began a gradual descent towards the sea. At first Curtis thought that he had missed and fired a second Sidewinder just before Teniente Eduardo de Ibáñez (25) and his navigator/bombardier Primer Teniente Mario Hipolito González ejected but they perished in the freezing cold sea. The AIM-9L failed to impact because B-110 hit the sea before being caught by the missile. The other Canberras jettisoned their bombs and wingtip tanks before breaking away in opposite directions; Mike Broadwater chased the leader and fired two Sidewinders at 4,000 yards but both fell short. Low on fuel, he had to break off and return to *Hermes*.

This first day's combat had proved that the Sea Harriers could be positioned correctly by the controllers on the ships; that AIM-9L worked as advertised; and that the Royal Navy's training emphasis on air combat had been worthwhile.

Sea Harrier FRS.1 ZA177 of 800 Squadron about to land on board HMS *Intrepid*. The temporary closure of the metal landing strip at San Carlos on 13 June caused two CAP Sea Harriers to divert to *Fearless* and *Intrepid* in San Carlos Water. On 8 June Flight Lieutenant Dave Morgan RAF destroyed two A-4B Skyhawks of Grupo 5 De Caza flown by Teniente Juan José Arrarás (KIA) and Alférez José Daniel Vázquez with Sidewinders fired from ZA177.

Stanley was used as an Argentine strongpoint throughout the conflict. Despite the 'Black Buck' and Harrier raids on Stanley airfield (no fast jets were stationed there for air defence) and overnight shelling by detached ships, it was never out of action entirely.[66] The Vulcan carried out a third conventional bombing attack on 29 May; then another (XM597) carrying AGM-4.5 Shrike missiles attacked a radar installation on 31 May (the radar was hit, but unfortunately repaired before 8 June). Vulcan XM597 aborted its second mission on 3 June after launching two Shrikes which destroyed an Ejercito (Army) Skyguard radar acting as a fire control unit for one of the GADA601 anti-aircraft batteries close to Port Stanley. Their critical fuel state forced the crew to leave the area and assisted by a Nimrod MR.2 made a successful rendezvous with its Victor tanker about half-way back to Wideawake. However, the tip of the Vulcan's refuelling probe broke off during the AAR and the crew had to divert to the nearest available airfield, at Rio de Janeiro in Brazil. The aircraft and crew were held in Rio for a week while diplomatic channels buzzed before being allowed to depart for Ascension.

In the early hours of Sunday 2 May the Argentine carrier *25 De Mayo* the Flagship of Task Force 20 with aircraft of 3 Escuadrilla de Ataque, Escuadrilla Antisubmarina and 1 Escuadrilla de Helicopteros embarked sent off a Grumman S-2E Tracker, which located a group of four British Task Force ships. At 0500Z preparations were underway on the carrier for a dawn attack by eight A-4Q Skyhawks of 3 Escuadrilla de Ataque. Before the attack could take place a second Tracker from the *25 De Mayo* had to be launched at 0828Z to update the position of the RN ships but its radar developed technical problems and the crew were unable to find the British fleet. At about 0900Z the Skyhawk mission was finally abandoned. Later that day the cruiser *General Belgrano* was sunk with the loss of between 321 and 368 crew members by the Royal Navy submarine HMS *Conqueror*. The *25 De Mayo* left the area to return to coastal waters and soon afterwards her air group disembarked and the carrier returned to Puerto Belgrano and thereafter posed no threat to the British Task Force.[67]

Fog persisted much of the time for the first three weeks of May, which reduced the level of flying activity on both sides. At times it was impossible to see across the decks of the carriers and 100 per cent humidity was experienced for up to six days at a time.

'On four days, 4-8 May' recalls David Morgan 'we flew patrols around the fleet and the odd harassing trip over the islands just to let them know we were still there - nothing major and no-one was shot down for a couple of days. The weather was appalling. At that stage we were pulled up to sleep above the water level because of the submarine threat, which made life very uncomfortable. I was sleeping on the floor of the Captain's day-cabin with five other people. Most of us had camp beds but some of us were just sleeping on the cushions. There were about forty people sleeping in the bar. We got some sleep and, as the days progressed, you got a bit more because you were a bit more tired, but there were nearly always two or three action stations to disturb you. It was irritating, but because you always knew that this might be the time you were going to get a torpedo through the side, you didn't actually get irritated. It was, however, debilitating because you never really got very much sleep. Over the first couple of weeks we all got very, very tired and people were asleep in the cockpit on the deck. While I was flying on 8 May I broke cloud at ninety feet and all I could see were grey sea, grey ship and grey clouds, everything ill-defined, so I had to do a quick circuit at about sixty feet and plonk on deck. That was one of the worst days.'

The few Royal Navy Sea Harriers were considered too valuable by day to risk in night-time blockade operations. However, they did conduct nightly combat air patrols. Although the Sea Harrier 'Blue Fox' radar was largely ineffective when looking down for targets over land, it was very effective over sea for both air and surface targets. It was admitted after the war, that many Argentine missions were aborted because their aircraft detected the 'Blue Fox' radar in search mode. Sea Harrier operations, hampered by a good deal of bad weather, continued throughout the first week in May. The first Sea Harrier was lost in the conflict on Tuesday 4 May when three Harriers from *Hermes* mounted a heavy attack on the airstrip at Goose Green. Flight Lieutenant

Ted Ball RAF of 800 Squadron witnessed the destruction of the Sea Harrier flown by thirty-two-year old Lieutenant Nick Taylor RN, who was hit by radar-controlled 35mm AA cannon fire and he crashed in flames to his death. Nick Taylor's body, still in its ejector seat, was recovered by the residents of Goose Green and buried under Argentine supervision with full military honours very close to where he came to rest. Nick lived in Ryme Intrinseca near Yeovil with his wife Clare, who was a serving WRNS second officer at the time, and their son Harry.

On the afternoon of 4 May Flight Lieutenant David Morgan was on deck on the *Hermes* when he saw 'this great ball of smoke. It was a ship turning, about ten miles away, with its side all glowing white. There was a hell of a lot of smoke.' The Type 42 destroyer HMS *Sheffield* had received a direct hit from one of a pair of Aerospatiale AM.39 Exocet missiles fired from a range of about five nautical miles by one of three Super Etendard aircraft of the ANA's 2a Escuadrilla de Ataque.[68] The missile failed to explode on impact but fires from its burning fuel got out of control and the ship was abandoned. Twenty-one officers and men died. 'Then the casualties started coming back on to *Hermes*, continues 'Mog' Morgan, and everyone was rather subdued and gritting their teeth and saying, 'Okay, this is it. Let's go and have those bastards.' I think that was when the guys suddenly realised that the Argentineans were going to fight back and we were going to lose a lot of people, so we'd really got to go for it. We'd gone into action, we'd heard of a death but we hadn't seen it; our first actual contact with war was the survivors from the *Sheffield*.' Taken in tow by HMS *Yarmouth* on 9 May, *Sheffield* sank in stormy seas the following day.

Further Sea Harrier losses occurred in the early hours of 6 May, when two aircraft from *Invincible* are believed to have collided in cloud. Lieutenant Commander John 'E-J' Eyton-Jones and Lieutenant Alan Curtis flying a night patrol in two Sea Harriers were vectored to investigate a suspicious radar contact near the stricken hulk of HMS *Sheffield*. The weather

Capitán Pablo Marcus Rafael Carballo with pilots of Grupo 5. L-R: Alférez (Ensign) Jorge Nelson 'Bam Bam' Barrionuevo; Alférez Leonardo Carmona; Primer Teniente (1st Lieutenant) Carlos Cachón; Teniente (Lieutenant) Carlos Rinke. Argentina deployed 48 Skyhawks (26 A-4P, 12 A-4C and 10 A-4Q). Armed with unguided bombs and lacking any electronic or missile self-defence, Argentine Skyhawks sank the destroyer *Coventry* and the frigate *Antelope* as well as inflicting heavy damage on several others: Navy A-4Qs flying from Río Grande, Tierra del Fuego naval air station destroyed the *Ardent*. In all, 22 Skyhawks (10 A-4Ps, nine A-4Cs and three A-4Qs) were lost during the six-week-long war (eight to Sea Harriers, seven to ship-launched SAMs, four to ground-launched SAMs and AA fire (including one to 'friendly fire') and three to crashes. (Editorial Perfil)

was appalling, with rain, fog and low cloud. Both pilots failed to return from this mission and were never seen again.[69]

On 9 May Dave Morgan went off with thirty-six-year old Lieutenant Commander Gordon W. J. 'Gordie' Batt to drop high-level bombs on Stanley airfield. 'We couldn't drop the bombs because there was total cloud cover and we'd been told not to drop if we couldn't see the airfield because we might put them into Stanley itself. So we turned out from there. I found a contact on the radar, went to investigate and found a big stern trawler called Narwal, which the Argentineans had been using to gather information. We asked what to do and the Navy said, 'Engage it'. 'Gordie' fired a few rounds across her bows to try and stop her, unsuccessfully. So we dropped our 1,000lb bombs - we couldn't land back on board with them, so we had to drop them somewhere! The weather was pretty bad, which meant we had to drop them at low-level and since they were fused for an 18,000-foot drop we knew they probably weren't going to go off. Mine, in fact, missed and we thought Gordie's had too but it went into the fo'c'sle, down two decks and stopped. It didn't actually go off so we didn't know we'd hit her at that stage. She still kept going, so we each emptied 200 rounds of 30mm into the side of the bridge and the engine-room. On the last pass she stopped and hove to, so we radioed back and some Sea Kings went in to capture her. Unfortunately, she was blown to pieces. The engine-room was completely knackered and there were holes below the water line from the 30mm, so we just let her sink.'

One bomb, which failed to explode, killed one of the crew. The crew abandoned ship and were picked up by RN helicopters. The Narwal was later boarded and her crew taken prisoner; she sank under tow the next day. Also on 9 May, other Sea Harriers bombed military targets around Stanley and turned back an Argentine C-130 escorted by two Mirages.

'So far we'd shot down nine, the Special Forces had got a Pucará and the ships had claimed a few more' continues Dave Morgan 'but I personally hadn't shot anything down. Unlike in the Second World War, we didn't put anything on the side of the aircraft. Instead, we covered up the glass tiles behind the bar with a bit of hardboard and one of the stewards put up a stencil for everything hit. People were coming down from sorties, rushing down to the bar and saying, 'Another A-4 on there!' So morale was pretty high.'

On 12 May three waves of four A-4s attacked the Task Force, two of the aircraft being shot down. As was usual, these attacks came in the late afternoon, so that Argentine aircraft approaching from the west would have the setting sun behind them, while British attacks from

A-4B Skyhawk C-250 of Grupo 5 de Caza at BAN San Julián which was deployed to Rio Gallegos in early April. (Museo Malvinas Oliva)

the Task Force in the east were mainly at dawn. Sea Harrier strikes on the main airfield resumed on 16 May, when two Sea Harriers on patrol from *Hermes* strafed two Argentine support vessels in Falkland Sound: the *Rio Carcarania* at Port King Bay and the *Bahia Buen Suceso* at Fox Bay. The former ship caught fire and was abandoned.

By 15 May major reinforcements of men and equipment were well on their way from Ascension to join the Task Force. The convoy routes were kept under constant surveillance by Nimrod MR.2 aircraft now fitted with improvised flight refuelling equipment, which enabled patrols of the South Atlantic in flights lasting up to nineteen hours. The mission on 15 May by MR.2P XV232 on 201 Squadron, flown by Flight Lieutenant J. A. Cowan with the Nimrod Detachment Commander, Wing Commander David Emmerson, OC 206 Squadron aboard, required three air to air refuellings by Victor tankers. Refuelling twice en route, XV232 flew to a point 150 miles north of Port Stanley, turned west until it was sixty miles off the coast of Argentina and then turned north-east to fly parallel with the coast, the crew making a visual and radar search of the areas near the major Argentine naval bases. XV232 flew at altitudes of between 7,000 to 12,000 feet so as to be a visual deterrent to ensure the Argentine fleet remained in port. The Nimrod recovered to Ascension after a flight of nineteen hours five minutes, during which it had covered over 8,300 miles and broken the record previously set up by the Victor flight to South Georgia. This reconnaissance confirmed that no major units of the Argentine Navy were at sea, but seven more similar flights were made during the days that followed. The original Nimrod had not been intercepted, but as an insurance against possible action by the Argentine fighters, the Nimrods undertaking subsequent missions were armed with Sidewinder AAMs for self-defence.[70]

On 18 and 19 May the Sea Harrier reinforcements and RAF Harrier GR.3s of 1 (F) Squadron on board the SS *Atlantic Conveyor* which had headed south from Ascension, transferred to the two carriers. Soon after their arrival, it was decided to remove the Sidewinder launchers from the Harrier GR.3s and use them in the ground attack role for which RAF Harrier pilots were well trained. The first such sortie, on the afternoon of 20 May, was a spectacularly successful attack on fuel dumps near Fox Bay on West Falkland by Wing Commander Peter Squire the Commanding Officer of 1(F) Squadron and Squadron Leaders Robert Iveson and Jeremy Pook the flight commanders. The three Harriers attacked with cluster bombs and recovered successfully to the carrier.

In all, 150 missions would be flown by GR.3s against well defended targets, which led to them sustaining considerable battle damage and further losses. To reduce the effectiveness of AAA and SAMs, chaff bundles were stuffed between the bombs and pylons to produce a cloud of aluminium strips on weapon release. Chaff was also stowed between the airbrake and fuselage and later an internal chaff/flare cartridge system was fitted. Losses were also reduced by the radar warning receiver, which detected radars in areas where they were not expected and gave the pilot the opportunity to fly even lower to break radar lock. Although the FINRAE[71] system gave some capability to align the inertial system, it was not sufficiently accurate for navigation and attack; the GR.3 pilots were thrown back on the use of stopwatch-and-compass and fixed aiming marks. The GR.3s were therefore guided to a pre-planned landfall by Sea Harriers, which also staged diversionary attacks and on return to the ships they were guided back by the carrier's radar. These problems were solved from 9 June by the opening of an 800 feet airstrip near San Carlos, using aluminium planking and equipped with refuelling facilities. Here the GR.3s could align their platforms accurately while waiting for Army calls for close support. To prevent accidental losses due to the Rapier batteries around San Carlos mistaking the Harriers for enemy aircraft, it was arranged that they should always make their approaches with undercarriages down and lights on. This airstrip was also used as a means to extend the Sea Harriers' time on CAP and as an emergency landing site for any friendly aircraft short of fuel. On one occasion the runway was temporarily made unserviceable by a helicopter's downwash lifting it off the ground, but two Sea Harriers about to land there simply diverted to the assault ships *Fearless* and *Intrepid*. As the land battle progressed, several grass strips became available as emergency landing fields for V/STOL aircraft.

On 21 May major landings by 3 Commando Brigade on East Falkland from San Carlos Water brought a sudden increase in air activity, both by Argentine Skyhawk and Dagger fighters and helicopters, the latter also taking part in a number of night raids in various parts of the Falklands. As anticipated, Argentine air attacks on the invasion force were heavy. They began at 1030 hours local time and, unlike missions flown early in the month, came in extremely low to minimise radar warning and the effectiveness of the defences. Some Argentine aircraft inevitably got through the fighters and SAMs and attacks were pressed home with vigour. Lieutenant Commanders' Mike Blissett and Neil Thomas on 800 Squadron on a CAP from *Hermes* had just arrived on station over Falkland Sound to start their patrol when the air controller ordered them to go after three Skyhawks of Grupo 5 led by thirty-four-year old Capitán Pablo Marcus Rafael Carballo that had attacked the Type 21 frigate *Ardent* whilst lying in Falkland Sound and supporting Operation 'Sutton' by bombarding the Argentine airstrip at Goose Green. The Sea Harriers descended below the puffs of cloud at 1,500 feet and headed out over West Falkland. They failed to find the Skyhawks, but suddenly as he passed about 3½ miles east of Chartres Settlement, Blissett saw four A-4Q Skyhawks pass below him from left to right. The Skyhawks, from Grupo 4, had just crossed the coast on their way in. When their pilots sighted the Sea Harriers, they broke formation and jettisoned their bombs and underwing tanks, pulling hard to the right to avoid the attack. Blissett, who had safely ejected from a Sea Harrier on 1 December 1980 when he struck the top of the ski-jump on HMS *Invincible* during a flying display, called a break to starboard and the Sea Harriers ended up 800 yards astern of the Argentinean aircraft. He recalled:

'I was in the lead with Neil to my left and about 400 yards astern, with all of us in a tight turn. The Skyhawks were in a long echelon, spread out over about a mile. I locked a Sidewinder on one of the guys in the middle and fired. My first impression was that the missile was going to strike the ground as it fell away - I was only about 200 feet above the ground. But suddenly it started to climb and rocketed towards the target. At that moment my attention was distracted somewhat as a Sidewinder came steaming past my left shoulder - Neil had fired past me' which I found very disconcerting at the time! I watched his 'Winder chase after another of the Skyhawks, which started to climb for a patch of cloud above; then the aircraft disappeared into the cloud with the missile gaining fast.'

Both Sea Harrier pilots had hit their targets; one exploding and the other burning and going out of control. Teniente Nestor Lopez ejected but his parachute failed to open and he was killed on impact with the ground. Teniente Daniel Manzotti's body was never found. Mike Blissett failed to get missile lock on his second target and fired all his 30mm ammunition to no obvious effect. Neil Thomas could not get missile lock on his second target either and stressed to pilots on *Hermes* on his return the need to fire both missiles when multiple targets appeared.

Throughout the day Argentine aircraft continued to attack the warships guarding the amphibious shipping. HMS *Brilliant* vectored Lieutenant Commander Nigel 'Sharkey' Ward and Lieutenant Steve Thomas onto fast-moving contacts as they crossed the coast from the west. Sharkey and Steve saw three Daggers approaching and carried out a copy-book attack using the Sea Harrier's low-level high-energy manoeuvrability to get behind the Argentine aircraft, whose pilots had no time to recover from their surprise: all three were destroyed.

As 'Sharkey' Ward turned to fly back to *Invincible*, he saw three Skyhawks heading down Falkland Sound towards a burning frigate; he alerted *Brilliant* and the CAP arriving on task from *Hermes*. This was flown by Lieutenant Clive 'Spaghetti' Morrell of 800 Squadron and Flight Lieutenant John Leeming RAF. They dived fast but were unable to intercept before the naval Skyhawks released their bombs on HMS *Ardent*. Morrell saw the bombs explode on the frigate. 'Having seen the bombs explode, I deduced that the attackers would probably exit going south-west down the Sound. I looked to where I thought they would be and they appeared, lo and

Capitán Pablo Marcos Rafael Carballo of Grupo 5 de Caza in the cockpit of A-4B Skyhawk C-239 with the yellow ship silhouette dated '12.5.82' denoting the claim for sinking HMS *Brilliant*, which was not sunk (Carballo did not take part in the action). On 23 May 'Cruz' Carballo, Teniente Carlos Rinke, Primer Teniente Luciano Guadagnini and Alférez Hugo Edgardo Gomez made attacks on HMS *Antelope* in San Carlos Water and they put two 1,000lb bombs into the Type 21 frigate. Neither bomb detonated but during attempts to defuse them in the early hours of 24 May one of the bombs exploded and subsequent fire reached a store of Sea Cat missiles. The explosions continued overnight and Antelope broke in half and sank that day. Carballo's Skyhawk was badly damaged in the action and he considered ejecting but managed to nurse the ailing jet home to Rio Gallegos safely. Guadagnini, in C-242, was shot down and killed by a SAM.

behold, below a hole in the clouds.' Near Goose Green Teniente de Fregata Marcello Gustavo 'Loro' Márquez in the last Skyhawk saw 'Spaghetti' Morrell's Sea Harrier drop in behind the aircraft ahead of him. Later Capitán de Corbeta Alberto Philippi reported: 'A couple of minutes after attacking I thought we had escaped, when a shout from Marquez froze my heart: 'Harrier! Harrier!' I immediately ordered the tanks and bomb racks to be jettisoned in the hope we would be able to reach the safety of cloud ahead of us.' Speeding through the narrows at low altitude, Marquez appeared to be concentrating his attention on the fate of the two Skyhawks in front of him. He did not notice John Leeming slide into position for a gun attack from behind on his aircraft. Leeming recalled: 'He was at about zero feet. I was at zero plus fifty. Still there was no sign that he had seen me; he was heading out as fast as he could. I fired a couple of tentative bursts and then my third splattered the sea around him. He must have realized what was happening then, because about a second later he rolled hard to starboard. But by then it was too late: I was within about 200 yards. Before he could start to pull round I put my sight on his cockpit, pressed the firing button and, as the first rounds struck, the aircraft exploded. I think the engine must have broken up because the aircraft just disintegrated.' Morrell's first Sidewinder destroyed the Skyhawk flown by Philippi, who ejected safely but his second missile would not lock and he had to close and use his guns on Teniente de Navio José 'Cacha' Arca, causing damage so severe that the Argentinean knew that he would not make the mainland. Arca flew to Port Stanley and he too ejected safely.

In the course of the main landing two Royal Marine Gazelles were brought down by ground fire, three of the four crew members were killed and a number of warships were damaged but no troop transports were hit and by nightfall 3,500 troops and nearly 1,000 tons of stores had been successfully landed around San Carlos Water and consolidating the beachhead began. That evening however, Aermacchi MB.339s from Stanley attacked HMS *Ardent* which was attacked by at least three waves of Argentine aircraft on 21 May, with bombs and 68mm rockets and the ship sank the next day.

Earlier in the day Squadron Leader Jerry Pook, accompanied by Lieutenant Martin Hare had taken off to fly in support of the amphibious assault in San Carlos Water. While Sea Harriers flew CAP the two GR.3 pilots were briefed to attack enemy helicopters in the Mount Kent area. They destroyed two Pumas and a Chinook on the ground before Hale was hit by several bullets and returned to the carrier, covered by Pook. Soon afterwards, two more Harrier GR.3s flown by Wing Commander Peter Squire and Flight Lieutenant Jeff Glover were briefed to provide close air support for the forces in the landing area. While searching for defensive positions at Port Howard, Glover's aircraft was destroyed by a 'Blowpipe' missile and was the first RAF Harrier G.3 lost in the conflict. Glover ejected, sustaining a broken arm and collar bone and a badly bruised face. He was captured by Argentine troops and flown to the military hospital at Comodoro Rivadavia, eventually being released on 8 July.

In mid-afternoon 'Fred' Frederiksen, leading a flight of two Sea Harriers with Sub-Lieutenant Andy George as his wingman, spotted a flight of four Dagger ground attack aircraft approaching the Task Force and closing behind the last of these, at low level and under a layer of cloud, he launched a Sidewinder to bring down Primer Teniente Héctor Luna's jet. He then sprayed the leader of the enemy formation with cannon fire. Luna ejected at low level and was lucky to land on the side of a mountain, from where he was rescued. The next day Frederiksen, now flying with Lieutenant Martin Hale, strafed the patrol vessel *Rio Iguazu*, which was carrying field guns and ammunition to reinforce the Argentine defences, driving it ashore among the kelp. He was mentioned in despatches.

Almost all the combats on 21 May took place at very low level - in most cases at about fifty feet. Sea Harriers and surface-to-air missiles were claimed to have destroyed nine Mirages and/or Daggers, five A-4s and three Pucará's. The Chief of Defence Staff later reported that 'the air battle was a complete victory'. Argentine air losses had amounted to five Skyhawks, five Daggers, two Pucarás and the helicopters knocked out by Pook and Hale.

On 22 May the Harriers of 1 Squadron attacked the airfield at Goose Green and two Sea Harriers found the *Rio Iguazu*, an Argentine patrol boat, in Choiseul Sound and strafed it, causing it to beach. On the following day the Harriers were detailed to bomb the airstrip at Dunnose Head on West Falkland, which was thought (wrongly) to be used by Argentine transport aircraft and the bombs caused some damage to local property. Flight Lieutenant David Morgan recalled:

'The morning of 23rd May dawned grey and overcast with regular heavy showers sweeping across the bleak landscape of the Falkland islands and making the flight deck of HMS *Hermes* a cold and even more inhospitable place than normal. I had been airborne before dawn to fly a Combat Air Patrol at low level over the slate grey waters of Falkland Sound in an effort to stop Argentine attacks on the armada of ships supporting the landings in San Carlos Water. The first sortie was uneventful, although it was very unnerving as we had been forced to fly our CAP below the 500 feet cloud base in poor visibility and at low speed to economise on fuel because of our range from the carrier. (By this stage we'd moved our CAP from round the fleet to around the landings, so we were actually capping at very long range - 200 miles plus - so we were pretty short of fuel). This made us very vulnerable to any enemy aircraft that might come across us in the mist and it was reassuring to know that my number two was as keyed up as I was, with his eyes constantly straining and his senses ready for instant explosive action, should we see a 'bogey'. We were both relieved when the time came to climb above the murk and head home into the early morning sun, to return to HMS *Hermes* and a hearty breakfast.

'By the time the sun was approaching its zenith, the weather had changed dramatically, leaving the islands bathed in bright sunshine with only small amounts of cumulus cloud scattered here and there in east - west lines. My wingman for this sortie was Flight Lieutenant John Leeming, an old buddy of mine from the RAF Germany Harrier force, who had volunteered for exchange service when the conflict had started, arriving five days earlier. John had only had a handful of hours in the Sea Harrier before heading for the South Atlantic and still had to get to grips with the weapons systems. Two days earlier he had been unable to fire a Sidewinder missile at a Skyhawk and eventually shot it down with guns, at very close range, nearly blowing himself to pieces in the process. We subsequently discovered that the reason for the missile not firing was that no-one had shown him how to select it properly! John was unfortunately killed in an accident after the Falklands.

'As we flew overhead Port Stanley on the way to our CAP station, we were greeted by a barrage of anti-aircraft fire, despite the fact that we were above 30,000 feet. The 35mm guns were not very accurate at this height and although the black mushrooms of their explosions looked rather frightening as they burst all around us, a gentle weave was all that was required to render them ineffective. In the distance we could see the silver specks of the ships in San Carlos Water and the toy-like outlines of Pucará attack aircraft on the grass strip at Goose Green. Once past Goose Green we let down to 8,000 feet and set up our patrol on a north-south axis over the 2,000 feet mountains of West Falkland, in an attempt to intercept any aircraft flying through the valleys to attack the landings. The Blue Fox radar was not designed for use over land, so we had to try to guess where the enemy would come from and put ourselves in a position to acquire them visually and engage them, before they reached their targets.

'Flying a medium level patrol is rather more relaxing than being at low level because it is easier to be sure that you and your wingman are not being threatened by a 'bogey'. It also gives you the opportunity to accelerate rapidly as you dive onto the tail of a low level raider and get a missile in the air before you are seen. What we did not realise, as we cruised back and forth, searching the rolling scree and peat bog for tell-tale flashes of movement, was that the enemy were not aware of the change in the weather and would not be airborne for another couple of hours. The Director who was controlling us, asked us to confirm our position from time to time and it was obvious that he, like us, was feeling that things were rather too quiet to last. He couldn't use his radar because of the surrounding hills and was relying on us to pick up and report any raids as they crossed the mountains. This would give them a maximum of three minutes warning of attack. Sooner him than us! There was a great feeling of empathy between us and we were very conscious of being the only ones standing between him and an enemy air attack.

'Unbeknownst to us, although the Argentine fighters were not airborne, there was, indeed, some air activity - and it was heading in our direction. A formation of three Argentine Puma helicopters had set off the previous evening, to transport a vital cargo of Blowpipe anti-aircraft missiles and mortar ammunition from Stanley to Port Howard. They had turned back in Falkland Sound when they stumbled across an unidentified ship in poor weather and spent the night at Goose Green. The following day, after the weather had improved, they set off once more for Port Howard. Because of the importance of their cargo, the lead Puma had the company commander on board and they were escorted by an Augusta 109A gunship, flown by the deputy commander. The Augusta 109A was a fast and very manoeuvrable helicopter which carried two pods of 2.75 inch rockets and a couple of forward firing machine guns. This could make life quite embarrassing for us in the right hands. Any fighter pilot who was shot down by a helicopter would never be able to hold his head up in a bar again! This formation crossed the Sound from Goose Green to Shag Cove and had just turned onto a northerly heading, with only about four minutes to go to their destination when their luck changed abruptly.

'John and I had just completed a turn at the southern end of the CAP over the Mount Maria area and were cruising slowly towards Port Howard at 8,000 feet when suddenly a movement caught my eye; a mechanical movement quite alien to the snipe-rich bogs and barren escarpments. The flash of sun on a helicopter rotor disc. There, a couple of miles south of me; was a helicopter skimming over a small inlet at Shag Cove, a few feet above the glassy water. I saw it! I yelled to John and asked the controlling ship to confirm that there were no friendlies in the area. At the same time I dived rapidly down to about 50 feet above the valley and accelerated to about 500 mph, running head-on towards the helicopter in an attempt to identify it.

A Harrier GR.3 safely down on the deck of HMS *Hermes* in adverse weather conditions.

Adrenaline pumped as the distance between us closed rapidly until, at about 500 yards I realised that it was a Puma and therefore, an Argentine.

'I yelled 'Hostile, hostile!' over the radio and John replied that he had a further three in a line behind the leader and was engaging the gunship escort. It was too late to get a missile off and I couldn't actually push the aircraft down low enough to get the guns on him so I just flew straight at it, passing as low as I dared over its rotor head. As I passed about ten feet above the enemy, I pulled the Sea Harrier into a 5G break to the left in order to fly a dumbbell back towards it for a guns attack. I strained my head back and to the left under the crushing pressure of the G forces and I saw the Puma emerge from behind me. It was flying in an extremely unstable fashion and after a couple of seconds, crashed heavily into the side of the hill, shedding rotor blades and debris before rolling over and exploding in a huge pall of black smoke. I was absolutely amazed! We had previously discussed using wing-tip vortices as a method of downing helicopters and it was obviously efficacious, although I had not particularly been aiming to try the method out at the time.

'As I reversed my turn to the west, I saw John diving down towards a deep stream bed running up into the mountains. As he recovered from the dive, the bottom of the ravine erupted in a storm of explosions from his 30mm cannon but I could not see the target. As I began my attack, John told me that it was an Augusta 109 helicopter gunship in the stream bed 100 yards east of his fall of shot. As I was squinting through the head-up display to find the target I wondered how he could have missed by such a massive distance. This was soon made clear by his next transmission: 'What the hell is the sight setting for guns Moggie?' We had discovered another hole in his briefing on the differences between the Harrier and Sea Harrier weapons system!

'My first attack missed, as the pilot manoeuvred his helicopter towards the relative safety of the mountains. I had also fired at rather excessive range in my excitement, which had degraded the accuracy of the guns. My second pass put explosions all around the Augusta 109A but didn't hit it. I pressed my third attack until the helicopter was filling the sight and I could clearly see the rocket pods attached to either side of the fuselage. As I pulled into a 5G recovery, I saw the target disappear under a hail of sparkling explosions from my cannon, followed shortly afterwards by the massive orange bloom of a secondary explosion from the fuel tanks at the rear of the aircraft. The pilot had failed in his task of defending the formation and had paid the price of running away, rather than trying to engage us with his rockets.

'As I turned away from the burning wreckage, John located a Puma near the smoke of the first helicopter and dived down towards it. He had emptied his cannon in his previous attacks but flew very low over the new target to show me its position. I followed him down towards the piece of heather that he had indicated but could see nothing. As I was about to recover, I realised that my gunsight was sitting directly over a Puma which had shut down on the rough ground and was being rapidly evacuated by a number of highly excited Argentine soldiers. I pulled the trigger to fire my cannon but only two rounds remained. By a combination of good luck and good shooting, one of these rounds impacted the tail of the Puma, rendering it unflyable. We rejoined over Falkland Sound in the climb to 36,000 feet for our return to *Hermes*. As we settled down, checked our fuel and began to think about our recovery, our replacement CAP from HMS *Invincible* called us on the radio. We passed them the location of the helicopters and they set off to complete the destruction of the second Puma.

'We had managed to destroy 20% of the enemy helicopter force at a time when they were desperately in need of such transport but I was not particularly happy at the destruction of the first Puma as I believed that the crew had perished in the crash. (A visit to the site of the action, after the conflict was over, showed the importance of the cargo - he'd had 200 rounds of 120mm mortar on board which explains why he'd gone bang! - and the subsequent information that the crew had survived also made me feel considerably better! It was also ironic that the aircraft I was flying on this sortie was the same one that I had been flying on the first raid of the war.

A Dagger making a run across the bows of British merchant vessels off the Falklands.

Then, the Argentines had put a hole through the tail with a 20mm anti-aircraft gun: This time, the boot had been on the other foot!')

'I reported to the bridge to brief the Captain on our achievements and was given information that made me even more concerned: the ship had intercepted a message saying that Jeff Glover was being transferred from Port Howard to Stanley by Puma at about the time of our engagement. For a couple of days I thought that we might have killed one of our own pilots but eventually, to my great relief, we received intelligence that he had been transferred to the mainland by Hercules.

Also on 23 May, 1 Squadron's Harriers carried out several armed reconnaissance sorties and made a three-aircraft attack on the airstrip at Pebble Island. The first Argentine attacks did not take place until about 1645Z and fewer than half of the planned 46 sorties were successful in reaching the target area. Shortly before 1900Z, a pair of Daggers were running in from the north of Falkland Sound when, presumably warned of the nearby presence of two Sea Harriers, they aborted the mission and returned along their outbound track. They were sighted over Pebble Island by Lieutenant Commander 'Andy' Auld and his wing-man Lieutenant Martin Hale. The leading Dagger was travelling too fast to be caught but C-437 flown by twenty-eight-year old Teniente Héctor Ricardo Volponi was well over a mile behind and within missile range of Hale who fired a Sidewinder from a distance of about 1,000 yards behind the Dagger. The missile exploded as it hit in the jet-pipe area. The Dagger disintegrated at low level, killing Volponi, the wreckage coming to ground on the western side of Elephant Bay two miles north of Pebble Island settlement.

That night a fourth Sea Harrier was lost, taking off with three other Sea Harriers from *Hermes* about an hour before midnight to attack Stanley airfield once more. Lieutenant Commander 'Gordie' Batt was last off the deck, but was then seen to explode ahead of the carrier. The cause of this accident, which occurred about ninety miles northeast of Port Stanley, was never established. His DSC was gazetted posthumously. Dave Morgan says 'I've got my diary for the day: 'Could've been a good day but this evening 'Gordie' Batt actually flew off the front of the carrier on a night-bombing raid, exploded and went into the water!' He was flying the aircraft in which I'd shot the helicopters down, which was also the one I'd been hit in over Stanley.'

Next morning four Harrier GR.3s on 1(F) Squadron carrying 1,000lb retarded bombs and two Sea Harriers flown by Neill Thomas and Mike Blissett on defence suppression attacked Port Stanley airfield. The Sea Harriers attacked from the north-east and toss-bombed, clear of the Argentine guns and missiles. They succeeded in distracting the defences for long enough to allow the first pair of GR.3's a clear run in from the north-west with their retarded bombs. The other pair attacked from the west and although bombs were dropped on the runway it was not put out of action. All the Sea Harriers and Harriers had recovered safely to *Hermes* by 1300Z.

800 Squadron's next action of the day came shortly afterwards when Lieutenant Commander 'Andy' Auld and twenty-seven-year old Lieutenant Dave Smith were launched for CAP.' 'Normally, an hour before launch time' recalled Smith, 'all the pilots involved crowd into Number One briefing room, where along with the helicopter crews launching at the same time, we receive a brief on the ship's position, course and speed and the various frequencies and call signs. After signing out and having aircraft allocated we go out onto the flight deck, which always seems to be absolute bedlam! Apart from the normal thirty knots of wind across the deck, there are helicopters landing and taking off, chiefs yelling and screaming at God knows who, aircraft being shuttled from one side of the deck to the other and back again (for no apparent reason). On top of all this, you are probably late because the engineers weren't ready and you've now got five minutes to start and get airborne.

'Damn! They've decided to move my aircraft just as I am doing my external checks. Never mind. I'll do them on the roll. Finally my plane checked and lined up on the centre line, with four minutes to go, I leap into the cockpit, frantically struggling with the tangle of straps and umbilicals and rush round the internal checks. I have to be especially careful now as it is when one is being hassled like this that one forgets something really important. Three minutes to go. I can see 'Wings' (Commander (Air)) looking at his watch - 'why isn't Red 4 started yet?' I bet he is saying... Well, here we go; checks complete; boosters on, start selected, master pressed. HP on - there she goes - jet pipe temperature rising - she's burning and turning. The navigation kit takes two minutes to align, so without further ado I initiate that process and sit it out. There are one-and-a-half minutes to go, with the sweat pouring off me.

'Right, they are unlashing me now; let's check my ejection seat pin's out; all takeoff checks complete and the navigation kit on line just in time with fifteen seconds to go. The flight direction officer is giving me the wind-up signal - I slam the engine to half power in three to four-and-a-half seconds - the nozzles checked and I accept the launch by showing the flat of my hand in the canopy. His hand drops and I smash the throttle to the firewall. Ten tons of angry power arrives in the small of my back in just under two seconds and the Harrier roars down the deck. A quick glance at the rpm and temperature - looking good - in less than three seconds my speed

Primer Teniente Luciano Guadagrini of Grupo 5 de Caza refuelling from KC-130 TC-70 en route to the Falklands. Guadagrini was KIA on 23 May in C-242 by a SAM during or immediately after the attack on *Antelope*. (Museo Malvinas Oliva)

is around ninety knots and here comes the ramp - whoosh - we're off! Nozzles rotated smartly to thirty-five degrees and hold everything. Trying to resist the temptation to touch the controls - she's reaching the end of the trajectory and I'm gently easing the nozzles forward, landing gear and flaps up and the aircraft is accelerating through 400 knots before I know it. A quick frequency change to call 'D' (the fighter direction officer), holding her down at 200 feet until I've got 600 knots and now pulling back on the stick and pointing the nose at the top of an enormous cloud above me. She passes through 15,000 feet effortlessly and I roll over on my back to bring my heaven-ward rate of ascent under control. 'D' has given me a vector and off I go looking for the attacking aircraft.'

By now HMS *Broadsword* and HMS *Coventry* had moved to a position north of Pebble Island in order to provide better radar cover to the north and north-west. Around 1415Z *Broadsword* directed the two Sea Harriers towards an incoming flight of four Grupo 6 de Caza Daggers flying low and fast over Pebble Island, heading towards San Carlos Water.

David Smith continues: 'The Boss and I arrived in the zone just as an air raid warning 'Red' was called. This is the call put across all radio nets when either radar or electronic surveillance has picked up the enemy inbound. You can imagine how the adrenalin starts to flow, as to date we had always been outnumbered two to one by the Argies. Suddenly, *Broadsword* called us and vectored us hard toward the west at full speed. They had detected a low-level raid of unknown strength at very high speed thirty miles away.

'Looking for the enemy is a 'cat-and-mouse' game. Who can see the other on his radar first and turn it to his advantage. I can hear his radar sweep on my warning receiver - it's telling me he is off to the right, slightly - and there he is - a tiny blip. Now we close each other with a closing speed of just under 1,000 knots. It is important that I see him by ten miles as I can then organise the fight to my advantage. Suddenly, through the radar lock cross in the head-up display, a tiny speck appears, initially stationary and then growing with incredible speed. He's obviously seen me too as I can see him turning towards. Seconds later there is a blue/grey blur less than 100 feet from my canopy as we cross and slam our aircraft into the first of a series of body-pounding combat turns, every muscle and sinew straining as we endeavour to fly the aircraft to its very limits under the crushing effect of seven 'G's. The most important thing is not to lose sight of him, even if it requires moving your head and neck into positions you wouldn't believe possible.

'By now my heart was beating away at full speed and my breathing almost to hyperventilation. I slammed the throttle to keep tucked in about 100 yards on the Boss' wing as he hauled round in a high 'G' turn and accelerated toward the threat. As we passed through about 550 knots we descended to about fifty feet above the sea and started a hard turn toward the now rapidly closing enemy. Suddenly the Boss called 'visual' with four Daggers very fast, very low. As I picked them up, the Boss fired his first missile, followed quickly by his second. Two Daggers erupted into enormous fireballs.' Mayor Luis Puga (in C-419) and Capitán Raul Diaz (in C-430) ejected successfully. Both of Auld's Daggers fell into the sea north of Pebble Island.

'No time to gawk - the second pair were breaking hard right and I was the only one with missiles to fire. I picked up the number three and pulled hard into his turns. As my missile 'cross' flashed across his tail, the angry growl of 'acquisition' pounded my ears. A quick press of the lock button and the missile locked and tracked - safety catch up and - fire. A great flash and the Sidewinder leapt off the rails, homing straight onto the target. Another flash and fireball. The Dagger broke up and impacted the ground in a huge burning inferno.' Teniente Carlos Castillo (in C-410) was killed. The wreck of that aircraft is thought to lie on the slopes of First Mount on the western edge of Elephant Bay near the Pebble Island settlement.

'The fourth Dagger was still about somewhere and as neither of us could see him, he was a threat. Then suddenly I saw him under the Boss, heading west at high speed. I turned hard, calling the Boss to break with me to cover my tail. We followed him flat out for several minutes, just out of missile range, until, short of fuel, we had to pull out.' The fourth intruder jettisoned its bombs and drop tanks and headed for home.

'I can see *Hermes* on my radar sixty miles away so I turn towards her and up the speed to 540 knots. A quick glance at the navigation computer confirms that it will take just over six minutes to reach her and use 1,000lbs of fuel. That will get me off *Hermes* with five minutes to 'slot' with 1,200lbs of fuel remaining. That in turn should give me about two to three minutes of fuel in the hover to sort myself out and land before the beast runs out of fuel!

'I returned to the ship with extraordinary mixed feelings. Delighted at having prevented the raid from getting through and at getting my first 'kill' but saddened and horrified at witnessing the savage, quick death of a fast jet combat at low level. There's no doubt - no one wins a war. Wasn't it the Duke of Wellington who said, 'The one thing more tragic than defeat is victory'?

'I see the ship and am cleared by the controller to the 'low wait.' This is an orbit off the ship's port quarter at 1,000 feet, where I now fly at endurance speed until my 'slot' time at 2½ minutes to 'Charlie' (land-on time) 'slot', which involves flying past the ship's bridge at 600 feet and break down-wind to land. It is from now on that the pilot of a Harrier has really to switch on and keep his act together. The flight profile has to change from being fully wing borne, as in a conventional aircraft, to fully jet borne in the hover, at the same time as flying a tight fuel critical circuit to land on a small, sometimes highly mobile deck.

'So, with my speed decaying reluctantly through 300 knots, I bang down full flap, steadying the jet downwind at 800 feet. Speed below 250 knots - landing gear going down and forty

Harrier GR.3s of 1(F) Squadron and FRS.1s of 800 and 826 Squadrons on the heaving *Hermes* flight-deck in late May. From bottom: GR.3 XZ997/31; XV789/32 and FRS.1 ZA194 (behind). The latter, flown by Lieutenant Martin Hale, destroyed a Grupo 6 de Caza Dagger (C-437) which crashed on the west side of Elephant Bay on Pebble Island on 23 May. The pilot, Teniente Héctor Ricardo Volponi, was killed. XV789 suffered battle damage during a rocket attack in the Port Stanley area on 31 May when it was flown by Wing Commander Squire and had to have an engine change on *Hermes*. (MoD)

degrees of nozzle selected. Turning finals now, checking 'four greens' to indicate landing gear down and locked, hydraulics okay and duct pressure reading to my roll reaction controls. Halfway round the turn and descending; glide path looks good, angle of attack pegged at 8 units and power coming on as I take sixty-degrees nozzle. Speed decaying through 200 knots, water injection coming on and rolling out on the final approach. Nozzles to the hover stop and the speed now rapidly decaying and power coming on to replace that wing lift with power. I am paying very careful attention to the angle of attack and the sideslip indicator now, as this is the most dangerous phase of flight in the Harrier. Coming up alongside the ship and stabilising in the hover.

'I glance to check the engine and fuel. The latter is rushing down now at about 200lbs a minute as I hold nearly full power to hold the hover. Once steady, I move sideways until over the deck and once established over my landing spot, quickly down. Bang on the deck - throttle slammed closed and nozzles fully forward - taxi into a clear area where I am once again lashed to the deck and can shut down.

'The air raids on the Fleet supporting the troops in the islands have been coming thick and fast and it has been our continuous task to provide a combat air patrol to get these guys. I simply cannot describe the moments of sheer, angry frustration when the raids slip our grasp and get through to do such dreadful damage to our brave ships. We are having to transit such long distances to reach the islands that we frequently have to depart just as a raid is coming in, in order to have sufficient fuel to get back to the ship. As it is, we are all recovering well below minimum and landing only with fuel for another few minutes of hover.'

Port Stanley airfield was attacked again on 25 May, but no serious damage was caused. Further Sea Harrier losses occurred on 29 May and 1 June: in the former case the aircraft slid off the deck while being positioned for take-off; the pilot, (Lieutenant Commander Mike Broadwater) ejected and was promptly picked up by a Sea King. In the sixth and last Sea Harrier loss, an 801 Squadron aircraft flown by Flight Lieutenant Ian 'Morts' Mortimer was shot down, by a Roland SAM and (because of enemy air activity in the area) he spent nine hours in his dinghy before being rescued by a Sea King.

The Sea Harrier's reliability and tolerance of adverse operating conditions was one of the

Harrier GR.3 XZ989/07 of 1(F) Squadron suffered an engine failure during its final approach to the FOB, north-west of Port San Carlos settlement, on 8 June. Wing Commander Peter Squire was shaken but otherwise unhurt in the crash-landing that followed. XZ989 was later moved to Port Stanley where it remained until airlifted to Ascension Island by Hercules on 20 November for onward conveyance to the UK by Heavylift Belfast.

The wreckage of Lieutenant Commander Nick Taylor's Sea Harrier FRS.1 XZ450, the first Harrier lost, on 4 May, when it was probably hit by 35mm automatic cannon fire from a GADA601 Oerlikon AA gun during a cluster-bomb attack on Goose Green airstrip and crashed south-east of the airfield. The disintegrating airframe's momentum carried it through a gate, across the Darwin road and through a fence before coming to a halt in a field adjacent to the eastern perimeter of the airstrip. Taylor was killed and the remains of his aircraft were later removed to a scrap area at Goose Green. The site is now fenced off and marked with a proper headstone, it is lovingly tended by the residents of Goose Green who hold an annual service on the anniversary of his death. Nick left a widow.

success stories of the conflict. *Hermes* regularly had thirteen out of fourteen aircraft serviceable at the start of the day, of which ten would still be available at the end, after forty-five sorties had been flown. Operations were never cancelled due to sea state. Due to the ships' ASW manoeuvres the aircraft had to operate in crosswinds far above peacetime limits, landing facing across the deck or even aft. Recovery took place down to 650 feet visibility and with a cloud ceiling down to 100 feet, the aircraft being guided by flares dropped over the stern. Out of 1,893 Sea Harrier sorties in the TEZ (Total Exclusion Zone) 282 were flown at night, though with limited success; the main targets were low-flying Argentine C-130s, which were extremely difficult to locate over land. Some were escorted by Mirages, but these always broke off before the Sea Harriers closed in.

The CAP mission was normally flown with a pair of Sea Harriers on station for twenty minutes at low level (after 21 May). Standard CAP stations were North or South end of the Sound and over the mountains west of the Sound. Their radars could detect aircraft flying low over sea, but not over land; hence many intercepts were made visually, assisted by the fact that the incoming aircraft could not vary their approach routes due to the need to check their navigation by reference to prominent land features.

Around the Task Force there was the no-go area of the ships' MEZ (missile engagement zone) broken only by a safety lane for the aircraft to recover to the carriers. Surrounding this was a cross-over zone of perhaps sixty nautical miles, which was also off-limits to the Sea Harriers. Outside this they could operate freely, controlled by the Local Air Warfare Co-ordinator on the carrier or a Type 42 destroyer.

On 26 May the breakout from the San Carlos beachhead began, with Commando and

Paratroop units setting out on the first stage of their advance on Port Stanley. 1 Squadron flew seven ground support sorties in the course of the day, one Puma being destroyed on the ground by Squadron Leader Jerry Pook. On 27 May the Squadron's Harrier GR.3s operated in support of the paratroops' advance on Goose Green and on one of these attacks the aircraft flown by Squadron Leader Bob Iveson was hit by 35mm fire and shot down. Iveson ejected over West Falkland and took refuge in the unoccupied Paragon House about seven miles west north-west of Goose Green. Jerry Pook took off from *Hermes* on a lone photo-reconnaissance sortie to try and locate Iveson but returned to the carrier an hour later after having no success. Iveson managed to evade capture and was eventually picked up by a 3 Commando Brigade Air Squadron Gazelle three days later, none the worse for his experience. After a night stop at the Brigade Headquarters he was flown back to *Hermes* by Sea King on 30 May.

Harrier attacks, which were heavy and very accurate, badly demoralised the enemy and played a major part in the subsequent British victory at Goose Green. Bad weather curtailed air operations on 29 May, but on the 30th, 1 Squadron made six sorties against targets near Mount Round, Mount Kent and Port Stanley. During one of these, Squadron Leader Jerry Pook's aircraft was hit and he had to eject at 10,000 feet over the sea, thirty miles from Hermes. He inflated and then got into his dinghy and was picked up by a Sea King after less than ten minutes on the water.

On 31 May 1 Squadron's Harriers carried out seven ground-attack sorties in the area around Port Stanley, softening up the enemy in preparation for the final phase of the ground operation. By this time 1 Squadron was down to three Harriers, but on 1 June two replacement aircraft flown by Flight Lieutenants Murdo Macleod and Mike Beech landed on *Hermes* after a non-stop eight hour twenty-five minute flight from Ascension, each aircraft supported by four Victor tankers. Later in the day, Flight Lieutenant Ian Mortimer had a lucky escape when his Sea Harrier was hit by a Roland missile several miles south of Port Stanley; he ejected over the sea and spent nine hours in his dinghy before being picked up by a Sea King.-

On 29 May an Argentinean C-130E of the Grupo 1 de Transporte Aereo Escuadrón 1 had made an unusual and unsuccessful bombing attack on the supply tanker *British Wye* well north of the TEZ. The C-130 first made a low reconnaissance pass and then, fifteen minutes later, returned to bomb her. The C-130 made its second run at an altitude of about 150 feet and eight 500lb bombs were dropped from the open ramp. Four of them fell into the sea without exploding; three exploded to port causing minor damage and one bounced off the foredeck without exploding. The C-130 climbed into cloud and left the area.

The only Argentine Hercules that was lost in the conflict was shot down on 1 June when TC-63 was intercepted by a Sea Harrier of 801 Squadron, fifty nautical miles north of Pebble Island in daylight when it was searching for the British fleet north-east of the islands. Capitán Ruben Mertel, Capitán Carlos Krause and Vicecomodoro Hugo Meisner constituted the flight crew while the rest of TC-63's complement comprised Suboficial Principal Julio Lastra, Suboficial Ayudante Manuel Albelos, Cabo Principal Miguel Cardone and Cabo Principal Carlos Cantenzano. Their C-130E departed Comodoro Rivadavia that morning at about the same time that a C-130H (TC-66) left Port Stanley for a long homeward run. The two aircraft were in occasional radio contact until about 1340Z, by which time the fighter controller on the British frigate HMS *Minerva* in San Carlos Water detected intermittent 'skin paints' to the north of Pebble Island by search radars when the Hercules 'popped up' for a quick radar sweep. Although low on fuel, two 801 Squadron Sea Harriers piloted by Lieutenant Commander 'Sharkey' Ward and Lieutenant 'Stevie T' (Steve Thomas) were diverted from the return leg of a routine CAP over Pebble Island. 'Sharkey' Ward picked up the target on his own radar and began a tail-chase after the C-130E below cloud. Possibly warned by Argentine ground radar at Stanley, the C-130E made off at high speed and low level towards the mainland but was easily caught by the Sea Harrier. Worried by his low fuel state, 'Sharkey' Ward fired his first Sidewinder out of range and it fell short but he hit with his second, which started a fire between the port engines. Unable

Ground crew wave off A-4B Skyhawks of Grupo 5 de Caza at Rio Gallegos. On 23 May A-242 (in foreground) was flown in the attack on HMS *Antelope* by Primer Teniente Luciano Guaqdagnini (KIA) and was brought down by a SAM in the San Carlos Water area. (Atilio Maggi)

to wait to see if the missile had taken out such a large target, he emptied 240 rounds of 30mm cannon into the Hercules at close range and saw a wing break off before the aircraft crashed into the sea in flames, fifty miles north of Pebble Island, eight minutes after it was detected. None of its crew survived. 'Sharkey' Ward and 'Stevie T' had only forty-five gallons of fuel left for their 180 mile transit to *Invincible*. They landed on safely which was just as well because both pilots did not have enough fuel for a further circuit.[72]

On the morning of 5 June the Harriers of 1 Squadron, together with Sea Harriers, began operations from a site at Port San Carlos, which considerably shortened the time it normally took them to reach their operational areas. By this time, essential spares were being airlifted to the task force by 38 Group's Hercules aircraft, which now had a flight refuelling capability and were consequently able to make the trip from Ascension; they had nowhere to land as yet, but they were able to make low-level supply drops. On 6 June bad weather again hampered Sea Harrier patrol missions. A pair of 1(F) Squadron Harrier GR.3s took-off from *Hermes*, which was at that time 240 miles east of Port Stanley, for a positioning flight to the Forward Operating Base (FOB) at San Carlos, where the poor weather limited operations to helicopters for most of the day. The strip was built by the Royal Engineers on the side of a hill overlooking Port San Carlos Water. It was known colloquially as 'Syd's Strip' after Squadron Leader Syd Morris who was in charge of the RAF's smallest airfield. It was very basic although the RAF ate royally, courtesy of the local farmer and his family. 'We waited here on call, ready to take off in support of the ground forces' recalled Flight Lieutenant Tony Harper. 'Unfortunately, communications were so bad that we often waited in vain all day before returning to 'Mother' for overnight re-tasking'. A two-aircraft CAP was launched from *Hermes* at 1415Z but, that apart, little of note happened to 800 Squadron that day. The 7 June proved to be a fine, clear day and one on which the FOB came into full use. The first CAP of the day was launched from *Hermes* earlier than usual in an attempt to intercept the regular early morning C-130 re-supply flight, but no Hercules was detected on this occasion.

'The morning of 8 June' recalls Flight Lieutenant David Morgan 'started much the same as any other. The ritual of a shower, putting on clean underwear and 'lucky' flying suit (by now rather high!) and a good breakfast before checking the briefing room for the day's commitments as dawn was breaking. I was unlikely to be needed before midday, as I was due to carry out the final part of my night qualification that evening. (Lieutenant Dave Smith and myself needed one more night-landing to make us night-qualified. We were both fairly new guys on the machines and we'd done our three night-launches - dawn, pre-dawn and 'inky-poo' (pitch dark) launch. We'd also completed a dusk landing and a fairly dark landing. This would be the last inky-poo landing before we actually became night-qualified). I therefore volunteered to fly in the right hand seat of one of the Wessex helicopters which had been saved when the *Atlantic Conveyor* was hit by an Exocet missile on 25 May. It had been nearly ten years since I had flown Wessex full time but I found it soon came back and I spent a happy couple of hours delivering mail and supplies around the fleet.'

After lunch Flight Lieutenant David Morgan had flown a mission patrolling to the north of Falkland Sound. 'The weather had cleared beautifully now, with very little cloud over the islands and just the odd thunderstorm over the sea. My sortie was completely uneventful.'

It was once again intended that the air defence Sea Harriers and ground support GR.3s would make full use of HMS *Sheathbill*, the Forward Operating Base at San Carlos. No enemy aerial activity was reported during the morning, but no chances could be taken and CAP was maintained. A detachment of GR.3s was sent to the FOB from *Hermes*, positioned about 250 miles east of the Falkland Islands, to support British ground forces, as and when needed. At this stage of the conflict the Harriers were normally using the metal landing strip at San Carlos to refuel between sorties. Upon arrival at Port San Carlos at about 1500Z the Harrier flown by Peter Squire, experienced an engine problem whilst landing there that morning and spread his aircraft all over the strip, coming to rest on top of a slit trench, effectively putting the FOB out of action for a few hours and all CAP cover by 800 and 801 Squadrons had to originate from the carriers with a corresponding reduction in continuous CAP cover and patrol loiter time. At the time of the FOB accident, two Royal Fleet Auxiliary landing ships, the *Sir Tristram* and the *Sir Galahad*[73] were both anchored at Bluff Cove (near Fitzroy), or, as Dave Morgan says, 'was actually at Port Pleasant which isn't the right name for a place to have a disaster. I was sitting on deck on alert when we were told there was an air-raid ashore.'

The air cover the Sea Harriers provided was intended only as a first line of defence and when Rapier SAMs were absent - as at Fitzroy on 8 June - the consequences could be disastrous. As both ships off-loaded troops and equipment, their activities were witnessed by Argentine observers and eight A-4B Skyhawks of Grupo 5 de Caza and six Daggers from Grupo 6 de Caza took off from Rio Gallegos in the Patagonian province of Santa Cruz and Rio Grande on the north coast of the eastern part of the Isla Grande de Tierra del Fuego to attack the ships. One of the Daggers was forced to return while the other five got embroiled with *Plymouth* at about 1700Z in Falkland Sound. The ship was damaged and the Daggers escaped unscathed back to the mainland despite ferocious gun and missile fire from HMS *Plymouth* and a subsequent chase by CAP Sea Harriers. In the meantime, the five remaining Skyhawks (three having returned to base with technical problems) tracked to the south of the Islands and then flew up the east coast of East Falkland to successfully bomb the two RFAs, with considerable loss of British life. The Skyhawks escaped back to the mainland as there was no CAP cover (it having been sent to the aid of Plymouth) and little effective ground fire.[74] The damage to *Plymouth* had not been serious.

Flushed with success, follow-up strikes were planned for that afternoon. Six Skyhawks of Grupo 5 were armed for an anti-shipping strike against the Royal Navy ships in Bluff Cove and the Skyhawks of Grupo 4 at San Julian were armed for an anti-personnel attack on the British troops at Fitzroy. Refuelling en route would be made with the KC-130H 'Chancha' ('Mother Sow') tankers of Grupo 1 de Transporte Aero at Rio Gallegos (which were used extensively in support of the Skyhawks and Super Etendards and frequently operated in a pair).

'We took off from Rio Gallegos around 15:00 hours with three 500lb bombs on each plane' recalled Primer Teniente Héctor 'Pipi' Sanchez, No.3 of 'Mazo' flight in Grupo 5. 'Our flight plan was to fly to the southeast of the Falklands but two of our aircraft suffered technical problems and had to return so we decided to form a single four aircraft unit. The leader was Primer Teniente Danilo 'Ruso' Bolzán, one of my closest friends and former classmate. The two other pilots were Teniente Juan Arrarás and Teniente Alferez Vázquez. Bolzán was the only one of us with Omega Low Frequency navigation equipment which allowed a more accurate navigation to the target area. The climate both in flight and on the islands was terrible, with low clouds and middle levels and heavy rains in some areas. When we made an aerial refuelling about 200 nautical miles from Rio Gallegos, I realized that one of my external tanks did not transfer all the fuel. But as we were so close to the goal, I decided to continue with the mission knowing the risk involved. We kept to a flight level of 15,000 feet and headed east until we were ninety nautical miles from the islands. There we descended to an extremely low level to avoid radar detection. We were flying so low that our engine efflux left wakes on the surface of the sea like power boats in a competition race. The scene left me stunned every time I flew a mission against the enemy. From the south of Falkland, we headed north to Fitzroy.

'Mazo' flight arrived from the south-west and overflew Fitzroy en route to the Port Fitzroy area. 'When we arrived at Bluff Cove' continues Héctor Sánchez 'we headed east and flew parallel to the Bay. We could see the thick black smoke from the *Sir Galahad* and *Sir Tristram*. The stern shone in a deep red by the heat from the fires burning below deck. Then we began receiving 20mm, GPMG, 'Blowpipe' shoulder-launched missiles and small-arms fire from ground troops and anti-aircraft artillery from the opposite shore. It was certainly deadly. At that point, Vázquez passed me while I felt the bullets of the enemy troops hit my plane. I tried in vain to shoot at them with my 20mm guns. Suddenly, at the mouth of Choiseul Sound, a landing-craft was sighted. Bolzán and Vázquez, his number two, dived down to attack. Bolzán lacked the time and airspace to line-up his aircraft properly and thus did not release any bombs on his pass but Vázquez, with more time available, caught the landing-craft with a direct hit.

'When we left to put to open sea due south, parallel to the coast of the island, I suddenly felt something was going on behind my plane. I looked back and saw a trail of explosions on the surface of the water behind my plane. I tried to identify the source of the shots, but nobody was shooting at me from the coast to my right or from any vessel at sea to my left. It would take me many years of reading to find the source of these shots.'[75]

On *Hermes* Dave Morgan and Lieutenant Dave Smith had strapped themselves into their aircraft to come to five minute alert, 'our minds fairly full of the night landing to come' recalled 'Mog' Morgan. 'Shortly before we were planned to launch, we were jolted back to reality by the broadcast 'Stand clear of intakes and jet pipes, scramble the alert five Sea Harriers!' We had a job to do. We were airborne [at 1850Z] within three minutes. For the next quarter of an hour we flew in silence, both wondering what we would find when we got to the islands. Finally, approaching the CAP station, I radioed the pair of Sea Harriers that we were relieving, who'd been there for about half an hour, to get an update and was told that they were 'over the action' to the north of our briefed station. My CAP area was Lively Island. As I approached it I called up the previous lot and said, 'Okay, where's the action?' As I came in I saw the two great columns of oily black smoke coming from the *Sir Galahad* and *Sir Tristram*. When we arrived overhead, the grim reality unfolded. They were at anchor in the bay, wreathed in a nightmare of smoke and explosions. From our perch, high in the sky, we could only watch with increasing concern and frustration as the living beetles of lifeboats crawled back and forth between ship and shore, with their desperate human cargoes. There was little we could do but search the lengthening shadows for further attackers, as we ploughed our parallel furrows back and forth, a couple of miles above their heads. To fly lower would have denied us radio contact with our controller in San Carlos and risked spooking the troops on the ground into thinking we were the enemy, returning to cause further chaos.

'Five miles to the south of our racetrack in the sky, I noticed a small landing craft ['Foxtrot 4' from Fearless], leaving Choiseul Sound and heading up the coast. On checking, this was identified as friendly and became a particular point to check, each time I turned back onto a westerly heading. I felt great empathy with them, as I imagined the crew, cold and tired in their tiny boat and I wondered if they had any idea that we were watching over them.

'The next forty minutes crept by as we circled, using the minimum possible amount of fuel,

Sea Harrier XZ499 of 800 Squadron flanked by two 1(F) Squadron Harrier GR.3s (including XZ133/10 in the foreground) about to take off on a CAP sortie from HMS *Hermes* in June 1982. (Lieutenant Commander R. C. Nichol RN)

neither of us talking and both very much aware of the tragedy being enacted below. Finally, making a routine check of the fuel gauges as I rolled into another turn to reverse track, I realised that I now had only four minutes flying before I had to turn east, into the rapidly darkening evening sky for Hermes. I flicked my eyes out of the cockpit and searched the gathering dusk below for the small landing craft and soon picked it out, butting its way through the South Atlantic rollers towards Port Pleasant, with white water breaking over its bows.

'It was in that instant that I spotted something which triggered the explosive action which lies, like a tightly coiled spring, beneath the outwardly calm carapace of the fighter pilot. My worst fears and fondest dreams had, in a single instant, been realised. A mere half mile to the east of the vessel was the camouflaged outline of a Skyhawk fighter, hugging the sea and heading directly for the landing craft which had become a very personal part of my existence for the last forty minutes. This was the very thing that we had been anticipating and dreading so much. I'd briefed Dave Smith beforehand that, if we saw anything at low-level, the guy who saw it would attack and the other chap would just try and hang on and clear his tail. I was at 10,000 feet and fairly slow. I stood the Harrier on its nose and jammed the throttle fully open, accelerating down towards this aircraft which was about eight miles away. I shouted over the radio 'A-4s attacking the boat, follow me down!' and peeled off into a 60° dive towards the attackers. Dave Smith wrenched his Sea Harrier around after me but lost sight of my machine as we plunged downwards with the airspeed rocketing from the economic 240 knots on CAP, to over 600 knots, as we strained to catch the enemy before he could reach his target.

'I watched impotently, urging my aircraft onwards and downwards, as the first A-4 opened fire with his 20mm cannon, bracketing the tiny matchbox of a craft. Unfortunately, I didn't get there in time to stop him, but I locked in to the guy with my eyes and saw him miss with his bomb and disappear off. My heart soared as his bomb exploded a good 100 feet beyond them but then sank as I realised that a further A-4 was running in behind him. The second pilot did not miss and I bore mute and frustrated witness to the violent fire-bright petals of the explosion which obliterated the stern, killing the crew and mortally wounding the landing craft.[76] All consuming anger welled in my throat - the most angry I've been in my life, because I knew from this huge great explosion that he'd killed people and because I hadn't been able to intercept and because he'd had the audacity actually to kill somebody while I was there. I determined, in that instant, that this pilot was going to die!

'As I closed rapidly on his tail, I noticed, in my peripheral vision, a further A-4 paralleling his track to my left. So I thought, 'Okay, you'll do'. I hauled my aircraft to the left and rolled out less than half a mile behind the third fighter, closing like a runaway train. I had both missiles and guns selected and within seconds I heard the growl in my earphones telling me that my missile could see the heat from his engine. My right thumb pressed the lock button on the stick and instantly the small green missile cross in the Head-Up Display transformed itself into a diamond, sitting squarely over the back end of the Skyhawk. At the same time, the growl of the missile became an urgent, high pitched chirp, telling me that the infra-red homing head of the weapon was locked on and ready to fire.

'I raised the safety catch and mashed the red, recessed firing button with all the strength I could muster. There was a short delay as the missile's thermal battery ignited and its voltage increased to that required to launch the weapon. In less than half a second, the Sidewinder was transformed from an inert, eleven foot long tube, into a living, fire breathing monster as it accelerated to nearly three times the speed of sound and streaked towards the nearest enemy aircraft. As it left the rails, the rocket efflux and supersonic shock wave over the left wing rolled my charging Sea Harrier above the sea. As I rolled erect, the missile started to guide towards the Skyhawk's jet pipe, leaving a white corkscrew of smoke against the slate grey sea. Within two seconds, the missile disappeared directly up his jet pipe and what had been a living, vibrant, flying machine was completely obliterated in a fraction of a second as the missile tore into its vitals and ripped it apart. The pilot had no chance of survival and within a further two seconds the ocean had swallowed all trace of him and his aeroplane, as if they had never been.'

('Mog' Morgan's first AIM-9L had in fact shot down Teniente Juan Arrarás (in C-226) who was killed, its debris tumbling into the Sound near Philimore Island. Héctor Sánchez saw 'a big explosion and then a cloud of black smoke and fire.' 'I could see the parachute fully open, swinging in the air as he descended into the water. Apparently no one rescued. He probably fell unconscious or injured and died from exposure in the cold water.')[77]

'There was no time for elation. I was going very, very fast - probably around the speed of sound. Because I was flying so much faster than the machine was supposed to be flown at and so much faster than the missile was supposed to be fired at, it rolled dramatically to the

Harrier GR.3 XZ963 which embarked on the *Atlantic Conveyor* off Ascension on 6 May 1982, sailing with the ship for the TEZ on 7 May and flown off to *Hermes* on 19 May. On 30 May, while being flown by Squadron Leader Jeremy Pook in search of enemy helicopters which had been reported west of Port Stanley, it was hit by small-arms fire resulting in a fuel leak. Pook ejected into the sea 30 miles short of *Hermes* when the aircraft ran out of fuel and was rescued by a Sea King after less than ten minutes in the water.

right which really took me by surprise as I was only 100 feet away from the water then. That was fairly startling. As I was righting my machine after the first missile launch, I realised that I was pointing directly at another Argentine aircraft at a range of about one mile; the one I had seen hit the landing craft. I mashed the lock button again, with strength born of righteous anger and my second missile immediately locked onto his jet efflux, as he started a panic break towards me. As I was about to fire, the homing head lost lock and the missile cross wandered drunkenly onto the sea, fifty feet below him. Cursing, I rejected the false lock, mashed the lock button again and fired, the missile whipping across my nose and taking a handful of lead to the left, to head him off.

'He obviously saw the Sidewinder launch, because he immediately reversed his break and pulled his aircraft into a screaming turn away from it. His best efforts were to no avail, however and the thin grey missile flashed back across my nose and impacted his machine directly behind the cockpit. The complete rear half of the airframe simply disintegrated, as if a shot-gun had been fired at a plastic model from close range. As the aluminium confetti of destruction fluttered seawards, I watched, fascinated, as the disembodied cockpit yawed rapidly through 90° and splashed violently into the freezing water.

'I felt a terrific surge of elation at the demise of the second A-4. I thought, 'That's the end of him' and started to scan ahead, in the murk, for the others.

'I had just picked out the next one, fleeing west, his belly only feet from the water, when a parachute snapped open right in front of my face. The pilot had somehow managed to eject from the gyrating cockpit in the half second before it hit the water and flashed over my right wing so close that I saw every detail of the rag-doll figure with its arms and legs thrown out in a grotesque star shape by the deceleration of the silk canopy. My feelings of anger and elation instantly changed to relief, as I realised that a fellow pilot had survived. (I suspect he was the victim of the escape seat ballistic spreader).[78] An instant later, immense anger returned as I started to run down the next victim before he could make good his escape in the gloom. One aircraft was still in front of me and beetling towards Goose Green, so I went in on him.

'Now that I had launched both missiles, I had only guns with which to despatch the remaining Skyhawks and as I lifted the safety slide on the trigger, I realised that my Head-Up Display had disappeared and I had no gunsight. This was a well known 'glitch' in the HUD software and could be cured easily by selecting the HUD off and then on again. This I duly did, but in the ten seconds it took for the sight to reappear, it was all over. The A-4 broke rapidly towards me as I screamed up behind him with a good 150 knots overtake. I pulled his blurred outline to the bottom of the windscreen and opened fire. The roar of the 30mm rounds leaving the guns at the rate of forty per second filled the cockpit. I kept my finger on the trigger and then I just relaxed the nose very, very gently back down, pulled it back and tried again, re-applying the G, in order to walk the rounds through him as best I could. I did that twice, didn't see any hits and didn't know where the bullets were going. I then ran out of bullets with this guy right in front of me, which was very frustrating. So I just rolled the wings level and pulled straight up because there was no point in hanging about there any more - I'd nothing left.

'Suddenly, over the radio came an urgent shout from Dave Smith, who was about a mile behind me, 'Pull up. Pull up, you're being fired at!' All he had seen of the fight up until now, because it was virtually dark, was two missile launches followed by two explosions. He then saw an aircraft only feet above the water, flying through a hail of explosions and didn't know whether it was me or the other guy, but then he saw me go up through the sunset. At Dave's cry, I pulled up into the vertical, through the setting sun and in a big lazy looping manoeuvre, rolled out at 12,000 feet heading northeast for Hermes.'

'Dave Morgan had suddenly shouted over the radio: Four Mirage! Follow me down, Dave.' recalled Dave Smith. 'I'm sure those were his actual words, but then discovered they were A-4 Skyhawk. I was very poorly positioned when the call came. We were in the middle of a turn and he was behind me. I applied full power with the throttle, turned, raising the nose and fell in a vertical dive toward the sea surface, Dave transmitting the attack from the front to about 240°, while I pulled the lever controls about forty-five metres above the sea at a speed of just over 600 knots. I could not see anything! I called Dave for more information and in response I could see the first of his missiles followed by the second. I must have been about two miles behind the fighting, unable to see Dave or the Argentine aircraft. That's when he approached the third A-4 and opened fire with his guns which not only showed me where the target was, but also showed me his position. It was right after that that I came close to colliding with the pilot who had ejected and was hanging from his parachute. It happened so fast that it's just a glint in my memory. Then I got a good solid infrared signal to engage and follow the A-4 which Dave had been shooting at. The two to three miles range seemed too far and I hesitated for a moment, wondering whether it was worth it. The Skyhawk was flying very low. I was about twenty-five metres off the water and exceeded the 1000 km speed but could not put it on the horizon. After a terrible moment of indecision I finally thought: 'Shit, it should be fine' and I fired. 'Sharkey' Ward, who was on patrol in a position south of ours with Steve Thomas, called on the radio and shouted 'Who made that shot?' I thought I had shot Steve Thomas! Steve's laconic answer was: 'It was not me Chief'. I sighed with relief. There was a big explosion and my Harrier veered wildly while the missile sped toward the target. It seemed to be fall short but it hit with devastating results.'[79]

In the vertical climb, Dave Morgan looked back down over Choiseul Sound and saw a white trail appear, accelerating towards the fleeing A-4. 'The trail was so low to the water that my first crazy thought was that it was a torpedo! I soon realised, however, that it was a missile and watched mesmerised as it headed for the enemy fighter. About halfway to the target, the rocket motor burnt out and for a few maddening seconds, I thought it had been fired out of range and would drop into the water. Dave had not misjudged it though and after seven seconds of flight, there was a brilliant white flash as the zirconium disc in the warhead ignited. The Skyhawk was so low that the flash of the warhead merged with its reflection in the water of the Sound. A fraction of a second later the aircraft disappeared in a huge yellow-orange fireball, as it spread its burning remains over the sand dunes on the north coast of Lafonia.'

The wreck of the Skyhawk was later found at Rain Cove near Island Creek and identified as C-204; its unfortunate pilot being Primer Teniente Danilo Bolzán.[80] Dave Smith concluded: 'The unfortunate pilot must have had less than a second before his plane hit the ground on the northern shore of Lafonia, exploding on impact.'

'Climbing rapidly through 20,000 feet', continues 'Mog' Morgan, 'I checked my engine and fuel gauges and realised that we were going to be very tight for gas. We used a figure of 2,000lbs of fuel overhead Port Stanley as a good rule of thumb for returning to the ship and my gauges were reading less than 1,400lbs. As I overflew the battered runway, climbing through 25,000 feet between the odd burst of anti-aircraft fire, my low-level fuel lights came on, indicating 1,300lbs remaining. At 40,000 feet, I called the carrier and told them that I was returning short of fuel and they obliged by heading towards us to close the distance. Even so, when I closed the throttle to start a cruise descent from ninety miles out, I was still uncertain whether I was going to make it before I flamed out and took an unwanted bath.

'At 40,000 feet the sun was still a blaze of orange on the western horizon but as I descended the light became progressively worse. By the time I had descended to 10,000 feet, my world had become an extremely dark and lonely place. The adrenalin levels, which had been recovering to normal during the twenty minutes after the engagement, now started to increase again in anticipation of my first night deck landing. To compound the problem and to give final proof of 'Sod's Law', *Hermes* had managed to find one of the massive thunder storms and was in heavy rain. I realised that I did not have sufficient fuel to carry out a proper radar approach and asked the controller to just talk me onto the centreline, whilst I adjusted my glide so that I would not have to touch the throttle until the last minute.

'With three miles to run, descending through 1,500 feet and still in thick, turbulent cloud, my fuel warning lights began to flash urgently, telling me that I had 500lbs of fuel remaining. At two miles, I saw a glimmer of light emerging through the rain and at 800 feet the lights fused into the recognisable outline of the carrier. I slammed the nozzle lever into the hover stop, selected full flap and punched the undercarriage button to lower the wheels. I picked up the mirror sight, which confirmed that I was well above the ideal glide path but dropping rapidly towards the invisible sea. With about half a mile to run, I added a handful of power and felt the Pegasus engine's instant response, stopping my descent at about 300 feet. The wheels locked down as I applied full braking stop to position myself off the port side of the deck and seconds later, I was transitioning sideways to hover over the centreline of the deck, level with the aft end of the superstructure. I knew that I had little fuel remaining, so finesse went out of the window as I closed the throttle and banged the machine down on the rain-streaked deck. Once safely taxied forward into the aptly named 'Graveyard' and lashed in place, I shut down the engine and heard Dave's jet landing on behind me. My fuel gauges were showing 300lbs - sufficient for a further two minutes flying!'

Héctor Sánchez too was low on fuel and desperately needed to rendezvous with a KC-130H 'Chancha' tanker if he were to get home. 'I ejected the empty tanks and bombs hanging on my plane and I began to escape at low altitude towards the islands. I saw lots of clouds and rain in front and headed there. I flew over Choiseul Sound at low altitude, knowing that rain could dissipate the heat produced by the Sidewinder and help confuse and therefore avoid the seeker heads of the missiles. I started closed evasive manoeuvres to avoid being tracked by the Sea Harrier radars while keeping an eye on the rear view mirrors for missile trails. When I reached East Falkland, I started heading south again. Even though I was in a state of deep shock due to what I had experienced during the minutes before interception I should concentrate on flying, not think about the climate and the circumstances in which I was piloting. I knew it was a difficult task trying to return home. I began to fly west, no more than a metre above the waves, just in case. I kept towards the southernmost point of the island Great Malvina for five threatening but less dangerous minutes that seemed like a century. I suddenly realized that I did not have enough fuel to reach Stanley. I had to make a decision and do it fast. If I decided to return to Stanley I could find several Harrier-hazardous areas, or anti-aircraft artillery could knock me down by mistake. I leaned back, knowing that the fuel was not enough but with the hope of finding the KC-130 Hercules for refuelling en route.

'I started to climb and radioed for someone to replenish me, but I received no responses. If there was none, I preferred ejecting in the middle of the ocean before returning to the Falklands. My blood ran cold at the thought. I was angry and shocked at losing my dearest friends in combat. However, it was not the day that God had in store for me. I had a surplus of 200lbs of fuel - nothing really - when finally my call for help was answered by Commodore and Capitán Alfredo Cano Rubich and the crew of a Hercules and it gave me a chance of life. But the bullets that had hit my plane had damaged the pressure system and the temperature made it extremely difficult to see out of the cockpit: I was flying blind. When I was high enough for refuelling, a thick layer of frost formed in the cockpit and I had to remove pieces of ice. That was one reason why I could not refuel on the first try. I was so desperate for fuel that I did not want to slow down my plane. I had to make a sharp turn to re-locate the Hercules and I had to fly until about West Falkland where at altitude I could see contrails and I could join the 'queue'. It was so risky just to give me a chance to live. We must not forget that the aircraft refuellers were an objective for the Harriers. They were very focused on their search and destroy mission. I will always feel that Capitán Rubich was like a father to me. They will never be enough words to explain how lucky I was to have survived the battle and for having been able to find the tanker. The whole operation lasted three hours. No one else had survived. I was deeply moved when I saw the faces of the mechanics. They were waiting for the arrival of my colleagues. They never returned. As long as I live, I will always appreciate the support they gave me. It was a black day for the British Task Force that day. For me too.'[81]

'Our debrief' concludes Mog Morgan 'took place in the Wardroom bar, which John Locke, the ship's universally loved and respected Commander, had kept open for us. Here we

After the war Capitán Héctor Sánchez (middle) became a Mirage IIIEA squadron commander in Grupo 8 de Caza at Mariano Moreno. The two other pilots in the picture are Capitán Marcelo Carlos 'Fibra' Moroni (left) and Primer Teniente Eduardo Adaglio (right). On 24 May Primer Teniente Sánchez of Grupo 5 de Caza attacked an unidentified 'frigate', causing no significant damage and fellow Grupo 5 pilot Alférez Moroni a RFA (probably *Fort Austin*).

Flight Lieutenant Dave 'Mog' Morgan all smiles after landing back on Hermes on 1 May after his FRS.1 Harrier (ZA192) had been holed by a 20mm shell, which had entered the left side of the fin at a grazing angle of about ten degrees and exploded, causing considerable damage to the right hand side of the fin and tail plane. The hole was cleaned up and patched with 'speed-tape', which might be described as heavy-duty aluminium kitchen foil with adhesive backing. The RN's first real experience of battle damage took 3-5 hours to repair, but similar holes were patched over within 1½ hours later in the conflict. ZA192 exploded shortly after taking off from *Hermes* on 23 May killing its pilot, Lieutenant Commander G. W. J. 'Gordie' Batt. (Martin Cleaver EMPICS)

In the summer of 1993 Morgan and Sánchez met in London and spent the afternoon at White Waltham airfield flying aerobatics. Sánchez and his wife stayed with the Morgans in their Somerset cottage and after several pints of scrumpy Morgan discovered that he had had ended up in front of Héctor in the heat of the engagement and had it not been for the fact that his gun had jammed, he might have been the only Argentine pilot to shoot down a Sea Harrier!'

discovered that a pilot from our sister squadron in *Invincible* had reported seeing four aircraft destroyed during our engagement. Neither of us could give a satisfactory explanation of the fourth kill but this version was sent back to UK, describing the mission as a night training sortie. This elicited the following amusing response from C in C Fleet: CONGRATULATIONS YOUR EVENING SORTIE. IF THIS IS WHAT YOU DO ON A TRAINING MISSION, I CAN'T WAIT TO SEE WHAT YOU DO WHEN YOU ARE OPERATIONAL!'

'That really was the last bit of excitement that I had out there, the last time I actually got engaged. But we did become night-qualified! The Argentine Air Force and Navy never really came out after that. There were a couple of quick raids but that was all.'

On 9 June 1 Squadron, now reinforced by two more Harrier GR.3s from Ascension, flew four sorties against enemy gun positions on Sapper Hill and Mount Longdon. Ground attack sorties against targets in the Port Stanley area continued the next day and some Harriers were damaged by small-arms fire, although none seriously. The Squadron flew eleven sorties on 11 June, of which ten were ground-attack sorties against Argentine positions and the other a toss-bombing attack on Stanley airfield. On 12 June 1 Squadron's Harriers flew six ground attack sorties against enemy positions around Sapper Hill; one aircraft, flown by Flight Lieutenant Murdo Macleod, was hit by small-arms fire bullets, creating a severe fire risk; he nevertheless managed to recover safely to HMS *Hermes*.

By 13 June, forward air controllers were in position on the hills around Port Stanley and this enabled 1 Squadron's GR.3s to use LGBs (laser-guided bombs) the next day on a highly successful attack against Argentine forward artillery positions designated by ground-based lasers. (None of the pilots had previously had experience with laser-guided weapons). The operation was carried out by the squadron's CO, Wing Commander Peter Squire, who scored a direct hit on an Argentine 155mm gun. A second strike was called off by General Moore in person, with Harriers only three minutes from weapons release; the designated target was an HQ on Sapper Hill, which was suddenly swarming with Argentine soldiers waving white flags! The next day saw the surrender of the enemy garrison in Port Stanley. Although the Sea Harriers continued to fly CAP for some time, 1 Squadron ceased offensive operations. The battle for the Falklands was over.

The Falklands conflict had lasted 74 days and ended with the Argentine surrender on 14 June 1982, which returned the islands to British control. During the conflict, 649 Argentine military personnel, 255 British military personnel and three Falkland Islanders died. In the air the Fleet Air Arm's Sea Harriers proved crucial to the success of the campaign. A total of 28 Sea Harriers and fourteen Harrier GR3s were deployed in the theatre. The Sea Harriers performed the primary air defence role with a secondary role of ground attack. The RAF Harrier GR.3 provided the main ground attack force. Although heavily outnumbered and without a single loss in air combat, the twenty-eight Sea Harriers of 800, 801, 809 and 899 Squadrons achieved 99% readiness and flew over 1,100 combat air patrols and ninety ground attack missions. In all, Sea Harrier pilots fired 27 AIM9Ls, scoring a success rate of around 90%, which resulted in twenty-one confirmed and three probable kills in air-to-air combat. Seven further confirmed kills were gained with Aden cannon. Sharkey Ward commanded 801 Naval Air Squadron, HMS *Invincible* and was senior Sea Harrier adviser to the Command on the tactics, direction and progress of the air war. He flew over sixty war missions, achieved three air-to-air kills and took part in or witnessed a total of ten kills; he was also the leading night pilot and was decorated with the Distinguished Service Cross for gallantry. Out of the total Argentine air losses, 28% were shot down by Harriers. Six Harriers were lost, two to ground fire and four to accidents. The total aggregate loss rate for both the Harriers and Sea Harriers on strike operations was 2.3%.[82]

A number of factors contributed to the failure of the Argentinean fighters to shoot down a Sea Harrier. Although the Mirage III and Dagger jets were considerably faster, the Sea Harrier was considerably more manoeuvrable. (Viffing was not used by RN pilots in the Falklands). Moreover, the Harrier employed the latest AIM-9L Sidewinder missiles and the Blue Fox radar. The British pilots had superior air-combat training, one manifestation of which was that they

27-year old Lieutenant Dave Smith of 800 Squadron climbing into his Sea Harrier on *Hermes* (and inset).

thought they noticed Argentinean pilots occasionally releasing weapons outside of their operating parameters. This is now thought to have been Mirages releasing external fuel tanks rather than weapons and turning away from conflict with the Sea Harrier. This later reduced their capability to fight an effective campaign against the Sea Harrier due to reduced range and lack of external fuel tanks.

British aircraft received fighter control from warships in San Carlos Water, although its effectiveness was limited by their being stationed close to the islands, which severely limited the effectiveness of their radar. The differences in tactics and training between 800 Squadron and 801 Squadron has been a point of criticism, suggesting that the losses of several ships were preventable had Sea Harriers from *Hermes* been used more effectively.

Both sides' aircraft were operating in adverse conditions. Argentine aircraft were forced to operate from the mainland because airfields on the Falklands were only suited for propeller-driven transports. In addition, fears partly aroused by the bombing of Port Stanley airport by a Vulcan bomber added to the Argentineans' decision to operate them from afar. As most Argentine aircraft lacked in-flight refuelling capability, they were forced to operate at the limit of their range. The Sea Harriers also had limited fuel reserves due to the tactical decision to station the British carriers out of Exocet missile range and the dispersal of the fleet. The result was that an Argentine aircraft could only allow five minutes over the islands to search and attack an objective, while a Sea Harrier could stay near to thirty minutes waiting in the Argentine approach corridors and provide Combat Air Patrol coverage for up to an hour. Dave Morgan recalls that 'at times, before the commissioning of the San Carlos strip, we only had five minutes on CAP.'

The Sea Harriers were outnumbered by the available Argentinean aircraft and were on occasion decoyed away by the activities of the Escuadrón Fénix ('Phoenix') or civilian jet aircraft used by the Argentine Air Force. They had to operate without a fleet early warning system such as AWACS that would have been available to a full NATO fleet in which the Royal Navy had expected to operate, which was a significant weakness in the operational environment. However, it is now known that Chile did provide early radar warning to the Task Force.[83] The result was that the Sea Harriers could not establish complete air superiority and prevent Argentine attacks during day or night, nor could they completely stop the daily C-130 Hercules transports' night flights to the islands.

Despite not being able to reach the speed of sound in level flight the Harrier more than proved its combat capability during the Falkland wars. Though it was faced by much faster enemy fighters these were not as modern, as well equipped and, most limiting of all, were operating at the very edge of their range - especially when carrying bombs. This meant that the Mirage and Dagger fighters could not take full advantage of their supersonic capability as it burned too much fuel. In-flight refuelling capability was limited to a few aircraft in the Argentinean inventory, not that they had enough tankers anyway. The most important factor in the success of the Sea Harrier was undoubtedly the all-aspect AIM-9L Sidewinder heat-seeking air-to-air missiles rushed into service as the Task Force sailed to the South Atlantic. The Argentinean's older rear-aspect AIM-9B Sidewinders, Matra Magic and Shafrir missiles could only be launched when directly behind their target as the seeker needed to lock onto the hot jet exhausts emerging from the tail pipe. The AIM-9L had a longer range and more importantly its more sensitive seeker meant it could be fired from any aspect. This, plus superior pilot training and better avionics enabled the British planes to employ a looser and more flexible formation than their opponents. Of twenty-seven AIM-9L Sidewinders fired by Sea Harriers, twenty-four hit their mark. Another six enemy planes fell to the Sea Harrier's 30mm cannons.

'When I think about the whole campaign' concludes Dave Morgan 'the most frightening fraction of a second was on the very first raid when I saw people actually firing at me and obviously trying to kill me. I think that's what really brought it home, made me absolutely scared stiff that fraction of a second. Then the old brain said, 'Sod it. We've got to get in there and drop the bombs anyway, so go do it.' I think everyone felt that on the first mission. Apart from that, the most uncomfortable times were during air attacks on *Hermes* when we were sitting down between decks with everything closed up round us, at almost perfect Exocet height, just waiting for a big rocket to appear through the wall. That was disturbing. When you're in the air, nothing matters, you're the master of your own destiny and you can do what you like, but sitting in that ship not being able to do anything was most disturbing.

'My saddest moment was on Ascension Island. There were about eight of us who stayed behind on the way back and we had a service the evening we were leaving. It was a lovely, still, tropical night and the old sun was setting and we had this very, very moving memorial service.

Though of short duration the Falklands Air War was a gruelling battle won in no small measure by the carrier-borne Harriers and their pilots and deck crews in often appalling weather conditions.

They'd flown out a whole lot of wreaths from the UK and one rose-grower had sent us a great box of roses and we stood on the back end of the ship and said a few words, tossed the wreaths over the back, scattered the roses and just sort of sat there with our own thoughts. When it was all over and it had all gone quiet and there was no shouting, hooting or roaring any more, we could just think about the guys who would not be going back. That was very, very sad.

'I don't think I ever felt that sort of remorse and sadness during the confrontation. Obviously, when you're in the flying world, you get used to losing friends; it never gets any easier, but the effects don't last quite so long. I've lost forty or fifty people, I suppose, since I've been flying, not all close friends, but people I've been on the squadron with. I must've lost fifteen or twenty real, good, close friends and it hurts like hell, but after a day or so, it's over, you know, life goes on. It's something you live with.

'And when we came back home, that was the most amazing moment of my life! We were all standing, lining the deck and everyone had tears streaming down their faces. At long last we could actually let it all go. That I think was the most amazing moment of my life, absolutely fantastic.'

Above: Having sailed for the UK on 4 July 1982 via Ascension Island, HMS *Hermes* sails into Portsmouth on 21 July to a hero's welcome.

Right: HMS *Invincible* is given an honour guard by small ships on arrival to Portsmouth on 17 September 1982 after 166 days at sea, the longest period ever for continuous carrier operations at sea.

Endnotes for Chapter 8

57   On 5 April 12 Sea Harrier FRS.1s sailed South with 800 Naval Air Squadron on HMS *Hermes*. Eight Sea Harriers sailed South with 801 NAS on *Invincible*. On 8 April 809 NAS formed with 8 Sea Harriers. On 31 April 6 Sea Harriers of 809 NAS flew to Ascension Island via Banjul, Gambia. On 1 May 6 Sea Harriers arrived at Ascension Island and two Sea Harriers of 809 NAS departed for Ascension via Banjul, arriving the following day. On 3 May 4 Harrier GR.3s took off from RAF St. Mawgan to join up with three Victor tankers. 1 'spare' Harrier (Flight Lieutenant John Rochfort) returned to base. 2 Harrier GR3s (Flight Lieutenants Tony Harper and Martin Hale) proceeded to Ascension. 1 Harrier GR.3 (Wing Commander Peter Squire) and 1 Victor diverted to Banjul due to technical problems, both arriving at Ascension later. On 4 May 2 Harrier GR.3s (Squadron Leaders Bob Iveson and Jerry Pook) arrived at Ascension Island 2 Harrier GR.3s (Squadron Leaders Bob Iveson and Jerry Pook) arrived at Ascension Island. 1 Harrier GR.3 (Flight Lieutenant John Rochfort) diverted to Porto Santo en route to Ascension. On 5 May 3 Harrier GR3s (Squadron Leaders Peter Harris and Tim Smith and Flight Lieutenant Jeff Glover) arrived at Ascension. 1 Harrier GR.3 (Flight Lieutenant Ross Boyens) diverted to Banjul. On 6 May 8 Sea Harriers and 6 Harrier GR.3s embarked on Motor Vessel (MV) *Atlantic Conveyor* at Ascension. On 18 May 4 Sea Harrier FRS.1s (Lieutenant Commander Hugh Slade, Lieutenant Bill Covington, Flight Lieutenant Steve Brown and John Leeming) and 4 Harrier GR.3s (Wing Commander Peter Squire, Squadron Leader Jerry Pook, Squadron Leader Peter Harris, Flight Lieutenant John Rochfort) transferred from *Atlantic Conveyor* to HMS *Hermes*. 4 Sea Harrier FRS.1s transferred from *Atlantic Conveyor* to HMS *Invincible*. On 20 May Harrier GR.3 (Flight Lieutenant John Rochfort) transferred from *Atlantic Conveyor* to HMS *Hermes*. On 1 June 2 Harrier GR.3s (Flight Lieutenants Mike Beech and Murdo McLeod) landed on HMS *Hermes* after a flight from Ascension. On 8 June 2 Harrier GR.3s (Flight Lieutenants Ross Boyens and Nick Gilchrist) landed on HMS *Hermes* after the flight from Ascension.

58   In April an arrester gear was fitted to support Skyhawks and there was always the possibility that A-4s or Super Etendards would be based at Stanley, using American-made hydraulic arrester gears; hence a continuing effort was necessary to disrupt aircraft operating areas.

59   Lockheed Hercules transport night flights brought supplies, weapons, vehicles and fuel and airlifted out the wounded up until the end of the conflict.

60   *The RAF In Action: From Flanders to the Falklands* by Robert Jackson (Blandford Press 1985).

61   Bob Tuxford was awarded the Air Force Cross for his part in the mission and his crew - 52-year old Squadron Leader Ernie Wallis MBE, Flight Lieutenant Mick Beer, Flight Lieutenant John Keable and Flight Lieutenant Glyn Rees - each received the Queen's Commendation for Valuable Service in the Air.

62   Lieutenant Commanders Gordie Batt ('Red Leader'): Tony Ogilvy ('Red 2'); and Neill Thomas ('Red 3') and Lieutenant Clive Morrell ('Red 4') 'who was tall and thin, with a rather Mediterranean complexion, hence his nickname 'Spaghetti' Morrelli'. Flight Lieutenant Bertie Penfold ('Red 5') was delayed by a fault.

63   *Jamás serán olvidados* by Claudio Meunier.

64   *Falklands: The Air War* (Arms & Armour Press 1986).

65   On one of these flights, on 7 June, a Fuerza Aérea Argentina Learjet was shot down by a 'Sea Dart' missile, killing the crew and the squadron commander, 43-year old Vicecomodoro Rodolfo Manuel De La Colina, the highest-ranking Argentine officer to die in the war.

66   'Black Buck 2' went ahead on the night of Monday 3 May and was flown by the same Vulcan with a crew from 50 Squadron captained by Squadron Leader R. J. Reeve who took off from Wideawake with a small group of Victor tankers. A larger formation of Victors left later and flew at a higher speed than on 'Black Buck I' to catch up with the Vulcan well along the route to Port Stanley. This operational change worked well enough but the runway was not hit though several Argentinean aircraft and buildings were very badly damaged. 'Black Buck 3' scheduled for 16 May was cancelled because of unexpectedly strong headwinds en route. 'Black Buck 4' flown on 28/29 May was the first anti-radar mission but five hours out from Ascension the HDU, the mechanism that winds and unwinds the refuelling hose, failed in the key Victor tanker before the penultimate fuel transfer and the mission was aborted. Two nights later, on 30/31 May on a mission to the Port Stanley area, 'Black Buck 5' (Vulcan XM597 flown by Squadron Leader Neill McDougall); supported by 18 Victor sorties and in conjunction with a Harrier attack on Port Stanley airfield, launched four AGM-45A Shrike missiles, which damaged the antenna of the Argentinean Westinghouse AN/TPS-43 surveillance radar installation. On the night of 2/3 June 'Black Buck 6' went ahead when Vulcan XM597 again captained by Squadron Leader McDougall, launched two Shrikes at

radar contacts but the Argentineans repeatedly switched off their radars. On the way home to Ascension, the Vulcan's refuelling probe fractured during a 'prod' at a Victor tanker and McDougall was forced to divert to Rio de Janeiro in Brazil. 'Black Buck 7' flown Flight Lieutenant Martin Withers to bomb Port Stanley airfield on 11/12 June was the last bombing operation involving a Vulcan. Fourteen Victor tankers carried out 18 refuelling sorties. This was a conventional bombing attack, the aircraft dropping a mixture of 1,000lb HE and anti-personnel bombs, fuzed to burst in the air, on enemy troop concentrations around Port Stanley, without hitting the runway, which was spared because the RAF would need it. The operation was held to be a partial success. Of the 63 bombs dropped, 42 landed hundreds of yards away from the aiming point and only one impacted the side of the runway - not the centre, as claimed. In the event, the Argentines never succeeded in landing fast jets on the airfield.

67   *Falklands: The Air War* (Guild Publishing 1987).

68   At least one and possibly two Super Etendards carried 'buddy-packs' to refuel the Exocet-armed aircraft in transit.) Reports indicate that the other missile may have been decoyed by chaff and that the successful round failed to explode. However, its remaining rocket fuel started fires which quickly spread thick smoke throughout the ship and cut off power supplies to fire-fighting equipment. The destruction of a Type 42 destroyer by a single hit is evidence of Exocet's lethality; but it is noteworthy that the missile was fired against a radar blip in the hope that this would prove a worthwhile target and that it happened to strike one of the most fire-prone areas of the ship. Various options to attack the home base of the five Argentine Etendards at Río Grande were examined and discounted (Operation 'Mikado'), subsequently five Royal Navy submarines lined up, submerged, on the edge of Argentina's twelve-nautical-mile (22 kilometres; 14 miles) territorial limit to provide early warning of bombing raids on the British task force.

69   John Eyton-Jones was born on 24 April 1943 in Northampton. He was the second of two brothers and two sisters. His father, John senior, served in the Royal Artillery during WWII. Educated at Northampton Grammar School, he joined the Royal Navy as a Fleet Air Arm pilot in 1964. Right from the start he was nicknamed E-J and displayed a special talent for the demanding world of fast-jet flying from carriers at sea. Specialising first on the all-weather Sea Vixen fighter, operating from *Eagle* and *Hermes*, he then moved on to the F-4K Phantom of 892 Squadron in the Carrier Air Group of HMS *Ark Royal*. By then, E-J had become an Air Warfare Instructor (AWI) and also completed a distinguished tour with the US Navy experimental squadron VX-4 at Point Mugu, California, where his record as an adversary in Air Combat Manoeuvering (ACM) was exceptional. On return to England in 1976 he converted onto the RAF's Harrier GR.3 and then joined No 1(F) Squadron at RAF Wittering, further enhancing his already unique reputation. When the Sea Harrier FRS.1 joined the Fleet, E-J, by now a Lieutenant Commander, returned to RN service and became an instructor with 899 Squadron NAC (Naval Air Command). He was heavily involved in ensuring that the Air Weapons tactics and training for this new VSTOL fighter were of the highest possible standard. On 5 April 1982 E-J was one of five 899 pilots seconded to 801 Squadron, which departed from England in HMS *Invincible*. E-J was a strong influence in the intensive work-up schedules that brought the embarked pilots up to operational standard by day and night. He also took part in a number of combat sorties. John Eyton-Jones left behind Sally, who he had married in 1966 and two young daughters, Sophie and Anna.

70   *The RAF In Action: From Flanders to the Falklands* by Robert Jackson (Blandford Press 1985). On the night of 20/21 May Flight Lieutenant Ford and a 206 Squadron crew with Wing Commander David Emmerson on board flew the longest maritime reconnaissance sortie so far, Nimrod XV232 covering 8,453 miles in a flight that lasted eighteen hours 51 minutes. *Falklands: The Air War*. In May XV232 returned to the UK briefly and was fitted with a 'Heath-Robinson' method of carrying and launching Sidewinder missiles - resulting in the aircraft earning the name 'the world's largest jet fighter' in various national newspapers of the day! After the war XV232 continued in RAF service, in the anti-submarine and search and rescue roles, until 11 May 2010 when it was acquired by the Classic Flight - the forerunner of the Classic Air Force.

71   Ferranti Inertial Navigation Reference and Attitude Equipment.

72   *See Fighter Supreme* by David Hobbs (*Flypast* magazine, April 2007).

73   On 1 June the 1st Battalion Welsh Guards went ashore on the Falklands with the Fifth Infantry Brigade at San Carlos. Without helicopter lift, they were sent forward to Fitzroy by sea, lead elements landing from HMS *Fearless* on the night of 6/7 June. Bad weather delayed the remaining guardsmen of 1 Battalion, who were embarked aboard *Sir Tristram* and *Sir Galahad*, to be caught by the air strike on Bluff Cove. By the end of 8 June, fifty-six British and Chinese servicemen had been killed, bringing the total losses so far in the conflict to 192 members of the British Task Force.

74   *Falklands;The Air War* (Guild Publishing 1987).

75   Quoted in *Malvinas Fuego En El Aire CAP.05* by Claudio Meunier.

76   The LCU - 'Foxtrot 4' from the assault ship HMS *Fearless* - heading towards Fitzroy from Goose Green was taken in tow, but sank before reaching the shore. The bombs killed four Royal Marines including Colour Sergeant Brian Johnston, coxswain of LCU F4 and two Naval ratings, while eleven were rescued. On 11 October 1982 the Posthumous award of the Queen's Gallantry Medal was made to Brian Johnston in recognition of gallant and distinguished service during the operations in the South Atlantic: Colour Sergeant Johnston was working in the vicinity of HMS *Antelope* on 23 May when her unexploded bomb detonated, starting an immediate fire which caused her crew, already at emergency stations, to be ordered to abandon ship. Without hesitation he laid his craft alongside *Antelope* and began to fight the fire and take off survivors. At approximately 2200Z he was ordered to stay clear of the ship because of the severity of the fire and the presence of a second unexploded bomb. Colour Sergeant Johnston remained alongside until his load was complete. In all LCU F4 rescued over 100 survivors from *Antelope*. 'Foxtrot 4' had also rescued 26-year old Teniente Ricardo 'Tom' Lucero of Grupo 4 after it was shot down in the waters of San Carlos on 25 May. Lucero was killed in a Piper PA-11/12 while he was spreading corn or soya fields in Cordoba, Argentina.

77   Quoted in *Malvinas Fuego En El Aire CAP.05* by Claudio Meunier.

78   Morgan's second missile brought down Teniente Alfredo Vázquez (in C-228) who managed to eject but he did not survive. The fuselage broke in two and fell into the sea two miles north of Middle Island. 'The 9L homing head used a liquid nitrogen cooled Antimony Sulphide seeker, which was able to detect much lower levels (and frequences) of IR radiation. This meant that it could guide onto the heat plume of the exhaust (as opposed to hot metal in the 9G). This, combined with a 360 degree laser fuse (as opposed to an IR fuse in the G) meant that the warhead went bang in the centre of the airframe no matter what the aspect. It also had a blast-frag warhead with a pyrophoric disc as opposed to the expanding rod of the 9G (if I remember properly). Altogether a much better weapon. Certainly my second shot would have been marginal if I had been carrying Gs.'

79   Quoted in *Malvinas Fuego En El Aire CAP.05* by Claudio Meunier.

80   When Dave Morgan inspected the wreckage later it revealed that the missile had exploded beneath the starboard elevator, causing catastrophic airframe damage.

81   Quoted in *Malvinas Fuego En El Aire CAP.05* by Claudio Meunier.

82   The Ministry of Defence give a total of 91 enemy aircraft of all types shot down, or destroyed or captured on the ground and eight 'probable' kills. These include Mirage/Dagger, 20 or 22; Skyhawk, 20 or 18; Pucara, 13; MB.339A, 2; Canberra, 1 or 2; C-130, 1; Super Etendard, 1 (?); Beech T-34C, 4; Puma, 12; Bell UH-1H, 16; Agusta A.109, 2; Chinook, 2; Bell 212, 2.

83   Chile was officially neutral during the Falklands War, but Chile's Westinghouse long range radar that was deployed in the south of the country gave the British task force early warning of Argentinean air attacks. This allowed British ships and troops in the war zone to take defensive action. Margaret Thatcher, the British prime minister at the time of the war, has said that the day the radar was taken out of service for overdue maintenance was the day Argentinean fighter-bombers bombed the troopships *Sir Galahad* and *Sir Tristram*, leaving 53 dead and many injured. According to Chilean Junta member and former Air Force commander Fernando Matthei, Chilean support included military intelligence gathering, radar surveillance, allowing British aircraft to operate with Chilean colours and facilitating the safe return of British special forces, among other forms of assistance. In April and May 1982, a squadron of mothballed British Hawker Hunter fighter-bombers departed for Chile, arriving on 22 May and allowing the Chilean Air Force to reform the No. 9 'Las Panteras Negras' Squadron. A further consignment of three frontier surveillance and shipping reconnaissance Canberras left for Chile in October. Some authors have speculated that Argentina might have won the war had the military felt able to employ the elite VIth and VIIIth Mountain Brigades, which remained sitting in the Andes guarding against possible Chilean incursions.

Chapter Five

'Tanker Trash', Tornadoes and The 'Buccs'

'As we progressed through the various phases of the war, from night low-level JP233 attacks to medium-level operations and finally to laser-guided bomb deliveries in concert with the worthy Buccaneers, we came to realize what a very good aircraft the Tornado is. Certainly, the aircraft never let us down and the now famous female 'art forms' that adorned them are testament to the affection that they inspired and we did ask an awful lot of them. The aircrew averaged twenty sorties or so apiece during the six-week campaign. The aircraft averaged about twice that number and, no matter what anyone tells you, machines do get tired after a while.'

Wing Commander Jerry J. Witts DSO MBIM, 31 Squadron OC Tornadoes, Dhahran.

Wing Commander Jerry Witts was sitting idly in a routine Station Executives' meeting in late October 1990 when the Station Commander suddenly announced that Bruggen was required to put together another Tornado detachment to go to the Gulf. 'My squadron was to take the lead and provide twelve crews and all my ground crew. We would be reinforced by personnel from the rest of the Station and I was to command the detachment. Needless to say, his announcement certainly grabbed my attention! Fortunately, despite the fact that my mind was a blur, I recalled some very sensible advice to the effect that, for the sake of one's career, it is better to appear unmoved by such exciting news rather than blurting out 'Beam me up, Scotty!' or other such unhelpful comments. Frantically, I tried to think of a sensible question:

'OK, Sir. Where are we going?'

'We don't know yet'.

'Oh. Do we know when we're going?'

'No'.

'Having thus exhausted my stock of sensible questions, the only thing to do was to start getting ready. But first things first, a cup of coffee and think through the likely problems. Fortunately, the Royal Air Force is blessed with a whole range of professionals who like nothing better than a task like this, so, in no time at all, the telephone was red-hot with a stream of callers giving me solutions to a whole bunch of problems that I would never have thought of.

'As events turned out, two months were to pass before we actually set off for the Gulf. Our new base turned out to be Dhahran in Saudi Arabia where we arrived at the turn of the year. Dhahran by this time was already home to an RAF Tornado air defence detachment, the Free Kuwait Air Force, several USAF units and, of course, resident Royal Saudi Air Force units. On top of that, the airfield was already an established major civil airport as well as being the primary airhead for the Allied forces in the region. Thus, shoe-horning my detachment into what claimed to be the busiest airfield in the world was not the easiest of tasks, particularly as we had only two weeks to run to the UN deadline on 15 January. As ever, the RAF rose to the occasion and, while it would be untrue to say that we never actually unpacked, we did manage to lay out our boxes in some semblance of order.'

When Iraq invaded Kuwait on 2 August 1990 and the Saudi Arabian Government requested assistance, air power was the only instrument at the disposal of the British Government which could get to the Gulf in time and with sufficient force to deter any further aggressions by Saddam Hussein. Because of this the RAF was from the outset at the forefront of the British effort and remained throughout hostilities. The RAF's contribution to air power in the Gulf - both in crisis and conflict - was second only in importance to that of the United States. Within 48 hours of the Defence Secretary Tom King's announcement that the Government was sending large scale forces to the Gulf in Operation 'Granby', a squadron of Tornado F.3s arrived in Saudi Arabia and two hours later they flew their first operational sortie. Flight Lieutenant M. E. Owens recalls:

'The Tornado F.3 was amongst the first aircraft to participate in Operation 'Granby', the British contribution to 'Desert Shield'/'Desert Storm'. 29 (Fighter) Squadron was completing its annual Armament Practice Camp (APC) at Akrotiri, Cyprus, when the invasion of Kuwait took place on 2 August 1990. Within ten days six F.3s from 29 (Fighter) Squadron, together with six F.3s from 5 Squadron (who had arrived at Akrotiri for their APC on the 7th), had deployed to Dhahran, Saudi Arabia and flown their first Combat Air Patrol (CAP) missions. The F.3 detachment at this stage consisted of the twelve aircraft with twenty-two aircrews, supported by over 200 ground crew. With the Iraqis massing a sizeable army in Kuwait and Saddam's intentions unclear, tension was high for the first few weeks. As forces from around the world rushed into Saudi Arabia to bolster the defences, the F.3s flew CAP missions just south of the Kuwait/Iraqi border. In conjunction with fighters from the US and Saudi Air Forces, these CAPS were manned 24 hours a day, guarding against a surprise attack.

'As time passed, the Allied Forces in Saudi Arabia built up rapidly and the situation stabilized. The MOD produced their first personnel rotation and the Coningsby crews were replaced by crews from RAF Leeming, who were by now equipped with the 'Granby'-modified Tornado F.3s. These improved aircraft had modifications to make them more suitable to the hot desert climate, as well as improvements to the aircraft's weapons, communications and countermeasures systems.'

'The initial two weeks in theatre was a particularly testing time for everyone' continues Wing Commander Witts 'and not least for my ground crew. On paper there was simply not enough time for them to service and maintain the aircraft during an intensive theatre-familiarisation flying phase, set up a sustainable wartime engineering operation from absolute scratch, develop and build self-protection facilities against the conventional, chemical and

RAF Tornado GR.1 ZD851/AJ Amanda Jane at Tabuk.

biological threat and train themselves in local procedures. In practice, of course, they achieved all of that and more. I still wonder, however, with no small amount of pride, how many other armed services would have coped with the challenge? Anyway, the deadline duly arrived and we were ready, after a fashion, to do whatever was required. If it is a soldier's right to complain, it is very definitely an airman's assumed right to speculate. In the final days and hours before hostilities commenced that speculation reached fever pitch as we waited to see Saddam's reaction. For some reason everyone seemed to think that I knew what was going to happen, whereas I very definitely did not or, at least, I knew no more than I had been told in the interests of being ready.

'Consequently, it was almost a relief when, in the closing hours of 16 January I was told that we would go to war that night. Even then, it was not a fact that could be broadcast to all and sundry so, for most of the detachment, the first they knew about the war was when my formation landed back from the first sortie at dawn on the 17th.

'From then on events took on a routine of sorts. The initial excitement soon disappeared and we settled down to the reality of war: working, eating, working, sleeping, working and then working some more. Fortunately, although we could never afford to get complacent about it, Saddam's chemical and biological weapons were never brought to use. However, our curiosity was more than satisfied by the regular Scud missile alerts and the resultant pyrotechnic spectaculars as our local Patriot defence missiles shot them down. As one high-ranking American officer commented ruefully 'It's a shame that Saddam Hussein's Scuds have intercepted every Patriot that we've fired against Iraq'. Such are the fortunes of war!

'So, for the ground crew at least, once we got started, the war became something of grind with not much to break the monotony. At times like this, British humour usually saves the day and so it was at Dhahran.'

Sergeant Adrean Davies in Dhahran writing in the *News from the Scudsophrenics,* said: Scuds! What an evocative word! Soon after the coalition forces initiated their first waves of bombing raids, one of the auxiliaries, a certain Colin Mathieson, was sitting outside drinking a non-alcoholic beer when we saw and so did a few others of us, a very bright flare, 'Must be a distress flare or something'. Then - BANG! 'No it isn't, GAS, GAS, GAS'. We all ran around putting on our respirators, dived into the Air Raid shelter, frantically squeezing ourselves into our chemical protection suits. Some were near panic and others more calm, helped the less capable. Our first Scud. It was taken out by the now famous and well documented Patriot system. It had reacted automatically and when we hear the fact announced on the radio there was a feeling akin to restrained euphoria. Since that first encounter we have had several experiences of midnight explosions.'

'For the aircrew, life was slightly different' continues Jerry Witts. 'There was absolutely no shortage of excitement as they returned again and again to whittle down the Iraqi's war fighting capability. The sorties were simple in profile but long and tiring in execution, as the euphoria of returning from yet another mission was replaced by bone-numbing fatigue as the adrenalin wore off. But, throughout, a marvellous relationship grew between the aircrew and the ground crew. Each person knew he was a vital part of the overall effort and everyone was giving 100% to make sure no one let the side down. As a commander, it was reassuring to see. As an aviator, it was a joy to experience, not only that we were fighting for a just cause but also that we had been given the tools to do the job properly. In the Tornado GR.1 we had an excellent aircraft that rightly earned itself a reputation for being rugged, flexible in operation and, most importantly, reliable. The aircraft had been modified in minor ways to cope with the desert environment, but the basic airframe and its capabilities were essentially unchanged from that which we normally operate in North-West Europe.'

All the RAF's re-fuelling assets were needed to deliver the Tornado GR.1s, F.3s and Jaguars from Europe to Tabuk and Dhahran in Saudi Arabia and the former RAF Muharraq, now Bahrain International Airport. In London on 9 August the MoD had announced the forthcoming

A Victor K.Mk.3 tanker with brake chute trailing returns to RAF Marham after a sortie in October 1993. (Author)

dispatch of a dozen each of Tornado F.3 air-defence fighters and Jaguar GR.1A attack aircraft. Operation 'Granby' had begun. In August 1990 55 Squadron's Victors were supporting RAF Jaguars at the Reconnaissance Air Meet in Texas when the recall of all tankers to the UK was ordered. Within 24 hours the 'Tanker Trash' was back at Marham and within 48 hours they were operating over France and Sicily to deploy fast jets to the Persian Gulf where conflict had begun on 2 August when Iraq's president Saddam Hussein's armies invaded Kuwait. On 7 August President George Bush ordered Operation 'Desert Shield' to liberate Kuwait. USAF Lieutenant General Charles A. Horner, the allied coalition's supreme air commander, began co-ordinating all air actions related to the build-up and within days, established HQ Central Command Air Forces (Forward) in Saudi Arabia. Initial Air Force planning was largely concentrated on defending Saudi Arabia from invasion and the first priority therefore was the neutralisation of advancing Iraqi tank and troop columns. The coalition air forces faced 750 Iraqi combat aircraft, 200 support aircraft, Scud missiles, chemical and biological weapon capability, 'state-of-the-art' air defences, ten types of surface-to-air missiles, around 9,000 anti-aircraft artillery pieces and thousands of small arms. The Iraqi air force had twenty-four main operating bases and thirty dispersal fields; many equipped with the latest in hardened aircraft shelters. As many as forty-five of the most important targets were situated in and around Baghdad, a city covering 254 square miles and one which was considered to be seven times more heavily defended than Hànôi had been in December 1972.

By the time the Gulf War began at 2340Z on Wednesday 16 January the Coalition had built an air force of 2,790 aircraft, over half of which were combat aircraft. Included in this total was the RAF contribution of 135 aircraft, which included 46 Tornado GR.1/IA attack and reconnaissance aircraft. The RAF had despatched almost its entire tanker fleet to the Gulf region.

The Tornado GR.Is were already halfway deployed in Cyprus for an APC. On 23 August plans for the dispatch of a Tornado GR.I squadron were announced. On 27 August twelve Tornado GR.Is in hastily applied 'Desert Pink' camouflage left Brüggen in Germany and were flown to Bahrain. A second squadron, of Laarbruch aircraft, but mainly Marham crews, left for Bahrain in two elements on 19 and 26 September, but transferred to Tabuk in the far west of Saudi Arabia from 8 October onwards. Finally, it was decided at Dhahran with twelve additional Brüggen GR.Is, the first of which arrived on 3 January. (Between 2 and 4 January 1991 a third Tornado squadron was deployed to Dhahran to complement the Tornado F.3s and six more Tornado GR.1As were received at the base between 14 and 16 January).

'On return to the UK' continues Flight Lieutenant M. E. Owens, 'it was soon decided that 29 (Fighter) Squadron would return to Dhahran just before Christmas, this time in company with 43 Squadron from Leuchars. To prepare for this deployment, the Squadrons carried out an extensive work-up programme to familiarise themselves with the new standard jets and hone their tactics against the Iraqi threat. One of the major modifications introduced to the F.3

was the ability to make use of Night Vision Goggles (NVGs). Much experience had been gained by the F.3 Operation Evaluation Unit in the use of NVGs and this was used by 29 (Fighter) Squadron to formulate new tactics for their use. Once the tactics had been developed, all crews flew a night work-up phase to ensure they were fully familiar with the NVGs. With the threat of chemical and biological weapons being used by Saddam, the crews also became fully practised in the use of the Aircrew Respirator AR5, worn in flight when a chemical agent had been used.

'The two squadrons deployed to Dhahran in December 1990 where they formed 'the F.3 Squadron' equipped with eighteen further-modified Stage 1+'Granby' jets. The crews had studied the enemy and had respect for the abilities of the Iraqi equipment, but were confident in their aircraft and tactics to defeat him by day or night, even under chemical attack.

'The situation in Dhahran was much the same as when 29 (Fighter) Squadron had left in September, with F3s manning CAPs just south of the Saudi/Iraq/Kuwait border. Christmas was a tense period, with extra aircraft held on ground readiness against an increase in the likelihood of a surprise attack by Saddam. Fortunately, this did not come about and all attention was now turned to the countdown to the UN deadline for Iraq's withdrawal from Kuwait on 15 January 1991. As diplomatic efforts continued, the Squadron used the time to prepare further for the worst eventuality. Squadron operations were moved to an underground concrete bunker and the aircraft were given protection by the use of concrete splinter-shields. On the flight line, sand- bag shelters were constructed to offer rapid protection to the air and ground crew in an air raid and men and machines alike were guarded round the clock by the RAF Regiment.

'With chemical/biological attacks still a definite threat, a decontamination facility was constructed to allow the Squadron to continue to operate even under heavy chemical/ biological contamination. By the time the deadline was reached the Squadron was literally ready for anything.

'As the deadline approached, several plans were drawn up which allowed for situations ranging from a mass attack by the Iraqis through to an all-out attack by the Allies to liberate Kuwait. Just prior to the commencement of Operation 'Desert Storm', the Squadron received the coded order to implement Plan 'Wolfpack' the offensive liberation of Kuwait; H-hour was defined as R0300 (local) 17 January 1991.

'With the plans already carefully prepared, the Squadron moved smoothly into war operations. The CAPs manned by the F.3s were situated just south of the Kuwaiti/Saudi border defending against a direct attack on Allied troops and installations. Controlled by US Airborne Warning and Control aircraft, the F.3s could also vector into Iraq/ Kuwait to engage Iraqi fighters intercepting friendly bombers. These Defensive Counter Air (DCA) CAPs were manned 24 hours a day throughout 'Desert Storm' by F.3s in conjunction with Saudi F.3s, Americans F-15s and French Mirage 2000s.

'In war fit, the F3s carried four Skyflash medium-range radar-guided air-to-air missiles (AAMs), three Sidewinder short-range infra-red AAMs and the internal 27mm Mauser cannon. To enable them to man CAPs at an extended range from base (up to 300nm), the F3s were fitted with 2 x 22501 drop tanks and supported by VC10, Victor and TriStar tankers. The F.3s also carried Chaff and infra-red flares for self-defence.

'On the ground, Dhahran came under many Scud attacks, which made life more difficult for air and ground crews, but did not prevent the Squadron from carrying out its task. The Iraqi Air Force's unwillingness to come up and fight soon became apparent to the aircrews as they continued to fly the CAPs and the decision was made to move the line of defensive CAPs forward. This resulted in the line of DCA CAPs being positioned just north of the Saudi/Iraq and Saudi/Kuwait borders, overhead the Iraqi army. With the defensive line established, American F-15s were free to patrol deep inside Iraq on Offensive Counter Air missions thereby denying the Iraqis the use of their own airspace.

'With virtually no movement from the Iraqi Air Force, the main threat to the F.3s came from the Surface-to-Air Missiles (SAMs) and Anti-Aircraft Artillery (AAA) used by the Iraqi army, over which they were now patrolling. Accurate intelligence allowed the F.3 crews to avoid the engagement zones of the larger SAMs, while flying high enough to be above the ceiling of the smaller SAMs and all but the largest AAA. On numerous occasions the F.3s were fired upon, but always successfully avoided being hit. Many times during this period the F.3 CAPs were vectored by AWACS to intercept and identify unknown radar contacts; however all but two turned out to be friendly. Of the unfriendly aircraft, the first contact was a pair of 'Floggers' that retreated deep into Iraq as the F.3s approached them and the second was a helicopter which landed at an Iraqi airfield before it could be engaged.

'The F.3s continued to man the CAPs 24 hours a day in conjunction with the other Allied fighters, until the start of the ground attack. At this time the CAPs were pulled back behind the Forward Line of Own Troops to allow Allied artillery freedom to fire without risk of hitting friendly fighters. As the round forces made their rapid progress the CAPs followed just behind, ready to deal with any Iraqi fighter/bomber resistance. 86

'The job of the F.3s on Operation 'Granby'/'Desert Storm' was DCA, preventing an air attack on friendly forces. At no time did any Allied forces or installations come under attack by Iraqi aircraft. Disappointingly perhaps, the F3s did not fire a single shot to achieve this, but, more importantly, no F.3 aircrew or aircraft were lost. Given the overwhelming strength of the Allied Air Defence system, it is really not surprising that the Iraqi aircraft had no desire to come up and fight, but the F.3 crews remain confident that they could have defeated any Iraqi fighters if the situation had arisen. Forced to stay on the ground or flee to Iran, the Iraqi Air Force took little part in the war and were dealt with most efficiently by our mud-moving colleagues.'

All the Tornado GR.I/IAs deployed to the Gulf were from RAF Germany, including even those held in reserve at Marham, as these were powered with the more powerful Mk.103 version of the RB199 reheated turbofan. At Muharraq Group Captain David Henderson was in command and XV Squadron commanded by Wing Commander John Broadbent, was the leading unit, although 9, 17 and 31 Squadrons and Marham's 617 'Dambusters' and 27 Squadrons provided crews.

By the time the Gulf War began at 2340Z on Wednesday 16 January the Coalition had built an air force of 2,790 aircraft, over half of which were combat aircraft. Included in this total was the RAF contribution of 135 aircraft, which included 46 Tornado GR.1/IA attack and reconnaissance aircraft. The RAF had dispatched almost its entire tanker fleet to the Gulf region. The initial requirement from Strike Command was that the Victor detachment should support the Tornado F.3 and the Jaguar missions only and the VC 10 detachment would support all Tornado GR.1 sorties. A maximum of nine VC 10 K.Mk.2/3s of 101 Squadron and two TriStar K.Mk.Is of 216 Squadron were at King Khalid Airport just outside Riyadh. On completion of their fighter-bomber positioning assignments one Victor arrived at Muharraq on 14 December for a formal handover from 101 Squadron VC 10 detachment, which had been operating at the Saudi base for three months. The next day three more Victors arrived, followed shortly by two more crews, as Wing Commander David Williams, OC 55 Squadron recalls.

'After all ground training was completed flying began on 16 December to air-refuelling 'towlines' scattered throughout the Saudi Arabian airspace. It became apparent that the rigid apportioning of receivers to tankers was impractical and the Victors supported all types of aircraft from the UK, Canada, France and the United States Navy and Air Force that were probe and drogue compatible. After two weeks of intensive flying, four crews returned to the UK so that the remaining four crews could be brought into the environment and be fully trained to a war footing by 12 January 1991. On this date additional Victor aircraft together with the two initial crews were positioned at Muharraq and by 16 January 55 Squadron was a total of six aircraft, eight crews and 99 ground crew. Further training sorties were flown until 16 January when at 2250 Zulu, two Victors led the first Muharraq Tornado GR.1 bombing mission into Iraq. The sortie was flown along 'Olive Low Trail', which was a track south of the Iraq border but concluded with a northerly heading to cast off the receivers into the heart of Iraq. Olive Trail then became the bread and butter for the rest of the war. To meet all contingencies and to ensure that fuel was available for the Tornadoes on their return from the mission, all Victor aircraft were refuelled to the maximum 123,000lb for takeoff. The early sorties were affected by very poor weather along the refuelling tracks and consequently, the aircraft consumed treble the normal fatigue. As experience grew, the take off fuel was adjusted and the fatigue penalty was reduced.'[87]

Wing Commander John Broadbent recalls.

'I knew that in the early stages of any conflict at least, the Tornadoes would primarily be used for night operations. This meant that most of my 24 crews were allocated to the night shift. As the UN deadline loomed I thought that it was prudent to initiate the night shift system so that our5 body clocks would adjust to the conditions. Then, in the afternoon of 16 January, whilst the night shift was sleeping, I got the 'phone call from Group Captain Dave Henderson the Bahrain Detachment Commander. He said, 'Bring everybody in'.

'In?' I queried.

'Yes'. 'Brief everybody.'

'In the first week of January I had lost the twelve Tornado crews who had the most theatre experience when 14 Squadron went home. (Aircrews changed over every six weeks in the Gulf). In their place I got six from 27 Squadron and six from 617 Squadron. 14 Squadron's ground crews, who were on a three-month detachment, stayed! XV Squadron, my squadron, plus attrition reserves from 9 Squadron, made up the rest of the Muharraq detachment. I was in charge of elements of five squadrons from three air bases in two commands: RAF Germany and Strike!

'I told the crews to rest but how could they now? There were some really serious looking young men around. We had all hoped it wouldn't come to this; that instead Saddam would come to his senses and back down. This was not our back yard. We weren't fighting for the White Cliffs of Dover. It's very difficult in the cold light of day in a distant land to fight for a principle. None of our people would choose to die in the desert, given the option, but their attitude was: 'Let's get it done, as professionally as we can and let's get home as soon as possible'. Ours was arguably the most dangerous mission going in the Gulf. Nevertheless, while there was a military reason for what they were being tasked to do, my people were determined to execute it to the best of their ability. Equally, I was determined too and knowing what the overall picture was, I knew I had a good chance of arranging it. Following the initial brief for the Operation, crews were assigned to their specific missions so that they could put the final touches to the plans. My position as Tornado Squadron Commander had entitled me to be one of the

Tornado GR.1 ZA491 *Nikki* (formerly *Nora Batty*) at take-off.

very few people at Muharraq to be involved in pre-planning missions for 'Desert Storm'. In peacetime training exercises we were used to picking up other people's plans and flying them at short notice. Of course, you would hardly expect to get shot at on a training flight on the North German plain and so the precise angle of cut on a runway was not life-threateningly critical. This was in marked contrast to the Gulf where we fully expected to be engaged by a well-equipped, battle-experienced enemy. Hence, our attitude to planning changed somewhat and we would pore for hours over maps deciding on best aiming points, approach directions, weapon loads and fuse settings to ensure maximum weapon effect at minimum risk.[88]

'One advantage of having been involved in the planning phase was that I had been able to set up the shift system in such a way as to ensure that I would be in a position to lead the first mission. I put XV Squadron crews into the first two waves. (27 and 617 Squadrons would cover the following night). Squadron Leader Nigel Risdale and I would lead the first eight Tornadoes. Our target was [Al] Tallil airfield in southwest Iraq, a huge airfield twice the size of Heathrow. We were to cut the two 11,000 feet parallel runways and the access taxiways leading from the HAS's [hardened aircraft shelters] with our JP233 anti-airfield weapons. Other, US packages were planned to strike the airfield first. Their time over target was 0400 hours; ours was eight minutes later at 0408 hours.[89]

'It was a funny feeling, emptying the contents of your pockets into little plastic bags to be collected by the pretty Squadron Intelligence Officer. It was an odd moment when she gave us our 'Goolie Chits', evasion maps and gold sovereigns before we trooped off. We gave ourselves plenty of time to prepare. Very few people in the detachment knew we were going to war at this stage. Not even the ground crews knew. We'd carried JP233 on night training missions before, so this appeared no different. We tried to make it look like a normal training mission. It worked.

'It was very lonely taxiing out with radio and lights out. Group Captain David Henderson and his OC Ops, Ray Horwood, gave us a brief wave. Our all-up weight of 30 tonnes with drop tanks and two JP233s (alone weighing 10,000lb) meant we could not taxi to the into-wind runway. The net result was a very short taxi followed by a tailwind take-off. All eight of us got airborne, checked in with the Airborne Warning and Control System (AWACS) aircraft and twenty minutes after take-off, met up with our VC 10 tankers who would take us to our entry point into Iraq. Tanking conditions on this first night were quite good, which was in sharp contrast to what was to occur over the following few nights. All eight aircraft refuelled successfully at around 15,000 feet and about one hour and twenty minutes after take-off we left the tankers and headed north. We descended to 500 feet in the black night sky towards Iraq and the unknown. Then we went down to 200 feet as we approached the target area. On the ingress frequency we heard the support packages of fighter sweep Wild Weasels and jammers and F-15s confirm that they too were on time. I could not of course see them in the darkness, but it was reassuring to hear them. The American package of about thirty aircraft was going to the same target and would bomb from medium altitude (around 20,000 feet). We were to bash through one minute after them, at 0408 local, so that our JP233 minefield would be undisturbed.

'Up until this point, it had been just like a training sortie but now came the real test. Would our tactics work? What would it be like to be under fire? Would we all come back? We all experienced some apprehension as the Iraqi border slid down our moving maps and we entered enemy territory for the first time. We had selected the crossing point because Intelligence had indicated that it was well clear of enemy threats and I for one was considerably relieved that they were proved right on the night. The early part of the low level phase proceeded uneventfully with just a few distant lights to be seen. The silence was broken only by the comforting call of 'picture clean' from the AWACS indicating that no enemy aircraft were airborne. However, this quiet scene was not to last.

'When we were about seventy miles from the target, Nigel could see through his NVGs [night vision goggles] the glow from a major battle, which was in progress in our 10 o'clock and as yet over the horizon from us. Nigel said, 'There's a bloody great punch-up going on,' or words to that effect. I wasn't wearing NVGs. I looked up and just saw darkness. Glancing at my watch, it was 11 o'clock - 4 o'clock local, the time the first American aircraft was due over Tallil. I had a quick look at my map to confirm that we would be shortly turning left to start our final run to the target. It seemed probable that the flak that Nigel could see was emanating from our target and was aimed at the American aircraft preceding us. This was confirmed minutes later as we turned towards the airfield and the flak moved into our 12 o'clock. It was obvious the firefight was coming from Tallil and that we'd have to fly through it. I asked, 'Just how fast can this Tornado go?' Nigel hit the burners and then took the burners out before we came over the visual horizon of the target. The firefight was right on our nose. Triple-A fire was hosing the sky. Occasionally, a friendly HARM high-speed anti-radiation missile was on its way down and distinctly unfriendly SAMs [surface-to-air missiles] would light the sky up. It was all just incredible. Many descriptions of what it looked like have been attempted but none do it justice. My own recollection is one of criss-crossing chains of multi-coloured, incandescent balls of tracer arcing up into the night sky. These were interspersed with masses of red speckles of what I assumed was small-arms fire. As far as we could tell, little if any of the fire was actually aimed at us, but it was difficult to convince your bowels of the truth or even relevance of that fact.

'As we approached the airfield, it seemed highly improbable that you could penetrate that seemingly bloody great wall of fire and hope to emerge unscathed out of the other side. My wave of four were converging on the airfield on a heading of 343°; the rear four on a heading of 078°. There would be one Tornado over target every twenty seconds, so that after two minutes twenty seconds all eight would have delivered their JP233s at low level and cleared the target at 550 knots. We rushed over the target wings level for 5-6 seconds to get the JP233s away. Balls of tracer and cannon fire were coming towards us like a pretty firework display. It was like trying to run through a shower without getting wet. I recall saying 'good luck' or something equally inane to Nigel and then putting my head down to make sure that I had the target marked perfectly on the radar. I motored my seat down so nothing could distract me. In peacetime our cockpit seats would have been high. Nigel pushed the speed up to as fast as we could go and got the height down to the absolute minimum compatible with the correct functioning of our JP233. Seconds later we were over the airfield and the cockpit was surrounded by tracer flashes. The JP233 started to dispense automatically with a thunderous roar; lighting up the undersurface of the aircraft with a dull red glow as it did so. Far more quickly than I had anticipated, since I had imagined that this part of the mission would appear interminable, the heavy thump of the now-empty weapon dispensers being automatically jettisoned signalled that the attack was over. The aircraft leaped forward freed of its huge weapon load and we were out the other side and safe. Feelings of relief and almost euphoria washed over us 'Holy Shit - I've survived,' I thought. Exhilaration! I felt ten foot tall - if not taller. Our attack was perfect.

'But our euphoria was soon to be cut short. I waited a couple of minutes before checking the rest of the formation in. All responded until I got to No. 5 - nothing. '5 Check'. Still nothing. 'We've lost 'Gordo' (Gordon Buckley), leader of the back four, I thought. 'We've lost him. I'm not surprised. Bloody good mate. Paddy Teakle too. Two really good hands. Never see them again.' My exhilaration was gone…In our Tornado clangers were going off WAH, WAH, WAH, red lights were flashing and 'Kojaks' (warning sirens) were blaring away. We were not going as fast as we should. We suddenly realized we had lost an engine. In the heat of battle we had not realized it. We did not jettison our tanks and in any case the aircraft was much lighter without the JP233s. We retraced our steps across the desert and turned back to the tanker. We were pretty quiet because we thought we had lost 'Buckers'. I was convinced that we had lost him when, despite repeated efforts to raise him on the radio, twenty minutes later we had reached the tanker with still no sign of him. Then, climbing up to the tanker, we heard him! He had heard us calling him but he had a weak transmitter and we could not hear him! I now have sympathy with those that say you have to experience pain to understand pleasure because when he did eventually check in my joy was complete. The rest of the mission was relatively uneventful; even having to shut down an engine on the transit back to Muharraq seemed totally innocuous after what we had experienced over Iraq. We were first back at Muharraq at six in the dawn sky, four hours and five minutes after take-off, to an enthusiastic welcome. And we were just in time to encourage the guys waiting to go out in the next wave [to Ar Rumaylah airfield for daylight lofting or 'toss-bombing' of 1,000 pounders]. Squadron Leader Pablo Mason looked grey. The world's press was waiting. Rupert Clark, my own No.4, told the press, 'It went on rails!' The guys couldn't have done better. I couldn't have asked them to do more. (Post-strike photos showed a very successful outcome and no more than a twenty feet error). There was lots of 'Biggles banter' with the troops. We said the usual, that it was 'a piece of piss,' 'nothing to worry about', etc! I rushed into squadron HQ still wearing my G-bags. Throwing open Dave Henderson's door I shouted: 'We're all back!'

'My formation was lucky, we all returned. Others were not so fortunate and over the next three days the Muharraq detachment was to lose three crews in quick succession, including John Peters and John Nichol from the formation we had waved off with such enthusiasm shortly after dawn on 17 January.[90] The leadership challenge following the losses at this time was not as great as one might imagine since I noted a marked stiffening of attitudes amongst the aircrews and a grim determination to get the job done. Nevertheless, we all felt a great deal of satisfaction and relief when the Allied forces gained air supremacy so swiftly. The effectiveness of the RAF's JP233 attacks certainly played its part in this achievement. My own formation flew its third and final JP233 mission on the night of 20 January and we moved medium level the following day. The rest, as they say, is history.'[91]

On the night of 17/18 January Marham crews formed a four-ship Tornado attack on Ubaydah bin al Jarrah airfield and another four were given Al Tallil airfield at Shaibah close to the city of Basrah as their target. Each of the eight Tornadoes was loaded with two JP233s. Other Tornadoes would return to take-out the taxiways the following day. The al Jarrah formation took off at midnight, local time and the 'Norwich' formation took off for Shaibah two hours later, as their shorter journey required just one pre-attack refuelling from a VC 10. One of the pilots on the Shaibah strike was newly promoted 24-year old Flight Lieutenant David Waddington on 27 Squadron. Waddington had been part of the original team of Tornado crews that had deployed to the Gulf essentially for training and on alert should the Iraqis invade Saudi Arabia. After six weeks, when it was decided to put more Tornadoes in theatre he and the rest

Jaguar GR.Mk.1A XX719 in Desert Pink scheme during the Gulf War.

Royal Saudi Air Force GR.4 Tornado coming into land.

of the 'Marham Group' had split from the 'Germany Group' and had moved to Tabuk. As part of the rotation of crews Waddington returned to England just before Christmas 1990. He was not scheduled to return to the Gulf until April 1991. His proposal to his fiancée Claire Holderness, a young nurse was accepted and they made plans for a summer wedding. But as the Gulf crisis escalated early in the New Year Waddington was called back and he had re-deployed to Bahrain in January. This time he and his fellow pilots sensed a definite increase in tension as the 15 January deadline approached.

After taking on fuel the four Tornadoes heading for al Jarrah dropped to 300 feet crossing the Iraqi border and steadily descended to 200 feet over the desert to the target, where the sky was lit up by AAA fire five minutes before they went in. Flying parallel to the runway in 'card four' formation the leading pair two miles apart, the trailing pair thirty seconds' flying time behind them, turned towards the airfield. The spacing was closed up to one mile and the interval to fifteen seconds, then ten. With one minute to go Flying Officer Nigel Ingle and Flight Lieutenant Paul McKernan of 617 Squadron in ZD744 felt a bump and thought they had been hit, but the Tornado was still flyable - just. Flight Lieutenant Beet and Flight Lieutenant Osborne and Flight Lieutenant Ruddock and Squadron Leader Crowley each dropped their two JP233s at one-fifth and three-fifths along the runway's length and Flight Lieutenant Waddington and Flight Lieutenant Hammans and Ingle and McKernan released their pair at the two-fifths and four-fifths points. After turning for home Ingle could not maintain control above 350 knots and when he eventually found the VC 10 tanker he could only maintain formation by adopting 45°-wing sweep. He managed to reach Muharraq safely where inspection revealed that the Tornado had suffered a bird strike that had removed a large section of the port wing's leading edge. The Tornado was immediately patched and flown back to Brüggen for repair. Three days later it was re-delivered to the Gulf and went on to complete 35 missions.

All went well as the 'Norwich' formation flew the ingress route over Iraq to Shaibah at 550 knots relying only on the radar altimeter to keep them 200 feet above the desert and a map to locate the electricity pylons to the north and east of the airfield. Firing started within two miles of the Iraqi border and continued remorselessly until the aircraft were back over the border into friendly territory again. All the JP233s were successfully released but there was heavy triple-A fire from the ground and the Iraqis sent up SAM missiles too. Waddington recalls.

'There were one or two missiles, which with the benefit of hindsight were probably unguided. I was just so focused on getting through that there was no real fear, more apprehension. We just wanted to get out the other side but we were busy doing our job in the cockpit. On leaving the target there was a huge explosion on the desert floor. Once the shooting stopped and we came out of Iraq and towards friendly territory we were over the sea climbing for our return to Bahrain and checked in with the AWACs. At that point they informed us that there were only three of us. There is a still a huge element of doubt over what happened and I do not think we will ever really know. [ZA392 flown by 27 Squadron's 39-year old CO, Wing Commander Nigel Elsdon and his 42-year old navigator, Flight Lieutenant Robert 'Max' Collier was hit three minutes after 'bombs away' and had crashed into the ground, killing both crew. The three other Tornadoes landed safely back at Muharraq after 1 hour 55 minutes in the air.] Even before then we knew that Peters and Nichol were missing because they had been flying from Bahrain in a different formation. So we knew this thing was dangerous and we knew that going against airfields was going to be dangerous by its very nature. I knew when I signed up that I could be called upon to do this sort of thing. It was under a UN mandate and it was war and although it was not the sort of thing we had envisaged I do not think there was any question as to why we were there. But this loss of Elsdon and Collier personally hit very, very hard together with the fact that the two Johns were missing. There was now an unspoken fear about who was going to be next.'[92]

The Tornado crews were flying night combat sorties only and at Muharraq on the 19/20th eight Tornadoes of 'Belfast' formation were made ready for a raid on Tallil air base in central Iraq. Four of the Tornadoes were armed with JP233s and another four were loaded with eight 1,000-pounders fused for an airburst fifteen feet above the Iraqi gun emplacements. At 1457Z seven Tornadoes (the eighth developed mechanical failure) headed for Tallil. The approach to the target was not as dangerous as before and the Tornadoes flew though the middle of Saudi Arabia meeting no resistance whatsoever. Tornado GR.I ZA396 was crewed by Flight Lieutenant David Waddington and his 44-year old navigator, Flight Lieutenant Robert 'Robbie' Stewart who was also from 27 Squadron. Waddington recalls.[93]

'We were only flying over Iraq for about thirty minutes until we hit the target. Absolutely pitch dark, nothing around us - just like doing a training sortie. I was the number two aircraft in the formation and consequently, with the tactics, among the first to arrive at the airfield. We were trying to do a surprise job dropping the 1,000 pounders to suppress the triple-A so that the last four aircraft, who were carrying JP233s, would have an easier time. It meant pulling the aircraft into a climb in a 'toss attack' and letting the bombs go at 30° climb about three miles from the target. We were just coming up to the pull-up point where we would release the bombs, three and a half miles from the target. I saw the bright yellow flame of a [Euromissile Roland SAM] launch at me, at 12 o'clock, which is the worst position. My exact words were 'Shit! Missile!' I broke left and shouted 'Chaff' at Robbie. All I could see was a flame like a very large firework coming towards me but once I banked the aircraft we lost sight of it. Then there was an enormous wind - I think I was unconscious very quickly. My last thoughts were that I was going to die. [The blast shattered the canopy, caused the hydraulics and started a fire in the cockpit]. Fortunately for me Robbie in the back seat had been protected because of the equipment and he used the command ejection system to eject us out [at 540 knots and only 180 feet above the ground]. My next memory after that was regaining consciousness on the ground. I have no recollection of the parachute landing but probably about half an hour later I came to. I realised that I had taken a lot of injuries, albeit superficial, to my face. Both arms were dislocated at right shoulder and left elbow. As a result of that I could not recover my parachute and because it was still inflated I could not recover my survival equipment. The pockets of my G-suit were blown away but my life jacket still had the radio and other essentials for short-term survival. The collective feeling of the rest of the formation was that we had not got out and they expected that we were dead.

'I realized that I could not stay where I was and had to put some distance between where I was then and where I wanted to be by daylight. At that stage I was still trying to make radio contact and although I suspected my radio was not working I kept trying to transmit. I was several hundred miles the wrong side of the border and had not been able to make contact with friendly forces. To be honest, the situation was still pretty poor. From where I was I tried to walk away. My legs were fine so I decided to try to escape and evade until daybreak. By then I had travelled four or five miles to a position where there were two pipelines. They were about forty feet apart so I tried to hide in the middle of them. But in the flat desert it was not too difficult for someone to follow a trail and some in the morning a couple of Iraqi soldiers spotted me. They started firing, pretty close to me. I don't think they were firing at me but they were sending me a clear warning. As they got closer I could see that they were quite scared of me. They knew I was armed and they kept gesticulating to me to put my arms above my head and surrender. But I could not do that. Both my arms had been dislocated and I could not raise them. There was a bit of a stand-off as they wondered what was going to happen but eventually they disarmed me, took away my pistol and then led me away to their barracks little more than a shed in the desert.'

Waddington was taken to Al Tallil airfield, his target the night before and he was then moved to Baghdad where blindfolded, he was interrogated by Ba'ath Party officials. His consistent refusal to answer questions apart from the 'big four' of name, rank, serial number and date of birth, was met with severe beatings with fists and sticks, which left him unconscious of on the verge of consciousness. Eventually his blindfold was lifted and the Iraqis showed him his aircraft checklist, which had his name and aircraft type on it. The physical elements of the beatings then transferred to the psychological phase but soon they became less intensive and eventually stopped. Waddington was taken to hospital in Baghdad and an operation was carried out on his damaged elbow. In prison his weight eventually dropped from ten and a half stones to just over eight stones. His only contact with other prisoners was when he heard the guards speak to them. He was aware that the American F-16 pilot Captain Jeff Tice and the captured Kuwaiti A-4KU Skyhawk pilot, Mohammed Mubarak were nearby.[94] He did not know what had happened to Robbie Stewart and considered that he had already made his escape on foot. But what had happened to him was that when he landed he broke his leg in three places and Iraqi civilians picked him up in the morning and handed him over to the military authorities in return for payment of $20,000. On or around 23 February the Americans bombed the prison holding the captured airmen but fortunately they hit the other half and not where the prisoners were and several guards were killed. Later, Waddington supposed that while the worst moment of captivity was when he realised he had been shot down the most frightening was the bombing of the prison and psychologically the worst thing was being kept in a pitch black cell for three weeks or so. Just after the explosions the prisoners were able to do a quick roll call and Waddington shouted 'does anyone know what happened to Robbie Stewart?' The reply came back, 'I'm here Dave'. Both men were repatriated after the end of the war.[95]

By 23 January five Tornadoes had been lost in action. On 20 January Squadron Leader Peter Battson and Wing Commander Mike Heath of 20 Squadron experienced a control malfunction aboard Tornado ZD893 just after take-off from Tabuk. They flew around for one hour twenty minutes burning off fuel, jettisoned eight 1,000lb bombs and made two landing attempts before they ejected. They were airlifted home on 24 January. On 22 January Squadron Leaders Gary Lennox (34) and Kevin Weeks (37) on 16 Squadron were killed when their Tornado (ZA467) was shot down during the attack on Ar Rutbah radar station. On 23 January Pilot Officer Simon 'Budgie' Burgess, at 23 the youngest pilot in the conflict and 40-year old Squadron Leader Bob Ankerson on 17 Squadron at Dharan took off in the early hours of the morning to bomb an airfield. After crossing the border it took them about forty minutes before they reached the target. At the release point they felt their bombs go. Seconds later there was an explosion and Ankerson could see six- or eight-feet flames 'leaping out' of the left wing. One of their bombs on release had detonated the others aboard Tornado ZA403/CO. They immediately jettisoned the fuel tanks but it was to no avail. Finally, Burgess called 'eject, eject, eject' and they banged out of the doomed Tornado. They were captured immediately. It was the start of several months of very unpleasant interrogation and solitary confinement before they were transferred to another prison which held Robbie Stewart, Dave Waddington, John Nichol, a Kuwaiti and an Italian. Though the Tornado force represented just four per cent of the Coalition air strength it had suffered 26 per cent of the casualties.

On 14 February the sixth and final Tornado lost in air combat occurred. Flight Lieutenant Rupert Clark (31) and Flight Lieutenant Stephen Hicks (26) of XV Squadron were flying ZD717 when they were the last aircraft in an eight-Tornado/four-Buccaneer package in an LGB attack on Al Taqaddum air base. Five seconds short of the bomb-release point Clarke noticed a brief burst of signals from a missile control radar on his RHWR. Clark continued with the attack however and there was no more radar activity until he reached the release point. One LGB left the wing rack but the second bomb refused to budge despite all efforts by Steve Hicks. Shortly after a panic radio call warned of a double missile launch over the target! Hicks called 'Break left!' and began releasing Chaff. Clark selected full power, lowered the Tornado's manoeuvering flaps and threw the aircraft into a tight turn. 'We were going through north when there was this huge explosion and I felt the blast wave hit the aircraft' he recalled later.' It was obvious what had happened. I shouted to Steve 'You OK?', but there was no reply.' The Soviet-built SA-3 'Goa' had detonated a few feet off the port side of the Tornado. Clark knew the second SAM was on its way and he moved the stick, overbanked the aircraft and pulled back. 'Then I saw the second missile coming at me. It was coming up vertically, waggling as it guided on to me. I pulled on the stick as hard as I could; there was nothing else I could do. The missile disappeared from view going behind and to the right of the aircraft. There was another explosion as it went off.' Again Clark shouted to ask how Hicks was and again there was no reply from his navigator.

Preparing GR.4 Tornadoes at RAF Marham for repainting in Desert Pink camouflage scheme prior to flying out to the Gulf.

After battling with the controls Clark finally pulled his ejection seat handle at 10,000 feet. He heard a loud bang and the aircraft filled with swirling black smoke as the rockets fired the canopy into the sky above. Then came another loud bang in the rear cockpit, as the navigator's seat fired. (The ejection seats are interconnected so that, if the pilot pulls his handle, the navigator's seat is fired first and the pilot's seat follows shortly afterwards). 'I got the kick up the backside as my seat fired. I heard or sensed each action in turn: the cartridges firing in my seat, my drogue gun going and my seat tumbling as I left the aircraft. I was fully conscious and I remember thinking, when are all these explosions going to stop? Then suddenly there was dead silence; absolutely no noise at all and I was hanging from my parachute.'

Clark could see Hicks' parachute land some distance away. The canopy deflated and there was no sign of life. Clark landed on the desert floor and took stock: 'You could have put a cricket pitch almost anywhere there and you wouldn't have needed to use the heavy roller. There was nothing at all to hide behind. Just off to the south were what

looked like some big sandstone blocks, land] I thought that was the best place to head. So I picked up the survival pack and started legging it in that direction. The pack was heavy and after about 200 metres I decided to get rid of the dinghy. I started to open the pack, very carefully so as not to inflate the dinghy, when psssssssss… the bright orange dinghy started to inflate itself!'[96] Clark remained at large for less than a quarter of an hour before a civilian on a motor cycle armed with a rifle came speeding across the desert towards him. With no chance of escape, Clark raised his hands in surrender and was taken prisoner. On 5 March the Tornado captives held in captivity were led out blindfolded, given a spray of cheap aftershave then led on to a bus and driven to a hotel in Baghdad and handed over to the Red Cross.

It was obvious to all that precision-guided weapons were the only salvation if the Tornadoes were to remain at medium level. Blackburn Buccaneers fitted with the 'Pavespike' pod, which provided a manually controlled TV picture by day only, were deployed to act as laser designators for the Tornadoes.[97] Despite a long operational life of thirty years, the Buccaneer prior to the Gulf War had never seen 'active service'. However, continual updating of the aircraft's avionic and weapons capabilities ensured that when the RAF required laser designation support for its Tornado aircraft during Operation 'Granby', the Maritime Buccaneer Wing of RAF Lossiemouth was suitably equipped and prepared for combat. Eighteen crews and twelve 'desert pink' Buccaneers deployed on 27 January 1991. Operational flying began on 2 February, when the first of many targets in Iraq was attacked using Paveway LGBs, delivered by Tornado and guided by the 'Pavespike' laser designation system of the Buccaneer.

Group Captain Bill Cope, the Buccaneer Force Commander in the war tells his story:

'In 1991 the RAF operated three Buccaneer squadrons, Nos. 12 and 208 Squadrons and 237 OCU (Operational Conversion Unit), all based at RAF Lossiemouth. The entire force consisted of about thirty airframes and the role was exclusively maritime attack, with the sole exception of 237 OCU which also had a reserve war role involving overland Laser designation (target marking), from low level, for Jaguar aircraft. Therefore the then AOC 18 Group - Air Marshal Sir Michael Steer - foresaw a possible requirement for overland Laser designation and instructed the Buccaneers to commence the appropriate low-level overland training. I was told that, in the unlikely event there was to be a Buccaneer contribution, he would be the commander. However, all the indications were that there would not be such a detachment, simply because there were already too many aircraft for the limited facilities and hardstanding area which existed at the airfields used by the RAF in the Gulf area.

'Of course, normal training continued and in mid January the two operational squadrons were on detachment, 12 Squadron in Gibraltar and 208 Squadron at RAF St Mawgan. About half-way through the planned 208 Squadron detachment and after two or three days of hostilities in the Gulf, Sir Michael Steer paid a visit to St. Mawgan. He arrived in the same aircraft that was to take Bill Cope (then Wing Commander OC 208 Squadron) home to Lossiemouth to go on leave. Sir Michael greeted Bill with the message that 'sadly, they (the Gulf War commanders) saw no need for Buccaneer involvement'. Bill climbed into the aircraft and returned to Lossiemouth, looking forward to his planned family holiday in Italy, knowing that a possible Gulf detachment was as distant as ever. The aircraft landed at Lossiemouth at 1900 hours, he bid farewell to the Station Commander and went home to pack. Needless to say, at 2230 hours he received a call to tell him the plans had changed and his Unit now had 72 hours to deploy to the Gulf.

'Three days of frantic preparation ensued. Virtually all of the Station was involved in the preparation of the detachment's six aircraft and its personnel and work continued non-stop, day and night, to the extent that the Station Commander, Group Captain (now Air Commodore) Jon Ford hardly slept for three days. The engineers had to prepare the first batch of six aircraft, installing wartime fits and repainting them in desert camouflage. Crews received anti-chemical and bacteriological warfare jabs, wrote wills and collected extra NBC (Nuclear, Biological and Chemical) clothing. Bill says: 'the Station's response to the short-notice deployment was magnificent; we had every support that they could think of and prepare in the time available. That splendid quality of back-up was maintained throughout the war, until everyone returned home.

'At 0400 hours on 26 January the first pair of Buccaneers, with Bill piloting one of them, departed Lossiemouth with the paint still wet on the aircraft. A nine hour direct flight with a TriStar tanker took the aircraft over Europe, Egypt and Saudi to the operating base at Bahrain. En route, Bill found himself, for the first time ever, piloting an aircraft carrying live-armed Sidewinder air-to-air missiles. The ground crew flew by Hercules, a nineteen hour flight.

'No sooner had the aircraft arrived than training began in earnest. A one week intensive training programme commenced, flying close formation sorties with Tornado bombers and acclimatising to desert conditions, which were completely different to overflying the sea, to say the least! The standard operating package was four Tornadoes and two Buccaneers carried the bombs, which were precision targeted using the Buccaneer Laser pod. As the Buccaneer only carries one pod, Laser failure would render the mission unworkable so all aircraft would have to return to base. Thus Buccaneers flew in pairs, to ensure that missions would not be compromised by such an eventuality.

'Only days after arriving in theatre, the Buccaneer Force flew its first mission, on 2 February. Two Buccaneers, crewed by Wing Commander Bill Cope and Flight Lieutenant Carl Wilson and Flight Lieutenant Glen Mason with Squadron Leader Norman Browne flew with four Tornadoes. They flew a route that was to become very familiar, popularly called 'Olive Trail', where they took some fuel on board from a tanker before heading towards the As Suwaira road bridge, at a height of 18,000 feet. The route was in cloud all the way until the final fifty miles where, just as the met team had predicted, there were clear skies. Although the crews knew that their aircraft had been illuminated by Iraqi owned Russian Air Defence systems, there was no enemy attempt to engage and allied AWACS aircraft regularly confirmed that there were no Iraqi aircraft airborne. The bridge was easily identified and the attack successful.

'A routine was soon established with daily taskings of mixed Tornado/Buccaneer packages to destroy road bridges over the Tigris and Euphrates rivers, to break the Iraqi resupply lines to their army in Kuwait. Within a week of commencing operations, nine crews were operational and success led to increased tasking. Indeed, the only constraint was the number of aircraft and daylight hours for, unlike modern systems, the Buccaneer Laser pod had no night-time capability. Although the equipment was dated - the navigator had to target the bombs using a roller ball for the forty seconds between release and impact - the Lasers achieved a 50% success rate which compares most favourably with modern equipment.

'In all, the Buccaneer Force is accredited with guiding bombs which destroyed approximately twenty bridges, varying from suspension to double-span motorway bridges. Unknown at the time, the Iraqis had located their fibre-optic cables along the same bridges, so every downed bridge also broke a communications line, resulting in disorder at the front line.

An RAF Jaguar, F.3 and GR.4 Tornadoes and a Buccaneer S.Mk.2B, all in Desert Pink scheme in formation.

'It has to be said that there was a lot of improvisation initially as the new aircraft packages were just that - new - and there was little experience on which to base operations. For example, although the squadron Qualified Weapons Instructors were adamant that the best aiming point for suspension bridges was the supporting towers, higher authority disagreed and instructed the crews to aim at the bridge abutments. However, almost immediately this decision was amended and the supporting towers targeted, to great effect. Another lesson quickly learnt was that the two sets of bombs had to detonate simultaneously; otherwise the second set of bombs would be blown off target by the first detonation.

'One of the more upsetting aspects of the campaign was having to drop bombs onto bridges without any means of warning road traffic. Sadly, from time to time, there were casualties, though there were also happier moments. On one occasion the navigator was observing a vehicle crossing a bridge when bombs destroyed the first and last sections, leaving the driver marooned but safe in the still intact centre. Alas, not all drivers were so lucky.

'It was after one week that Bill saw his first SAM. This was not as frightening as it may sound, as a missile which is receiving guidance signals - which is a serious threat - kicks in its trajectory so is easy to recognise. On the other hand, non-guided missiles followed a straight path and are no longer a risk to the target aircraft. Given the presence of American Wild Weasel aircraft - who would shoot their anti-radar 'HARM' rockets straight into a guided missile radar unit; during the raids, the Iraqis were highly reticent to switch on the radar; if they had, they quickly switched it off, preferring to launch wildly their weapons. Thus, the allied aircrew could see when the SAMs were not guided and consequently very unlikely to hit.

'Throughout the seven weeks of hostilities morale was very good. Of the eventual eighteen aircrews in theatre, not one mission was cancelled due to illness or aircraft unserviceability, compared to the peacetime norm whereby an average of one sortie per week would have been lost to sickness alone. The aircrews had been specially selected, resulting in one senior officer for every aircraft, to maximise experience levels. Despite this and the fact that no aircraft were lost, of course walking to the aircraft prior to a mission was always a sobering time and you could not help but compare the contrast between those setting out and those returning.

'The ground crew deserves a special mention. Under the sterling leadership of Squadron Leaders David Tasker and George Baber, aircraft serviceability was indeed impressive and only bettered by the Jaguar Force. There was always at least one spare aircraft and usually two, not bad for an aircraft older than the majority of the personnel in theatre. Indeed, in its thirty years in operation, never had Buccaneer serviceability been better. In fairness, the ground crew had to put up with a lot, including highly stressed aircrew from time to time. Even Bill confesses to occasionally having been less than a perfect gentleman and was most grateful to Flight Sergeant (now Warrant Officer) 'Chalky' White for his good grace following one particular incident, details of which are best kept secret.

'Once the land offensive commenced, the Buccaneer role switched from bridge bombing to airfield attacks, specifically against Hardened Aircraft Shelters, runways and any aircraft on the ground, to ensure the Iraqi Air Force stayed out of the battle. In fact, the Iraqi Air Force showed no inclination to engage and the Buccaneers actually stopped flying with air-to-air defence missiles and carried bombs instead. They still flew in packages with Tornado bombers and provided Laser guidance, but in addition would bomb opportunity targets afterwards. Such bombing would be done at steep dive angles of up to 40%, which necessitated applying airbrakes to prevent the aircraft going supersonic, which it was not cleared to do. It certainly raised the hairs on the back of the neck!

'One notable successful opportunity target that presented itself was on 21 February at Shayka Mazar when several Russian built 'Cub' transport aircraft were sighted on the aircraft pan. Both Buccaneers dive bombed the aircraft and were delighted to see two of the targets destroyed. The first enemy aircraft received a direct hit but the bombs failed to explode; none the less, the momentum of the bomb did the trick and the aircraft split in two. The second Buccaneer - under the guidance of navigator Flight Lieutenant Carl Wilson - also scored direct hits and TV viewers back in the UK were treated that night to the spectacle of the fully fuelled aircraft exploding in a ball of fire.

'Buccaneer crews were accommodated in a five star hotel with en suite facilities. They would work two days on and one day off. During the day off they were free to explore but, in reality, usually relaxed by the swimming pool. In some respects, it all seemed a little unreal. Crews would awake at 0300 hours, shower, put on civilian clothing - uniform was forbidden in the hotel - and drive in the hire car the five miles to Bahrain.'

Squadron Leader W. N. Brown 'A' Flight Commander on 12 Squadron who was awarded the Distinguished Flying Cross for service in the Gulf recalls:

'The tactics employed by the Buccaneer force during Operation 'Granby' were evolved for the 'unique' war with Iraq. Prior to the deployment, routine training for Buccaneer crews mainly involved flying tactics at very low level and high speed. Operations during the conflict, however, were all conducted at high level and involved techniques, new and untried, being used by the Buccaneer crews. Fortunately, training over the years for 'the worst case' enabled everybody to adjust quickly to the demands of a new scenario and the capability of the Buccaneer was easily absorbed into the large-scale co-ordinated operations of the Allies.

'On all missions two Buccaneers would accompany four Tornados to their allocated target. After long transits to Iraq, tanking en-route, the package would split into two Tornados and one Buccaneer. The Tornados would approach the target and release their 1,000lb Paveway Guided Bombs. The Buccaneer crew would then be responsible for guiding these bombs to the target. In order to accomplish this, the crew had a number of objectives:

1.   The target had to be acquired visually.
2.   The pilot had to point the Pavespike pod at the target.
3.   The navigator had to identify the target and continue to track it with his pod.

4. The laser had to be fired from the pod and held on the aiming-point until bomb impact.

When listed as above these objectives may appear relatively easy to achieve, but the reality of course was very different. The necessity of the Buccaneer pilot visually acquiring each target from high level meant that meticulous study and planning for every target took many hours. Tornado crews, as the leaders of each package, took the brunt of most of the planning, with the Buccaneer crews concentrating on the actual attack details. Planning began the day prior to a mission and crews usually reported for briefing six hours prior to take-off. Co-ordination with Airborne Warning and Control, Tanker support, Electronic Counter Measure support aircraft and fighter aircraft all had to be arranged before sortie briefing, with lots of time left afterwards for Intelligence and Combat Survival updates. Most operational missions involved long transits before entering enemy airspace; this time was gratefully used to ensure that all aircraft systems were synchronized with the accompanying Tornados and that they were all working. Once into enemy territory everything focused on completing the task. All of one's senses were heightened, but as the target approached one seemed to get tunnel vision and nothing mattered more than finding the aiming-point and marking it until the bombs impacted. The Pavespike pod encases a television camera which gives the Buccaneer navigator a small picture on a screen in the rear cockpit. Once his pilot his pointed the camera at the target the navigator can watch the aiming-point and fire the laser beam at it. Seconds after 'bombs gone', although it often seemed like an eternity, the Buccaneer crew were able to evaluate the success of their attack and have the results recorded on a video tape.

'Now the pilot and navigator could revert to being a crew again and all eyes were out of the cockpit, looking for enemy surface-to-air missiles and anti-aircraft artillery, as all haste was made towards friendly territory.

'On the ground, life was just as hectic. Engineering support worked flat-out in limited space and time to ensure that the Buccaneers were always ready for action. 'Nose Art' and missions completed in the form of painted bombs were welcome additions to the aircraft, always mysteriously appearing after a night in rectification. High temperatures, Scud alerts and rapidly constructed support bays were all hindrances the engineers coped with, as they do on many Squadron detachments. Field catering and letters to and from home filled in any spare time available and at the end of each day's flying the ground crew were able to share the aircrews' success by viewing the video debriefs of the day's missions.

'During Operation 'Granby' the Buccaneer Wing flew over 200 sorties against a variety of targets. The majority of the missions were flown to guide bombs dropped by Tornados, but towards the end of the conflict the Buccaneer crews were also self-designating their own bombs to the target, having released them from a high-angle dive. This method of attack needed much less co-ordination, but it could not deliver the weight of bombs needed to destroy hardened targets. Operation 'Granby' proved to be hugely successful for the Buccaneer Wing. Aircrew learnt many valuable lessons about themselves, their aircraft and their weapon systems. They were supported totally by Squadron ground crew, who never failed to produce a serviceable aircraft for a mission. Continued support from all sections at RAF Lossiemouth meant that 'war ops' could be carried on as if a normal detachment was in progress. In short, twelve Buccaneers were deployed on Operation 'Granby' and twelve Buccaneers returned unscathed.

'High-level operations over the desert against a land-locked country were never envisaged as a setting for the Buccaneer to go to war. However, it happened and the aircraft and crews reacted to the challenge superbly. The aircraft performed outstandingly in a role that was never foreseen; the well-publicised destruction of military targets in Iraq is testament to the professionalism and flexibility of all RAF personnel involved in the operation.'

What was needed urgently was a laser designator for use on the Tornado to direct Laser Guided Bombs (LGBs) on to the target at night. Ferranti had been involved in the development of such a system since 1973 and this culminated in the production of a Thermal Imaging

Airborne Laser Designator (TIALD) pod which had been under flight development on a Buccaneer at RAE Farnborough since early 1988. To permit day and night operation under varying weather conditions, TIALD was equipped with thermal imaging and a TV camera, which were mounted in a pod carried beneath the aircraft. The designator was integrated into the aircraft's navigation and attack (nav/attack) system to enable it to be directed and controlled and the thermal or visual images were recorded by the infrared recce recorder in the Tornado GR.IA. Before TIALD the RAF's ability to use LGBs depended on designation of the target by a manually controlled laser marker. This was operated either from a ground based designator, as was used in the Falklands conflict, or from the air. In the latter case, the marker equipment was fitted to a Buccaneer and controlled by the navigator. Although it was employed successfully during the Gulf War, there were several limitations to this system. The main one was that the navigator needed to see the target visually, thus limiting its use to good weather by day: Additionally, it could not be integrated with a modern nav/attack system. Also, having located the target the navigator had to track it visually - not easy in turbulence or if the aircraft was taking evasive action. During the preparations for 'Granby', Ferranti were asked to accelerate development of TIALD and its integration into the Tornado system, the main problem being the extensive computer software changes required by this integration. This problem was overcome and it was planned to complete the work within six weeks, starting from 30 November 1990. Within three weeks a modified pod was delivered to Boscombe Down and the RAF had allocated five Tornado GR1s for modification to carry the TIALD pod. 13 Squadron were selected to introduce TIALD into service and four experienced crews carried out development trials at Boscombe Down. Five aircraft were modified at Honington with the necessary wiring to link the main computer and the system control panel in the rear cockpit with the front of the left shoulder pylon, where the TIALD pod was to be mounted. The aircraft also had the other special modifications required by all Operation 'Granby' aircraft. These included the 'Have Quick' frequency hopping, anti-jamming radio and the Mode IV Identification Friend or Foe (IFF)

Tornado GR.1 ZD707/BK of 31 Squadron under shelter at Muharraq, Bahrain with AIM-9 Sidewinder missiles in the foreground. This aircraft normally operated out of Dhahran in Saudi Arabia.

A TIALD pod attached to an RAF Tornado during the Gulf War. TIALD as an air interdiction targeting pod performed reasonably well, as was proved in 'Deliberate Force' (1995), 'Allied Force' (1999) and Operation 'Telic' (2003). However The TIALD pod was sidelined in RAF service by the introduction of the stand-off 'Storm Shadow' missile, GPS-guided Enhanced Paveway and the LITENING pod. Experience in Afghanistan led to the realisation that TIALD was outdated. It was designed in the 1980s, to allow pilots to drop laser guided bombs on targets like bridges, big buildings and aircraft hangars but what was needed was a sensor that is geared more towards urban close air support, where the need is to defend particular targets that are very similar to others, such as compounds within small towns or villages.

equipment for compatibility with that used by the US Forces and their Airborne Warning and Control System (AWACs) aircraft. All engines had to be fitted with single crystal turbine blades, as early experience in the desert revealed problems with sand melting on the original blades and blocking their cooling air ducts.

On arrival at Tabuk the TIALD team was taken over by OC 617 Squadron. Wing Commander Bob Iveson, probably the only RAF officer to have flown on operations in both the Falklands and Gulf Wars. (During the Falklands War he was shot down flying a Harrier and had ejected). The normal procedure was for two bomber aircraft to fly at about 20,000 feet in close proximity to the Tornado, which carried the TIALD pod but no bombs: this allowed two sticks of bombs to be dropped on two targets in a single pass by the TIALD aircraft. Each of the bombers carried a maximum of three LGBs. On the run up, the TIALD aircraft fired its laser designator for a period of about thirty seconds to illuminate the target. The laser energy was reflected back over a large area in the general direction of the designator. Within these reflections was a region in the form of an inverted cone known as the 'basket' (not to be confused with the AAR basket). It was necessary for the bomber aircraft to drop their bombs within this 'basket' if the laser seeker in the nose of the bomb was to receive signals of sufficient energy to acquire the target. It was also necessary for the canard control fins and tail wings to be able to deflect the bomb onto it from its normal trajectory. As soon as the bombs were observed to burst on the first target, the designator was aligned on the second target and fired to guide the bombs, which had already been released, from the second aircraft. Later, with experience, it became possible for the TIALD aircraft to designate four targets in a single pass.

Arrival of the TIALD-equipped Tornadoes allowed Tabuk to switch to precision missions on 30 February and from then until the end of the Gulf War the Tornadoes at all three bases flew few free-fall-bombing missions.[98] Flight Lieutenant Adrian Frost a navigator on 617 Squadron who carried out the first operational TIALD sortie[99] recalls.

'The RAF's capability for the airborne designation of LGBs provided by the PAVESPIKE pod fitted to the Buccaneer was a twenty-year-old design and was fitted with only a TV camera. Hence it could provide only a daylight capability. The necessity for night operations meant that TIALD would be rushed into service as soon as possible. The only TIALD pods available at the time were two flight demonstrator pods with TI only, which had been flying on a Buccaneer test-bed aircraft. These had never been designed for carriage on the Tornado. Indeed, there were no Tornado aircraft capable of carrying the pods either. However, a rapid development programme, TAP (Tornado advanced programme) was undertaken at the Aeroplane & Armament Experimental Establishment (A&AEE), Boscombe Down. The two pods, affectionately called Sandra and Tracy [after the 'Fat Slags' cartoon characters in Viz magazine] entered operational service on 10 February, flying from Tabuk and destroying hardened aircraft shelters at the H3 south-west airfield complex in north-west Iraq. As testament to their outstanding success, the two pods flew 91 missions in eighteen days, scoring 229 direct hits. Overall their success rate was bettered only by the F-117A Stealth Fighter.'

Flight Lieutenant Kevin Noble and Jerry Cass on 13 Squadron had been one of the four experienced crews that had carried out TIALD development trials at Boscombe Down. They flew eleven TIALD sorties in the Gulf. The normal procedure was for two bomber aircraft to fly at about 20,000 feet in close proximity to the Tornado, which carried the TIALD pod but no bombs: this allowed two sticks of bombs to be dropped on two targets in a single pass by the TIALD aircraft. Each of the bombers carried a maximum of three LGBs. On the run up, the TIALD aircraft fired its laser designator for a period of about thirty seconds to illuminate the target. The laser energy was reflected back over a large area in the general direction of the designator. Within these reflections was a region in the form of an inverted cone known as the 'basket' (not to be confused with the AAR basket). It was necessary for the bomber aircraft to drop their bombs within this 'basket' if the laser seeker in the nose of the bomb was to receive signals of sufficient energy to acquire the target. It was also necessary for the canard control fins and tail wings to be able to deflect the bomb onto it from its normal trajectory. As soon as the bombs were observed to burst on the first target, the designator was aligned on the second target and fired to guide the bombs, which had already been released, from the second aircraft. Later, with experience, it became possible for the TIALD aircraft to designate four targets in a single pass.

Kevin Noble's and Jerry Cass's first TIALD mission was on 8 February, against an airfield in Western Iraq known as H3 North West, which was near the Jordanian border The first two bombers thundered off into the night at thirty second intervals, with their twin blue afterburner flames fading into the distance as they accelerated. These then disappeared as the burners were cancelled, leaving only the flashing navigation lights visible; meanwhile Kevin counted down the seconds on the stopwatch, before taking off in pursuit. They climbed up to level out at just above 20,000 feet, checking with the duty AWACs as they left Tabuk and he then gave regular reports of 'picture clear', meaning that there were no enemy fighters airborne. It was a fine clear night and all the formation was in sight as they climbed. After about thirty minutes they were approaching the Iraqi border and completed the 'fence checks' before entering enemy airspace: these included arming the guns and AIM-9 Sidewinder missiles and switching all external lights out. Everything was going smoothly, the aircraft was fully serviceable and the formation was in good shape and on time. Below it was completely dark, as there was no habitation in the desert. Soon after crossing the border, they saw bomb flashes some miles to the East as another target was attacked and these were immediately followed by the first sight of AAA. This consisted of dense, multi-coloured white, red and blue flashes and was fairly typical in that the defences only opened fire after the first bombs had landed. However, it all seemed to explode well below them, so AAA did not appear to present much of a threat at medium level. 'Meanwhile', recalls Kevin Noble 'Jerry was giving a good confidence-building commentary from the navigation system. He had identified all the fixes accurately on radar, the TIALD pod was working properly and he was also able to track other aircraft ahead on the radar. The Radar Homing and Warning

Receiver (RHWR) remained pretty quiet throughout with mainly friendly fighter indications, although a couple of short duration strobes from enemy SAM systems appeared. Chaff was dropped and we manoeuvred, looking for the threat, but nothing was seen so we continued on our way. Apparently a long streak of rocket flame indicated that the SAM was not heading for us: however a wobbling red dot would show that it was coming our way and it was time to take drastic action.

'Soon we were approaching the target and Jerry identified the airfield from over twenty miles away, zooming in on the TIALD to the North West corner for the first Hardened Aircraft Shelter (HAS). All went smoothly as we approached and went through the pre-planned procedures in preparation for the attack. These culminated in the first bomber releasing his load of three LGBs on time. Meanwhile we were already in the turn to fly past the airfield, following our own route to one side of and above the bomber. We flew high as we were lighter than the bombers and also did not wish to have bombs whistling past our ears in the darkness. As the first bomber called 'bombs gone', I started my stopwatch to give Jerry the count-down. By this time, Jerry was tracking the side of the target HAS and fired the laser for the last part of the bombs' flight, while I then gave the count-down to impact which was 40 seconds after release. As the count reached zero, Jerry called, 'Splash', as he saw the bombs impact on his TV TAB screen. But there was no time to waste since the second stick of LGBs was already in the air. Jerry zoomed out on the TIALD pod viewing head and 'walked' the tracking cross out of the HAS site, down the runway, up the fourth taxi-way to the HAS at the end and zoomed in again to commence tracking. All this only took about five seconds and was done from memory - there was no time to study maps at this stage. Meanwhile I continued the countdown to the next impact, calling every ten seconds and cross-checked with Jerry that he had started firing the laser at the correct time. As Jerry was concentrating on his equipment, I looked down towards the target as best I could, whilst monitoring the RHWR and taking care not to dip a wing or drop-tank in the way of the TIALD's view of the target. All was quiet and the AAA was silent. Again, as I reached zero on the second ten-second countdown, Jerry saw the bombs impact on the target before zooming out to look back at the airfield to obtain good video coverage for bomb damage assessment. By this stage we were a couple of miles beyond the target on the way out, so the pod was looking back at quite an angle. As we were departing, with our two bombers somewhere out there in the dark, we could hear the second phase of the attack going in behind us as the next two bombers and TIALD aircraft went through. Soon, they too were pulling out behind us and our bombers and we were all heading for home.

'As we crossed back into Saudi airspace, I made the weapons switches safe and turned the navigation lights on; many other lights also appeared up and down the border as various other aircraft crossed out of Iraq. For some reason, the crews often referred to Iraq as 'sausage side',

Buccaneer S.Mk.2B XX901/N *The Flying Mermaid-'Kathryn, Glen Elgin,* which flew nine missions in the Gulf War. The red bomb, which denotes an attack by the Buccaneer itself, represents one of two An-12s bombed at Shayka Mayhar and destroyed on 27 February 1991.

but the origin of this appellation is not known. The return to base was uneventful and we were soon in the stream of aircraft landing at Tabuk. I felt great elation and relief that everything had gone according to plan and the results for their formation appeared to be good. This first operational mission into Iraq had been successful and we had all returned: it was a big hurdle to have crossed and we now knew roughly what to expect in the future. The whole trip had only lasted an hour and 40 minutes, so it was a relatively short introduction to operations. It was pleasant to climb out of the aircraft into the cool night desert air and, having signed in on the aircraft servicing documents, we gathered back at Operations for the 'hot debrief' on the mission. This was quite short and provided the first Intelligence information on the success of the mission and of any threats encountered. The Detachment Commander was there to meet us as we came in and he remained for the debriefing, as he did on most subsequent occasions. Then came the item we had all been waiting for - the showing of the aircraft video tapes to see how the attack had gone. This provided a great change for the bomber crews following the earlier frustration of dropping dumb bombs into the darkness: we could now actually see where the bombs had gone. On the videos from both TIALDs it was just possible to see the bombs as dots sliding across the screen to hit the big earth-covered HAS in a great hot flash which showed up well on the IR picture, the blast shooting out from both ends of the HAS. The mission was definitely successful.

'The second trip was very similar to the first; the target being HAS on H2, another airfield in Western Iraq. By now, experience had shown that dropping three LGBs on a HAS was wasteful and two were found to be sufficient. The HAS on this airfield were bare concrete, like their NATO counterparts and as bombs impacted through the roof the massive doors, weighing several tons, were blasted away at great speed. Anything inside would have been completely destroyed with aircraft inside being barely recognisable.

'Our third mission targeted the runway at Mudaysis, just over 100 miles West of Baghdad. For maximum effect, the bombs were aimed to hit the junction where the taxiways joined the runway. The attack went well except that the second set of bombs failed to detonate - they were

Right: Buccaneer S.Mk.2B XX885/L
Hello Sailor/Caroline Famous Grouse,
which flew seven missions in the
Gulf War.

Below: Buccaneer S.Mk.2B XV863/S
Sea Witch/Debbie Tamnavoulin which
flew six missions in the Gulf War.

JP233 being loaded under the fuselage of a Gulf War Tornado.

Retarded JP233 runway-cratering bomblets exploding on target.

seen to impact on the runway in a small hot flash under the TIALD cross-hairs, but this was far too small to be bombs exploding and it was very disappointing. Our fourth operational mission was our first day sortie and was against more HAS, this time on the airfield at Jalibah South East in South Eastern Iraq, near the border with Kuwait. A large sandstorm covered the whole area and when we arrived over Jalibah, cloud prevented the TIALD seeing the target area, so the attack was called off and we headed back to base feeling somewhat dejected. The fifth mission came on 17 February: this time it was a night sortie against the Ar Ramadi highway bridge approximately 70 miles West of Baghdad. This was our first bridge and it carried dual carriageways over a river. At take-off I could not get one of the afterburners to light on the runway. The engine 'war rating' switch was wired in the rear position, so I moved it forward to get extra power from that engine without the afterburner and, by selecting 'combat', I raised the turbine temperatures still further to increase power. With full afterburner on the good engine, the take-off roll was rather longer than normal, but otherwise it was satisfactory. The route took us to the North of the target before turning South on to the attack heading. This time we were designating for the second pair of bombers, so Jerry could see the hot area on the bridge from the first pair's attack. There was some AAA over the target as the bombers knocked down one side of the dual carriageway, but the other side remained standing. The return to base was uneventful until I selected flaps on a long final approach - the slats came down but the flaps did not, so I left the circuit to sort out the problem. When I was still unable to lower the flaps, I elected to carry out a landing with both slats and flaps retracted, as detailed in the Emergency Procedures, as this was safer than with slats down but no flaps. I then dumped fuel to reduce the aircraft's weight and landing speed to a minimum. Even so, the calculated speed at the runway threshold was 190 knots - about 40 knots faster than normal - but the extra speed only became apparent at touch-down, when it was very noticeable. It then seemed to take ages to slow down using reverse thrust and brakes. However, I had dealt competently with what could have been a difficult situation and the aircraft was not damaged. Initially the engineers rectified both problems but, although there were no further difficulties with the flaps, that engine was later to give trouble. The same afterburner problem subsequently happened on a number of occasions until finally a pilot was approaching the tanker for AAR about twenty minutes after take-off when his wingman reported white sparks spitting from the exhaust. These were turbine blades, which had obviously had enough of being subjected to very high temperatures. A loss of thrust followed by the appearance of an engine vibration warning caption caused the aircraft to slow down and start to lose height, so the pilot jettisoned tanks and returned to base. An engine change was then required and this cured the problem.

'We did our sixth mission on 19 February. This was our second in daylight and was against the Bin Al Jarrah airfield approximately seventy miles South East of Baghdad. The second TIALD aircraft became unserviceable so, as before, Jerry and I reverted to the back-up plan to designate for both pairs of bombers. It was a beautifully clear day as we approached for the attack around midmorning and, for a change, I could see the target area during the run up. The first pair of targets was large earth-covered, semi-buried fuel tanks. Unfortunately both bombers misidentified the offsets on the radars and released the bombs outside the basket. This was a good demonstration of why the TIALD crew needed to count down accurately, as when the count got to 45 seconds we knew that the bombs must have landed - even though Jerry could not see them on his screen. However, we then had to leave the first target and move to the second without delay, where the same thing happened again. This was very disappointing, but Jerry and I had to put this out of their minds as we had to make a second run to pick up the following pair of bombers - the targets were large concrete ammunition bunkers to the South of the airfield. On the run in the distinctive 'wah-wah-wah' of the RHWR was heard, plus guidance indications for the SA-3 SAM missile system, so Jerry immediately dispensed chaff while I took evasive active and scanned the sky. However, the indications ceased and nothing was seen, so we continued the run. This happened on another couple of times during the attack, but the warnings

Two Victor K.Mk.2 tankers of 55 Squadron in formation. Nearest aircraft is XH672 *Maid Marian*.

were only of short duration of a second or so. The first bombs hit the target with a moderate flash on the TV screen and Jerry moved the designator on to the next bunker, but the second strike was altogether more impressive. There was an exclamation from Jerry as a huge fireball filled his screen and after rolling out on the escape heading, I dipped a wing to look at the target. A huge mushroom cloud, resembling that from a nuclear weapon, was rising: it was very spectacular and could still be seen from 80 miles away on the way home and by that time the smoke cloud had reached a height of about 15,000 feet.

'Our seventh mission took place on 20 February and it was to attack the runways at the former RAF base at Shaibah just North of the Kuwaiti border, a three hour round trip with much of the time spent over Iraq. However it was safer to spend longer over the quiet regions of Iraq than take the shorter route near the 'hot area' of Kuwait. Patchy cloud made it difficult for Jerry to acquire the target, but eventually he got the TIALD locked on and the bombs struck home. On the way back we had to do a night AAR. Joining the tanker was quite exciting because, as usual, there was a myriad of lights from aircraft coming out of Iraq and several of these were visible in the tanker stack. Initially it was difficult to tell which was our tanker until we got closer and were able to identify the correct one since it was at the briefed height. It was a VC 10 and we made contact without difficulty before going home. This was to be our last trip on night operations.

'On 22 February, for our eighth mission we went back to the airfield at Bin Al Jarrah, again by day, but this time we attacked the runways and the mission was successful. For our ninth mission the following day the target was the runway at Ghalaysan, which was directly South of Baghdad but only about 70 miles in from the Saudi border one of our bombers was unserviceable, so we only had to designate for a single aircraft. The attack was in the late afternoon, the weather was pretty poor and we were the third wave tasked against this airfield on 23 February. All the others had aborted because of bad weather, but Jerry and I were lucky. Having flown past large thunderstorms on the way in we initially thought that we also would fail. Luckily, as we approached there was a gap in the weather, just enough to see the target. This time we were second to designate and I saw the bombs from the leading pair exploding on the runway; meanwhile Jerry had directed the TIALD onto their part of the runway and saw the bombs from their single bomber strike home.'

On 25 February, the target for Kevin Noble's and Jerry Cass's tenth mission was the railway bridge at Samawah approximately 120 miles South East of Baghdad and only about fifty miles from the Iranian border. The bombers tanked on the way to the target but with less weight the

TIALD aircraft carried a third tank on the right shoulder pylon and did not need to refuel. However, to reduce drag, the third tank, when empty, was jettisoned over Iraq and they later estimated that it might have been over the French held sector. 'This was the only drop-tank that I ever jettisoned. Again the weather was poor, with much cloud and rain, but we met up with the bombers precisely on time before entering Iraq. The weather continued to be terrible all the way to the target. As we had been briefed that there were probably only light defences and the RHWR was quiet on approaching the area, we let down to 8,000 feet in an attempt to see the ground or the target. We found only torrential rain and could not see anything, so we aborted the mission and climbed back up for an uneventful return to base. The round trip had taken two hours and 40 minutes and was a complete anti-climax, as we had achieved nothing.

'Our eleventh and final mission came on the morning of 27 February, although at the time we did not know it. The targets were the fuel storage installations at Al Asad airfield, which was approximately 150 miles northwest of Baghdad. It was a crystal clear morning after the rains: the wadis were wet and showed up darkly, looking like the veins of a leaf, while the surrounding desert was dry and light in colour En route, a few blackened and burned out targets, including an oil refinery, appeared. Our targets were large semi-buried fuel tanks on the airfield and good hits were obtained on both, but the strikes were not as spectacular as we had expected and certainly did not compare with the ammunition store at Bin Al Jarrah. The return to base was uneventful.'

The end of the war came suddenly and unexpectedly when a cease-fire was declared on 28 February 1991. Following the expiry of the United Nations ultimatum for Iraq to withdraw from Kuwait by 15 January, air operations had started on 17 January and had continued for a total of 42 days, while the ground war - starting on 24 February - had lasted only for 100 hours. However, these operations resulted in the complete defeat of the Iraqi forces.

During 'Granby' and 'Desert Storm' ten of 55 Squadron's Victor K.2s, the oldest aircraft in the campaign, flew 299 sorties and by 18 March 1991 all had returned to Marham. On 15 October that same year 55 Squadron was disbanded and the last Victor flight was made six weeks later on 30 November when XH672 *Maid Marion* was flown to Shawbury to be dismantled for transportation to the RAF Museum at Cosford. During the Victors' 37 years of flying from

617 Squadron 'The Dam Busters' are welcomed home at Marham following the end of the Gulf War in 1991.

Norfolk aerial warfare had changed out of all recognition. During the 1991 Gulf conflict, nine out of ten expended weapons were unguided 'dumb' bombs and about 75% of the weapons were precision guided. In the next war as far as the bombers - Tornadoes included - were concerned, weapons delivery would largely be laser- or satellite-guided. Air superiority had been replaced by a desire for air dominance.

Endnotes for Chapter 5

86 'When the end of offensive combat operations was declared, the F.3s continued to man CAPs in Kuwait 'policing' the airspace, while holding aircraft on Quick Reaction Alert (QRA) in case hostilities resumed. The cease-fire held and the Allied forces began to return home. The F.3s involvement in Operation 'Granby' ended on 10 March when two F.3s finished their last duty on Quick Reaction Alert.'

87 'On 19 January an additional Victor was sent to supplement the other six. Up to a maximum of 14 sorties were flown over the Persian Gulf in support of attack missions and air defence patrols and together with 138 OLIVE TRAILs and numerous other patrols, 299 sorties were flown over the 42 day war, an average of 33 missions per crew. The Victor detachment achieved every objective and did not fall down on any operational sortie. It was tight at times and the need for flexibility, excellent engineering support and good airmanship saved the day and produced a 100% success rate.'

88 On 18 October Tornado GR.I ZA466/FH flown by Squadron Leaders Ivor Walker and Bobby Anderson of 16 Squadron ejected following a take-off collision at Tabuk with a wrongly raised arrestor barrier at the approach end of the runway. On 13 November Jaguar GR.1A XX754 flown by Flight Lieutenant Keith Collister of 54 Squadron was killed on a low-level training flight over Qatar. On 13 January 1991 Flight Lieutenants Kieran Duffy and Norman Dent of 14 Squadron were killed when Tornado ZD718/BH crashed during a low-level training sortie.

89 Wing Commander Jerry Witts of 31 Squadron would also lead four Tornadoes from Dhahran to the same target.

90 One of ZD791's AIM-9L Sidewinders was hit by flak, exploded and 'took out' the engine, forcing Flight Lieutenants John Peters (26) and Adrian 'John' Nichol (27) of XV Squadron to eject. They were captured by the Iraqis and endured a brutal imprisonment before their release on 4 March 1991.

91 Author's interview with Wing Commander John Broadbent/Presentation to the RUSI on 23 October 1991 by Wing Commander Broadbent, Royal Air Force Staff College, Bracknell. ©RUSI Journal August 1992. John Broadbent was awarded the DSO.

92 The bodies of Wing Commander Elsdon and Flight Lieutenant Collier arrived in the UK on 19 March 1991.

93 In an interview with Mark Nicholls of the EDP, January 2001.

94 Mohammed Mubarak was shot down on 17 January when eleven out of the twelve A4KU Skyhawks despatched from Dhahran dropped their bombs on Saudi territory. Major Jeff Scott Tice and Captain Harry M. 'Mike' Roberts of the 401st TFW (Tactical Fighter Wing) were flying F-16A/Cs on a combat strike from Doha AB on 19/20 January when they were shot down over Baghdad when SAMs detonated close to their aircraft. Both Roberts and Tice parachuted to safety but became PoWs. Another F-16 went down on 21 January when a MK-84 bomb detonated before release. US Navy helicopters rescued the pilot at sea. All told eight USAF pilots and three USN pilots became PoWs in the Gulf War.

95 Dave Waddington and Claire Holderness were married in the chapel at RAF Cranwell on 17 August 1991. Promoted Wing Commander, Dave Waddington assumed command of IX (B) Squadron in June 2006.

96 Quoted in *Sky Battles: Dramatic Air Warfare Actions* by Alfred Price (Cassell 1998).

97 218 Buccaneer-Tornado missions were flown and 24 bridges and 15 airfields were attacked during which 169 LGBs were dropped (48 by Buccaneers).

98 Between 10 and 27 February 72 successful TIALD sorties were flown and 23 were aborted.

99 On 10 February Flight Lieutenants Gareth Walker and Adrian Frost plus the four bombing aircraft accompanied Wing Commander Iveson and Flight Lieutenant Chris Purkiss in ZD848.

Chapter Six

Buffs and The Gulf War
1990-1991

'Undeniably, the B-52 remains the longest living bomber in US military aviation history.'
General Christopher S. Adams

Conflict in the Persian Gulf began on 1 August 1990 when Iraq's president Saddam Hussein's armies invaded Kuwait. On 7 August President Bush ordered Operation 'Desert Shield' to liberate Kuwait. USAF Lieutenant General Charles A. Horner, the allied coalition's supreme air commander, began coordinating all air actions related to the buildup and within days, established HQ Central Command Air Forces (Forward) in Saudi Arabia. From this headquarters the air actions that would bring an end to the war ('Desert Storm') were put into operation. Within 35 days the Air Force deployed a fighter force that equalled Iraq's fighter capability in numbers. In total the Coalition built an air force of 2,350 aircraft, over half of which were combat aircraft. Initial Air Force planning was largely concentrated on defending Saudi Arabia from invasion and the first priority therefore was the neutralization of advancing Iraqi tank and troop columns. The B-52H units remained on alert in the United States and did not deploy during 'Desert Storm' though some B-52H aircrew underwent a quick conversion onto the older model. (Plans to deploy some B-52H-models in a hastily adopted conventional fit were well advanced as the war drew to a close).

The coalition air forces faced 750 Iraqi combat aircraft, 200 support aircraft, Scud surface-to-surface missiles, chemical and biological weapon capability, 'state-of-the-art' air defences, ten types of surface-to-air missiles, around 9,000 anti-aircraft artillery pieces and thousands of small arms. The Iraqi air force had twenty-four main operating bases and thirty dispersal fields; many equipped with the latest in hardened aircraft shelters. Colonel John A. Warden, deputy director of doctrine, strategy and plans for the USAF, devised an overall target plan

B-52G-130-BW 59-2599 *Thing* in the 93rd Bomb Wing at Morón AB.

originally called 'Instant Thunder' in which ten sets of targets were selected for the war against Saddam. As many as forty-five of the most important targets were situated in and around Baghdad, a city covering 254 square miles and one which was considered to be seven times more heavily defended than Hànôi had been in December 1972. So, although the B-52G crews could have dropped GBU-10 or GBU-12 Paveway III laser-guided-bombs (LGBs) flying with F-111Fs which could laser-mark targets for them using their Pave Tack laser/FLIR pods, America was not about to repeat the 'Linebacker II' offensive which cost so many B-52s. This time an enemy capital was the sole domain of more than forty F-117A Nighthawk Stealth Fighters, which arriving in Baghdad virtually undetected could release 2,000lb GBU-27 laser-guided bombs with unprecedented accuracy and impunity. However, once the coalition had gained air superiority it was planned to use the B-52Gs in a conventional role aimed at 'preparing the battlefield'. Echoes of Viêtnam resounded in the media who talked in terms of 'surgical strikes' in contrast to the use of 'carpet-bombing'. General Norman Schwarzkopf the ground commander certainly favoured the use of B-52s in strikes on massed Iraqi Republican Guard positions near the border with Saudi Arabia but he rejected the term 'carpet bombing', which he said, 'tends to portray something totally indiscriminate, en masse with regard to the target'. At a CENTCOM briefing in Riyadh on 27 January he declared that the allied campaign was much more carefully organized and the choice of weapons was a most important consideration. Ten days earlier this had been amply demonstrated by B-52Gs of the 596th Bomb Squadron, 2nd Bomb Wing during the opening round of Operation 'Desert Storm' but for reasons of military secrecy the operational details were not made public until a year later.

Five months of preparations and planning for Project Senior Surprise, the bombing of Iraqi targets from the mainland USA by B-52Gs carrying conventionally armed Boeing cruise missiles had begun at Barksdale AFB in August 1990. At the time B-52G/Hs were known to carry AGM-86B ALCMs, which were nuclear tipped, but Boeing had created the AGM-86C by replacing the W80-1 nuclear warhead of the AGM-86B with a 992lb HE blast-fragmentation version at the expense of some fuel carrying capacity. Global Positioning System (GPS) navigation replaced the terrain contour matched (TERCOM) version in the ALCM. The new missile, which had better penetrating power against hardened targets than the AGM-109 Tomahawk Land Attack (Cruise) Missiles (TLAM), was called the XLRB (extra-long-range bomb) or 'Secret Squirrel', after a cartoon character (the 'crusader against evil'). AGM-86C cruise missiles fitted with conventional warheads and the GPS was a closely guarded secret because arms-control negotiations with the USSR were at a sensitive stage.

On a mission during Operation 'Desert Storm' two B-52Gs prepare to take off from Prince Abdulla Air Base at Jeddah in Saudi Arabia.

Top: Loading three AGM-86 ALCMs at Minot AFB.

Right: Lieutenant General Ellie 'Buck' Schuler, 8th Air Force.

Below, right: The 'Secret Squirrel' patch.

Seven B-52Gs armed with 39 AGM-86C missiles were placed on heightened alert on 11 January 1991. With the start of the Gulf War imminent Lieutenant Colonel Jay Beard the mission commander received the 'go' order at midnight on 16 January. By 3:00 am he had called all fifty-seven members of his handpicked crews. (The normal crew of six men was augmented with one extra pilot and one extra radar navigator so some could rest en route). At 0400 they were called and met by several generals including Lieutenant General Ellie 'Buck' Shuler, 8th Air Force. For many arriving in the 'vault' for their final brief, it hit home for the first time that they were really going to war. Major Blaise Martinick, a radar navigator on the mission, recalled, 'As we all started filtering in with our flight suits half zipped and so on, there stood the 8th Air Force commander, the squadron commander and the wing commander and we realized that this was it.' The crews were briefed that they were bound for Iraq, a round trip of more than 14,000 miles. Their launch windows were to destroy key Iraqi targets before the initial push by NATO forces. Launched at precisely the right moment, the CALCMs could avoid aircraft leaving Iraq and arrive over their targets at midmorning, destroying or damaging infrastructure targets and further

Line up of wrecked Iraqi MiG-29s.

degrading air defences. Eight targets, including powerplants at Mosul, a telephone exchange in Basra and other electrical generating facilities, were picked for CALCM attack. Iraq's electrical grid and communications nodes were 'soft targets,' - ones not needing special penetrating bombs - and so CALCMs were ideal to use against them.

After the flight briefing, General Shuler likened this mission to that flown from the carrier USS *Hornet* against Tokyo in 1942 by the B-25 crews of the famous 17th Bomb Group led by General Jimmy Doolittle, who had all trained at Barksdale. 'After that, we were really pumped up,' Colonel Beard said.

Colonel Beard was asked for a last-minute favour to help some of the men make out wills, which they had neglected to prepare. Beard had to get the base Judge Advocate General out of bed and he had a lieutenant colonel in the alert facility doing wills at 3:00 in the morning. Colonel Beard did not mind, however. There were few other favours he could do for his crews. To maintain security he could not let them into the chow hall and give them a warm meal or even extra box lunches because it would tip off the kitchen. He had therefore pre-positioned some low-residue, low-gas meals 'fit-for-flight' aboard the B-52Gs, as well as five-gallon jugs of water and some jugs of 'tepid coffee'. In addition, he had instructor seats removed and put in air mattresses and sleeping bags, one 'upstairs' and one 'downstairs.'

A hard rain was falling as Colonel Beard and his crews went to their jets at 0500. Their last bad fuses replaced and their radios coaxed into operation all seven B-52G taxied out to the runway. Each B-52G weighed a gross weight of 244 tons, the heaviest that most of the pilots had ever flown and they needed more than 9,000 feet of runway to get airborne from Barksdale shortly after 0600 in three formations about ten minutes apart (2/2/3). Lieutenant Colonel Warren Ward, a graduate of Louisiana Tech, looked down at his alma mater as the sun was coming up. 'I could see Wylie Tower down at Ruston and I was thinking, 'Am I ever gonna see that again?' It was one of the thoughts running through my mind.'

Over the Atlantic, the three cells headed toward their first of two aerial refuelling rendezvous, with KC-135s out of Lajes Field, Azores. Major Marcus Myers of the 96th Bomb Squadron, an aircraft commander on the mission, recalls, 'Up in the boom pod window, they held up a sign that said, 'Good hunting'. 'So even though they weren't sure what we were doing, they kind of had an idea.'

Colonel Beard, in the lead plane, 'Doom 31,' called the aircraft commanders on secure frequencies to check in. He quickly got an audio thumbs-up from five of the six other B-52Gs but not from 'Doom 34.'

'We're working something right now and we'll get back to you, 'Captain Bernie Morgan and co-pilot Lieutenant Mike Branch radioed. Patiently, Colonel Beard waited as an hour passed. Finally, past the point where any planes could turn back, B-52G 57-6475 Miami Clipper II 'Doom 34' called to say they had shut down an engine on takeoff due to fluctuating oil pressure. Normally, this would have been an air abort, but the crew refused to be left behind.

'That's OK,' Colonel Beard said. 'They did exactly what I would have done. I expected nothing less. I wanted them to be gung ho.' It had been determined beforehand that a B-52G could complete the mission with just six of its eight engines.

Over the Mediterranean, with KC-10s out of Moron AB, Spain, the B-52s were refuelled a second time. Timing was crucial. The CALCM mission had been set back a couple of hours because it was feared Libya might track the B-52s and warn Iraq. They were not to pass Libya until F-117A stealth fighters had hit their first targets in Baghdad. Flying lights-out and in radio silence, the B-52Gs crossed the Mediterranean, the Red Sea and arrived over Saudi Arabia, where the three lead B-52Gs flew to their northern launch area and four flew to their southern launch area. From about sixty miles south of the Iraqi-Saudi border near the town of Ar Ar, in a sequenced launch over ten minutes, spread out so the missiles wouldn't hit each other or their launching craft, the CALCMs dropped off their rails, extended their wings, lit their engines and headed north. Thirty-five of the thirty-nine CALCMs were launched successfully against the eight high priority targets in central and southern Iraq, which included a power station at Mosul, the Basrah telephone exchange and other electrical generating facilities. Four CALCMs failed airborne pre-launch testing (the Williams F107 turbofan on one CALCM failed to develop power on launch) but thirty-one missiles fired hit their targets with precision and the other four exploded close enough to cause serious damage. (Later reconnaissance revealed that CALCMs had hit a number of targets dead-on. One CALCM had snapped its aim point, a telephone pole, in half. The raid achieved between eighty-five and ninety-one per cent of its objectives, well above an expected eighty-per cent, since ALCMs had never before been volley-launched or operated under real-world conditions with GPS. One missile fell unexploded in the launch area, later to be found and destroyed. Another was never accounted for and might have been shot down.) When the last missile was away, the B-52Gs turned west, reformed and headed back to Barksdale. The B-52Gs had been airborne for fifteen hours but the mission was far from over.

Heading back toward the Mediterranean, the seven bombers hit severe weather. Visibility dropped to below two miles, the minimum required for a desperately needed aerial refuelling. With only thirty minutes of fuel remaining, conditions improved enough to carry out the refuelling with KC-10A Extenders from Spain. Had the weather remained

M117 750lb bombs on the underwing stores station of B-52G-95-BW 58-0182 *What's Up Doc?* of the 379th Bomb Wing at RAF Fairford at the time of the Gulf War in 1991 when it flew two missions from Moron AB, Spain. A total of twenty-four M117 bombs could be carried on the two underwing positions fitted with the redundant Hound Dog pylon and MERs (via Tony Thornborough)

bad, the B-52Gs would have had to fly to a divert field. Two B-52Gs were flying with a pair of seized engines; sharply increasing drag and two other B-52Gs had fluctuating oil pressure readings. In addition, four of the aircraft were carrying 2,500lb hung missiles.

As they headed for the Atlantic, some of the crews tried to sleep. Most had been up long before the mission even started. It wasn't really sleeping, it was more like lying down and dehydrating for two hours. On the lower deck, cramped quarters forced an unfortunate choice: One could lie down with either one's head or boots in the urinal.

The weather turned very nasty again and the B-52Gs were hit by 130-140-knot headwinds. They had planned on a worst-case headwind of ninety knots. Colonel Beard kept searching for a way to get out of the wind. First they went high, then they tried low, but there was no relief. The wind at Lajes was so harsh that the KC-135As, which were to give them their last fill-up, were grounded. With fuel running low the B-52Gs radioed Moron AB for help. A flight of KC-10As dashed out and found them and Colonel Beard asked them to give them everything they could.' The Extenders stayed with the bombers as long as they could but finally had to pull away or they would not have made it back to Spain. The heavy drag and wind continued to eat up gas. The B-52Gs with hung missiles and seized engines would need another fill-up to get back to Barksdale. Colonel Beard was determined that they would not resort to a divert field. B-52s showing up unannounced at an East Coast base, carrying what looked for all the world like unexpended nuclear missiles would mean big trouble. Finally, he raised the 8th Air Force command post on a secure frequency and two 'strip tankers' (kept ready for just such emergencies) were launched from Robins AFB, Georgia. They met the B-52s just over the coast but one of the bombers developed a faulty radio and was unable to communicate with the tanker. Colonel Beard, through a special plane-to-plane communication system, could talk to the other pilot and messages were relayed to the tanker.

It was almost dark when the B-52Gs arrived back at Barksdale. They wasted no time getting down and, once on the ground, taxied directly into their shelters, exposing their hung missiles to as few unauthorised eyes as possible. By the time that 'Senior Surprise' was over the B-52G crews had been in the air for over thirty-five hours. It was the longest-ranging combat mission in the history of aerial warfare. (The previous longest-range bombing mission in history was during the Falklands War. On the night of 30 April/1 May 1982 a RAF Vulcan supported by eleven Victor tankers made the first 'Black Buck' sortie from Ascension Island to Port Stanley airfield in a mission time of fifteen hours 45 minutes). After a perfunctory debrief, they headed home for much-needed sleep. A year and a day later all the crews involved in 'Senior Surprise' were awarded Air Medals by Lieutenant General Martin J. Ryan, 8th Air Force Commander and the mission was finally revealed to the public.

An eventual force of seventy-three B-52Gs participated in 'Desert Storm'. Twenty organised as the 1708th Bomb Wing (P) were based at Prince Abdullah AB (King Abdul Aziz international Airport), Jeddah in Saudi Arabia. Another twenty organised as the 4300th Bomb Wing (P) were at Diego Garcia in the British Indian Ocean Territories. The 4300th was made up of elements of the 62nd Bomb Wing at Carswell AFB, Texas, the 69th Bomb Squadron at Loring AFB, Maine and a handful of crews from Griffiss and Castle AFBs. The remainder flew from Moron AB, Spain (801st Bomb Wing (P) and RAF Fairford in England (806th Bomb Wing (P). Most B-52G missions against Iraqi targets were flown from Diego Garcia, over 3,200 miles from Baghdad. Both the 1708th and 4300th Wings (P) were controlled by the 17th Air Division (P) at Riyadh, Saudi Arabia. At first the B-52G force was used for night strikes employing the Electro-optical viewing system using FLIR (Forward Looking InfraRed) and low-level-light TV sensors to improve low-level night penetration. Then, as air supremacy was gained and areas were found where the air forces could operate without air-to-air threats, the Buffs began operating around the clock. Bombing of airfields and Command, Control and Communications' targets would also feature in the B-52Gs' target list.

On 16 January Phase I of the Gulf Air War began when fourteen crews in the 4300th Bomb Wing (Provisional), a unit pieced together from various B-52 units: Loring, Griffiss, Castle and Barksdale, launched out of Diego Garcia. The mission is recalled by one of the B-52 pilots who took part:

'I'm biased of course, but I've never felt that the B-52 community got much credit for what we did in the 1991 Gulf War. I learned from the History Channel, back when it still had history, that the F-117 pretty much won the war all by itself. Watching cable news back then you might have come away with the idea that we weren't even there. It seemed like the Pentagon mostly wanted to show off all the cool high-tech stuff like smart-bombs going down the air vent of the bunker. 'Look how clean and surgical our air war is!' They didn't really want to highlight a bunch of Eisenhower-era aircraft dropping iron bombs left over from the Vietnam War.

'This gives me a chance to relate one of the lesser known stories of that war. Most people don't know that B-52s flew low-level strike missions on the first nights of the Gulf War. These were the first, and may well be the last, B-52 low-level combat missions. What we came to call 'Night One'. I make no claim to heroics. What I went through was a walk in the park compared to Berlin or Hànôi. Still, if you get shot over Iraq you're just as dead as one of those other places. All it takes is for one bad-guy to get lucky. I make no claim to any great humanitarian motivations either. I was there because the powers that be thought I needed to be there. I just wanted to bring my butt home in one piece along with the other five guys on my plane.

'First a little background. In August of 1990, two days after the invasion of Kuwait, I was dumb enough to answer my phone on a Sunday morning. My squadron commander said 'Be here in 4 hours with your bags packed. You're going away indefinitely.' Gulp.

'Pretty soon my crew and I found ourselves halfway around the world on Diego Garcia. A tiny strip of coral in the Indian Ocean. Our home for the next 7 months. Our initial tasking would have been to make low-level runs against Iraqi tank columns if they'd pushed into Saudi Arabia. Not sure how survivable that scenario would have been. Glad I didn't have to find out. Fortunately we were able to spend much of the next five months training for what was probably coming. Wasn't much else to do on an atoll in the Indian Ocean. Note that tropical islands are no longer on my list of vacation spots.

A B-52 taking off from RAF Fairford during 'Desert Storm'.

'I looked forward to flying, mostly as a break from the mind-numbing boredom. It's funny how you start to really take your training seriously when you know the real deal is likely to happen soon. Oh, and I spent a lot of time thinking to myself: 'I'm going to get shot down. I'm going to be a PoW. They're going to beat the crap out of me. THIS SUCKS!' Like I said before, I'm not claiming hero status here.

'I know the war seemed rather one-sided but that's not what we were expecting going into it. General Horner himself told us to expect the loss of six aircraft from our unit. The KC-135 crews were told to expect 20% losses on the first night. Gee thanks General. Great pep talk. I feel much better now.

'January 16th around 5:00 pm somebody's knocking on our door saying 'You guys are going in an hour. Get your stuff together.' I walked over to the chow hall and tried to eat something but my stomach had squeezed itself into a tight ball so I sipped some ice tea and went back to the room to wait for our ride down to the Operations building. At Operations we received our initial briefings. We already knew our targets for the first night so it was mostly a rehash of what we already knew. We'd be briefed on things like what threats to expect and best places for evasion in case we got shot down (bad). We'll be in a 3-ship 'cell' attacking an Iraqi airfield. It's one of their secondary airfields, not too terribly far into Iraqi territory. The main airfields have fortunately been tasked to fast-movers like F-111s and

Wreckage of a downed Iraqi MiG-29 (inset) and a Frogfoot.

The 'Highway of Death' from Kuwait City to Basra where thousands of Iraqi armoured fighting vehicles fleeing bumper to bumper from Kuwait were destroyed.

British Tornadoes. We get a final pep talk from the Wing Commander - 'Don't run into the ground'. OK, good advice. I'll try to remember that Colonel.

'After all the briefings we gathered all our gear and headed out to the jet. Unlike a normal launch, we did everything radio silent. I don't think there were any Iraqi submarines hiding in the lagoon snooping on our conversations, but no sense advertising that you're on your way.

'We launched something like 31 bombers and tankers that night. The primary strike aircraft plus airborne spares. We did all this purely based on timing. We started engines at our assigned time, taxied on time and took off on time. We launched into absolute crap weather. There was a line of storms hitting the island right around that time and we ploughed right through it. Golly, that was fun. And we haven't even gotten to the good stuff yet.

'OK, we're out of the freakin' monsoon at least. Now we've got six hours or so to target and a couple of air refuellings to get through. We're carrying bombs on the wing pylons (27 internal + 24 external) so the extra drag is really making us burn fuel. After the second refuelling it's time to put our gear on. Survival vests and side-arms (like that's going to do much). We took our heavy, Vietnam-era flak vests and positioned them around the cockpit for extra protection. We didn't wear them because we weren't sure what the extra weight would do to us in an ejection. Later we got modern police-style vests that we did wear.

'Soon we're 'feet dry' over Oman and headed up towards Saudi Arabia. I remember seeing lights everywhere as hundreds of aircraft were heading towards the Iraqi border. And then I fell asleep. I wish I could say that I was such a steely-eyed warrior I was able to sleep through danger - in reality I was just exhausted. A long day plus two refuellings on top of all the additional stress must have taken its toll on me. My co-pilot woke me up an hour or so later saying 'Hey, we need to get ready to go low.'

'We have some housekeeping to do first. The Night Vision Goggles are sensitive to anything except green light. We turn off the red instrument lights, tape over all the warning lights with black electrical tape and tape up green chemical light-sticks to serve as our instrument lighting. We turn off all the exterior lights. Our dark-green aircraft should be very difficult to pick out on a dark night like this.

'Now the other two aircraft in the cell (formation) go their separate ways. We've been flying 2-mile spacing off each other up to this point. Now we'll be taking separate routes to the target. This is called a 'multiple axis of attack'. It's a relatively new tactic for us and we've only practiced it a few times. The plan is to cross the target from 3 different directions with 45 seconds between aircraft. We've never even practiced it this tight. We always used 60 seconds in training. We need to make our time-over-target to zero second tolerance. We don't want the plane behind us flying into our bombs.

'We drop down to a few hundred feet off the ground well before crossing the border into Iraq. My aircraft is carrying cluster bombs filled with mines. The idea is to sow mines over the airfield to make it difficult to repair the damage our two wingmen are going to do. They're carrying British 1,000lb runway cratering bombs. These things will dig a hole and then wait to blow up later on at various intervals. The bad thing about dropping cluster is we'll have to pop up to 1000 feet to release the weapons. 1000 feet is a bad altitude. You either want to be really low or really high. Anything in between is a good place to get shot. They've planned for us to be first across the target, hoping the additional element of surprise will make up for being that exposed.

'It's very dark. Not really enough light for the NVGs to do much good. I'm flying the terrain trace and watching the FLIR, which is doing a decent job of picking up the warm desert.

'We cross into Iraqi airspace and now the NVGs start to work. They're picking up all that anti-aircraft fire you probably saw on cable. The goggles now actually work too well. It's hard to tell how close this stuff is. I suspect it's further away than it looks and I pass that on to the crew because they're starting to get a bit excited. I am too, but I don't want to let on. I'm supposed to be the cool, fearless Aircraft Commander (ha!).

'I'm seeing everything from small arms up to the big 57mm stuff. I can't tell if they're really shooting at anybody or just hoping someone will fly through it.

'And now my EWO is telling me he's picking up what he thinks is a MiG-25 search radar. Great.

'The MiG never locks on to us. I doubt he even knew we were there. His radar wasn't worth much down low and neither was he (they didn't train for it). Plus there are F-15s at least in the general area so I figure they'll keep him busy. The guns worry me more, but so far nothing is coming anywhere close to us.

'Finally we hit the Initial Point for our bomb run and we're inbound to the target. The navigator is calling airspeeds for me to fly to make the timing work. I'm making sure to keep the Course Deviation Indicator centred so that the bombs go where the radar navigator is aiming. A typical bomb run lasts about a minute from start to finish:

'60 seconds'

'RCD connected, light's on' (The final arming step is complete. No sense going through all this trouble and have the bombs stay on the plane!)

'30 seconds'

'Stepping out to my final offset' (This is the Radar Navigator adjusting his aim point)

'20 seconds - climb!'

'I climb to 1000 feet. It's dark. I can't see a damn thing out here.

'10 seconds - doors'

'The bomb doors open.

'5, 4, 3, 2 1 bombs away'

'The bombs start to ripple off the aircraft.

'Flash! Flash! Flash! Flash! Flash! Oh this is not good!

'I think they're shooting at me and I can't do a damn thing about it while the bombs are releasing! The flashes are just the right rate of fire to be a medium sized AA gun. I'm waiting for what I think are 37mm shells to come ripping through the plane - nothing. Either they're not a very good shot or it's something else. I'm not going to stick around to find out.

'The bomb doors close, I push the throttles up and the nose over. I start violently gun-jinking the plane around in three dimensions. We're headed back down and passing 390 knots (limiting airspeed), 410, 420! 430!

'The plane is now starting to mach-tuck. The faster we go the more the nose wants to go down which makes it go faster which makes the nose go down more. Not what you really want to be doing a few hundred feet off the ground on a very dark night.

'I'm suddenly remembering a conversation I had with one of the Vietnam-era guys 'You can fly this thing faster than 390 but she'll mach-tuck on you so be sure to run some nose-up trim'.

'I give the trim switch on my yoke a quick burst of nose-up and sure enough problem solved.

'Dear Lord please don't let me get shot coming off the target.

'OK, we're finally out of the target area and I haven't managed to kill us evading the real or imagined guns. It's quite possible that what I saw was the little explosive charges that opened our cluster bombs but I didn't realize it at the time.

'Now during all the excitement the navigator has lost his situational awareness and has got us turning back towards the target. Not good. That's about the last place I want to be right now. The radar nav (the senior navigator) fortunately gets us pointed back in the right direction.

'Shortly after our wingmen come off target a flight of F-15Es come in to finish what we started. Scratch one airfield.

'The rest is mercifully uneventful. We egress at low-level, rejoin the formation and head for home.

'We're alive! Woo hoo!

'Years later I would always get a little antsy right around January 16th. I'd be thinking to myself 'Why do I feel so weird today?' Eventually I'd remember what day it was and think 'Oh yeah, that's why.'

'Nobody ever did ask why I was going so fast. My answer would have been 'Because it wouldn't go any effing faster!'

From 0239 to 0525 hours (local time) on 17 January the five strike packages carried out area denial attacks on four key airfields - As Salman, Glalaysan, Wadi al Khirr and Mudysis - in southern Iraq and a 'highway strip' dispersal base just north-east of the Saudi-Iraqi border. These five installations could be used by Iraqi fighters to mount operations against AWACS aircraft, which were especially vulnerable to enemy aircraft or to make NBC attacks on coalition forces massing south of the border. Three were assigned to each of the four airfields and two in each package carried British 1,000lb GP to cut vital taxiways while the other carried CBU-89 cluster bomb units. Two more B-52Gs, which operated against the highway strip, carried CBU-52s or CBU-58s. Making their attacks at 500 feet or lower the B-52Gs dropped their delayed-action bombs and scattered the minelets from CBU-89, CBU-52 and CBU-58 cluster bombs that denied the Iraqis' use of huge areas of the bases.

On 18 January two B-52Gs carried out a low-level strike on the Al Sahra Undergraduate Pilot Training airfield and Air Force Academy in northern Iraq. That same night thirteen B-52Gs of the 1708th Bomb Wing (P) formed from complements at Barksdale, Castle and Wurtsmith AFBs, Michigan, took off from Wurtsmith and headed for Jeddah. In a show of force four of them bombed the Republican Guard's Tawalkana Division in Southwest Kuwait en route. During their stay at Jeddah one of the wing's B-52s flew twenty-nine missions, the most of any bomber crew in the theatre. B-52Gs based at Jeddah flew three-

or four-hour missions, sometimes two a day. They carried up to fifty-one 500lb and 750lb bombs (with twenty-seven housed internally) at a time, Gator anti-tank mines and other CBUs. On 22 January an E-8A J-STARS detected an armoured division's assembly area and a seventy-one vehicle convoy moving towards Kuwait. Coalition aircraft devastated the convoy but when on the night of 29/30 January the Iraqis tried again there was no early detection and three Iraqi battalions crossed the Kuwaiti border and headed for the abandoned Saudi coastal town of Khafji twelve miles away. Three mechanised divisions massed near Wafra to support the Iraqi advance units. The enemy land and sea incursions were met with attacks by Coalition aircraft but the town fell and Coalition forces were forced to counter-attack. Near Wafra the B-52Gs bombed three Iraqi mechanised divisions comprising 240 tanks and 60,000 troops which were making its way through Kuwait to reinforce the original incursion and soon the ten-mile long column was in full retreat. On 30 January raids on the Hammurabi and Madinah divisions of the Republican Guard reached their peak when B-52s dropped 470 tons of bombs on Guard positions in twenty-eight strikes.

During the first few days of the war six B-52Gs attacked the North Taji Logistics Centre and an ammunition plant after F-117As flying ahead of the strike destroyed all fifteen SAM sites ringing the targets. A further strike by nine B-52Gs bombed part of Baghdad's radar early warning network. At its height B-52Gs bombed Republican Guard concentrations (estimated to total 150,000 troops dug in over an area of 4,000 square miles and any other targets required, in Kuwait and Iraq, every three hours. (In all, Coalition aircraft carried out 5,600 sorties against the Republican Guard, out of a 35,000 total directed against the Iraqi Army). After the first few days, low-level attacks gave way to high-level missions, mainly against Republican Guard divisions and troop concentrations and against bunkers and other logistic complexes. They were also used to breach the huge berms the Iraqis had built up to fend off the expected amphibious attack. Interdiction missions continued against ammunition factories, storage areas, Iraqi oil refineries and fuel depots, Scud missile storage and production facilities, industrial sites and air bases. Other B-52G crews waited on alert, ready to react to any Iraqi invasion of Saudi Arabia by flying out to the invaded area at low altitude, seeking out and bombing Iraqi forces before egressing over the Persian Gulf.

The Northrop Grumman E-8 Joint Surveillance Target Attack Radar System (Joint STARS) Airborne ground surveillance, battle management and command and control aircraft tracks ground vehicles and some aircraft, collects imagery and relays tactical pictures to ground and air theatre commanders.. The two E-8A development aircraft were deployed in 1991 to participate in Operation 'Desert Storm' and accurately tracked mobile Iraqi forces, including tanks and Scud missiles. Crews flew developmental aircraft on 49 combat sorties, accumulating more than 500 combat hours and a 100% mission effectiveness rate. These Joint STARS developmental aircraft also participated in Operation Joint Endeavour, a NATO peacekeeping mission, in December 1995.

B-52Gs and other aircraft often received information on Iraqi targets from airborne E-8A Joint STARS (USAF/USAFE/Army Joint Surveillance and Target Attack Radar System developed by prime contractor Grumman, now Northrop Grumman) which made its debut in 'Desert Storm'. J-STARS undertook ground surveillance, targeting and battle management missions. One of the two E-8As (a 707-320 airframe modified by Boeing) was airborne every night of the Gulf War. On the night of 13 February J-STARS detected an Iraqi armoured division and a cell of B-52Gs was directed to attack the target. Another time B-52Gs attacked a marshalling yard when Scud missiles were discovered on flat cars. B-52Gs were also used to deter Scud launches, flying along roads known to be used by the Scud launchers to get to their launch points, especially in the western box, where Scuds had been launched against Israel. The B-52Gs would drop a bomb or two every fifteen-twenty minutes throughout the night. These together with F-15E Eagle operations kept Scud movements to a minimum. On 3 February B-52G 59-2593 crashed into the Indian Ocean fifteen miles south of Diego Garcia after a catastrophic electrical system failure returning from its mission. It was rumoured that combat damage was responsible. Three crewmembers safely ejected but three others ejected too late and were killed. Several B-52Gs were damaged and one damaged by a SAM hit returned safely. Another lost two engines resulting from a near miss by a SA-3 missile and shrapnel from AAA fire damaged another. 58-0248 lost most of its 50-calibre machine gun package when a AGM-88A HARM anti-radar missile fired by another US aircraft on defence suppression support locked onto the B-52G's tail-mounted gun-laying radar but the B-52G landed safely at Jeddah and was sent to Guam for repair.

Jim Clonts, a B-52 navigator based at Barksdale I AFB. Louisiana, who was TDYd to Diego Garcia, recalls: 'A typical mission during Desert Storm lasted about 17 hours from take-off to landing. We would take off from a small island called Diego Garcia, located in the Indian Ocean. Our formation of three B-52s would fly northwest toward the Persian Gulf, topping off our tanks from Diego tankers about an hour after take-off. Four hours later hours we would meet up with six KC-135 tankers from Oman or Bahrain. We would air refuel for another hour, topping off our tanks again before we flew into battle. We would take two hours to cross Saudi Arabia and get to Iraq or Kuwait. Once we got close to the border we would call our AWACS plane on the radio and check in with our strike controller. He or she would tell us what the tactical situation was, what threats were in the area (like fighters or surface to air missiles) and would pass any target changes to us. Most of the time we would get a new target when we checked in. The targets were usually things like ammunition dumps, rail road yards, airbases, armoured and mechanized infantry divisions (tanks), etc. Sometimes the targets were 'troops in the field'; basically large concentrations of Republican Guard soldiers. Usually the targets were real easy to find on radar. They tended to be in the middle of nowhere (in the desert).

'Some of the threats we encountered surface to air missiles and anti-aircraft artillery. Enemy fighters were driven off by our own fighters, which were near us most of the time. Our electronic warfare officer could jam many of the Iraqi radars, but we also had F-4G Wild Weasels with us carrying AGM-88 anti-radiation missiles. If a missile-radar turned on they could shoot a missile at it. A few B-52s got hit by enemy missiles and anti-aircraft artillery (AAA), but they all managed to return to base safely.

'We would usually spend anywhere from fifteen minutes to forty-five minutes over Iraqi territory. We would fly our bomb run, drop our bombs and turn around to go home. We had a target timing window in which our bombs had to hit within a certain time period. You see when all our bombs go off shrapnel fills the air up to 2,000 feet high, 2000 feet wide and a half mile long. Any plane flying through that would be shot down so we had to drop our bombs on time, less we kill a friendly plane flying through the area. That was my job as navigator, get the plane to the target and air refuellings on time. There were a few times we had to change course to get out of range of some missile that was aimed at us and we did get AAA shot at us, but we never got hit. A buddy of mine did come back with a hole in the nose of his plane. They found a piece of shrapnel inside the nose. After we crossed back into Saudi Arabia, we'd fly another two hours and refuel again for the trip home. We'd land five hours later and spend the next three hours debriefing the mission.'

As in Viêtnam a generation earlier, B-52 raids proved a great psychological weapon, especially a few days before the land battle began. Aircraft dropped psychological warfare leaflets to warn Iraqi forces that the B-52s were coming. After the attack, more leaflets reminded the Iraqis where the bombs had come from and said that the B-52s would be back. Most missions against Iraqi targets involved the delivery of up to 40,000lbs of conventional 'iron' bombs (a co-ordinated weapons release of 153 750lb bombs by a cell of three B-52Gs could wipe out an area 1.5 miles long by one mile wide). Despite some inaccuracy it was estimated that the devastating effects caused by B-52 bombing influenced twenty-forty per cent of Iraqis who deserted. F-117A stealth fighters would attack and knock out the Iraqi air defences around the bombers' targets before the huge payload B-52Gs and FB-111Fs destroyed them. On 28 February just before a cease-fire came into effect, over fourteen F-111Fs followed sixteen B-52Gs in the bombing of al Taji, a storage area fifteen miles north-west of Baghdad about twice the size of the USAF Air Logistics storage areas at Oklahoma City, Sacramento and Ogden, combined. Al Taji was hit repeatedly.

Despite their age the B-52s held a mission-capable rate of more than eighty per cent throughout the war. In all 102 B-52Gs flew 1,625 sorties (just over three per cent of the USA's combat mission total) from their bases in England, Saudi Arabia, Spain and Diego Garcia. They dropped 72,289 bombs for a total of 25,700 tons or thirty-one per cent of all US bombs (and forty-one per cent of the Air Force bombs) dropped during the Gulf War. These are impressive statistics but the results of the B-52 attacks were sometimes disappointing. In post-war analyses, accuracy has been criticised, due to the high winds, which affected unguided bomb ballistics and by an error introduced, by a contractor in misidentifying the ground co-ordinates of (some) targets.

By 25 February 1991 airpower had forced thousands of Iraqi soldiers to abandon their stockpiles of equipment, weapons and ammunition and surrender. On 27 February Kuwait was liberated although it was not until 11 April when the conflict was declared officially over. Aerial superiority once again had been instrumental in an early victory but in 1996 William J. Perry the then US Secretary of Defense declared that, 'For decades we've described our objective as air superiority. In 'Desert Storm' …what we had was not air superiority but air dominance'. He added, 'We liked it and we want to continue to have it. This meant an ever-spiralling budget for new stealth aircraft like the high-technology Lockheed Martin YF-22 Raptor and the Northrop Grumman B-2 Spirit two/three seat long-range strategic bomber, which first flew on 17 July 1990. The B-2 is the costliest warplane ever built (around $900 million per copy) and though the Air Force would have liked 132 aircraft they had to settle for just twenty-one B-2A Spirits, the last being delivered on 14 July 2000.

Chapter Seven

The War Against Terror

'The chances of being shot at on the average sortie were high, as Saddam Hussein's Air Defence personnel were active and looking to bring down an expensive American or British jet.'

Tim McLean, a pilot on 6 Squadron

After the cease-fire in the Gulf War the RAF Jaguars[100] returned home to RAF Coltishall in Norfolk to a hero's welcome but soon another detachment was being prepared to fly back to the Gulf region. Saddam Hussein had begun attacks against the Kurdish population in the mountainous regions in the north of Iraq bordering Iran, Turkey and Syria which resulted in massive refugee problems for those three countries. The UN responded by establishing a safe haven and Security Zone for the Kurdish people. An area of Iraq above 36 degrees North was also designated an air exclusion zone to Saddam Hussein's Air Force. To ensure compliance with the UN resolutions, a Coalition Task Force comprising the USA, UK and France was formed to patrol the area primarily to discourage Iraq from infringement but also to respond in the event of any flagrant disregard of the UN edict. Turkey agreed to join the coalition force for Operation 'Warden' as it was called and operations were to be conducted from the Turkish Air Force Base at Incirlik. 'Warden' was the UK contribution to the US-led Operation 'Provide Comfort' relief operation for the UN 'Safe Haven' for the Kurds of Northern Iraq, established in July 1991 following their failure to overthrow Saddam Hussein. The USAF provided the air defence and fighter-bomber role, shared with the Turkish Air Force, whilst the UK and France provided tactical photographic and reconnaissance cover as the UASF did not have this component in Europe. The UK

Bombs from a B-52 begin an assault against the Taliban in northern Afghanistan in October 2001 when Taliban tank positions were hit.

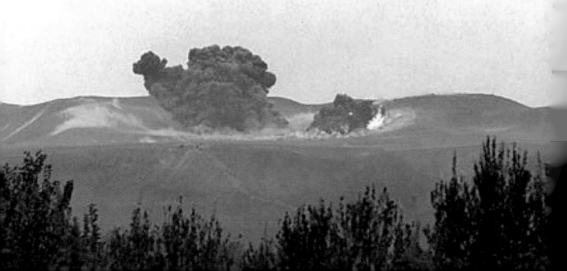

committed eight Jaguar GR.1A aircraft and France a similar number of Mirage F1CR-200s both dedicated to observe and record Iraqi military activity within the exclusion zones. The Jaguar GR.1A was selected as the most suitable aircraft as their BAe and Vinten VICON LOROP pods recorded their imagery on film unlike the Tornado GR.1A that used video cameras. The UK commitment was formed during August 1991 under the command of Group Captain John Morley.

The eight Jaguars were drawn from all three squadrons at Coltishall and were painted in the now familiar 'Desert Pink' scheme. Although 41 Squadron was the only Jaguar unit dedicated to photographic reconnaissance, both 6 and 54 Squadron pilots had been trained to undertake this role as each squadron providing aircrew and ground crew on a two monthly rotation. The first four aircraft departed Coltishall on 4 September followed by the remaining aircraft five days later. 41 Reconnaissance Intelligence Centre (RIC), plus support personnel and equipment were flown out to Turkey by C-130 Hercules aircraft. In addition, the VC 10 tankers of 101 Squadron, which supported the initial deployment of the Jaguars in their non-stop flight, were to remain in theatre to provide air to air refuelling cover for the duration of Operation 'Warden'.

The Jaguars, generally operating in pairs, one armed with CBUs, a second configured for reconnaissance, were required to regularly overfly all known military sites and photograph the activities to provide constantly updated intelligence. Targets included Iraqi troop concentrations, air defence sites, military airfields, at least five were located within the no fly zone), railway terminus, barracks and vehicle parking areas. All of the targets were located within Iraqi territory and were potentially hostile. Therefore the Jaguars carried defence packages consisting of overwing mounted AIM-9L Sidewinder missiles, 30mm Aden cannons and an electronic countermeasures suite which included the PHIMAT Chaff/flare dispenser and an ALQ-101 jamming pod on under wing hard points. Periodically the Recce Pod was replaced by 1,000lb bombs to demonstrate to the Iraqis that the coalition was ready and willing to respond with force if needed. The Mirage F1CR-200s invariably performed their recce task in the mornings whilst the Jaguars flew slots later in the day. The location of each target to he photographed was carefully plotted on large maps to determine their exact positions. The number of aircraft required to perform the mission was also determined by the quantity of subjects that needed to be photographed, although the normal sortie rate saw the Jaguars working in pairs with up to six aircraft flying per day. Missions usually lasted two hours and were flown with support packages provided by USAF F-16s or F-15s, defence suppression F-4G Phantoms and ECM-jamming EF-111 'Spark Varks' or USN EA-6B Prowlers and tanker support.

It was with a certain amount of trepidation that Tim McLean, a pilot on 6 Squadron, stepped on to the tarmac at Incirlik Air Base, near Adana, in the southern reaches of Turkey.

'The long and slightly painful, Hercules flight from RAF Lyneham had given me ample time to consider what was in store in the forthcoming weeks. Within a few days the years of training I had undergone would be put to the test, as I would fly over hostile Iraqi territory for the first time. The chances of being shot at on the average sortie were high, as Saddam Hussein's Air Defence personnel were active and looking to bring down an expensive American or British jet.

'I was welcomed by a couple of my fellow squadron members, Graham Duff and Andy Millikin, who quickly showed me the ropes and handed me an obligatory beer. The weekend would be available to acclimatize and read up on the extensive orders, rules of engagement and standard procedures that had to he understood and of course signed for, before taking to the air. The amount of information to be assimilated was daunting, to say the least. There was also the chance to socialise with the Squadron ground crew and it was here that I first saw the camaraderie that I will always remember from my time on operations with 6 Squadron. Although everybody was relaxed and made the most of the excellent facilities at the base, it was evident from the start that there was a focus beyond what is seen on the standard training deployment. With that focus the entire squadron was brought closer together making for an excellent work and social environment.

'Monday morning saw us rise at 0430 which was a most pleasant 0230 UK time if the body had not quite adjusted its circadian rhythms. The main briefing room was large to accommodate crews from over forty aircraft. The amount of assets employed on each mission was awe-inspiring for one who had not been in this environment before. Crews from Airborne Warning and Control, Tankers (UK and US), Electronic Intelligence platforms ('Rivet Joint'), Electronic Warfare Jammers (US Navy Prowlers), Offensive Counter Air (F-15Cs), Suppression of Enemy Air Defence (F-16s) and Emergency Defence Suppression (F-l5Es) were all in attendance. 6 Squadron's Jaguar pilots were also there to brief on the Reconnaissance Plan for the day. Good for morale was the presence of the Combat Search and Rescue (F-16s and 'Pave Low' Helos) personnel who would he responsible for defence and pick up of any downed airmen.

'The aims for the day were covered along with the important logistics of managing to get those 40 aircraft out and back from Incirlik in good order. Expansions were made on the Air Tasking Order and the crews then cleared off for individual briefs. It was here that the Squadron Intelligence Officer, Judith Graham, updated the political and tactical picture and the sortie-lead covered the Jaguar specific details. Particular attention was paid to 'Green Lanes' which were lines of least resistance to vacate the Iraqi airspace in case of fighter launch. The time available was more than sufficient, which was a marked contrast to the training environment of home. It was then that we donned the flying equipment, which could prove crucial if one was unlucky enough to end up on Iraqi soil 'sans Jaguar'. The Combat Survival Waistcoat contained everything but the kitchen sink and the loaned pistol was also reassuring (as to whether it could repel advancing hordes was debatable). After being dropped off at the Hardened Aircraft Shelters we were able to pre flight the jets and check the various systems that would be required for each mission. Updates were broadcast on the package common frequency and, if there were no late injects, were spooled up and the long taxi commenced.

'It is hard to describe how I was feeling as I joined the long queue of aircraft with their strictly choreographed take-off times: an edifying wave from the pilot of a heavily armed F-15 Eagle saw us onto the active runway and away. The long transit to the eastern part of turkey enabled us to check and double check our aircraft and to picture build from the various radio transmissions of the formations ahead of us the nerves were starting to settle and concentration was brought to bear on the hours ahead. Fuel was taken from a RAF VC 10, final checks completed and the Iraqi border beckoned. It was surprising how mountainous terrain was but this was soon left behind as we conducted a circular route over the desert area to the North of the 36th parallel. The reconnaissance pod was pre-programmed to take footage of certain targets as requested by higher command. The frequent radio transmissions advised of anti aircraft fire in a host of areas but I have to admit that I saw nothing to alarm. It was only minutes later that we flew back into Turkish airspace ready to refuel and reconfigure our jets for further runs. These were duly completed and a westerly heading taken up for Adana. Once on the ground the tapes were taken from the reconnaissance pods for exploitation by the Intelligence community. Sortie duration for the Jaguars could be as much as five hours with the Offensive Counter Air F-15s closer to seven, which made for some long days.

'The mission flows, with time, could become routine. However, there is no doubt that the near certainty of being shot at and the knowledge of what could await if Iraq was via parachute counterbalanced this. The sorties flown while on 6 Squadron as part of 'Northern Watch' will remain with me for a long time. The knowledge that the Squadron did its part, in protecting the Kurds of Northern Iraq from an oppressive regime for such a sustained

A USAF B-52H refuelling from a tanker during 'Enduring Freedom'.

period, is reward for the extended periods away from home and some heart-in-mouth moments. The feeling of comradeship with the 6 Squadron members that served in Turkey is also something I will always value.'

The personnel on 41 Squadron were the first to deploy on Operation 'Warden' during the late summer of 1991 and were the last of Coltishall's squadrons to participate prior to being replaced by the Harrier Force in April 1993. Flight Lieutenant C.R. Soffe BSc, 1(F) Squadron Harrier GR.7 pilot, recalled:

'Nos 1(F), 3(F) and IV(AC) Squadrons were responsible for providing the UK Offensive Support Contribution, primarily tactical air reconnaissance, within the Area of Responsibility (AOR). No. 1(F) Squadron deployed to Incirlik, Turkey on rotation with the other two Harrier GR.7 squadrons... Once deployed, the more senior pilots led the first few sorties, but from then on the lead was rotated between all the pilots. Flying over Iraq, with the huge array of hostile SAM systems and AAA deployed on the ground, certainly concentrates the mind and improves your lookout. Even with the Harrier's excellent integral electronic warfare suite, the ZEUS system, all pilots were constantly looking out for that telltale plume of smoke from a SAM missile launch. An early 'spot' could make the difference between flying home and walking home! As was shown by an incident that occurred on 24 November 1993, the Kurds were obviously very aware of our presence in the AOR and of its protective benefits. A Harrier pilot had to eject over the Kurdish area of Northern Iraq after his aircraft suffered an engine failure. The people of the village of Bishiel witnessed this and sent out men to help the pilot. The Muktar of the village sent a handwritten letter in barely understandable English to the coalition forces. In thanks for the help given by the village people, they received a bountiful supply of livestock and equipment. The village must now be one of the most prosperous in the area.'

Meanwhile, Operation 'Jural' had begun in August 1992. Air assets from France, the United States and the UK, in the form of Tornado GR.1s, were sent to enforce a UN no-fly zone in southern Iraq, south of the 32nd Parallel. Flight Lieutenant D. J. Knowles BA on 9 Squadron, RAF Bruggen recalled:

'Throughout the operation the RAF has had a dual role. Equipped with the Ferranti thermal imaging airborne laser designator pod, the Tornado force has been tasked with carrying out reconnaissance of Saddam Hussein's operations against the Marsh Arabs south of the 32nd Parallel and with providing a capability to deliver LGBs on to point targets. This latter capability was ably demonstrated during the Gulf War and during the raids on Iraqi air defences in early 1993. The RAF contingent based in the Arabian Peninsula must stand ready to repeat these operations at short notice should the situation require it. On almost every day since the beginning of the operation, RAF aircraft have been operating inside Iraq, south of the 32nd Parallel, gathering information on the deployment of Saddam Hussein's forces. The squadron was fortunate in having a number of aircrew with considerable combat experience in operation 'Desert Storm'. Even so, flying deep into Iraq with known SAM systems deployed is not to be taken lightly. Enemy radars and triple-A systems are keen to play cat-and-mouse with coalition aircraft - sometimes to their cost, as the launching of a USAF anti-radar missile in support of one of our missions demonstrated.'

On 22 February 1993, twelve Jaguars of 6 Squadron departed Coltishall for the Italian Air Force base at Gioia del Colle in southern Italy when Coalition forces were once again tasked to support an international operation designed to help maintain the United Nations Protection Force (UNPROFOR) in Bosnia-Herzegovina in the former Yugoslavia. 'Deny Flight', for which the UK's participation was known as Operation 'Grapple', was a large force drawn together by the UN and NATO began on 7 April 1993 with the deployment of RAF Jaguars, Tornado F.3s, E-3D AEW aircraft, TriStar tankers and Nimrods to forward bases in Italy.

Flight Lieutenant A. G. Tait BSc AMI MechE, an F.3 Tornado navigator on XI Squadron recalls one of the missions he flew.

'The mission was slated for the small hours. After a week and a half of waiting, this was to be my first. The brief was a model of economy, the delivery of a monotone. It was not a pep talk. It was the full stop at the end of a professional's sentence, expressionless and matter-of-fact. I dressed in slow time, reluctantly collected a pistol and two clips of ammunition and stood out on the porch, watching the moon rise above a thin veil of cloud. Over Bosnia, only scattered rafts of stratus interrupted the view. Glancing down at the lights in towns and villages, it seemed as quiet as any country marooned in the very depths of night. I reached for my night-vision goggles. NVGs are little image-intensifying binos that fit to the front of a modified helmet on a lever arm so that they can be swung down over the eyes. Whilst light to the hand, NVGs are still heavy to the head and, like most backseaters, I prefer to use them as a captain's spyglass. I switched them on and peered down at the quiet scene 20,000 feet below. Through the pebble-dashed liquid green light of the NVGs I looked down at the bright flare of street lamps and for the first time saw the still brighter flares of fires.

'We shifted our combat air patrol to the south as the second pair split to the tanker, perched over the Adriatic. Overhead Sarajevo we witnessed a war in progress, coloured pea green; fires, explosions, tracer fire. For a moment I started, thinking I saw an aircraft flying low and fast across the battle lines, but when it bloomed into a sudden flash of light I realized it was a shell I'd been watching. In my guidebook, it says: 'Sarajevo is a deeply attractive city where the   region's three historical ingredients - nationalism and Turkish and Austrian occupations - underscore a buoyant individualism'. It's the target for any trip here. A buoyant individualism that made this last remark the quote of the decade.

'To the north, storm clouds were gathering and our view of the battle below grew dim before their riding and colossal bulk. These were the real gods of war, the genuine article, wearing white, flickering with fire and light, they sang out their rage across a land consumed by rage. We skirted their edges, slipped through the gaps; we were inconsequential by their side. Storms like this one would still be sweeping the skies of Bosnia long after the last shells had been expended, the last bullets fired, the last homes torched, the last villages surrounded and mortared and cleansed, the last escaping victims turned to refugees. Long after Bosnia had teetered to the very edge of abandon and tumbled headlong into the abyss, such a storm as this would still be customary across the night skies, a summer storm brewed from the midday heat.

'The radar homing warning receiver lit up and my head was filled with the trilling alarm of a triple-A battery target tracking. The target was tracking us. I stared mesmerized at the screen, feeling nothing. Fumbling in the dark, I reached for the chaff button and pressed it. The green run light flashed four times. Still the alarm sounded inside my head.

'Are you going to call that?' asked my pilot impatiently. I pressed the foot switch.

'Three One Bravo, targeted, one two seven.' The alarm died. The screen cleared. I flew my final mission six weeks later. The trip spanned a sparkling, clear-skied midday. After seventy hours of live armed inactivity, we were finally vectored into low level to search for helicopters hidden near Tuzla and almost missed them. Almost. I looked down the left side of the jet and saw a pair of 'Hips' [Mil Mi-8s] nestling in a sand quarry, dressed with insulting prettiness in coats of blue-striped white paint.

'I do not know if finding those two helicopters served a purpose. I do not know if it helped a country stumble along the dark path to peace. I only know that I would like to believe it.'

At Gioia del Colle 6 Squadron shared the manning of the detachment with 54 and 41 Squadrons. The Jaguars at Gioia were representative of the Coltishall Wing, although with the application of a new colour scheme, ARTE light grey designed for medium level operations, the only method of determining squadron ownership of the aircraft was by the two letter code on the tail and nose wheel door. The aircraft were fitted and prepared to Operation 'Granby' standard, which included overwing AIM-9L Sidewinder launchers, Tracor flare dispensers, Phimat chaff dispenser and AN/ALQ-101 ECM pod and tweaked' engines, with the only addition being an extra radio to allow for communications with in-

Harrier GR.9 at Kandahar airfield in 2009.

RAF technicians attaching a Paveway guided missile to a Tornado in Afghanistan.

theatre command and control agencies. Two of the aircraft (XZ364/GJ and XX720/GB) were permanently configured for 'wet film' photographic sorties; one with a LOROP (LOng-Range Oblique Photography) pod (which was later substituted for the GP-1 pod) and the other with a BAe pod, which carried the F.126 general survey camera. A Reconnaissance Intelligence Centre (RIC) was set up at Gioia to handle wet film processing and subsequent interpretation. This information was then passed to the 5th Allied Tactical Air Force for future mission planning, particularly in the event of a Close Air Support requirement. Unlike the Tornadoes, the Jaguars were tasked during the daytime only and they could fly anything between four and eight sorties a day including reconnaissance missions. The medium-level reconnaissance sorties were flown with two to three aircraft with up to ten targets per sortie. One GR.1A flew as the 'photo-ship' and the others, both standard GR.1As, acted as the 'stinger' to provide vital visual cross-cover for any aerial SAM threats.

In July 1993 nine Jaguars left for Gioia del Colle supported by 36 C-130 loads of personnel and equipment. Pilots were rotated to Gioia del Colle throughout 1994 while back at Coltishall station life, exercises and other duties had to fit in with the detachments to Italy. Wing Commander Tim Kerss MBE BSc, OC 54 (F) Squadron recalls the events of 1994.

'Throughout the detachment, tension in Bosnia remained high and on 2 May, the third day in theatre, the operational HQ at 5 ATAF in Vicenza, Northern Italy, tasked three Jaguars to be re-roled into an anti-shipping fit. The chosen weapon was the CRV-7 rocket; the aircraft re-role, which included the removal of bombs and underwing fuel tanks, fitment, filling and testing centre-line fuel tanks and preparation and loading of the rocket pods, was achieved in minutes rather than hours. In the event, the situation which had led to the call for these weapons was defused and the Squadron was not required to use them in anger; however, the exercise had proved the flexibility of the Jaguar and professionalism of Squadron personnel.'

The detachment ended on 10 June and the pilots returned to Gioia shortly thereafter.

A RAF Tornado GR.1 of II (AC) refuelling from a VC-10.

On 22 June the Operation 'Deny Flight' commitment was again handed to 6 Squadron and 54 returned to Coltishall having accomplished 100% of its tasked sorties. The Squadron's third deployment to Gioia del Colle took place on 12 October at a time when tension was running high in Bosnia. Initially operations continued at a normal pace with a mixture of reconnaissance and CAS sorties. However, at the beginning of November the World's attention fell on the Bihac Pocket in the North West of the Country. The use of missiles in the surface-to-surface role against a UN protected area caused particular concern. But it was the attack on 19 November against the town itself by two Orao[101] aircraft from Udbina airfield in the RSK that finally provoked a NATO air strike.'

In response to a UN request, a NATO raid on Udbina was planned by the Dutch contingent using photographs taken by the Jaguars on previous reconnaissance sorties. The raid itself was planned for 20 November but it had to be cancelled because of high cloud over the target area. The following day a strike package of over fifty aircraft was tasked to strike the runways and taxiways on the airfield from the direction of the Dalmatian Coast. The package consisted of US, Dutch, French and RAF aircraft - including four Jaguars - and was supported by the airborne controllers in their E.3 Sentrys together with USAF EF-111A Ravens and USN EA-6B Prowlers in the ECM role. Two Jaguars of 54 Squadron, one of which was flown by Wing Commander Tim Kerss, dropped 1,000lb bombs on the airfield. The other pair was tasked to carry out post-strike Bomb Damage Assessment photographs using the Long Range Attack Pod. Flight Lieutenant Chris Carder, one of the Jaguar recce pilots, recalls. 'Funny thing, it was meant to be my day off. I was going to play golf (we did six days on, two days off). I got a telephone call at about 0830 telling me to come in. At briefing we were told that in the afternoon we would be raiding Udbina and I was to lead the Jaguar post-attack recce pair. Basically, I was to get post-strike BDA (Bomb Damage Assessment) photos using the LOROP at a height above 15,000 feet, 4-5 miles off the target.

'We tanked from a TriStar on the way in. Tanker after tanker was stacked up to refuel the American F-16s and F-18s and French Mirages. It was a gorgeous day. You could see for miles. AWACS cleared the package to push through and then we got specific clearance to go in. An F-18, relaying the clearance from AWACs to us, said: 'You are cleared to press. 'Manpads' (man-portable shoulder launched missiles) and triple-A are in the area.' If flak was heavy we could always get the pictures later but there was only light triple-A. The raid went in and pails of smoke were rising from the airfield, which was at the base of a mountain. The wingy asked: 'What speed are you going through?'

I said: 'As fast as I can get.'

'I couldn't look out that much. I had to maintain level height to get good pictures and was using the HUD [head-up display]. My back-up was there just to watch my six. That was it. I got the photos and we all headed back to Giola del Colle. We didn't need the tanker on the way home.'[102]

Tim Keress continues.

'The results of the attack are now history but it was indeed a proud moment for the Squadron to represent the RAF in the largest air operation ever undertaken by NATO. The following days saw the planning and even launching of similar packages. Again, the Jaguars provided reconnaissance support but no further bombs were dropped in anger. Amid the flurry of subsequent diplomatic activity the threat of immediate air strikes abated and, by the time that the Squadron returned to Coltishall during the first week of December, tasking was back to normal.

'Following a welcome but brief rest 54(F) Squadron took to the skies once again in force over the UK, an invaluable and necessary opportunity to rekindle academic and tactical skills in the air and to re-acquaint the ground crew with the challenges of running a full flying programme. When it came, the Christmas break was welcomed by all, a chance to reflect upon a truly memorable year and to contemplate what 1995 would bring. Already the programme was filling, with the promise of exercises in the USA and Norway, a missile-firing camp at RAF Valley and a squadron exchange to Portugal. The Cold War might have been over but with so much instability in the World the Squadrons had never been busier! Mobility and flexibility were the keys to the emerging role and, while life could be hectic, it certainly wasn't boring!'

During 'Grapple' the Jaguar Force had flown 3,000 operational sorties over Bosnia, culminating in more than 5,000 flying hours. Not a single Jaguar was lost due to enemy action during this time. However, one aircraft, XZ373/GE, was lost on 21 June 1995 during a training

RAF C-17 of 99 Squadron during a trooping flight. RAF C-17s were used extensively to and from Afghanistan.

The Tornado F.3 made its combat debut in the 1991 Gulf War with 18 aircraft deployed to Dhahran, Saudi Arabia. The aircraft deployed to the region were later upgraded in a crash programme with improved radar and engines, better defensive countermeasures and several adaptions to the weapons systems to improve combat performance in the Iraqi theatre; however, they still lacked modern IFF and secure communications equipment. They therefore flew patrols further back from Iraqi airspace where encounters with enemy aircraft were less likely, and did not get the opportunity to engage any enemy aircraft. From August 1990 to March 1991, the RAF's F.3 detachment flew more than 2,000 combat air patrol sorties. In 2003 the F.3 was one of the assets used in Operation 'Telic', Britain's contribution to the Iraq War. An expeditionary force composed of 43 and 111 Squadrons (known as Leuchars Fighter Wing) was deployed to the region to carry out offensive counter-air operations. The Tornado F.3s of Leuchars Fighter Wing operated all over Iraq, including missions over and around Baghdad, throughout Operation 'Telic'. Due to a lack of airborne threats materialising in the theatre, the F.3s were withdrawn and returned to European bases that same year.

sortie whilst being flown by a USAF exchange pilot with 6 Squadron. After a successful ejection over the Adriatic Sea, the pilot was eventually rescued by a Royal Navy Sea King, which had been scrambled from the NATO base at Split. On 31 January 1995 6 Squadron left Gioia del Colle and Operation 'Grapple' air operations were taken over by the Harrier force from RAF Wittering. At Coltishall two TIALD Jaguars (XX962 and XZ725) and crews were put on 48-hour standby ready to deploy to Italy to designate for the Harrier GR.7s against Serb targets in Bosnia if and when required. 6 Squadron took over the standby commitment on 24 August 1995 and shortly thereafter Operation 'Deliberate Force' began when an artillery shell exploded in a market square in Sarajevo. On 29 and 30 August the TIALD Jaguars were flown to Gioia del Colle by Squadron Leader Alex Muskett (XX725) and Squadron Leader Simon Blake (XX692) respectively. One of the Jaguars had a TIALD pod owned by GEC Marconi and the other was borrowed from a Tornado squadron at Brüggen. Operations began on 30 August when the two TIALD Jaguars and four Harriers each armed with a pair of 1,000lb Paveway II LGBs attacked an ammunition storage depot near Sarajevo. Altogether, Squadron Leaders Muskett and Blake flew 25 operational TIALD sorties, guiding 48 PGMs onto their targets and acquiring a number of other targets for Harriers attacking with 1,000lb iron bombs. In January 1997 the Jaguars returned to Gioia del Colle to take over the 'Grapple' detachment from the Harriers with 41 Squadron leading the way.[103]

In December 1993 the 917th Bomb Wing deployed its B-52Hs, personnel and equipment to Aviana Air Base, Italy to support the UN no-fly rule over Bosnia-Herzegovina. After Operation 'Deny Flight', it was decided that three of the five remaining first-line B-52H units (92nd, 410th and 416th Bomb Wings) would be deactivated by the end of 1994 and their aircraft reassigned to the 2nd and 5th Bomb Wings. The 917th Wing meanwhile, returned to Aviana Air Base in August 1994 and again in May 1995 to uphold the UN ban on military flights in the Bosnia-Herzegovina airspace.

In September 1996 Operation 'Desert Strike' went ahead in Iraq after three divisions of Iraqi Republican Guard troops were ordered by President Saddam Hussein to seize the northern town of Irbil on 31 August. Northern Iraq had been independent of Saddam Hussein since the end of the Gulf War and under protection of coalition air forces (Operation 'Provide Comfort II'). In response the 2nd Bomb Wing that same day deployed four B-52H aircraft and crews of the 96th Bomb Squadron led by the CO, Lieutenant Colonel Floyd L. Carpenter and over 170 personnel (carried by a C-5) to Andersen AFB, Guam. At around 1700 hours the first of the B-52Hs took off from Barksdale for the 15.8-hour flight to Guam. En route two air-refuellings were carried out just off the West Coast and near Hawaii and the four B-52Hs landed at Andersen at around midnight on 31 August. Crews had not been told that they were to launch a combat strike against targets in Southern Iraq at 1900 hours on 1 September, nineteen hours after landing on the island! Three of the aircraft were to launch with the spare returning after the first air refuelling and the remaining two continuing on to launch conventionally armed AGM-86C cruise missiles against targets in southern Iraq. Lieutenant Colonel Floyd L. Carpenter in *Mud Buff* and the other B-52H flew on and were refuelled in mid-air twice more. During their approach to the Gulf region two Mirage interceptors were launched and gave chase but they were diverted from their task by F-14D Tomcats from the USS *Carl Vinson*. As the two B-52Hs approached the southern coast of Kuwait they separated and began launching their CALCMs. The first three launches were 'uneventful' and by the time corrective action had been taken they were at the limits of their launch boxes so the B-52H crews had to turn back having launched only half their loads. However, Carpenter decided they would turn around and launch the rest of their CALCMs. The move was popular with crews and command alike and *Mud Buff* launched six CALCMs and the other B-52H, seven.[104] On the way home the B-52Hs were threatened with interception once more but the Tomcat escorts did their job well and none came within forty miles of the bombers, who returned safely to Guam after a 33.9 hour, 13,600-mile round trip. The mission resulted in the fourteen crewmembers in the 96th Bomb Squadron winning

A laser guided weapon being fitted to a Tornado during Operation 'Jural'. The mission was to monitor and control airspace south of the 33rd parallel in Iraq, in support of Operation 'Southern Watch'. Coalition forces in the region monitor Iraq's compliance with United Nations Security Council Resolutions.

the Mackay Trophy, which is awarded annually by the National Aeronautic Association to US Air Force aircrew in recognition of the most meritorious flight of the year. On 15 September two of the B-52Hs and over 140 personnel re-deployed from Guam to the British Indian Ocean Territory of Diego Garcia in case further strike missions were ordered. The remaining pair of bombers returned to Barksdale from Guam and two additional B-52Hs were later deployed to Diego Garcia bringing the total aircraft to four again. On 12 October 1996 all 2nd Bomb Wing deployed assets returned to Barksdale.

On 13 November 1997 when Iraq demanded that American citizens working for UNSCOM leave the country immediately and three days later President William J. Clinton directed a military force build-up in Southwest Asia. On 19 November the 2nd Bomb Wing began deploying an air expeditionary group of six, later eight, B-52H aircraft and over 200 personnel to Diego Garcia in response to the crisis. On 12 February 1998 the 2nd Bomb Wing increased the air expeditionary group at Diego Garcia with an additional six B-52H aircraft and sixty personnel bringing total deployed assets to fourteen B-52Hs and over 260 personnel.

Diplomacy seemed to deter Iraq and on 30 May HQ Air Combat Command directed all deployed forces to stand down from alert and prepare for redeployment to home stations. On 3 June the first three B-52Hs returned to Barksdale and the remaining deployed aircraft and personnel returned Stateside over the next two weeks. Iraq's continued non-compliance with UN Security Council resolutions marked a crisis point and on 11 November, as the last UNSCOM inspectors departed Baghdad, President Clinton ordered a military force build-up in Southwest Asia under the codename Operation 'Desert Thunder'. On 14 November the 2nd Bomb Wing deployed an air expeditionary group of seven, later nine, B-52H aircraft (one went unserviceable on Guam) and 180 personnel to Diego Garcia. There they formed the 2nd Air Expeditionary Group (AEG), commanded by Colonel Robert A. Bruley, Jr. They were joined on 11 December 1998 by seven B-52Hs of the 5th Bomb Wing based at Minot AFB. During 16 to 19 December 1998 the US and Great Britain launched Operation 'Desert Fox' - a series of strong, sustained air and cruise missile attacks against military and suspected NBC related sites in Iraq. Allied aircraft flew 1,075-1,165 sorties. During the second and third nights of the attack the B-52Hs of the 2nd AEG fired ninety AGM-86C CALCMs against targets in Iraq. On the second night of 'Desert Fox' (the first night of B-52 participation), the B-52Hs flew in two flights of six aircraft each separated by six hours between them (each flight also included an initial seventh spare). The lead flight, led by Lieutenant Colonel Thomas J. Griffith, commander of the 96th Bomb Squadron

In September 1996 Operation 'Desert Strike' went ahead in Iraq after three divisions of Iraqi Republican Guard troops were ordered by President Saddam Hussein to seize the northern town of Irbil on 31 August. That same day two B-52H aircraft and crews of the 96th Bomb Squadron on Guam led by the CO, Lieutenant Colonel Floyd L. Carpenter in *Mud Buff* launched conventionally armed AGM-86C cruise missiles against targets in southern Iraq. *Mud Buff* launched six CALCMs and the other B-52H, seven. The bombers returned safely after a 33.9 hour, 13,600-mile round trip.

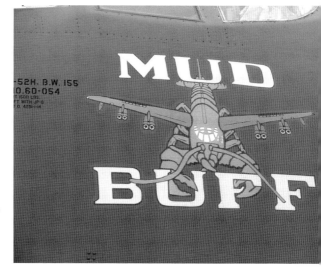

A RAF Typhoon FGR4 of 1(F) Squadron and a French Armee De L'Air Mirage 2000N of the Escadron de Chasse 2/4 'La Fayette' during Exercise 'Capable Eagle' in 2013.

and manned by 96th Bomb Squadron crews fired forty-one CALCMs. The second flight, led by Lieutenant Colonel Douglas C. Haynor, commander of the 23rd Bomb Squadron and manned primarily by 23rd Bomb Squadron crews (three individual 2nd Bomb Wing crewmembers were in the mix) entered the launch box in the early morning hours of 18 December 1998. Haynor's flight fired thirty-three CALCMs. All told, seventy-four CALCMs were fired by the two flights that night. In the evening of 18 December 1998, the 2nd AEG launched a two-ship follow-up strike mission. Manned by mixed 20th Bomb Squadron and 96th Bomb Squadron crews, Major Keith W. Anderson of the 96th Bomb Squadron served as the flight mission commander. The two-ship flight launched a final sixteen CALCMs against Iraqi targets. The 'Desert Fox' grand total for the B-52H stood at ninety AGM-86C CALCMs. 1st Lieutenant Cheryl A. Lamoureux, a 20th Bomb Squadron EWO, became the first woman flier in US Air Force history to fly a combat mission when she participated in the two-ship CALCM strike on the night of 18/19 December 1998.[105]

On 17 February 1999 eight B-52Hs at Barksdale forward deployed to RAF Fairford forming the 20th Expeditionary Bomb Squadron (part of the 2nd Air Expeditionary Group) to take part in Operation 'Allied Force'. This NATO operation was aimed at bombing Serbia in an attempt to halt the ethnic cleansing of Kosovo and force the Yugoslav army to withdraw from Kosovo. On 24 March six of the B-52Hs took part in the first wave of air strikes, firing CALCMs against Serbian targets. Four additional B-52Hs of the 5th Bomb Wing at Minot were deployed to Fairford on 27 March and the deployment built up to peak strength of fourteen aircraft. In all, 25 individual aircraft deployed during the 78-day Campaign, which lasted from 24 March to 20 June 1999. During 57 days of actual air strikes the B-52Hs and B-1Bs at RAF Fairford dropped 11,000 bombs and launched sixty-two ALCMs in 270 sorties.

In April 2001 41 (F) Squadron RIC returned to Incirlik in Turkey to support the Jaguar Wing Detachment which had once again taken over the task of policing the Northern No Fly Zone in Iraq, now called Operation 'Resinate' (North). This was a busy period operationally as Iraqi air defence units became noticeably more hostile in response to coalition air activity in the run up to Operation 'Telic' in early 2003. Two of 6 Squadron's pilots were decorated for their contribution to operations over Northern Iraq. In November 2001 Flight Lieutenant James Head was the formation leader of a two-aircraft reconnaissance mission patrolling the 'No Fly Zone'. As the Jaguars crossed into hostile territory on their

234

first 'recce run'; they were met with far higher levels of anti-aircraft fore than usual. Having observed AAA exploding close aboard, Head called his formation to take evasive manoeuvres and modified the planned route. Subsequently, a further ten concentrated AAA airbursts were seen close to the Jaguars. Despite this he calmly continued the run whilst ensuing that the updated threat was passed to all other coalition aircraft. On returning to Turkish airspace and following air-to-air refuelling, he was immediately given a complex airborne re-task. After ensuring his new wingman was fully prepared Flight Lieutenant Head calmly led the formation back into hostile territory for a second reconnaissance run. His actions earned the award of the DFC. The last such medal awarded to a 6 Squadron pilot was to Warrant Officer M. Gelbhauer in 1946.

Flight Lieutenant Graham Pemberton, who completed six operational tours on Operation 'Resinate' (North) patrolling the No Fly Zone over Northern Iraq, received the Queen's Commendation for valuable service in the air. In November 2002 he was detailed to carry out a tactical reconnaissance sortie. Having crossed into hostile airspace, he spotted intense anti-aircraft artillery fire that was a clear threat to his formation and F-16 aircraft in the vicinity. Pemberton directed immediate defensive manoeuvres and positively controlled the F-16s ensuring all aircraft avoided the artillery airbursts. Subsequently, it was revealed that this had been the heaviest day of hostile fire since the Operation commenced. During his operational tours, Graham Pemberton played an important part in developing coalition tactics and procedures.

International political wrangling forced the rapid withdrawal of the Jaguar Force detachment from Turkey only days before operations began to topple Saddam Hussein. Ultimately, although the Jaguar Force was not required to take any further part in the operation the JRP and the RIC deployed to Al Jaber in Kuwait to support reconnaissance operations by the Harrier during the war. At the end of hostilities in 2003 JRP and GIES were re-deployed to the Tornado GR.4 detachment located initially at Ali Al Salem in Kuwait and subsequently at Al Udeid in Qatar.

Despite its defeat in the Gulf War, Iraq continued to present the biggest obstacle to peace

A Tornado GR.4 of XIII Squadron taking off from Kandahar in Afghanistan.

Armed RAF Tornadoes at dispersal.

in the Gulf region and there were other trouble spots to police. During 1996 the US Navy maintained a constant global presence supporting national interests and reinforcing international policy as Enterprise, Nimitz, Kitty Hawk, Theodore Roosevelt, George Washington, America and Carl Vinson deployed in support of Operations 'Joint Endeavor' over Bosnia-Herzegovina, 'Desert Strike', 'Southern Watch' and 'Sharp Guard'. America was decommissioned on 30 September after 31 years of service. On 28 June the venerable A-6 Intruder deployed with VA-75 'Sunday Punchers' on Enterprise to the Mediterranean, for its final deployment (both VA-196 and VA-75 were scheduled to disestablish in spring 1997, ending more than thirty years of medium attack service to the Navy's carrier force) and VA-75 bid farewell to the 'Blue Blasters' of VA-34, the only other Intruder Squadron on the East Coast. The 'Blasters' were headed home to transition to the F/A-18s.[106] after the mandatory familiarization flights, the 'Sunday Punchers' went in-country to fly defence suppression, CAP and FAC[107] (airborne) missions over Bosnia-Herzegovina for a week and half before heading for Mallorca and calling at Cannes in southern France, Souda Bay in Greece and for liberty at Haifa in Israel. After participating in Exercise 'Juniper Hawk' in Israeli airspace, Enterprise sailed to the Persian Gulf to join the Carl Vinson in support of Operation 'Southern Watch' and 'Desert Strike'.[108] This was the first time since 'Desert Storm' that carrier battle groups from the Pacific and Atlantic fleets formed together in the Persian Gulf. The Carl Vinson battle group, with Carrier Air Wing 14 embarked had been on station in the Gulf since early summer to enforce the No Fly Zone in southern Iraq. The 'Jolly Rogers' of VF-103 on board Enterprise added their LANTIRN-equipped[109] F-14Bs to the operation. When the call came to strike Iraq south of the 33rd Parallel with cruise missiles carried by two B-52s based on Guam, the 'Tomcatters' of VF-31 and VF-11 'Red Rippers' F-14D Tomcats flew as fighter escorts and defensive air patrol. VF-31 also took post-strike imagery with their TARPs-equipped Tomcats. E-2C Group II Hawkeyes of VAW-113' Black

RAF Jaguar GR.1As of 54 Squadron on a mission during Operation 'Northern Watch' in September 1999.

Eagles' provided AEW to the B-52s, which flew for nineteen hours to reach the Gulf because allies in the region did not take part. The Hawkeyes also controlled the escort fighters from the air wing.

The 'No Fly' Zone over southern Iraq, originally established south of the 32nd Parallel was extended further. Also, 'Desert Strike' weakened Saddam Hussein's hold on Iraqi forces by further restricting Iraqi freedom of movement in the air. Finally, Saddam Hussein backed down from military actions against the Kurds and the Carl Vinson battle group transited the Strait of Hormuz in early October.

On 11 September 2001 nineteen operatives of Osama bin Laden's al-Qaeda terrorist network launched a co-ordinated and devastating attack on the United States of America. Hijacking four US civilian jetliners, the terrorists deliberately flew one aircraft into each tower of the World Trade Centre in New York City and dived a third aircraft into the southwest side of the Pentagon in Washington DC. The fourth hijacked jetliner crashed in rural Pennsylvania after a courageous band of passengers overpowered the terrorists. Over 3,100 people lost their lives in the worst terrorist attack in America' history. Within days of the attacks America prepared for combat operations in the so-called 'War Against Terror' aimed at eliminating the repressive Taliban regime of Afghanistan and Osama bin Laden's al-Qaeda leadership and training infrastructure in the country. B-52Hs of 20th Bomb Squadron from Minot AFB and Air Force Reserve Command's 93rd Bomb Squadron from Barksdale AFB (and a number of B-1Bs) deployed to Diego Garcia as part of Operation 'Enduring Freedom'. The B-52Hs formed the 28th Air Expeditionary Wing at Diego Garcia where they operated under the auspices of the 20th EBS from 7 October 2001-March 2002. Aircrew were better prepared than in previous operations. During 'Allied Force' many of the aircrew had not had the chance to train with night vision goggles (NVG), which caused some problems. By the time of 'Enduring Freedom', however, deployed pilots had already received realistic night training and aircrew were closer to the USAF's ideal of experiencing the first ten days of combat in a familiar environment. The deployed B-52Hs were fitted with the Combat Track II datalink system, an interim system used instead of the more advanced Joint Tactical Information Display System (JTIDS) Link 16, which proved popular among aircrew. This allowed mission planners to pass new target intelligence and information to aircraft in flight and even to change targets or upload entire new missions while the aircraft was en route to the target.

There was some 'traditional' B-52 'carpet-bombing' of the Taliban front line north of Kabul, capital of Afghanistan, especially as part of 'softening up' before allied ground attacks were made against defended enemy positions: B-52Hs carpet-bombed Taliban positions outside Bagram AB on 31 October 2001, for example. The B-52Hs were also used as a psychological weapon, dropping leaflet bombs backed up by the threat of carpet bombing attacks. The B-52Hs typically flew 'figure of eight' patterns while waiting for

Security forces spring into action at Barksdale AFB to form a perimeter as Air Force One carrying President George Bush prepares to land at the base on 11 September 2001 following the suicide attacks on the World Trade Center in New York and the Pentagon in Washington DC. Within a month, B-52Hs like 61-0029 SAC Time of the 93rd Bomb Squadron, 917th Wing, Air Force Reserve Command (behind) would be deployed on bombing missions against the Taliban and Al-Qaida in Operation 'Enduring Freedom,' October 2001-March 2002 (Reuters 2001/Win McNamee).

238

targeting data from a special operations controller on the ground, equipped with a laser rangefinder, a digital map system and GPS system. The FACs, who accompanied US and allied troops - including Afghan Northern Alliance forces - would radio target co-ordinates to the B-52H, whose crew entered these co-ordinates into a Joint Direct Attack Munition [JDAM] or precision-guided bomb. The B-52H would then typically use a single JDAM against its intended target, rather than a whole stick of twenty-seven or fifty-one conventional unguided 'dumb' bombs.

'Enduring Freedom' was a much less 'intense' air campaign than 'Desert Storm' had been. But whereas the Air Force had needed about ten aircraft to destroy a single target during 'Desert Storm', according to Central Command's commander, General Tommy Franks, in 'Enduring Freedom' a single aircraft was often used to take out two targets. He also said that the 200 sorties a day flown in 'Enduring Freedom' hit roughly the same number of targets, which had been hit with 3,000 sorties in 'Desert Storm'. The type of targets hit were a so very different, fewer of them being static targets such as troop concentrations and bunkers. This forced a major shift in tactics, with a move away from pre-planned missions against pre-briefed targets towards much more reactive missions in which B-52Hs loitered in the general target area before being called in to attack evolving targets identified by Forward Air Controllers (FACs).

In January 2003 the spotlight in the 'War Against Terror' 'turned to Saddam Hussein's regime in Iraq. It was evident that Saddam Hussein had failed to account for his biological and chemical weapons and 29,984 other prohibited weapons. Planning for Operation 'Iraqi Freedom', the Second Gulf War, began. In the months leading up to the war aircraft patrolling Iraqi 'no-fly' zones bombed eighty air defence sites. In early March B-52Hs were deployed to RAF Fairford, Diego Garcia and Andersen AB, Guam to be used as part of the coalition's 'shock and awe' campaign against Iraq, initially attacking and eliminating military and air defence targets in and around Baghdad. The aircraft were subsequently used against deployed Iraqi Army and Republican Guard formations and targets. On 19 March almost 467,000 US personnel were in the Middle East, 61,296 of them from the US Navy, which moved the carriers USS *Theodore Roosevelt* and USS *Harry S. Truman* into the eastern Mediterranean. Iraqi Freedom began with Coalition aircraft conducting strikes to prepare the battlefield. On 20 March six US warships in the Persian Gulf and Red Sea and two F-117A Stealth Fighters with no jamming or fighter support attacked leadership targets of opportunity in Baghdad. The F-117As dropped four EGBU-27 LGBs and the warships fired more than forty AGM-109 Tomahawk Land Attack (Cruise) Missiles (TLAM). Next day the B-52Hs took part in what has been described as the largest CALCM strike in history, launching 76 of more than 140 missiles fired. In all, coalition air forces commenced nearly 1,000 strike sorties marking the beginning of A-Day, the air campaign. Coalition forces seized an airfield in western Iraq and advanced 100 miles into Iraq. Over the first three weeks of the war USAF crews flew nearly forty per cent of the combat sorties and delivered two-thirds of the munitions tonnage. The rest was divided between the USN, USMC, RAF and RAAF. In all, 15,000 precision guided munitions were dropped and 750 cruise missiles were launched. In contrast to the 1991 war, when nine out of ten expended weapons were unguided 'dumb' bombs, about 75 per cent of the weapons were precision guided..

After an agreement had been reached with Turkey concerning over-flight rights, the air offensive on the northern front opened on 24 March with strike packages being launched around the clock from the *Truman* and the *Roosevelt*. For almost three weeks of continuous operations, the carriers' air wings maintained a 24-hour round the clock presence over northern Iraq. The 400-mile flight from the eastern Mediterranean meant that US navy fliers oftenspent between five and six hours in their cockpits during these flights. The *Truman* flew mainly daylight strike missions while the *Roosevelt's* were flown at night.

By 25 March Defense Chief Donald H. Rumsfeld could claim 'total dominance of the

The Northrop-Grumman B-2 Spirit Stealth Bomber made its combat debut in 1999 during the Kosovo War. It was responsible for destroying 33% of selected Serbian bombing targets in the first eight weeks of US involvement in the War, during which, six B-2s flew non-stop to Kosovo from their home base in Missouri and back in 30 hours. The B-2 was the first aircraft to deploy GPS satellite-guided JDAM 'smart bombs' in combat use in Kosovo. In Afghanistan, B-2s struck ground targets in support of Operation 'Enduring Freedom'. With aerial refuelling support, the B-2 flew one of its longest missions to date from Whiteman AFB, Missouri to Afghanistan and back. During Operation 'Iraqi Freedom' B-2s operated from Diego Garcia and an undisclosed 'forward operating location'. In March 2011 B-2s were the first US aircraft into action in Operation 'Odyssey Dawn', the UN mandated enforcement of the Libyan no-fly zone. Three B-2s dropped 40 bombs on a Libyan airfield in support of the UN no-fly zone. The B-2s flew directly from the US mainland to Libya; a B-2 was refuelled by allied tanker aircraft four times during each round trip mission.

air'.[110] Like the Afghanistan campaign in 2001 the 'long-distance' war against Iraq often involved small teams of Special Forces troops (and their Kurdish allies) directing US Navy attack aircraft and B-52s to blast Republican Guard positions and other Iraqi ground forces with anti-vehicle and anti-personnel weapons[111] and satellite-guided Joint Direct Attack Munitions (JDAMs) respectively.[112] Those who were not killed had their morale destroyed by the strikes. TLAMS could also now be launched against targets in northern Iraq and were used on 28 March to blast the mountain base of the Ansar al-Islam group before Kurdish peshmerga fighters, backed by US Special Forces, stormed the base. The final advance towards Baghdad by the US Third Army was supported by a massive force of 800 strike aircraft and attack helicopters, which included F/A-18 and F-14 strike aircraft on the three US Navy carriers in the Gulf, which were also tasked to support the ground offensive. By the afternoon of 9 April US troops had reached the centre of Baghdad and Saddam Hussein and his cohorts had disappeared. On 16 April CENTCOM officials declared the end of major combat action in Iraq.[113]

Endnotes for Chapter 7

100 See *SEPECAT Jaguar: Tactical Support & Maritime Strike Fighter* by Martin W. Bowman (Pen & Sword 2007).

101 SOKO/Iav Craiova J-22/IAR-93 lightweight close-support and ground attack aircraft, the result of a collaborative Yugoslav and Romanian project and which emerged with a configuration reminiscent of the Jaguar and powered by two Turboméca/ORAO-built Rolls-Royce Viper turbojets.

102 Chris Carder flew the Jaguar with 54(F) Squadron from 1992 to 1996. He then became a Jaguar QFI at RAF Lossiemouth and he was the Jaguar display pilot in 1999. Earlier in his career as a Hawk QFI at RAF Valley he was twice the winner of the No.4 Flying Training School aerobatic competition. He was also the 1991 solo Hawk display pilot. In 2000 he joined the Red Arrows as Red 4.

103 When UNPROFOR changed its role to become the United Nations Implementation Force (IFOR), Operation 'Deny Flight' became Operation 'Decisive Endeavour' and in December 1996 IFOR's role changed again to become the United Nations Stabilization Force (SFOR) and Operation 'Decisive Edge' then became Operation 'Deliberate Guard'.

104 At the same time as this mission, AGM-109 Tomahawk Land Attack (Cruise) Missiles (TLAM) were fired from the destroyer USS *Laboon* and from the cruiser USS *Shiloh*. The next day, more missiles were fired from US Navy ships against targets that had been undamaged during the previous attack.

105 After Operation 'Desert Fox' the Iraq forbid any more weapons inspections and denied the existence of the UN No Fly Zones. During the first days of 1999 two USAF F-15s and four US Navy F-14D (VF-213) were engaged by about thirteen Iraqi MiGs and Mirage F.1s above the No Fly Zone in southern Iraq. In accordance with the UN resolutions, both the F-15s and F-14s fired missiles at long distance at the Iraqi. No Iraqi aircraft were hit, but one Iraqi fighter is said to have crashed on approach to its airbase because of a lack of fuel. After this incident the UN continued to control the No Fly Zones, undisturbed by Saddam's forces ... eventually firing at Iraqi installations if provoked.

106 The Navy received the first F/A-18E/F Super Hornets and the LANTIRN (low-level altitude navigation and targeting infrared radar for night)-capable F-14B Tomcat. The island was installed on the flight deck of (CVN-75), the Navy's newest carrier on 11 July, bringing the carrier, which on 7 September was christened *Harry S. Truman*, one step closer to completion.

107 Forward Air Control (FAC(A)).

108 *1996 The Year in Review* by William T. Baker, *Naval Aviation News July-August 1997* and *The Hook, winter 1996*.

109 Infrared and laser-guided bombing system.

110 Out of 2,565 aircraft deployed, 863 were USAF, 372 USMC and 408 USN. The US Army deployed 700+ helicopters. By comparison, in Desert Storm the USAF had deployed 830 fixed-wing aircraft, the USN 552 aircraft of all types and the USMC, 242 fixed-wing aircraft and 324 helicopters and the US Army, 1,193. In total the Pentagon committed 1,624 fixed-wing aircraft and 1,537 helicopters to Desert Storm. Air War Iraq by Tim Ripley (Pen & Sword Aviation 2004).

111 Navy and Marine attack aircraft dropped Mk 81/82 Snakeye bombs, Mk.7 GATOR mines, Mk.20 Rockeye, PLU-77/B APAM, CBU-24 and BLU series cluster/fragmentation bombs. Due to range and fuel tanking requirements, aircraft often had to fly missions with only two or three dispensers/bombs underwing.

112 See *Air War Iraq* by Tim Ripley (Pen & Sword Aviation 2004)

113 In March 1999 NATO decided to strike against Serbian forces due to continuing ethnic expulsion and massacres against the Albanian people in Kosovo. To end Yugoslavian terror NATO bombed Serbia for weeks day and night. The US sent among others the aircraft carrier USS *Theodore Roosevelt* which also meant launching F-14s. The role of the F-14s was enemy fighter suppression, forward air control, aerial reconnaissance and also precision laser-guided air-to-ground attacks. When airstrikes ended, the role of the allied fighters was changed to fly cover for the international KFOR troops who occupied Kosovo. Between 6 April and 9 June CVW-8 fighters flew 4,270 total sorties and 3,055 combat sorties with zero losses. The F-14s, EA-6Bs and F/A-18s of CVW-8 destroyed or damaged a total of 477 tactical targets and 88 fixed targets. Among others, VF-14 F-14s dropped 350 laser-guided bombs (a total of 350,000lbs) and the 'Tophatters' flew also FAC(A) missions for other coalition strike aircraft.

Chapter Eight

Inherent Resolve

Unlike previous US combat operations, no name had been given to the American intervention against the Islamic State of Iraq and the Levant (ISIL), including both the campaign in Iraq and the campaign in Syria until it was announced in mid-October 2015 that the operational name would be Inherent Resolve.

Following the start of the Arab Spring in 2011, protests in Syria against President Syria Bashar al-Assad were suppressed and became violent. In 2012 the al-Nusra Front was established by the Islamic State of Iraq as the official branch of al-Qaeda in Syria. Starting in November 2012, 18 months after the beginning of the Syrian Civil War and four months after the beginning of air raids by fixed-wing SAF aircraft, Su-24 medium bombers were filmed attacking rebel positions. The SAF suffered its first Su-24 loss, an upgraded MK2 version, to an Igla surface-to-air missile on 28 November 2012 near the town of Darat Izza in the Aleppo Governorate. One of the crew members, Colonel Ziad Daud Ali, was injured and filmed being taken to a rebel field hospital. Also, Syrian 'Fencers' were reportedly to have been involved in near-encounters with NATO warplanes. The first of such incidents occurred in early September 2013 when Syrian 'Fencers' of the 819th Squadron from Tiyas airbase flew low over the Mediterranean and approached the 14-mile air exclusion zone surrounding the British airbase in Akrotiri, Cyprus. The jets turned back before reaching the area due to two RAF Eurofighter Typhoons being scrambled to intercept them. Turkey also sent two F-16s. The 'Fencers' were possibly testing the air defences of the base (and their reaction time) in preparation for a possible military strike by the US, the United Kingdom and France in the aftermath of the chemical weapons attack in Ghouta, Damascus allegedly committed by the Syrian government. On 23 September 2014 a Syrian Su-24 was shot down by an Israeli Air Defence Command MIM-104D Patriot missile near Quneitra after it had penetrated 800 metres into Israeli controlled airspace over the Golan Heights. The missile hit the aircraft when it already re-entered into the Syrian air space. Both crew members ejected safely and landed in Syrian territory.

In June 2014 US forces started undertaking reconnaissance missions over northern Iraq. By the end of September that year the United States had conducted 240 air strikes in Iraq and Syria, as well as 1,300 tanker refuelling missions, totalling 3,800 sorties by all types of aircraft. A tactical arrangement with Kurdish and Iraqi forces, and drone videos are being used to coordinate close air support without needing US troops in ground combat. On 7 August President Obama gave a live address describing the worsening conditions in Iraq and that the plight of the Yazidis particular had convinced him that US military action was necessary to protect American lives, protect minority groups in Iraq and to stop a possible ISIL advance on Erbil, the capital of the Kurdish Autonomous Region. On 8 August the United States began bombing ISIL targets in Iraq. By 10 August, assisted by these air attacks, Kurdish forces claimed to have recaptured the towns of Mahmour and Gweyr from Islamic State control. Additional Iraqi air strikes conducted in Sinjar were reported to have killed 45 ISIL militants and injured an additional 60 militants. On 11 August a spokesman for The Pentagon said the air strikes had slowed down ISIL's advance in northern Iraq, but were unlikely to degrade ISIL's capabilities or operations in other areas. Between 8 and 13 August, US air strikes and Kurdish ground forces enabled 35,000 to

On 20 March 2011 ten Typhoon aircraft deployed from RAF Coningsby to Gioia Del Colle (GDC) in Southern Italy as part of Operation 'Ellamy' - an international coalition (18 nations provided air or maritime assets) aimed at enforcing a no-fly zone proposed during the Libyan Civil War to prevent government forces loyal to Muammar Gaddafi from carrying out air attacks on anti-Gaddafi forces. By lunchtime the next day two Typhoons were flying Combat Air Patrols in support of the No Fly Zone (designated by the US as Operation 'Odyssey Dawn'; the Canadians as Operation 'Mobile' and the French as Opération 'Harmattan'). On 22 March Typhoons patrolled the no-fly zone while Tornado GR.4s from RAF Marham flew an armed reconnaissance sortie. The first Typhoon multi-role sortie was flown in mixed formation with a Tornado GR.4 on 7 April. On 12 April Typhoons were used operationally in a ground attack role for the first time. A Typhoon destroyed two main battle tanks near Misrata with Paveway II whilst a Tornado destroyed the third with Paveway IV. In total, RAF aircraft destroyed eight main battle tanks on 12 April. Since the start of Operation 'Ellamy' up until 12 April, RAF aircraft had engaged over 100 main battle tanks, artillery pieces, armoured vehicles and SAMs.

RAF Raytheon Sentinel R1 ZJ692 seen taking off from the Mojave Spaceport during a visit to the National Test Pilot School is the RAF's only long-range wide area battlefield surveillance asset, providing critical intelligence and target tracking information to British and Coalition forces. The aircraft was deployed operationally in Afghanistan from 2009 and provided vital intelligence during NATO operations in Libya in 2011 and French operations in Mali in 2013.

A Tornado over the desert during the first RAF air strike on Iraq on 27 September 2014.

45,000 of Yazidi refugees to escape or be evacuated from the Sinjar Mountains. On 16 August US air power began a close air campaign aimed at supporting the advance of Kurdish fighters moving toward the Mosul Dam. Kurdish sources commented that it was the 'heaviest US bombing of militant positions since the start of air strikes'. On 8 September the Iraqi Army, with close air support from the US retook the key Haditha Dam and recaptured the town of Barwana, killing fifteen ISIL fighters.

On 26 August 2014 the US began sending surveillance flights, including drones, over Syria to gather intelligence on ISIL targets in Syria. The flights began gathering intelligence that would aid future air strikes; however, air strikes were not yet authorized at that point and no approval was sought from the Assad government for flights entering Syrian airspace. On 2 September ISIL released a video threatening to behead British citizen David Haines. Prime Minister David Cameron reacted by saying that ISIL will be 'be squeezed out of existence'. On 10 September Foreign Secretary Philip Hammond stated in Berlin that 'Britain will not be taking part in any strikes in Syria'. This remark was quickly contradicted by a spokesman of Prime Minister David Cameron who said that the Prime Minister had 'not ruled anything out' as far as air strikes against ISIL were concerned. On 10 September President Barack Obama gave a speech indicating his intent to 'degrade and ultimately destroy' Islamic State of Iraq and the Levant (ISIL), saying, 'I have made it clear that we will hunt down terrorists who threaten our country, wherever they are. That means I will not hesitate to take action against ISIL in Syria, as well as Iraq.' For the first time, he authorized direct attacks against the militant group in Syria. In his address, he said the United States was going on the offensive, launching 'a steady, relentless effort to take out' the group 'wherever they exist.'

On 5 and 15 September and 3 December the United States, United Kingdom, France, Germany, Italy, Canada, Turkey and Denmark came together to discuss concerted action against ISIL. The coalition of 5 September (ten countries) decided to support anti-ISIL forces in Iraq and Syria. On 15 September French Air Force Dassault Rafale fighter aircraft operating from Al Dhafra Air Base in the United Arab Emirates began flying reconnaissance missions over Iraq as part of Operation 'Chammal', France's contribution to the international effort to combat Islamic State (IS) militants. Six (later nine) Rafales were initially tasked with identifying IS positions in support of US air strikes. On 18 September Rafales joined American operations in conducting attacks, launching four strikes near the Northern Iraqi town of Zumar that destroyed a logistics depot and killed dozens of IS fighters. On 19 September France conducted its first air strike which targeted an ISIL depot, making it the first Western coalition partner to conduct air strikes in Iraq. Two Rafale jets armed with GBU-12 Paveway II conducted the air strikes on an ISIS depot in Mosul, dropping four GBU-12 bombs. Over the following few days, pairs of Rafale jets

Royal Australian Air Force F/A-18 Hornets and a KC-30A MRTT of 33 Squadron RAAF over Iraq on 23 December 2014.

flew reconnaissance missions. On 25 September, a day after the beheading of a French hostage, two Rafales conducted France's second air strike while in a reconnaissance mission, destroying four warehouses of ISIS near Fallujah. French/American jets conducted air strikes at night in Kirkuk, killing fifteen ISIS fighters and injuring thirty. Reconnaissance missions were conducted by two Rafales and an Atlantique 2 over Ninawa Province on 26 September.[114]

On 22 September the United States, Bahrain, Jordan, Qatar, Saudi Arabia and the United Arab Emirates began to strike targets of the Islamic State of Iraq and the Levant (ISIL) inside Syria, as well as the Khorasan group in the Idlib Governorate to the west of the Aleppo Governorate and the al-Qaeda-affiliated al-Nusra Front around Ar-Raqqah, as part of the Military intervention against ISIL. During the first night of air strikes, the United States' force deployed with HARM missiles as a precaution, as it was uncertain how Syria's air-defence network would react. Pentagon Press Secretary Rear Admiral John Kirby confirmed that the United States and other partner nations had undertaken strikes in Syria using fighters, bombers and Tomahawk missiles in strikes authorized by President Barack Obama. The initial strikes were coordinated by United States Central Command and targeted about twenty Islamic State of Iraq and the Levant targets, including headquarters buildings. Sources in Syria claimed that among the targets was also Brigade 93, a Syrian army base that the militants had recently captured and targets in the towns of Tabqa and Tel Abyad in Ar-Raqqah Province. F-22 Raptor stealth fighters were reported to be among the US aircraft striking targets in Syria on the first night of the campaign, carrying out their first combat missions since entering service in 2005. A number of Raptors dropped 1,000lb GPS-guided bombs on Islamic State targets in the vicinity of Tishrin Dam. Combat operations by F-22s were planned to continue into the foreseeable future. While some missions involve striking targets, the F-22's main role is intelligence, surveillance and reconnaissance (ISR) gathering. By January 2015 the F-22 accounted for three percent of Air Force sorties during Operation 'Inherent Resolve'. Between September 2014 and July 2015 F-22s flew 204 sorties over Syria, dropping 270 bombs at sixty locations. On 23 June 2015 a pair of F-22s performed the aircraft's first close air support (CAS) mission after receiving a short-notice request for air strikes in close proximity to friendly forces.

In Britain on 26 September Parliament was recalled to debate the authorization of British air strikes against ISIL in Iraq. David Cameron told MPs that intervention at the request of the Iraqi government to combat a 'brutal terrorist organisation' was 'morally justified'. He went on to state that ISIL was a direct threat to the United Kingdom and that British inaction would lead

Armée de l'Air (French Air Force) Rafales over Iraq on 19 September 2014.

to 'more killing' in Iraq. Parliament voted overwhelmingly in favour of air strikes. Although the House of Commons only authorized air strikes in Iraq, Prime Minister David Cameron argued that there was also a 'strong case' for air strikes in Syria but this would require another House of Commons vote. Operation 'Shader' (the code name given to the British participation in the ongoing military intervention against the Islamic State of Iraq and the Levant (ISIL) went ahead and the RAF began conducting armed sorties over Iraq immediately after the vote, using six Tornado GR.4s stationed at RAF Akrotiri in Cyprus. The first air strike occurred on 30 September when a patrol of two GR.4s attacked an ISIL heavy weapons position using a Paveway IV laser-guided bomb and an armed pickup truck using a Brimstone missile. On 3 October the six GR.4s were increased by an additional two aircraft. The same day it was reported that the Royal Navy had tasked Type 45 destroyer HMS *Defender* to escort the US Navy aircraft carrier USS *George H. W. Bush* (CVN-77) while she launched aircraft into Iraq and Syria. On 16 October the Ministry of Defence announced the deployment to RAF Akrotiri in Cyprus of an undisclosed number of General Atomics MQ-9 Reaper unmanned combat aerial vehicles to assist with surveillance. However, Michael Fallon stated that the Reapers could also conduct air strikes alongside the Tornado GR.4s. On 21 October the MoD confirmed that RC-135W Rivet Joint (a large, all-weather electronic surveillance aircraft based on the C-135 airframe) and MQ-9 Reaper surveillance flights were occurring over Syria, making the UK the first Western country other than the United States to operate in both Iraq and Syria simultaneously. The first air strike conducted by a Reaper occurred on 10 November and were believed to have been flown by pilots nearly 3,000 miles away in rural Lincolnshire where pilots seated behind banks of screens in an air-conditioned cabin, in a high security hangar, use satellite links to control the unmanned aircraft flying nearly constant armed reconnaissance missions over Iraq and Syria. By 26 September 2015 Tornado and Reaper aircraft had flown over 1,300 missions against ISIL and had conducted more than 300 air strikes, killing more than 330 ISIL fighters. According to Defence Secretary Michael Fallon, the UK had conducted a 'huge number of missions' over Iraq by 13 December 2014, second only to the United States and five times as many as France. By 5

Voyager KC.2 refuelling two Tornado GR.4s over Iraq on 18 November 2015.

February 2015 the UK had contributed 6% of all coalition air strikes in Iraq - a contribution second only to the United States. In March 2015 the MoD revealed that the Reapers had conducted eight surveillance missions over Syria during January.

Operation 'Okra' meanwhile, the Australian Defence Force (ADF) contribution to the military intervention against the Islamic State of Iraq and the Levant (ISIL), had commenced on 31 August 2014. Its stated aim was to combat ISIL threats in Iraq. The Australian government announced on 14 September that an Air Task Group (ATG) of up to eight F/A-18F Super Hornets, an E-7A Wedgetail AEW&C aircraft and a KC-30A air-to-air refuelling tanker, along with a Special Operations Task Force, would be deployed to the Middle East in preparation for possible operations against ISIL forces. The ATG commenced operations on 1 October and on 3 October, Prime Minister Tony Abbott announced that his country would commence air strikes. In late September an Air Task Group (ATG) of 400 RAAF personnel was deployed to Al Minhad Air Base in the United Arab Emirates as part of the coalition to combat Islamic State forces in Iraq. Australian aircraft have also been reported to have been operated out of Al Dhafra Air Base south of Abu Dhabi. The initial commitment of aircraft included six F/A-18F Super Hornet strike aircraft from 1 Squadron RAAF, an E-7A Wedgetail Airborne Early Warning and Control aircraft from 2 Squadron RAAF and a KC-30A Multi Role Tanker Transport from 33 Squadron RAAF. The ATG began operations on 1 October. Between 6 and 17 October, Australian aircraft flew 54 sorties. In at least two of them, a number of ISIL fighters were killed. Australian F/A-18Fs attacked ISIL military equipment and facilities in support of Iraqi and Kurdish troops on the ground. In late December Australian Super Hornets were involved in assisting Kurdish ground forces free Yezidi people trapped on Mount Sinjar along with other coalition aircraft. During their seven months of operational flying over Iraq, the 1SQN F/A-18Fs flew over 400 sorties and 2,900 flight hours. A second ATG arrived in the UAE in early January 2015 to replace the first group of personnel and operate the aircraft originally deployed. Six single-seat F/A-18As of 75 Squadron RAAF at Tindal deployed to the Middle East to replace the six dual-seat F/A-18Fs in March 2015. On 30 June the Department of Defence reported that the ATG had dropped more the 400 weapons in support of Iraqi forces since the commencement of operations with the F/A-18A Hornets and F/A-18F Super Hornets flying nearly 5,000 hours, the E-7A Wedgetail completing 100 operational sorties and the KC-30A air-to-air refuelling aircraft providing 25 million pounds of fuel to Australian and coalition aircraft. Air strikes were extended to Syria in September 2015.

Operation 'Impact', Canada's contribution to the military intervention against the Islamic State of Iraq and the Levant began on 4 September 2014 when the Canadian government announced that it would deploy up to 100 Canadian Special Forces to Iraq in a non-combat advisory role. On 3 October Canada's role in the intervention increased when Canadian Prime Minister Stephen Harper announced that Canada would be deploying nine aircraft, including six combat aircraft to Iraq. Canadian air strikes in Iraq began on 2 November. Canadian air strike operations in Syria began on 8 April 2015 when two CF-18s attacked an ISIL garrison near Raqqa. The Canadian jets were joined by six US aircraft in the strike. Prior to the attack, Canadian aircraft had performed three sorties into Syrian airspace. On 20 May two Canadian jets bombed an ISIL staging area north of Ar-Raqqa. In June CF-18s attacked near Al-Hasakah in eastern Syria.

On 24 September the Dutch government sent six F-16AM/BM fighter jets to contribute to the 'international battle against ISIS (ISIL)' in Iraq. On 7 and 8 October, Royal Netherlands Air Force fighters operating from Shaheed Mwaffaq Air Base in Jordan dropped their first bombs in the north of Iraq, hitting at least an ISIL vehicle. On average, RNLAF F-16s conducted one or two sorties per day. By 17 November they had dropped 75 bombs on ISIL targets in Iraq such as camps and command posts and were also giving air support to Iraqi and Kurdish ground forces. In June 2015 the RNLAF flew its 1,000th sortie over Iraq. During the first nine months of the mission 575 strikes had been carried out.

Morocco in late November 2014 became the first Arab state to join the American-led military intervention in Iraq, responding to an American appeal to send several F-16 jets to the fight against ISIL. Four F-16s of the Royal Moroccan Air Force reportedly carried out air strikes against ISIL positions on the outskirts of Baghdad, among other areas, around 10 December. The Moroccan warplanes were to focus on hitting fixed targets, including training camps, oil refineries and weapons depots. The Jordanian Air Force on 4 February 2015 began targeting ISIL positions in Iraq in retaliation for ISIL's brutal burning of Jordanian pilot Muath al-Kasasbeh,[115] beginning the campaign with a large air strike campaign centred on Mosul, which killed 55 ISIL militants, including ISIL's top senior commander of Mosul known as the 'Prince of Nineveh'. On 25 March the American-led Coalition joined the Second Battle of Tikrit, launching its first air strikes on ISIL targets in the city centre. That night, US aircraft carried out 17 air strikes in the centre of Tikrit, which struck an ISIL building, two bridges, three checkpoints, two staging areas,

HMS *Defender* escorting the USS *George H. W. Bush* on 1 October 2014.

two berms, a roadblock, and a command and control facility. The US-led Coalition continued conducting air strikes in Tikrit until 31 March, when Iraqi forces entered the city centre. On 8 April Iraqi forces, building on their advances in the Saladin Governorate, launched an offensive to liberate the Anbar Governorate from ISIL occupation, beginning with an offensive in the region around east Ramadi, backed by Coalition aircraft. In retaliation, ISIL executed 300 people in the western Anbar Province. On 12 April the Iraqi government declared that Tikrit was free of ISIL forces, stating that it was safe for residents to return home. By mid-April ISIL had lost 5,000 to 6,500 square miles in Iraq since their peak territorial influence in August 2014 to Iraqi and American coalition forces, leaving them still possessing 15,000 square miles in Iraq.

On 23 February 2015 the French Navy deployed its Task Force 473 carrier strike group to the Persian Gulf to conduct air strikes from the aircraft carrier *Charles de Gaulle* which contributed twelve Rafale fighters, nine Dassault-Breguet Super Étendard strike aircraft and 2 E-2C Hawkeye airborne early warning and control aircraft. The task force also included the French frigate Chevalier Paul (D621), a Rubis-class submarine, a Durance-class tanker, and the British frigate HMS *Kent*. After eight weeks of operations, the task force left the Persian Gulf on its way to India, heralding the end of its contribution to Operation 'Chammal'. On 5 November 2015 it was announced that the *Charles de Gaulle* would resume operations in Syria to fight ISIL.

As of October 2015 Canada had made 172 air strikes against ISIL targets in Syria and Iraq, making up 2.3 percent of all Allied attacks since the onset of the war. However, since June, there had been a decline in the number of strike missions being performed by Canadian aircraft. Twenty air strikes were performed that month, climbing to 30 in July, then down to twelve in August and ten in September. Canadian aircraft left for the Middle East to join in air strikes on 21 October 2014. In total, six CF-18 fighter jets, an Airbus CC-150 Polaris air-to-air refuelling tanker and two CP-140 Aurora surveillance aircraft were sent, along with 700 military personnel. Canadian CF-18 fighter jets completed their first operational flights departing from Kuwait on 31 October. The first Canadian air strikes began on 2 November. Canada also flew an extra CF-18 to Kuwait to be used as a spare if the need arose. On 4 November RCAF CF-18s using GBU-12 bombs destroyed ISIL construction equipment being used to divert the Euphrates River to deny villages water and to flood roads, diverting traffic to areas with IEDs. On 12 November Canadian

A F-16 refuelling from a KC-135 during 'Inherent Resolve'.

Boeing 737-7ES Wedgetail N3788C Airborne Early Warning and Control aircraft of 2 Squadron RAAF.

jets destroyed ISIL artillery just outside the Northern Iraqi town of Baiji. Air strikes continued throughout December and into January 2015 totalling 28 strike missions. It was then reported that Canadian Special Forces troops, which had been highlighting targets for air strikes, had engaged in fighting after coming under attack. On 30 March 2015 the Canadian Parliament voted to extend deployment of its military for one year and extend the mission to targets in Syria. No additional forces were announced. On 8 April Canada initiated air strikes in Syria with two CF-18 fighters bombing a former military installation of the Syrian government that was captured by ISIL near its headquarters in ar-Raqqah. From 2 November 2014 to 13 May 2015 the Canadian armed forces struck eighty ISIS fighting positions, 19 ISIS Vehicles and ten storage facilities. As part of his election campaign, Mr. Justin Trudeau pledged to bring home the CF-18 fighter jets that were deployed to the region until March 2016. On 20 October 2015 the Canadian Prime Minister designate informed Barack Obama of Canada's intention to pull out of air strikes in Syria while keeping its ground forces in Iraq and Syria.

Targets in Syria bombed by the United States and assisted by Saudi Arabia and the United Arab Emirates included ISIL forces laying siege to Kobanî, a primarily Kurdish city in Syrian Kurdistan, in support of the People's Protection Units (YPG) and Free Syrian Army, who were defending the city. On 12 October the Turkish government approved the use of Turkish military bases by coalition forces fighting ISIL in Syria and Iraq. These installations would include key bases only 100 miles from the Syrian border and important US military bases in Turkey such as the Incirlik Air Base. On 19 December US General James Terry announced that the number of US air strikes on ISIL had increased to 1,361. Since November 2014 the Islamic State of Iraq and the Levant (ISIL) had suffered the loss of at least a dozen senior leaders due to coalition air strikes. On 25 December Hassan Saeed Al-Jabouri, the ISIL governor of Mosul, who was also known as Abu Taluut, was killed by a US-led Coalition air strike in Mosul. It was also reported that the US planned to retake the city of Mosul in January 2015. On the 15th it was reported that over 16,000 air strikes had been carried out by the Coalition. The US Air Force has carried out around 60 percent of all strikes. Among them, F-16Gs performed 41 percent of all sorties, followed by the F-15E at 37 percent and then the A-10 at 11 percent, the B-1 bomber at eight

An RAF Reaper MQ-9 remotely piloted air system.

percent and the F-22 at 3 percent. The remaining 40 percent had been carried out by the US Navy and allied nations. On 20 January the SOHR reported that al-Baghdadi, the leader of ISIL, had been wounded in an air strike in Al-Qa'im, an Iraqi border town held by ISIL and as a result, withdrew to Syria. On 21 January the US began coordinating air strikes with a Kurdish launched offensive, to help them begin the planned operation to retake the city of Mosul. On 21 July it was reported that nearly 44,000 sorties had been flown since August 2014.

On 30 June 2015 Prime Minister David Cameron once again made calls for air strikes in Syria, following the Sousse attacks which left thirty Britons dead. On 17 July it emerged that British pilots were taking part in air strikes in Syria whilst embedded with US and Canadian forces. On 19 July, during a television interview with NBC, David Cameron stated that Britain was committed to destroying the caliphate in Syria and Iraq. On 21 August three Islamic State fighters, two with UK nationality, were targeted and killed in Raqqa, Syria by a RAF MQ-9 Reaper strike. One of the British nationals targeted had been plotting attacks in the United Kingdom. Another British national was killed in a separate air strike by US forces in Raqqa on 24 August. On 7 September Prime Minister David Cameron announced that two British Islamic State fighters were targeted and killed in Syria by a MQ-9 Reaper drone strike.

By early June ISIL had lost over 13,000 fighters to Coalition air strikes in Iraq and Syria, with 10,800+ of the deaths in Iraq. By July ISIL had lost over 15,000 fighters to US-led Coalition air strikes in Iraq and Syria, with 12,100+ fighters killed in Iraq. An independent monitoring group reported that air strikes had killed about 15,000 ISIL militants. The CIA estimated that Islamic Group had about 31,000 active fighters. Other groups such as the Syrian Observatory for Human Rights claimed there may be as many as 100,000 fighters. In August it was reported that coalition aircraft had flown a total 45,259 sorties in the previous twelve months of operations, with the USAF flying the majority, accounting for 67 percent and dropping more than 5,600 bombs in the campaign to date. The countries that participated in the strikes in Iraq included Australia, Belgium, Canada, Denmark, France, Jordan, The Netherlands and the UK. In Syria nations that took part included Australia, Bahrain, Canada, France, Jordan, Saudi Arabia, Turkey and the UAE. Including Saudi Arabia, Jordan, United Arab Emirates and Kuwait, 62 countries had joined the coalition against the group, but only 21 provided air and military support and just twelve had launched air strikes. Nearly four out of five air strikes on ISIL territories had been conducted by the US which had spent $3.5 billion dollars on the operation, an average of nearly $10 million dollars a day.

On Wednesday 12 August the US launched its first air strikes from Incirlik air base in southern Turkey when six F-16G fighter jets from the 31st Fighter Wing based at Aviano, Italy attacked Islamic State targets in Syria. Earlier that month the US had begun flying armed drones from Incirlik. At the time most US aerial combat missions over Iraq and Syria were being flown from more distant air bases in Qatar and elsewhere in the Persian Gulf region, although the US also was flying F-16s from Muwaffaq Salti air base in Jordan. The Incirlik-based F-16s are equipped with surveillance and reconnaissance equipment in addition to weapons and thus can be used to verify targeting information that may be provided by local Syrians or Iraqis cooperating with the US.

On 30 September Russia began military intervention in the Syrian Civil War, consisting of air strikes primarily in north-western Syria by Russia against militant groups opposed to the Syrian government, including al-Nusra Front (al-Qaeda in the Levant), the Islamic State and the Army of Conquest. According to Russian and Syrian officials, in July President Bashar al-Assad had made a formal request to Russia for air strikes to combat 'international terrorism'. After a series of major setbacks suffered by the Syrian government forces in the first half of 2015 a political agreement was reached between Russia and Syria to intensify the Russian involvement. Over fifty Russian aircraft and helicopters (later increased to 69), including Sukhoi Su-24M2 'Fencer', four Su-30CM 'Flanker-C' jet fighters to protect ground support aircraft and bombers attacking ISIL, at least a dozen Su-25 SM 'Frogfoot' armoured subsonic close air support/attack aircraft and six Su-34 'Fullback' multirole fighter/bombers comprised a part of aviagroup based

A USAF F-22 strike in Syria on 18 November 2015.

A Tupolev Tu-22M taking off from Soltsy-2 on 19 November 2015.

at the Hmeymim airbase, outside Latakia. With its maiden flight having taken place in 1970 the Su-24 was the first Soviet/Russian jet to feature a variable-sweep wing which allow for perfect manoeuvrability during flights at subsonic and supersonic speeds. The Su-24 became the first Soviet jet designed to operate at extremely low altitudes. The upgraded Su-24 carries the R60M air-to-air guided missile, the Kh-29L and Kh-25 ML air-to-surface missiles, as well as guided bombs, regular bombs and non-guided missiles. The Su-34 'Fullback' is an all-weather combat aircraft capable of carrying all available types of high-precision air-to-surface weapons. According to Western military analysts, despite its age the Su-25 is still the perfect war machine to attack ISIL positions in Syria. The Su-25SM underwent modernization in recent times; it was equipped with a GLONASS navigation system and advanced avionics which allow for the use of high-precision weapons.

In the morning of 2 October Su-24M, Su-34 and Su-25s of the Russian Air Force launched four air strikes on ISIL in the ancient Syriac city of Al-Qaryatayn and the T4-Palmyra highway, Homs province. An ISIL command and control centre was destroyed in a single air strike in Al-Qaryatayn, while an ISIL convoy on their way to the Teefor-Palmyra highway was attacked. Following the air strikes, the Syrian Army and National Defence Forces pushed ISIL out of the town of Mheen towards Al-Qaryatayn after a two-hour engagement that killed 18 militants and destroyed two technicals mounted with ZU-23-2s. Syrian forces then launched a counter-attack

A Sukhoi Su-34 at Latakia on 3 October 2015.

A Soviet Su-34 'Fullback' attacking Raqqah and Aleppo in Syria in October 2015.

south-west of Al-Qaryatayn to recover the main road. In the same day, the Russian Air Force began bombing Al-Nusra Front positions in al-Rastan and Talbiseh in the Homs province. Later, they proceeded with bombing Al-Nusra in Kafr Zita, Al-Ghaab Plains, Kafr Nabl, Kafr Sijnah, and Al-Rakaya in the Hama province. The Syrian Air Force and the Russian Air Force jointly bombed Al-Nusra in Jisr al-Shughur. At night, the Russian Air Force targeted ISIL with eleven air strikes over Al-Raqqah while targeting electrical grids outside it, two air strikes over Shadadi-Hasakah highway and three air strikes in Al-Mayadeen, Deir ez-Zor province. The primary ISIL military base in Tabaqa Military Airport was also attacked, with the barracks being destroyed in two air strikes. Near the Military Airport, an ISIL weapons supply depot in Al-'Ajrawi Farms was also bombed. At the same time, the ISIL primary headquarters in Tabaqa National Hospital was heavily damaged in a Russian air strike. In Al-Hasakah province, the Russian Air Force targeted ISIL in Al-Shadadi and Al-Houl, while the Syrian Air Force attacked an ISIL convoy along the Deir ez-Zor-Hasakah highway.

On 3 October nine ISIL positions near the group's de facto capital in Raqqa were bombed. During the day, the Russian Air Force made four air strikes over Al-Nusra controlled Jisr al-Shughur and additional ones in Jabal Al-Zawiya and Jabal al-Akrad. One of the targets was an Al-Nusra reinforcement convoy heading from Jisr al-Shughur to the northeast countryside of Latakia province. On 7 October Syrian ground forces were reported to carry out an offensive under Russian air cover. On 8 October the number of air raids increased significantly up to over sixty sorties a day, a tempo maintained for the next two days. The Russian defence ministry announced on 9 October that up to sixty ISIL targets were hit in the past 24 hours, supposedly killing 300 militants in the most intense strikes so far. The Russian Defence Ministry declared that within the period from 30 September to 22 October, the Russian aircraft carried out 934 sorties from the Hmeymim air base and destroyed 819 targets. On 17 November Russia employed the Russia-based Tupolev Tu-160 'Blackjack' supersonic, variable-sweep wing heavy strategic bomber armed with Kh-101, Tu-95MSM 'Bear' armed with Kh-555 and Tu-22M3 'Backfire' armed in FAB-500 strategic long range bombers as well as cruise missiles launched from a submerged vessel in the Mediterranean to hit what were claimed were the IS targets in Raqqah, Deir ez-Zor as well as targets in the provinces of Aleppo and Idlib. In just three days in

Soviet Su-24 bombers on a mission in Syria on 22 November 2015.

mid-November Russian aircraft carried out a staggering 394 sorties, hitting 731 rebel targets across Syria.

Since 31 January 2015 there had been a combined 8,378 close air support, escort and interdiction sorties flown by US and coalition aircraft in support of 'Inherent Resolve'. In addition, there had been 8,194 weapons released, making it harder for ISIL to sustain itself as a fighting force. The US and coalition had flown a total of 8,125 strikes on ISIL (and occasionally Al-Nusra). Some 5,321 hit targets in Iraq while 2,804 hit targets in Syria, killing over 20,000 fighters and damaging or destroying 16,075 targets. The rest of the Coalition had flown 1,772 strikes in Iraq and Syria (1,626 Iraq / 146 Syria). As of 14 November US and partner nation aircraft had flown an estimated 57,301 sorties in support of operations in Iraq and Syria.

In October and November 2015 the US intensified its air strikes on ISIL-held oil facilities in an operation named 'Tidal Wave II', after the World War II campaign against Axis oil targets in Romania. The US strategy aimed 'to knock out specific installations for six months to a year' by focusing on facilities near Deir el-Zour. The Pentagon believes that area of eastern Syria is where the heart of ISIS' oil operation is located and generates as much as two-thirds of its oil revenue. The Omar oil field, which produced 30,000 barrels of oil per day and $1.7 million to $5.1 million in revenue per month at full capacity, was hit on 21 October, reducing it to roughly a third of its capacity. French aircraft also participated in the strikes. On 16 November Operation 'Tidal Wave II' destroyed 116 IS fuel tankers clustered near Abu Kamal, a town on the Syrian border near Dayr al Zawr. Four A-10 Thunderbolt IIs and two AC-130 Spectre gunships were used to bomb and strafe the vehicles. In an effort to minimize potential civilian casualties, two F-15 fighter jets dropped leaflets an hour prior to the air strike , warning drivers to leave the almost-300 vehicles gathered in the target area.

On 14 November ISIL claimed that the coordinated attacks that took place in Paris the previous day that killed more than 130 people were in retaliation for Operation 'Chammal'. On 15 November the Armee d'l Air launched its largest air strike of the bombing campaign in Syria to date, sending ten Dassault Rafales and Mirage 2000s, launched simultaneously from the United Arab Emirates and Jordan that dropped twenty bombs in training camps and ammunition facilities in Al-Raqqah, the de facto capital of Islamic State. The operation, carried out in coordination with US forces, struck a command centre, recruitment centre for jihadists, a munitions depot and a training camp for fighters. The first target destroyed was used by Isis as a command post, jihadist recruitment centre and arms and munitions depot. The second held a terrorist training camp. On Tuesday 17 November two Canadian CF-18 Hornets successfully struck three Islamic State fighting positions near the Iraqi city of Ramadi with precision-guided munitions during two separate air strikes. The French nuclear-powered aircraft carrier Charles De Gaulle set sail for the Persian Gulf on Wednesday 18 November, as was announced before the attacks on Friday. The aircraft carrier will make more planes available for use against IS and will also dramatically cut the time it takes for French fighter jets to reach their targets in the region. The Charles De Gaulle is capable of carrying up to forty jets and helicopters and will 'bolster Paris' firepower in the region,' as President Francois Hollande said. He called the Paris attacks an 'act of war' and said 'France will be merciless towards these barbarians." Prime Minister Manuel Valls also vowed to 'destroy' those behind the attacks.

On 20 November the United Nations Security Council called on all countries that could do so to take the war on terrorism to Islamic State-controlled territory in Syria and Iraq and destroy its safe haven, warning that the group intended to mount further terror attacks like those that devastated Paris and Beirut the previous week. In a unanimously adopted resolution, the fifteen-member body declared the group's terrorist attacks abroad 'a global and unprecedented threat

Left: Russian ground staff members attach a Kh-25L high-precision missile to a Sukhoi Su-30CM 'Flanker-C' at the Khmeimim airbase near Latakia, Syria on 20 October 2015.

Below: Two Su-25 SM 'Frogfoots' taking off from Latakia, Syria for a mission in late 2015.

to international peace and security' following the 'horrifying terrorist attacks' it perpetrated recently in Sousse (Tunisia), Ankara (Turkey), over Sinai (Egypt) with the downing of a Russian airliner and in Beirut and Paris. 'By its violent extremist ideology, its terrorist acts, its continued gross systematic and widespread attacks directed against civilians, abuses of human rights and violations of international humanitarian law, including those driven on religious or ethnic ground, its eradication of cultural heritage and trafficking of cultural property,' ISIL constitutes 'a global and unprecedented threat to international peace and security,' the Council stressed.

On Monday 23 November taking off from the *Charles de Gaulle* French jets struck Islamic State (IS) group targets in Syria and Iraq, destroying targets in Ramadi and Mosul in Iraq in support of Iraqi forces on the ground fighting the jihadist group. Later on Monday, another raid was carried out over Raqqa, Syria, where several facilities including a command centre for the IS group were destroyed. French President Francois Hollande said earlier on Monday in Paris: 'We will intensify our strikes, choosing targets that will do the most damage possible to this army of terrorists.' The *Charles De Gaulle*, the largest western European warship currently in commission, has 26 fighter jets, more than doubling France's strike capacity in the US-led mission against IS group.

On Wednesday 2 December under the light of a half moon, three Tornado GR.4s left RAF Akrotiri just before 11.30pm UK time, just 57 minutes after MPs in the House of Commons had approved extended bombing campaign against the so-called Islamic State in Iraq and the Levant from Iraq into Syria. Supported by a Voyager air refuelling tanker and a Reaper and operating in conjunction with other coalition aircraft they dropped Paveway IV guided bombs in strikes against six targets within the extensive oilfield at Omar, 35 miles inside Syria's eastern border with Iraq. The Omar oilfield is one of the largest and most important to IS's financial operations and represents over 10 per cent of their potential income from oil. Before conducting their attacks they used the Tornadoes advanced sensors to confirm that no civilians were in the proximity of the targets. The Tornadoes returned a little more than three hours later. Initial analysis of the operation indicated that the strikes were successful.

Endnotes for Chapter 8

114 In November 2014 the French strike force was augmented with six Dassault Mirage 2000Ds based in Jordan. Between 18 December 2014 and 7 January 2015, French aircraft performed 45 missions in total. Rafales and Mirages performed 30 of those missions neutralising ten targets. On 14 January François Hollande declared that the aircraft carrier *Charles de Gaulle* would deploy to the Persian Gulf with its strike group and that it was capable of supporting airstrikes against ISIL. French aircraft hit targets in Syria for the first time in early October 2015.

115 King Abdullah II vowed revenge and temporarily took the lead in the bombing raids on ISIL during February 2015. On 8 February Jordan claimed that during the course of 3 days, from 5-7 February, their airstrikes alone had killed 7,000 ISIL militants in Iraq and Syria, and also reportedly degraded 20% of the militant group's capability.